Edinburgh University Library

D1757852

Edinburgh University Library

University of Edinburgh

30150   027678611

Social Inequality in
Iberian Late Prehistory

Edited by

Pedro Díaz-del-Río
Leonardo García Sanjuán

BAR International Series 1525
2006

EDINBURGH UNIVERSITY LIBRARY
WITHDRAWN

This title published by

Archaeopress
Publishers of British Archaeological Reports
Gordon House
276 Banbury Road
Oxford OX2 7ED
England
bar@archaeopress.com
www.archaeopress.com

BAR S1525

Social Inequality in Iberian Late Prehistory

© the individual authors 2006

ISBN 1 84171 962 5

Printed in England by The Synergie Group

All BAR titles are available from:

Hadrian Books Ltd
122 Banbury Road
Oxford
OX2 7BP
England
bar@hadrianbooks.co.uk

The current BAR catalogue with details of all titles in print, prices and means of payment is available free from Hadrian Books or may be downloaded from www.archaeopress.com

List of contributors

AFONSO MARRERO, José Andrés
Departamento de Prehistoria y Arqueología
Universidad de Granada
Campus Universitario de Cartuja s/n. 18071.
Granada. Spain
jaamarre@ugr.es

BALBÍN BEHRMANN, Rodrigo
Sección de Prehistoria
Universidad de Alcalá de Henares
Antiguo Colegio de Málaga
Colegios, 2. 28801. Alcalá de Henares, Madrid.
Spain

BERNABÉU AUBÁN, Joan
Departamento de Prehistoria y Arqueología
Universidad de Valencia
Avenida Blasco Ibáñez, 28. 46010. Valencia. Spain
juan.bernabeu@uv.es

BUENO RAMÍREZ, Primitiva
Sección de Prehistoria
Universidad de Alcalá de Henares
Antiguo Colegio de Málaga
Colegios, 2. 28801. Alcalá de Henares, Madrid.
Spain

CÁMARA SERRANO, Juan Antonio
Departamento de Prehistoria y Arqueología
Universidad de Granada
Campus Universitario de Cartuja s/n. 18071.
Granada. Spain
jacamara@ugr.es

CASTRO MARTÍNEZ, Pedro V.
Departamento de Prehistoria
Universidad Autónoma de Barcelona
Edificio B. Campus UAB. 08193. Bellaterra
(Barcelona, Spain)
Pedro.Castro@uab.es

DÍAZ-DEL-RÍO, Pedro
Departamento de Prehistoria
Instituto de Historia
Consejo Superior de Investigaciones Científicas
Serrano, 13. 28001. Madrid. Spain
diazdelrio@ih.csic.es

DÍEZ CASTILLO, Agustín
Departamento de Prehistoria y Arqueología
Universidad de Valencia
Avd. Blasco Ibáñez, 28. 46010. Valencia. Spain

ESCORIZA MATEU, Trinidad
Departamento de Historia, Geografía e Historia del
Arte
Universidad de Almería
Edificio Departamental de Humanidades y Ciencias
de la Educación II (Edif. C). Ctra. Sacramento s/n.
La Cañada de San Urbano. 04120. Almería. Spain.
tescoriz@ual.es

GARCÍA SANJUÁN, Leonardo
Departamento de Prehistoria y Arqueología
Universidad de Sevilla
María de Padilla s/n. 41004. Sevilla. Spain
lgarcia@us.es

GARRIDO-PENA, Rafael
Departamento de Prehistoria, Arqueología,
Antropología Social y Ciencias y Técnicas
Historiográficas. Fundación Arcadia.
Universidad de Valladolid.
Prado de la Magdalena s/n. 47011. Valladolid. Spain

MARQUÉZ ROMERO, José Enrique
Departamento de Ciencias y Técnicas
Historiográficas, Historia Antigua y Prehistoria
Universidad de Málaga
Campus de Teatinos. 29071. Málaga. Spain
jemarquez@uma.es

MOLINA BALAGUER, Lluis
Departamento de Prehistoria y Arqueología
Universidad de Valencia
Avenida Blasco Ibáñez, 28. 46010. Valencia. Spain
lluis.molina@uv.es

MOLINA GONZÁLEZ, Fernando
Departamento de Prehistoria y Arqueología
Universidad de Granada
Campus Universitario de Cartuja s/n. 18071.
Granada. Spain
molinag@ugr.es

ONTAÑÓN PEREDO, Roberto
Grupo de Prehistoria
Universidad de Cantabria
Edificio Interfacultativo. Avenida de los Castros,
s/n. Santander. Spain
ontanonr@unican.es

OROZCO KÖHLER, Teresa
Departamento de Prehistoria y Arqueología
Universidad de Valencia
Avenida Blasco Ibáñez, 28. 46010. Valencia. Spain
teresa.orozco@uv.es

Contents

CHAPTER 11. GARCÍA SANJUÁN, Leonardo – *Funerary ideology and social inequality in the Late Prehistory of the Iberian South-West (c. 3300-850 cal BC)*

CHAPTER 12. MARQUÉZ ROMERO, José E. – *Neolithic and Copper Age ditched enclosures and social inequality South of the Iberian Peninsula (IV-III millennia cal BC).*

List of figures

CHAPTER 11

CHAPTER 10

CHAPTER 12

List of Tables

Prologue

Juan Vicent
Consejo Superior de Investigaciones Científicas

This book is the result of a session held at the Congress of Peninsular Archaeology (Faro, 2004). The organizers of that session (i.e., the editors of this volume) did me the honor of inviting me to participate as a discussant and have now renewed their confidence in me by asking me for these introductory pages. In them I will not attempt to review either the material presented in the book or the overall argument which gives it coherence (since the editors do this more than well enough in their introductory article). Instead I will try to present some of the reflections with which, on that occasion, I attempted to determine the main lines of the contributions and to frame the lively discussion with which the session ended, thereby connecting what occurred in Faro (insofar as this is reflected in my notes) with its bibliographic consequences. Thus, I must advise the reader that these remarks have a rather subjective character: they attempt to reflect the spirit of the debate in which I was privileged to participate rather than to present an academic critique of the actual contents of the present volume. Finally, one should note that, as often occurs in these cases, the materials gathered together in this book do not reproduce completely the contributions presented at the session. At least three of the papers presented at Faro were not developed into publishable form for a variety of reasons that have more to do with the complex obligations of their authors rather than with substantive causes. In some cases this absence may be due to some of the remarks that follow, as I will point out where necessary. Conversely, two contributions (those of Bernabeu *et. al.* and Balbín & Bueno could not be presented at the session but were eventually able to enrich this volume.

Having made these initial clarifications, I will begin by pointing out the significance of the Faro session within the setting of recent research into the recent prehistory of Iberia. As the editors point out, it is the first monographic session on a decidedly sociological subject to be held at a gathering of Spanish and Portuguese researchers to appear in the form of a book. This reflects, not the real development of research in our countries, but some of the oddities of our academic traditions, such as the format of scientific meetings. Sociologically informed research on the prehistory of the Peninsula by now has a long trajectory going back to the 1980s. At that time the contributions of certain notable Anglo-American researchers began to influence a generation of archaeologists that was trying to bring about in archaeology the "transition" that the two Iberian countries had undertaken in the previous decade in the political and social spheres. Since then, two further generations of "post-traditional" archaeologists have succeeded one another, each increasingly involved in interpreting the archaeological record in socio-economic terms and each, at least formally as we shall see, free of the constraints and rigidities of the culture-historical paradigm. As the editors point out, most of the contributors to this volume belong to the third of these generations, one that is currently achieving academic security, that was trained after the reincorporation of our scientific community into an international circuit characterized by its post-processualism, and that has had no need to combat the inertia of the autochthonous and autarchic culture-historical tradition against which the two preceding generations had to struggle. Significantly, members of the previous two generations — the writer of these lines among them — are not absent from the group of authors who appear in this volume; this establishes a certain continuity that also should be taken into account.

I should devote a final contextual comment to a fact pointed out by the editors in their introductory article and discussed at the session following upon some remarks by Professor Jorge. This is the absence of Portuguese contributors to a session that was announced as being Peninsular in scale and that many scholars of that nationality participated in as members of the audience. Probably this absence was due to particular circumstances from which no general conclusion should be drawn. Professor Jorge, however, put forward some suggestive reflections about the differential development of theoretical and interpretative approaches in each national tradition. His remarks constituted an interesting contribution to the discussion, but one on which, for obvious reasons, I should not comment. In any case, the absence of Portuguese papers in this volume shows how much remains to be done to integrate the two Peninsular archaeologies, in spite of the progress that has been made along this line (thanks in large part to the initiatives of Professor Jorge himself and of other Spanish and Portuguese colleagues). One must also keep Professor Jorge's remarks in mind when one reads these comments, which do not refer to the theoretical situation in Portuguese archaeology.

Although it is clear that Spanish and Portuguese researchers are fully integrated into the main currents of present-day archaeological thought, it is also clear that our academic traditions limit the expression of this integration, and this points out the exceptional nature of this volume. For the most part, our scientific meetings follow the obsolete model of the old *Congresos Nacionales*, in which the sessions (almost always "general" ones) are grouped by chronological periods or at most by general thematic areas ("economy", "environment", etc.), as in the interesting series of *Congresos del Neolítico en la Península Ibérica*. Here, I must underline the importance of the series of congresses on Iberian prehistory, in the latest of which this session was held, the more flexible format of which permits monographic sessions on special topics. This is a necessary condition for the appearance of books such as this, in which the contributions reflect theoretical and interpretative debates, rather than "recent advances" in the development of empirical knowledge that, albeit necessary, do not in themselves reflect the present state of research.

Going beyond this specific comment on the character of our scientific meetings, I wish to underline how the general weight of academic tradition affects the expression and development of the theoretical aspects of archaeological thought. Perhaps the most powerful inertia derived from the traditional culture-historical paradigm is the perpetuation of the chronological sequence as the framework for specialization in university education and (consequently) in archaeological investigation. Researchers consciously dedicate themselves to a particular chronological period and, less consciously, limit the reach of their theoretical and interpretative projects to that framework, even though their work may be informed by a broader paradigm. Thus, the call by the editors of this volume for us to "use long chronological frameworks" has a value that goes beyond broadening the variability of the archaeological record. I think that it is evident that the subject examined in this volume (namely, the origin and early development of social inequality) can be addressed only within a chronological framework broad enough to overcome the artificial breaks that archaeological periods impose on the logic of history. Insofar as periodization is based on normative cultural features (ceramic styles, funerary practices, etc.), it contradicts the predominantly materialist orientation of the discourse that, as we shall see below, animates debates on inequalities. Taking into account, furthermore, that the very nature of inequalities presupposes that "social being" determines "consciousness", to invoke once again the spirit (but not the "ghost", *pace* Derrida) of old Marx, we cannot suppose that the products of "consciousness" would permit us trace the causes and embodiments of that "being". Joking aside, however, I believe it is evident (at least to most of the authors in this volume) that it is, for example, by contrasting the social structures of the Copper and Bronze Ages that we shall grasp the expressions of social history of the Peninsula's communities. Without such comparative analyses we run the risk of overlooking things that are really important. One is the possibility, only hinted at by the contributors, that the same "social formation" may be found in different archaeological periods and not be confined to a particular "archaeological culture". This should cause us to reconsider some of the terms now commonly used, such as the "Argaric social formation", that may be, paradoxically, rather "idealist" formulations.

In any event, I believe that this book, like the session that was its origin, constitutes a great step forward in the right direction: it reasserts the logic of history in the face of the immanent idealism of the culture-historical inertia that still, unfortunately, dominates Iberian prehistoric studies. In this sense, the title's recovery of the term "recent prehistory" is significant in that it gives a name to the ambit in which the historical processes that we seek to understand can actually be observed. "Recent prehistory"—a term foreign to Iberian academic traditions, at least with respect to its analytical implications—is becoming more and more common as a framework for discussion. It may be premature, therefore, to question its validity by asking whether the great historical cycles we seek to understand extend far beyond its limits. Thus, for example, is it possible for us to understand what we mean by "social inequality" without taking into consideration pre-Neolithic hunter-gatherers? Can we evaluate the degree of hierarchy in Bronze Age societies without comparing them to the first unquestionably tributary social formations that arose as a consequence of the integration of parts of the Peninsula into the Mediterranean "world economy" in the first millennium BC? Discussion of these issues would be out of place here, but they hovered over the debate at Faro and are noted in some of the contributions.

Following up on the above, I would like to add that adopting a unified chronological framework is not the only preliminary adjustment required by the current direction of our discussions. We also need, urgently, to extend our comparative framework beyond the limits of the Peninsula. Up to now, reference to European and Mediterranean prehistory has been dominated by the culture-historical paradigm, which used it as a source of archaeographic parallels to support more or less diffusionist accounts of culture change. Our idiosyncratic archaeological "transition" reacted against these practices by emphasizing the necessity of understanding the development of the Peninsula's prehistory in terms of its own local processes, to the point of discrediting *a priori* any recourse to comparisons beyond its bounds. Perhaps the time has come to propose a rehabilitation of comparative archaeology, on new foundations of course. The problem is not just that phenomena such as Beakers occur beyond the geographic limits of Iberia. It is, rather, that the methodology of the new theoretical and interpretative paradigms demands an extra-Peninsular comparative framework. The culture-historical orientation, based as it was on the exceptional nature of each local historical trajectory, gave immediate ontological value to formal parallels. Replacing it with a project based on theories (in the strong sense of the term) that are social or anthropological involves making our assessments of the archaeological record "case studies" of general phenomena. To evaluate them correctly we need to establish scales of comparison. Otherwise we may be observing reality with magnifying lenses without being aware of it. I cannot resist an example that has little to do with what was discussed in Faro: as Gilman (1996) has observed, a few parishes in Bronze Age Denmark can produce more metal objects than whole provinces in south-east Spain. Leaving aside Gilman's interpretation of this fact, it seems to me evident that some such evaluation of the overall scale of production should be a matter of high priority for any interpretative hypothesis that considers control over metal resources to be the basis of the establishment of Bronze Age states, no less, in the Peninsula. Similar considerations of scale, not always in the same direction, might be obtained by comparing other important elements of our archaeological record: megaliths, for example. By all this I do not mean that the relatively modest amount of metal or of human labor invested in monuments apparent in the Peninsula's archaeological record is significant in and of itself. What I do mean is that, by not assessing those amounts comparatively, we shut ourselves off from assessments that may be very important and from a real understanding of the specificity of the historical trajectories of the Peninsula's social formations.

In any event, the comparative approach suggested in the previous paragraph must be preceded by a comparative focus within the Peninsula. This is precisely one of this volume's most interesting features. In the 1980s Spanish archaeology (I cannot speak with the same knowledge of Portugal) underwent a process of regionalization. This was the result of several factors: the increased influence of anthropological models emphasizing local integration; the widespread adoption of methodological approaches derived from "spatial archaeology" (that would crystallize in the following decade into the variety of approaches under the rubric of "landscape archaeology"); and a research agenda increasingly marked by the necessities of public archaeology, arising from changes in heritage legislation that were part of the administrative and political decentralization of the Spanish state. The take-off of public archaeology led first to the widespread preparation of regional site registers and subsequently of intense, though uneven, archaeological activity guided, not by specifically academic interests, but by the demands of urban growth and large-scale transformation of the countryside. The conjoined result of these factors has been a sharp growth of archaeological knowledge of parts of the Peninsula that previously had been almost unknown (the interior, the northwest, the Cantabrian facade) and the appearance of new categories of evidence (i.e, both the reevaluation of aspects of the archaeological record that hitherto had received little attention and the multiplication of lines of evidence that went beyond the limits of relevancy set by traditional approaches. The best example of this is the widespread recognition in various geographic contexts of sites like the ditch enclosures amply discussed in various chapters of this book. The "unique" character of phenomena like Los Millares has been belied by the appearances of other site complexes of equal or larger size (Marroquíes Bajos, La Pijotilla, Valencina de la Concepción, and so on). It has also lengthened the time over which we must consider the causes of the monumentalization of space, since at Mas d'Is this seems to go back to the Neolithic (Bernabeu *et al.*, this volume).

As a result of all this, and with "recent prehistory" as the unit of analysis, we are now, perhaps for the first time, able to evaluate the real complexity of the Peninsula's historical setting. Our understanding of that complexity arises precisely from the confrontation of the separate regional processes, rather than their concrete archaeographic differences, against a background of interpretative problems that demand theoretical frameworks capable of making sense of the diversity. The principal theoretical proposals formulated during the initial development of a post-traditional archaeology were tied to the case of the Peninsula's south-east. The contributions to this volume and the discussion at the session in Faro bear witness to the effort to adjust, or surpass, this theoretical heritage in order to address the diversity that seems to be the most salient characteristic of the archaeological record taken as a whole. Indeed, as the contribution by Bernabeu *et al.* notes, it is now as important to explain why the supposed development of class societies did *not* take place in most of the Peninsula as it is to explain why it *did* arise in some areas (the south-east and south-west).

The general orientation of the discussions in the Faro session suggests two centers of attention: one theoretical, involving the proposal of general interpretative models; the other empirical, subordinated to the former, involving the redefinition of the archaeological indicators of social inequality. Indeed, what is most notable about this volume is that the majority of the contributions have a number of presuppositions in common. It is most significant that the topic of reference of this session — the in principle ambiguous notion of "inequality" — should have been unanimously interpreted by the participants as a synonym for "exploitation", with few references to other possible social or political interpretations (e.g., "hierarchy" or "social stratification"). Consistently with this, most contributions share a certain number of terms with distinctly Marxian roots ("means of production", "social relations of production", and so on). In fact, the choice by the editors to use the term "inequality", rather than other possibilities such as the "complexity" normal in the Anglo-American processual tradition, indicates a certain wish to link the session's work to the core of the Marxian tradition.

In my role as discussant I suggested that this convergence, in part generated by the way the session was set up, permitted us to identify an "emergent paradigm" in the field of later Iberian prehistory, a paradigm whose theoretical core makes reference to what may be termed the "Marxist tradition", but one that defines a "scientific community" broader than what might be identified as Marxist and constitutes a research agenda of general value. We might term this current of thought, increasingly influential in the development of research, the "materialist paradigm".

I do not intend to propose a "paradigmatic interpretation" of the history of research on later Iberian prehistory, but I think that a flexible use of some of the ideas once put forward by Thomas Kuhn (even accepting all their limitations and the wear and tear produced by their popularity) may help clarify the current dynamics of that research from the point of view defined in this volume. In its most general (and ambiguous) acceptation a paradigm is "the entire constellation of beliefs, values, techniques and so on shared by members of a given community" (Kuhn 1970:175). The "scientific community" is identified by the practice of a specific type of research, defined by shared elements, referred to as "normal science". In Kuhn's (1979:513) reformulation, the shared elements that define "normal science" (and this the scope of a paradigm or, more precisely, a "disciplinary matrix") are: a theoretical language, a set of "models" (general theoretical assumptions about how and where this language is to be applied), and a series of "examples", or normative applications "accepted by the group as paradigmatic in a general sense". Externally, a paradigm is characterized by its opposition to rivals within the general scope of the discipline with which it competes to become the "dominant paradigm", a success that defines a "scientific revolution". I believe all of this can be seen in the current setting of research into later Iberian prehistory, as reflected in the contributions and references contained in this volume.

As we have seen, most of the contributions share certain basic ideas that define stand in contrast both to normativist culture-historical practice, on the one hand, and to functionalist processualism, on the other. The general assumptions that define this type of "materialist" research (and distinguish it from its culture-historical and processualist alternatives) can, simplifying drastically, be expressed in two propositions:

1.   The important variability in the archaeological record for later Iberian prehistory should be interpreted in social terms (as opposed to the "cultural" ones of the preceding normativist approach) characterized by the emergence beginning in the Neolithic of forms of political and economic inequality within communities.

2.   Social relations of production based on the appropriation of surplus labor (i.e., exploitation) are the determinant of these inequalities.

These shared principles identify a "materialist paradigm" in research on later Iberian prehistory, but that paradigm does not constitute a single theoretical model. On the contrary, the internal dynamic of that research is quite diverse and marked by competition between "models", in Kuhn's sense defined above. I believe this dynamic can be characterized by the existence of a dominant model, rather clearly defined by a series of normative applications (or "examples") and by a series of "emergent models", proposed in principle as applications for different problems. The process of "normal" competition between models should consist of attempts by each of them to appropriate the applications of the others and convert them into "examples", that is to say normative applications accepted by the entire community.

The dominant model is what we might term the "initial class society model" [ICSM], whose most notable, but not its only, examples are F. Nocete's (2001) interpretation of the Copper Age of the Guadalquivir valley and the Southeast as "state"-type class societies and the interpretation by V. Lull and his associates (Lull & Risch 1995) of the Argaric likewise. These are independent and not always compatible interpretations that are based on differing methodological approaches, and they operationalize fundamental categories of Marxist analysis differently. They share, however, a common interpretation of the two propositions enumerated above, namely, the identification of the archaeological markers of inequality in the record of their two cases as demonstrative of the existence of social classes.

The remaining elements of the ICSM, among the question of the "state", derive from this basic supposition. If one is dealing with class societies, we must suppose that its underlying social relationship, the one that determines the totality of the social structure, is class exploitation: a limited social segment, constituted as the dominant class, appropriates the surplus labor generated by the rest of the members of the society. For this to be possible, there must be surplus production and conditions that guarantee the dominant class privileged access to it and/or permanent control of how it is produced. Following Marx (1978), in precapitalist societies, unlike capitalist ones, the mechanism that guarantees the appropriation of surplus labor is non-economic coercion (physical or ideological) exercised by the dominant over the subordinate class. Under such conditions, the reproduction of the dominant class depends on its ability to maintain permanently its coercive capacity. Since this cannot depend on individual capabilities, but must rely on a political organization that controls the whole society and perpetuates itself over time, the "state" is defined as the sum of the conditions that make this possible. The existence of the state is, then, as much a consequence of, as a condition for, the existence of a class society. Thus, the analytical unit that makes the social processes of later Iberian prehistory intelligible is the problem of the origin of the state.

The paradigmatic nature of this conception (as applied to the Argaric "example") is clearly expressed in the following passage from Castro & Escoriza's contribution to this volume:

> Years ago [there] was debate about "chiefdoms" or "gangster-elites" in the Argaric political system, however it is now generally accepted that there was a state system. The institutionalisation of violence and its control enables us to define the political structure as a State... Only those who associate the "state" with governmental institutions ... comparable to those of the ancient Middle East doubt the State nature of the system ... Scientific debate today is centered on the mechanism of social exploitation, the existence of which cannot be doubted.

No doubt is possible about the existence of a mechanism of social exploitation because it is assumed as a general criterion for the interpretation of the archaeological evidence (proposition 2 *supra*): it is the delimiting criterion of the paradigm and cannot be questioned. Thus, the entire paradigmatic structure inevitably rests in one form or another upon dogmatic metaphysical assumptions (Kuhn 1979). Questioning the dogmatic nucleus would occur in one of Kuhn's revolutionary periods, but it is not part of normal investigation. This consists of reducing new case studies to the condition of "examples". Here the reduction is carried out by specifying the conditions under which new archaeological contexts can be described as belonging to initial class societies.

Some participants in the session (Castro & Escoriza, Cámara & Molina, as well J. Ramos, whose paper was not incorporated into the volume) presented papers defending the ICSM. These were all theoretical and critical essays, not proposals for new applications. This too characterizes a dominant model that needs more to defend the territory it has won against external criticism and internal contradictions than to gain new ground that might give rise to new contradictions. One must note, however, that one positive effect of these efforts at "theoretical refinement" is to make the internal contradictions of the ICSM evident: see, for example, Castro & Escoriza's critique of Nocete's use of the ICSM on chalcolithic data sets, a critique that makes plain the radical heterogeneity of the ICSM's principal "examples".

At the same time one can identify models that do or may challenge the ICSM for primacy within the "materialist paradigm". These assume that exploitative relations may exist in prehistoric societies that do not involve the formation of classes. This involves disagreement with the ICSM at the highest theoretical level, since it involves a differing interpretation of the very terms of the theoretical language. What we have termed "emergent models" involves proposals along this line with respect to different examples than those to which the ICSM is applied. Limiting ourselves to this volume, the contributions of Díaz del Río and Garrido are representative of this current. These and others that are theoretically less explicit (e.g., Ontañón and Bernabeu et al.) assume that structures of permanent exploitation exist within social formations, but at the same time recognize that there are structural limitations that hinder the development classes in the sense proposed by the ICSM.

In my view the opposition between a dominant ICSM and an emergent model (which we might describe generically as "models of pre-class development) currently constitutes the fundamental structure of the dynamics of normal research within the materialist "paradigm". This opposition carries on a division that already characterized the formative stage of the materialist, since the debate between class and pre-class interpretations of the Bronze Age of the South-east (exemplified by the respective claims of Lull [1983] and Gilman[1987]) goes back more than twenty years. The dynamic undoubtedly involves large theoretical issues that concern some of the basic principles of the Marxist matrix, such as the applicability of a Marxian notion of "social class" in precapitalist contexts, the Marxist theory of the state and that of modes of production.

That said, however, the proper establishment of a paradigmatic logic, with the consequent development of "normal" scientific research based on a series of minimal points of agreement, opens up perspectives for competition between theories that go beyond fairly dogmatic disputes over different readings of Marx of little interest outside the materialist paradigm itself. The ability of a materialist conception of archaeology to attract more support than the dominant external paradigmatic rivals with which it competes (namely, processualism abroad and culture-history within Iberia) depends on the capacity of its various "models" to account coherently for the new results of empirical investigations. As we have seen, these recent advances require us for the first time to address geographic and temporal scales beyond the bounds of single cases. As we have said, competition between models within a paradigm are resolved by the respective ability of each to reduce the examples of the others to its own terms, that is to say, by proposing more general hypotheses that show how the fundamental variability of the contexts to be explained are manifestations of a single process. To return to the point made by Bernabeu et al., the question facing the ICSM is not so much explaining all the social formations of recent Peninsular prehistory as state-type class societies, as to explain why probably many of them cannot be described in those terms. This involves acknowledging a process of differential development within the Peninsula.

The new setting produced by these empirical developments urgently raises the necessity of redefining the archaeological bases for the application of theoretical concepts. This is a point on which almost all the contributors to this volume seem to agree, no matter what their theoretical orientation. In fact, most of the contributions address in one way or another the necessity of establishing archaeological indicators for theoretical categories. This occurs because the indicators used by existing models have lost some of their significance as the archaeological record has expanded. This is what has happened to Nocete's (2001) identification of ditch enclosures and fortified settlements as the crucial marker of early class societies. The increased geographical and chronological extent of the known cases makes any single explanation of them impossible and converts them into polysemic signifiers whose meaning depends on other factors, as several of the contributors (Bernabeu et al., Díaz del Río, Márquez) point out. The same occurs with respect to funerary variability (García Sanjuan), "art" (Bueno & Balbín), etc. In this sense it is significant that the direct supporters ICSM are precisely the ones who insist on the need to redefine the archaeological indicators of exploitation.

In any event, this not the place to delve more deeply into the internal contradictions of the various models that have been proposed. I limit myself to offering a framework for interpreting, with the purely heuristic assistance of certain Kuhnian categories, what I believe to be the current dynamics of research on recent Iberian prehistory as reflected in this volume. A more systematic elaboration and formal justification of this reconstruction would require much more space and depth than seems reasonable in a prologue. Indeed, a critical review of my paradigmatic reconstruction would probably raise many more problems than I have resolved. Many of these problems would require specific investigation: How did the materialist disciplinary matrix in Iberian archaeology arise? Why has Marxism played such an important role, to the point of practically displacing processualism? Why hasn't Marxism pushed aside the culture-history that continues to be the real dominant paradigm in our archaeology?

Be that as it may, I believe that it helps clarify matters to organize the different competing approaches in the Iberian debate on social inequality as normative applications of theoretical models within a common paradigm. It makes it possible to appreciate some of the challenges presented by the growth of the archaeological record, to identify the nuclei of dogmatic thought that impede our progress, and to understand what I consider to be an exceptional case of how archaeological thought is formed.

I wish to close by thanking the organizers of the session and editors of this volume for having made possible the collection of so rich a set of materials.

El Escorial, 23 June 2006

References

GILMAN, A. 1987: "El análisis de clase en la Prehistoria del Sureste". *Trabajos de Prehistoria* 44: 27-34.

- 1996: "Craft specialization in late prehistoric Mediterranean Europe". En: B. Wailes (ed.) *Craft Specialization and Social Evolution: In Memory of V. Gordon Childe.* Unniversity Museum of Archaeology and Anthropology, University of Pennsylvania. Philadelphia: 67-71.

KUHN, Th. S. 1970: *The Structure of Scientific Revolutions.* 2nd ed. Enlarged. The University of Chicago Press, Chicago and London

- 1979: "Segundas reflexiones acerca de los paradigmas". In F. SUPPE (Ed.): *La estructura de las teorías científicas.* Translation by P. Castillo & E. Rada. Editora Nacional. Madrid: 509-533.

LULL, V. 1983. *La "Cultura" de El Argar* Akal. Madrid.

LULL, V. & RISCH, R. 1995: "El Estado Argárico". *Verdolay* 7: 97-109.

MARX, K. 1978: *El Capital. Crítica de la Economía Política. Volumen III.* Translation by W. Roces. Fondo de Cultura Económica. México D.F. 2ª edición, 13ª reimpresión.

NOCETE, F. 2001: *Tercer Milenio a.n.e. Relaciones y Contradicciones: Centro-Periferia en el Valle del Gualdalquivir.* Bellaterra. Barcelona.

CHAPTER 1

Advances, problems and perspectives in the study of social inequality in Iberian Late Prehistory

Leonardo García Sanjuán
Universidad de Sevilla
Pedro Díaz-del-Río
Consejo Superior de Investigaciones Científicas

Abstract

This paper attempts a general assessment of the contributions included in this volume. We examine three main kinds of problems related to the research on social inequality in Iberian Late Prehistory. These are theoretical, empirical and interpretative. Among the first, we comment upon the very definition of social inequality, the taxonomical categories employed in social evolution, as well as the main factors causing inequality, with special attention to labour force mobilisation. Among the second, we highlight some weaknesses of the Iberian archaeological record for the investigation of the subject matter, such as the limitations of the absolute chronology or the settlement record. Finally, we discuss the propositions that have been put forward to understand the forms that social inequality took among Neolithic, Copper and Bronze Age communities, concluding that Iberian archaeologists would much benefit from a comparative perspective.

Key words: Social inequality; Neolithic; Copper Age; Bronze Age; Iberian Peninsula; Historiography; Archaeological Theory; Labour Mobilisation.

Resumen

En este trabajo realizamos una valoración general de las aportaciones incluidas en este volumen. Distinguimos y comentamos una serie de problemas relativos a la investigación de la desigualdad social en la Prehistoria Reciente peninsular. Estos son teóricos, empíricos e interpretativos. Entre los primeros, destacan la discusión del concepto mismo de desigualdad social, las categorías taxonómicas relativas a la evolución social y los factores que la causan, con especial atención a la movilización de la fuerza de trabajo. Entre los segundos, se discuten las principales debilidades del registro arqueológico ibérico para el estudio de este tema, por ejemplo limitaciones de la cronología absoluta y del registro de asentamientos. Finalmente, se valoran las diferentes propuestas en relación con las formas en que se expresó la desigualdad social entre las comunidades del Neolítico, la Edad del Cobre y del Bronce de Iberia, concluyendo que sería beneficioso para los arqueólogos ibéricos un enfoque más comparativo.

Palabras clave: Desigualdad Social; Neolítico; Edad del Cobre; Edad del Bronce; Península Ibérica; Historiografía; Teoría Arqueológica; Movilización de Fuerza de Trabajo.

1.1.- Introduction

This volume is the product of a one day Session organised as part of the IVth *Congresso de Arqueología Peninsular*, held in Faro (Portugal, 14-19 September 2004). The aim of this meeting was to discuss the subject matter of prehistoric social inequality, a topic that had never before been at the centre of a session in an Iberian archaeology conference.

The geographic coordinates of the volume were already defined by the very title of the conference. Although from the onset our purpose was to embrace all of Iberia, the inevitable limitations on the availability of various colleagues have finally claimed their toll. Despite our interest, the resulting volume does not include contributions dealing specifically with regions like the Atlantic façade,

the North-west or the Balearic Islands. This makes the book slightly unbalanced, geography-wise, towards the South-eastern half of Iberia. However, this does not mean that the Western regions of Iberia are altogether absent from the discussion, as various chapters deal with them more or less specifically (*e.g.* Bueno & Balbín; Ontañón; García Sanjuán). In any case, the picture drawn by the twelve chapters is fairly representative of the geographical variability of the issue under discussion.

In chronological terms, all papers look at Late Prehistory. In Iberia this means the period encompassed between the second half of the Sixth and the beginning of the First millennia cal BC (Neolithic, Copper and Bronze Ages). The chronological framework is justified more on practical grounds, such as a limited availability of time for a one day Session, than on theoretical or thematic reasons.

Undoubtedly, it would have been of the greatest interest to examine the subject matter from the Upper Palaeolithic down to the pre-Roman Iron Age. We nevertheless chose to focus on Late Prehistory, in itself a coherent historical period, and therefore all papers deal with the first farming and metallurgical societies. Contributors were explicitly asked to use long chronological frameworks for their discussions. In the present state of knowledge, this is probably a wise approach to take, since the evidence often lacks enough detail or quality to examine variability within shorter periods of time.

From a thematic viewpoint, the authors of this volume tackle a wide series of issues. These include theoretical problems -like for example, applicability of social evolution taxonomies, centre-periphery relationships, or the sets of factors causing inequalities-, empirical problems - critical assessment of the validity of systems of empirical indicators, empirical testing of hypothesis, quality of the available data-, as well as interpretative problems - comparative inter-regional and diachronic analyses of the economic, social and ideological process involved in social inequality. The second and third sections of this chapter discuss further some of these issues, commenting on the attention and treatment they have received throughout this volume.

A volume such as this is in itself justified not only because of the intrinsic interest of the subject matter, but also because of the lack of a synthesis in English dealing with the entire Iberian Peninsula. The low presence of Iberia within global studies of European and Old World Prehistory has been a recurrent complaint -it could almost be said that a *historical* one- among Spanish and Portuguese colleagues. Of course, there is little doubt that this is partly due to the limited international impact that Iberian archaeological research has had in the past, mainly a consequence of its relatively low presence in English speaking journals. Within the last decade, the international impact of Iberian prehistoric research has improved thanks to initiatives such as the *Journal of Iberian Archaeology*, the increase in the pace of publication of syntheses and collective books in English (*cf.* Fernández Castro 1995; Lillios 1995; Cunliffe & Keay 1995; Díaz-Andreu & Keay 1997; Balmuth *et al.* 1997; Arnaiz *et al.* 2001; Chapman 2003), specialised subject monographs (Ramos Millán *et al.* 1991; Merideth 1998; Peña-Chocarro 1999; Forenbaher 1999; Rodríguez Díaz *et al.* 2001; Hunt Ortiz 2003; etc.) and a growing number of papers in international journals. However, there is still a long way to go. For many specialists both in Spain and Portugal, the practice of addressing research results to an international audience by means of their publication in English is still rather alien. Hence, this volume targets those scholars interested in both theoretical issues and Old World Archaeology, through the presentation of the current state of the art on prehistoric social inequality in Iberia.

The list of contributors suggests in itself the existence of a certain generation of scholars aware of the need to give Iberian Prehistory a wider international resonance. Although some contributors are senior academics, the majority are younger scholars that have developed their research careers well after the end of Franco's dictatorship. Trained by the first Spanish non-normative archaeologists, they have also had a more direct exposure to foreign research institutions and traditions. This is an aspect of the configuration of this volume that is worth assessing within its adequate historiographic context.

Despite some interesting precedents (*e.g.* Arribas 1968), the first studies specifically devoted to the subject of social complexity and inequality within Iberian Late Prehistory were published between the end of the 1970s and the early 1980s (Chapman 1978; 1982; Chapman *et al.* 1987; Gilman 1976; 1981; 1987a; 1987b; Gilman & Thornes 1985; Lull 1983; Lull & Estévez 1986; Mathers 1984a; 1984b; Ramos Millán 1981). These works had two fairly well defined features. First, their almost exclusive chrono-geographical focus was on the Copper and Bronze Ages (Los Millares and El Argar *cultures*) of the Spanish South-east, at that time the only area for which an extensive archaeological record was available. Secondly, the great influence that processual archaeology had on this line of research through the works of British and US scholars like A. Gilman, R. Chapman and C. Mathers. The process of consolidation of research on social complexity in the Late Prehistory of the Spanish South-east has already been sufficiently analysed from a theoretical and historiographical viewpoint (Martínez Navarrete 1989; Román 1996; Hernando 1999) and we shall therefore not dwell on it.

Over the last decade, several Portuguese and Spanish archaeologists have joined this line of work (*e.g.* Díaz Andreu 1991; Micó 1993; García Sanjuán 1999; Guerrero Ayuso 1999; Santos Gonçalves, 1999; Garrido-Pena 2000; Villoch 2000; Cámara 2001; Díaz-del-Río 2001; Nocete, 2001; Ontañón 2003). The interest on the subject matter of inequality has gradually expanded to other Iberian regions, where a more suitable archaeological record has been gradually built. As Garrido-Pena points out in Chapter 7, one of the main efforts made by specialists has consisted in the adaptation of theories and methods previously applied in the research of the Spanish South-east, to the newly recovered archaeological record of other Iberian regions. One of the aims of this book is precisely to reflect those efforts.

In general, contributors to this volume belong to the so-called second and third generations of Spanish post-normative archaeologists (Vicent 2001: xi). These scholars were the first ones to develop a theoretically oriented archaeology, no longer concerned with the critique of culture-history paradigms. Most of them develop processual arguments, occasionally informed by Marxian thought. Some have explicitly Marxist frameworks, while

2

others -the least- draw on certain postprocessual insights. The impact of non-Spanish archaeology in all of these perspectives can be traced through the most cited foreign authors: Robert Chapman, Antonio Gilman and Richard Harrison, the first three processual archaeologists to work on Iberian Prehistory.

Nevertheless, some discussion is now centred precisely on this theoretical perspective. Interestingly, the issues under discussion are not a direct result of the impact of postprocessualism (which in Spain has had comparatively little penetration) in the study of social inequality, but of the weight of some specific schools of Marxist thought in the current Iberian (especially Spanish) archaeological scene. The first, associated with the Universidad Autónoma de Barcelona, is known for its outstanding contribution to the current knowledge of the El Argar 'culture', among others. The second involves colleagues from the Universities of Granada, Jaén and Huelva that have published some important studies on Southeastern prehistory throughout the last decades. The reader will have a chance to decide whether their criticisms have a broader interest, beyond contemporary Spanish archaeological debates.

Altogether, a number of relevant theoretical, methodological and empirical issues emerge from the pages of this book. What follows is a preliminary attempt to evaluate them.

1.2.- Theoretical issues

As it often happens with very general (and debated) theoretical concepts, the notion of social inequality is not entirely straightforward – see for example Gilman 1995: 235. Not surprisingly, Raymond Williams *Keywords* (1983) and Tom Bottomore's *Dictionary of Marxist Thought* (2001) lack entries for "inequality" (although they do so for "equality"). An explicit definition is also absent in Price and Feinman's *Foundations of Social Inequality* (1995). In Chapter 2 of this volume, P. Castro Martínez and T. Escoriza Mateu provide an enlightening discussion of the problems attained in defining *inequality* (or need thereof), and some of its archaeological implications. As a human phenomenon, social inequality is sharply present in today's world, and therefore is bound to shape different approaches in one way or another. This is an epistemological issue that underlies much of the theories addressing human social inequality from Anthropology, Archaeology, or History.

It is commonly accepted that at an individual level all human beings are different (*unique*, *unequal*), mainly due to differences in biology, talent and ability. Suggesting a discussion of prehistoric social inequality in Iberia, our aim, however, was not to engage in a discussion on the irreducible individuality of human identity (or, for that matter, on the non-egalitarian nature of human individu-

als). Instead, our main aim was to discuss social forms of inequality that are specifically human and, furthermore, *why* have they only occurred within *certain* (and not among all) human societies (Anderson 1990: 187; Webster 1990: 346). This is obviously a formidable task that has been at the core of much discussion in political anthropology and prehistoric archaeology throughout most of the XXth century, and this book can only reflect some of the relevant issues involved.

Historically, social forms of inequality have been originated by socially and politically institutionalised mechanisms of economic exploitation. In their most extreme versions, these inequalities (entailing severe differences in the access to the resources and material means that sustain human life) cause, in those people at the lower statuses, serious life threats such as malnutrition, starvation, propensity to diseases, privation of freedom and other forms of mental and physical suffering. As M. Fried affirms "dangerous deprivation of individuals in non-stratified societies usually does not occur until there is a sharp reduction in the standard of living of all. All individuals physically capable of securing food can attempt to do so for there are no barriers between them and the basic resources (…) in stratified societies some members of the society face problems of subsistence different from those who enjoy direct access to basic resources…" (Fried, 1967: 188).

In our view, two elements must be mentioned as part of the notion of social inequality.

Firstly, economic exploitation may, in principle, occur in class and class-less societies. Individuals are exploited when they are forced to spend in production more time than the necessary to produce the goods they consume or when all or some of their productive output is exacted by others against their will. When producers produce their own consumption goods, the exploitation criteria would be to know if and how they also produce for the consumption of others (Elster 1986). Needless to say, this definition creates serious challenges for archaeologists.

In strongly socially-stratified societies, exploitation may cause individuals to be deprived of some of the basic elements that sustain life, hence making inequality insufferable. This leads us to the second element to be taken in to account, namely that human social inequality is a matter of degree: in some societies, inequalities are very mild and rather tolerable for those who suffer them, whereas in some other societies inequalities are brutal and cause extreme suffering to large numbers of people: "gentle, hidden exploitation is the form taken by man's exploitation of man whenever overt, brutal exploitation is impossible" (Bourdieu 1999: 192). Inequality and exploitation have also qualitative and quantitative aspects strongly related to the prevailing political conditions: social inequality has political, economic and ideological dimensions that are not necessarily coterminous (Price & Feinman 1995: 4).

As Castro and Escoriza suggest in Chapter 2 of this volume, we might just as well want to abandon the use of terms such as *equality-inequality*, favouring the *symmetry-asymmetry* dichotomy, and calling inequalities 'social exploitation'. But when confronted with such concepts, we may also feel the need to categorise them. The above cited authors suggest their own terminology: 'relative', 'partial' and 'extensive' exploitation. Although welcome, these concepts may have both theoretical and operational problems when dealing with the archaeological record and may therefore be as open to criticisms as the term 'inequality' itself.

Whether we call them *inequalities* or *asymmetries*, the fact remains that there are and have been forms of extreme social inequality derived from economic exploitation, like slavery, serfdom, caste or class systems and that there is a need to understand the circumstances and factors under which some human societies have developed them while others have not. With such aim in mind, the investigation inevitably arrives to the inception (and early development) of agrarian societies, when options for differential surplus appropriation increased and, consequently, new options for social exploitation developed. The original accumulation of surplus is crucial to understand the origins of aggressive forms of social inequality: without surplus production there are no movements in the concentration and expression of power and no qualitative shifts in economic relationships (Haldon 1993: 46).

To prehistoric archaeology, this field of research poses great challenges. The present book reflects the variety of different solutions and sensitivities to deal with it. We could for example highlight the relative absence in most contributions of explicit discussions on the taxonomic categories widely applied within prehistoric archaeology by neo-evolutionary or Marxist traditions (*e.g.* bands, tribes, chiefdoms, states, or modes of production). These categories are present, but not subject to specific scrutiny regarding their contents, scope and limitations. Some of them were certainly discussed in-depth by Iberian archaeologists in the 1980's: such was the case, for example, of the controversial notion of *chiefdom* (Ramos Millán 1981; Nocete 1984; González Wagner, 1990; Alcina Franch, 1990) or the Asiatic mode of production (Ruiz Rodríguez, 1978; Gómez Fuentes, 1985). Nowadays, however, the emphasis seems to have shifted towards the discussion of specific factors that motivated and embodied social inequality. These are, for instance, labour control and the monopolisation of the means of production (Díaz-del-Río 2004; Cámara & Molina in this volume), or forms of exploitation and inequality based on gender, to which little attention had been previously paid (Castro & Escoriza in this volume).

Another aspect worth highlighting is the pervasiveness of the current controversy regarding the extent and form of social inequalities among south Iberian Copper Age communities (*c.* 3300-2200 cal BC). There are two rather opposed views on this matter. According to the first, Chalcolithic social formations were *tributary states* in which central settlements, the residence of the elites, controlled in an exploitative way the agrarian and metallurgical production of peripheral and dependent communities (Nocete, 1984; 2004; Arteaga 1993; 2001; Cámara & Molina this volume). Some of these authors regard the set of communities settled along the lower basin of the Guadalquivir river as a *civilisation* (Arteaga 2001). This somewhat problematic term, frequently used for empire-state social formations based on urban systems, is also occasionally applied in a much more general manner, almost as a synonym of *culture* (*e.g.* by some French prehistorians to Upper Palaeolithic hunters-gatherers). For the second view, these societies did not develop highly institutionalised forms of power and social inequality. Instead, they were organised on communal economic principles, with collective access to means of production and products, and presented undifferentiated funerary ideologies. They would be therefore best described as pre-state societies (Ramos Millan 1981; Gilman 1987a; 1987b; Chapman 1990; García Sanjuán 1999; Castro *et al.* this volume).

Similarly, there is ongoing discussion over the character of Early Bronze Age societies (*c.* 2200-1500 cal BC). For example, the south-eastern El Argar 'culture' is regularly described as tributary and stratified, a class society at a State level according to some Marxist views. This State would have been controlled by strongly militaristic elites. Some other authors, including one of us (PDR), disagree with this perspective (*e.g.* Gilman 1998; Vicent 1998). At present, the focus is also set on the extent and intensity of the interaction between such a seemingly pristine tributary state and its neighbouring communities, especially in terms of exchange, metallurgy and militaristic ideology (and practice).

Nevertheless, this controversy becomes less prominent in current research when one moves towards Central and Northern Iberia. Although some disagreements do exist over the scale of complexity, there seems to be a wide agreement that Copper Age societies experienced less sharp inequalities (*e.g.* Díaz-del-Río, Ontañón or Garrido-Pena in this volume). The debate turns in this case to the nature of inequalities in what have been defined as 'middle-range societies'. The fact that this debate has frequently centred on the 'State controversy' can be misleading. Most prehistoric Iberian societies were far from being at the verge of statehood. The analysis of their social dynamics, and their material evidence, should be instructive when compared to the scale of complexity in the so-called states.

One key feature in the study of Iberian prehistoric social inequality is precisely the striking regional variations of social complexity. When observed from a comparative perspective, one of the emerging issues of this volume is the means by which labour force was mobilised and controlled throughout Late Prehistory. This is particularly clear for the Copper Age, when regional variability in the archaeological record is most salient. The III millennium BC is assumed to comprise the consolidation of a village way of life (but see Márquez in this volume), and most of all, the first generalised horizon of non-funerary monumentalisation crosscutting Iberia.

The existence of powerful chiefs, elites, or dominant social classes is frequently suggested when interpreting this archaeological evidence. All Neolithic, Copper and Bronze Age Iberian societies abound in examples of monumental infrastructures, only achievable through the involvement of a significant amount of labour force. Some contributors consider this evidence as the result of a society that mobilises labour through coercion. They suggest two relatively simple pathways: direct violence, and the generalisation of dependency ties and obligations through debt. Both are conceivable, although not always easy to demonstrate with the currently available evidence. And when so, they are frequently difficult to generalise to all of southern Iberia. Furthermore, as several authors have pointed out, an unavoidable background question arises: why, when placed at the brink of economic exploitation, would producers not just vote with their feet, ostracise the chief or, when persisting, kill him? (Harris 1982: 120-121; Haas 1982: 175; Clastres 1987:116). In the context of the Copper Age, land did not seem to be a limiting factor: fissioned segments could have colonised available areas, reproducing themselves with limited but efficient investments. As suggested, an increase of intergroup conflict could have triggered aggregations, something plausible in some parts of southern Iberia, where fortified settlements arose simultaneously, somehow following a dynamic of *sympathetic explosion* (Díaz-del-Río 2004). However, these means of mobilising social labour are questionable for most of Iberia, where aggregations seem to have preceded any evidence of overt conflict.

In most cases, aggregation patterns result in the construction of monumental enclosures, but these potential centres lack close-by similar neighbours that could suggest inter-group conflict as the triggering cause. In fact, these sites incorporate a significant number of features that are difficult to understand from a defensive logic. As a result, some authors have suggested their role as *monumentalised spaces*. Although pertinent, the emerging debate over the function of enclosures may obscure what we understand as the key aspect in this whole process: the concentration and immobilisation of vast investments of labour.

Our frequent difficulty to argue for effective means of coercion would require exploring other more persuasive means of mobilising social labour. Many of them do not necessarily lack coercive qualities: religious forms are often kind with the believer, but implacable with the sceptical. Structural power, as defined by Eric Wolf (1999), may not be easily traceable in the archaeological record, but its potential should not be dismissed. Not surprisingly, the majority of Late prehistoric materialised symbols come into play in Iberia precisely during the Copper Age, and their geographical concentration corresponds to those areas with largest enclosures. All this evidence disappears by the Bronze Age transition. It thus seems that certain ideologies were required to facilitate the *massing effect* (Sahlins 1961) of late prehistoric segmentary societies.

Nevertheless, many contributors do acknowledge the importance of analysing *tactical power*: the specific forms "used by individuals and groups to gain resources or advantages over others" (Wolf 1999: 290). Out of all, feasting is the preferred. Recent North American anthropological literature on the topic (*e.g.* Dietler & Hayden 2001) has been quickly assumed by many scholars. Different feasting mechanisms are used to explain a variety of archaeological cases. Work-feasts, competitive feasts, even potlatch, are mentioned when explaining enclosure building or bell beaker social dynamics.

These interpretations will probably mark future debates, and thus require some comments. The strength of feasting as a generalised explanatory argument depends on the strength of its archaeological evidence. As Hayden (2001: 35) notes, there is a wide range of feasts, all of which leave broad archaeological signatures. Nevertheless, although there are notable exceptions (*e.g.* Kelly 2001), impressive unambiguous evidence may not be that frequent. In order for feasting to become a powerful explanation, we should previously know what a feasting context would look like. For instance, and among others, a considerable amount of food remains and cooking utensils could be expected, somehow proportional to the amount of individuals gathered. This would be a good device when comparing regional evidence. Variability should inform us on the different effect of feasts as political economic mechanisms. Evidence may be in front of us, and must be highlighted. In the meantime, the use of feasting as a generalised argument can be an illuminating but misleading metaphor.

Altogether, a good deal of the debate concerning the social organisation of Iberian Copper and Bronze Age societies stems from openly diverging interpretations of the same archaeological evidence. The next section comments of the empirical problems posed by an archaeological record that is often fragmentary and ambiguous and to which highly demanding and complex questions are being increasingly asked.

1.3.- Empirical issues

Virtually all authors of this book formulate, at some point or another, a more or less bitter complaint about the limitations of the available archaeological evidence to tackle the study of social inequality. Four main reasons may account for those limitations.

First, for a long time Iberian archaeology had to devote vast efforts to build a chronological frame of reference in which to insert the events and attributes observable in the archaeological record. Until the extension of radiocarbon dating, that did not occur in Spain and Portugal until the late 1970's, the construction of a time frame by means of the formal study of well stratigraphically-documented artefacts (i.e. pottery typologies) was the main and most time-consuming challenge of Iberian prehistorians. This explains, for example, the stratigraphic approach followed in the excavation of a majority of settlements and, consequently, the remarkable scarcity of open-area recordings until the 1980's. Second, the study of wide segments of the archaeological record is a recent phenomenon. Within Iberian Culture-History archaeology, human, botanical or faunal remains were often considered of little or, at most, secondary epistemological value. Thirdly, although the 1980's was the period of the *awakening* of regional surveys and spatial archaeology in both Spain and Portugal (e.g. *Arqueología Espacial* 1984), the energy invested in these projects has often resulted in a relative void when it comes to current interpretations. This seems strange, considering that the analysis of polities is of key relevance to a reasonable understanding of socioeconomic relations in and between groups. Finally, Culture-History perspectives favoured the excavation and study of funerary sites. When confronted with the available evidence, one of the most limiting factors in the study of social inequality is precisely this frequent bias towards the funerary record, as the case of southern Iberia suggests (García Sanjuán 1999).

Yet, the archaeological study of social organisation in general, and of the social forms of inequality in particular, demands a wide and robust archaeological evidence capable of supporting empirical testing relative to multiple economic, social and ideological aspects. Prominent among these are variations in the accumulation of food resources and labour within and between communities, patterns of consumption, gender roles, hierarchical status of settlements, the ideological role of conspicuous consumption, or the accumulation of value in funerary spaces (both in architecture and artefacts).

Interestingly, and despite the limitations highlighted above, a common trait in several contributions of this book is precisely the use of settlement evidence. An excellent example of this can be found in Chapter 8, where Bernabeu, Molina, Díez and Orozco analyse differential labour investments in Neolithic ditch enclosures of the Spanish Levant. In fact, the last decade has witnessed the publication of an important series of monographs that account of extensive and multi-disciplinary research in a number of important Neolithic, Copper and Bronze Age settlements, like, to name but a few, Leceia (Cardoso 1994; 2003), Moncín (Harrison *et al.* 1994), El Castillo (Harrison *et al.* 1998), Gatas (Castro Martínez *et al.* 1999), Fuente Álamo (Schubart *et al.* 2000), Peñalosa (Contreras 2000) or Cabezo Juré (Nocete 2004). This is a

limited but promising evidence of the shift in the way future Iberian research will be carried out.

Undoubtedly, the publication of high quality research on single sites will produce increasingly sophisticated interpretations on the subject of social inequality. For the time being, it is not hard to perceive that the quality of data is rather limited. Although scholars may have highly structured research agendas and robust methodologies, empirical support must be obtained from fragmentary and ambiguous evidences. The currently available record calls for hypothesis building, but rarely allows conclusive testing. This conveys two risks that all contributions to this volume are likely to reflect in one way or another. The first involves the generation of interpretations that lack or have a poor connection between the theoretical formulation of the problem and the supporting data. The second is the temptation to perform disproportionate or openly biased evaluations. Narratives are easily built, but their strength depends on qualified support: often, the gap between hypothesis building and empirical support is too obvious to hide, and too many things have to be taken for granted.

It is quite tempting to apply theoretical models based on anthropological analogies to explain social inequality among prehistoric societies. They frequently create narratives that are coherent in themselves. However, archaeological explanations are not necessarily formulated in this manner. Anthropological and archaeological research carried out over the last century suggest the diversity of intervening causes, situations and trajectories of social inequality. They both call for historically rooted analyses. Theoretical frameworks have key importance introducing structure and rationality in the underlying research premises, but they are important insofar as they vertebrate hypotheses that can be empirically tested. If theoretical formulation is confounded with interpretation, then research becomes a hollow narrative. We should keep a *clinical* relationship with the data: precipitated or excessive interpretations of the data lead to the puddle of sterile discussion.

The imbalance between questions and theoretical formulations, on one hand, and the available information on the other, allows radically different interpretations on the same topics. This probably reflects the early, incipient, character of the archaeological research on this subject matter. It is, however, obvious, that a comparative project requires increased efforts towards high-quality analyses of the archaeological record at both regional and local scales.

Over the last 20 years Iberian Archaeology has learned the kind of empirical record required in order to discuss issues of social inequality. Iberia is a large, complex, and ecologically diverse region. Prehistoric societies, although not necessarily determined by environmental diversity, inevitably had to cope with it. Social and economic processes, and their resulting archaeological record, were also diverse. Hence, this can be a key conclusion that any non-iberian reader could draw from the present book. Although this diversity of processes may seem obvious, it has not received proper attention in the context of Iberian archaeological practice: the comparative project put forward by North-American Anthropology has had few supporters in both Spanish and Portuguese archaeologies. Historical -and occasionally cultural-contingency dominates current interpretations, something not necessarily contradictory with a comparative archaeology. While regional studies have allowed an increasingly detailed understanding of local dynamics, comparative analyses beyond them have not been regularly practised. Fragments of past histories can be followed throughout the book, and their variability will come to forth, suggesting both striking regularities and indicative differences. Some contributors do take into account this variability, and their suggestions should have challenging effects in future research. As editors, we think that Iberian archaeology would benefit greatly from one such comparative project. It is true that in the current state of the research of prehistoric social inequality we probably have many more questions than answers. Nevertheless, we do have a rational and legitimate need for a scientific knowledge that can help us to understand such a potent and present human problem.

Acknowledgments

We would like to acknowledge the support and help of Nuno Ferreira Bicho, University of Faro, during the celebration of the Session of which this book gives account, and for having enabled its independent publication. We would also like to thank Juan M. Vicent and Tatiana Andronova for their useful comments on the first drafts of this paper.

Professor Antonio GIlman kindly translated Dr. Vicent's Prologue, while Ruth Taylor translated various chapters and made the final revision of the manuscript. Thank you also to Jose Luis Garcia Valdivia for various editing and indexing tasks. Finally, we must thank the contributions of A. Ramos Millan, J. Ramos Muñoz, L. Oosterbeek and Victor Hurtado Perez, who participated in the session held at the Faro Congress, but, due to various contingencies of academic life, have been unable to see their valuable contributions reflected in this book.

1.4.- References

ALCINA FRANCH , J. 1990: "Las jefaturas en perspectiva arqueológica." In J. Adánez Pavón, C.M. Heras Martínez & C. Varela Torrecilla eds.: *Espacio y Organización Social*. Madrid. Universidad Complutense: 35-56.

ANDERSON, D. G. 1990: "Stability and change in chiefdom-level societies. An examination of Mississippian political evolution on the South Atlantic slope". In M. Williams & G. Shapiro eds.: *Lamar Archaeology. Mississippian Chiefoms in the Deep South*. Tuscaloos. The University of Alabama Press: 187-252.

ARNAIZ VILLENA, A.; MARTÍNEZ LASO, J. & GÓMEZ CASADO, E. Eds. 2001: *Prehistoric Iberia. Genetics, Anthropology and Linguistics*. Plenum Publishers. New York.

ARQUEOLOGÍA ESPACIAL 1984: *Arqueología Espacial. Coloquio sobre la distribución y relaciones entre los asentamientos*. Vols. 1-6. Seminario de Arqueología y Etnología Turolense. Colegio Universitario de Teruel. Teruel.

ARRIBAS, A. 1968: "Las bases económicas del Neolítico al Bronce". In M. Tarradell Ed.: *Estudios de Economía Antigua de la Península Ibérica*. Vicens Vives. Barcelona: 33-60.

ARTEAGA, O. 1993: "Tribalización, jerarquización y Estado en el territorio de El Argar". *Spal* 1 (1992): 179-208.

- 2001: "La sociedad clasista inicial y el origen del estado en el territorio de El Argar". *Revista Atlántica-Mediterránea de Prehistoria y Arqueología Social* 3 (2000): 121-219.

BALMUTH, M. S.; GILMAN, A. & PRADOS-TORREIRA, L. Eds. 1997: *Encounters and Transformations. The Archaeology of Iberia in Transition*. Monographs in Mediterranean Archaeology 7. Sheffield Academic Press. Sheffield.

BOTTOMORE, T. ed. 2001: *A Dictionary of Marxist Thought*. Blackwell. Oxford.

BOURDIEU, P. 1999: *Outline of a Theory of Practice*. Cambridge University Press. Cambridge.

CARDOSO, J. L. 1994: *Leceia 1983-1993. Escavações do Povoado Fortificado Pré-histórico*. Estudos Arqueológicos de Oeiras, Nº especial. Câmara Municipal de Oeiras. Oeiras.

- 2003: *O Povoado Prè-histórico de Leceia no Quadro da Investigaçao e Valorizaçao do Patrimonio Arqueológico Portugués. Síntese de Vinte Anos de Excavaçoes Arqueológicas (1983-2002)*. Câmara Municipal de Oeiras. Oeiras.

CASTRO MARTÍNEZ, P.; CHAPMAN, R. W.; GILI, S.; LULL, V.; MICÓ, R.; RIHUETE, C.; RISCH, R. & SANAHUJA, M. E. 1999: *Proyecto Gatas 2. La Dinámica Arqueoecológica de la Ocupación Prehistórica*. Junta de Andalucía. Sevilla.

CHAPMAN, R.W. 1978: "The evidence of prehistoric water control in Southeast Spain". *Journal of Arid Environments* 1: 261-274.

- 1982: "Autonomy, ranking and resources in Iberian Prehistory". In C. Renfrew & S. Shennan Eds.: *Ranking, Resource and Exchange. Aspects of Archaeology of Early European Society*. Cambridge University Press. Cambridge: 46-51.

- 1990: *Emerging Complexity: the later prehistory of south-east Spain, Iberia and the west Mediterranean*. Cambridge University Press. Cambridge.

- 2003: *Archaeologies of Complexity*. Routledge. London.

CHAPMAN, R.; LULL, V.; PICAZO, M. & SANAHUJA, M. E. Eds. 1987: *Proyecto Gatas: Sociedad y Economía en el Sudeste de España c. 2500-800 a.n.e. La Prospección Arqueológica*. British Archaeological Reports. International Series 348. Oxford.

CLASTRES, P. 1987: *Investigaciones en Antropología Política*. Gedisa. Barcelona.

CONTRERAS, F. Ed. 2000: *Análisis Histórico de las Comunidades de la Edad del Bronce del Piedemonte meridional de Sierra Morena y Depresión Linares-Bailén. Proyecto Peñalosa*. Arqueología. Monografías 10. Junta de Andalucía. Sevilla.

CUNLIFFE, B. & KEAY, S. Eds. 1995: *Social Complexity and the Development of Towns in Iberia*. Proceedings of the British Academy 86. Oxford University Press. Oxford.

DÍAZ-ANDREU, M. 1991: *La Edad del Bronce en el NE de la Submeseta Sur. Un Análisis sobre el Inicio de la Complejidad Social*. Universidad Complutense de Madrid. Madrid.

DÍAZ-ANDREU, M. & KEAY, S. Eds. 1997: *The Archaeology of Iberia. The Dynamics of Change*. Routledge. London.

DÍAZ-DEL-RÍO, P. 2001: *La Formación del Paisaje Agrario. Madrid en el III y II Milenios BC*. Comunidad de Madrid. Madrid.

- 2004: "Factionalism and collective labor in Copper Age Iberia." *Trabajos de Prehistoria* 61 (2): 85-98.

DIETLER, M. & HAYDEN, M. Eds. 2001: *Feasts. Archaeological and Ethnographic Perspectives on Food, Politics, and Power*. Smithsonian Institution Press. Washington.

ELSTER, J. 1986: *An Introduction to Karl Marx*. Cambridge University Press. Cambridge.

FERNÁNDEZ CASTRO, M. C. 1995: *Iberia in Prehistory*. Blackwell. Oxford.

FETSCHER, I. 2001: "Equality". In T. Bottomore ed.: *A Dictionary of Marxist Thought*. Blackwell. Oxford: 177-178.

FORENBAHER, S. 1999: *Production and Exchange of Bifacial Flaked Stone Artifacts during the Portuguese Chalcolithic*. British Archaeological Reports. International Series 756. Archaeopress. Oxford.

FRIED, M. 1967: *The Evolution of Political Society. An Essay in Political Anthropology*. Random House. New York

GARCÍA SANJUÁN, L. 1999: *Los Orígenes de la Estratificación Social. Patrones de Desigualdad en la Edad del Bronce del Suroeste de la Península Ibérica (Sierra Morena Occidental c. 1700-1100 a.n.e./2100-1300 A.N.E.)*. British Archaeological Reports International Series S823. Archaeopress. Oxford.

GARRIDO-PENA, R. 2000: *El Campaniforme en la Meseta Central de la Península Ibérica (c. 2500-2000 a.C.)*. British Archaeological Reports. International Series 892. Archaeopress. Oxford.

GILMAN, A. 1976: "Bronze Age Dynamics in South-East Spain". *Dialectical Anthropology* 1: 307-319.

- 1981: "The development of social stratification in Bronze Age Europe". *Current Anthropology* 22 (1): 1-23.

- 1987a: "Unequal development in Copper Age Iberia." In E.M. Brumfiel & T.K. Earle eds.: *Specialization, Exchange and Complex Societies*. Cambridge University Press. Cambridge: 22-29.

- 1987b: "El análisis de clase en la Prehistoria del Sureste". *Trabajos de Prehistoria* 44: 27-34.

- 1995: "Prehistoric European Chiefdoms. Rethinking 'Germanic' Societies". In T.D. Price and G.M. Feinman eds.: *Foundations of Social Inequality*. Plenum Press. New York: 235-251.

- 1998: "Reconstructing Property Systems from Archaeological Evidence". In R.C. Hunt & A. Gilman eds.: *Property in Economic Context*. Monographs in Economic Anthropology 14. University Press of America. Lanham: 215-233.

GILMAN, A. & THORNES, J. B. 1985: *Land Use and Prehistory in Southeast Spain*. George Allen & Unwin. London.

GÓMEZ FUENTES, A. 1985: "El estado minoico y el modo de producción asiático". *Zephyrus* 37-38: 249-254.

GONÇALVES, V. S. 1999: *Reguengos de Monsaraz. Territorios Megalíticos*. Ministerio da Cultura. Lisboa.

GONZÁLEZ WAGNER, C. 1990: "La jefatura como instrumento de análisis para el historiador: cuestiones teóricas y metodológicas." In J. Adánez Pavón, C. Heras Martínez & C. Varela Torrecilla Eds.: *Espacio y Organización Social*. Universidad Complutense de Madrid. Madrid: 91-108.

GUERRERO AYUSO, V. M. 1999: *Arquitectura y Poder en la Prehistoria de Mallorca*. Editorial El Tall. Palma de Mallorca.

HAAS, J. 1982: *The Evolution of the Prehistoric State*. Columbia University Press. New York.

HALDON, J. 1993: *The State and the Tributary Mode of Production*. Verso. London

HARRIS, M. 1982: *El Materialismo Cultural*. Alianza. Madrid

HARRISON, R. J.; RUPÉREZ, T. A.; MORENO LÓPEZ, G. Eds. 1998: *Un Poblado de la Edad del Bronce en El Castillo (Frías de Albarracín, Teruel)*. British Archaeological Reports. International Series 708. Oxford.

HARRISON, R. J.; MORENO, G. C. & LEGGE, A. J. 1994: *Moncín. Un Poblado de la Edad del Bronce (Borja, Zaragoza)*. Diputación General de Aragón. Zaragoza.

HAYDEN, B. 2001: "Fabulous Feasts. A Prolegomenon to the Importance of Feasting". In M. Dietler & B. Hayden eds.: *Feasts. Archaeological and Ethnographic Perspectives on Food, Politics, and Power*. Smithsonian Institution Press. Washington: 23-64.

HERNANDO GONZALO, A. 1999: *Los Primeros Agricultores de la Península Ibérica. Una Historiografía Crítica del Neolítico*. Síntesis. Madrid.

HUNT ORTIZ, M. 2003: *Prehistoric Mining and Metallurgy in South West Iberian Peninsula*. British Archaeological Reports. International Series 1188. Archaeopress. Oxford.

KELLY, L.S. 2001: "A Case of Ritual Feasting at the Cahokia Site". In M. Dietler & B. Hayden eds.: *Feasts. Archaeological and Ethnographic Perspectives on Food, Politics, and Power.* Smithsonian Institution Press. Washington: 334-367.

LILLIOS, K. Ed. 1995: *The Origins of Complex Societies in Late Prehistoric Iberia.* International Monographs in Prehistory. Archaeological Series 8. Ann Arbor University. Michigan.

LULL, V. 1983: *La "Cultura" de El Argar. Un Modelo para el Estudio de las Formaciones Económico-Sociales Prehistórica.* Akal. Madrid.

LULL, V. & ESTÉVEZ, J. 1986: "Propuesta metodológica para el estudio de las necrópolis argáricas". *Homenaje a Luis Siret (1934-1984).* Diputación Provincial. Sevilla: 441-452.

MATHERS, C. 1984a: "Linear regression, inflation and prestige competition: 2nd millenium transformations in SE Spain". In W. Waldren, R.W. Chapman, J. Lewthwaite & R.C. Kennard Eds.: *The Deyá Conference of Prehistory. Early Settlement in the Western Mediterranean Islands and their Peripheral Areas.* British Archaeological Reports International Series 229. Oxford: 1167-1196.

- 1984b: "Beyond the grave: the context and wider implications of mortuary practice in South-east Spain". In T.F. Blagg, R.F. Jones & S. Keay Eds.: *Papers in Iberian Archaeology.* British Archaeological Reports International Series 193. Oxford: 13-46.

MARTÍNEZ NAVARRETE, M. I. 1989: *Una Revisión Crítica de la Prehistoria Española: La Edad del Bronce como Paradigma.* Siglo XXI. Madrid.

MERIDETH, C. 1998: *An Archaeometallurgical Survey for Ancient Tin Mines and Smelting Sites in Spain and Portugal. Mid-Central Western Iberian Geographical region 1990-1995.* British Archaeological Reports. International Series 714. Archaeopress. Oxford.

MICÓ PÉREZ, R. 1993: *Pensamientos y Prácticas en las Arqueologías Contemporáneas: Normatividad y Exclusión en los Grupos Arqueológicos del III y II milenios cal ANE en el Sudeste de la Península Ibérica.* Universitat Autònoma de Barcelona. Barcelona.

NOCETE, F. 1984: "Jefaturas y territorio: una visión crítica". *Cuadernos de Prehistoria de la Universidad de Granada* 9: 289-304.

- 2001: *Tercer Milenio a.n.e. Relaciones y Contradicciones Centro-Periferia en el Valle del Gualdalquivir.* Bellaterra. Barcelona.

- Ed. 2004: *Odiel. Proyecto de Investigación Arqueológica para el Análisis del Origen de la Desigualdad Social en el Suroeste de la Península Ibérica.* Junta de Andalucía. Sevilla.

ONTAÑÓN PEREDO, R. 2003: *Caminos Hacia la Complejidad. El Calcolítico en la Región Cantábrica.* Universidad de Cantabria. Santander.

PEÑA-CHOCARRO, L. 1999: *Prehistoric Agriculture in Southern Spain during the Neolithic and the Bronze Age. The Application of Ethnographic Models.* British Archaeological Reports. International Series 818. Archaeopress. Oxford.

PRICE, T.D. & FEINMAN, G.M. 1995: "Foundations of Prehistoric Social Inequality". In T.D. Price and G.M. Feinman eds.: *Foundations of Social Inequality.* Plenum Press. New York: 3-11.

RAMOS MILLÁN, A. 1981: "Interpretaciones secuenciales y culturales de la Edad del Cobre en el Sur de la Península Ibérica. La alternativa del Materialismo Cultural". *Cuadernos de Prehistoria de la Universidad de Granada* 6: 203-256.

RAMOS MILLÁN, A.; MARTÍNEZ, G.; FERNÁNDEZ, G.; RIOS JIMÉNEZ, G. & AFONSO MARRERO, J. A. Eds. 1991: *Flint Production and Exchange in the Iberian Southeast, III millenium BC.* University of Granada. Granada.

ROMÁN DÍAZ, M. P. 1996: *Estudios sobre el Neolítico en el Sureste de la Península Ibérica. Síntesis Crítica y Valoración.* Universidad de Almería. Almería.

RODRÍGUEZ DÍAZ, A.; PAVÓN SOLDEVILA, I.; MERIDETH, G. & JUAN I TRESSERRAS, J. 2001: *El Cerro de San Cristobal, Logrosan, Extremadura, Spain. The Archaeometallurgical Excavation of a Late Bronze Age Tin-Mining and Metalworking Site. First Excavation Season.* British Archaeological Reports. International Series 922. Archaeopress. Oxford.

RUIZ RODRÍGUEZ, A. 1978: "Elementos para un análisis de la fase asiática de transición". In VVAA: *Primeras Sociedades de Clase y Modo de Producción Asiático.* Akal. Madrid: 9-39.

SAHLINS, M.D. 1961: "The Segmentary Lineage: An Organization of Predatory Expansion". *American Anthropologist* 63(2): 322-345.

- 1977: *The use and abuse of Biology. An Anthropological Critique of Sociobiology.* University of Michigan Press.

SCHUBART, H.; PINGEL, V. & ARTEAGA, O. Eds. 2000: *Fuente Álamo. Las Excavaciones Arqueológicas (1977-1991) en el Poblado de la Edad del Bronce.* Junta de Andalucía. Sevilla.

SOUSA, A. C. 1998: *O Neolítico Final e o Calcolítico na Área da Ribeira de Cheleiros.* Ministerio da Cultura. Lisboa.

VICENT, J.M. 1998: "La Prehistoria del Modo Tributario de Producción". *Hispania* LVIII-3 (200): 29-36.

- 2001: "Prólogo". In P. Díaz-del-Río: *La formación del paisaje agrario. Madrid en el III y II milenios BC.* Arqueología, Paleontología y Etnografía 9. Comunidad de Madrid. Madrid: ix-xiii.

VILLOCH VÁZQUEZ, V. 2000: *La Configuración Social del Espacio entre las Sociedades Constructoras de Túmulos en Galicia.* Universidad de Santiago de Compostela. Santiago de Compostela.

WEBSTER, G. S. 1990: "Labor control and emergent stratification in Prehistoric Europe." *Current Anthropology* 31 (4): 337-366.

WILLIAMS, R. 1983: *Keywords. A Vocabulary of Culture and Society. Revised Edition.* Oxford University Press. New York.

WOLF, E.R. 1999: *Envisioning power. Ideologies of Dominance and Crisis.* University of California Press. Berkeley.

CHAPTER 2

Labour, inequality and reality. Arguments not to perpetuate fictions about prehistory

Pedro V. Castro Martínez
Universidad Autónoma de Barcelona
Trinidad Escoriza Mateu
Universidad de Almería

Abstract

We make a critical reflection on concepts such as Origin and Development (linked to notions of Progress and Process) and Social Inequality (a formal approach without real content). Similarly, we review various concepts derived from the former which are widely used within Archaeology, evaluating their inherent problems and limitations. Finally, we attempt to make a contribution for a historical sociology which, from Archaeology, contemplates the objective conditions of social life. We regard production and social life as the necessary departure point from which to assess the social reality of men and women. We believe that the main aim of a Social Archaeology is to know, in every historical situation, whether sexual and social groups maintain symmetrical or asymmetrical social relations and whether those relations are presided by reciprocity or by labour exploitation.

Key words: Inequality; Origins; Development; History; Labour; Production; Social Archaeology.

Resumen

Proponemos una reflexión crítica sobre los conceptos de Origen y Desarrollo (vinculados a ideas de Progreso y Proceso) y de Desigualdad Social (aproximación formal sin contenido real). Igualmente revisamos diversos conceptos derivados de los anteriores y de amplio uso en arqueología, evaluando sus problemas y limitaciones. Finalmente, intentamos, desde la arqueología, aportar argumentos para una sociología histórica, que contemple las condiciones objetivas de la vida social. Consideramos la producción y el trabajo social como el punto de partida imprescindible para valorar la realidad de las mujeres y los hombres. Porque creemos que el objetivo prioritario de una Arqueología Social es conocer en cada situación histórica, si los colectivos sexuales y sociales mantienen relaciones simétricas o disimétricas, si prima la reciprocidad o si se impone la explotación del trabajo.

Palabras clave: Desigualdad; Orígenes; Desarrollo; Historia; Trabajo; Producción; Arqueología Social.

2.1.- Introduction

Marx said, *"Right, instead of being equal, would have to be unequal"* (Marx 1875), an affirmation that moves away of the currently dominant ideology. The main principle of dominant liberalism evaluates all types of inequality of rights (but not in fact) in a negative light. Vindicating inequality, even discrimination, can be qualified as immoral and is always discredited, if not sanctioned. However, recovering the old affirmation could be the only way to open a path that roots out the privileges of social reality. We are talking about privileges that are hidden behind a veil of formal equality, about social dissymmetry that the homogeneity of rights not only does not resolve but actually favours.

Reflections that are based on the equality-inequality dichotomy are not yet part of the political agendas, nor do they form part of the majority of social theories that have been translated into the realms of Archaeology. However, in this paper we intend to put forward the following argument: we must stop talking about Social Inequalities. It is often a concept that falls short of what we really want to communicate. While, at other times, we have to stop and think if when we use it we really mean something. It would be much more relevant to talk about social and material realities, abandoning this formal euphemistic terminology that is only good for maintaining fictitious sociological knowledge.

Such a theory requires concepts such as Origin and Development. These are terms that undoubtedly contribute to relativist and subjective perspectives of historical-cultural roots. Nevertheless, they can whittle away a correct approximation to the knowledge of past societies, whilst restricting the focus to paths of unidirectional historical change.

Perhaps a great deal of what we are saying here may seem obvious, but we believe that the obvious is the first thing that should be remembered. To transfer something into the realms of the obvious often entails forgetting it. The next step is to think and act without being aware of it. The result is that the fruit of social theorisation (or of social interpretations) translates into fiction something that is a far cry from reality, past or present.

2.2.- Origins, Developments and Processes

Origins and Developments are concepts that are directly related to a dominant line of thought that gives priority to the principles of Evolution, Progress or Process. Origins are understood as singular, and once they become (whatever they come to be) their continuity to present day is set in motion. Developments are, without exception, processes that from these origins head towards the establishment of a phenomenon, whatever that phenomenon may be.

In Prehistoric Archaeology, some of the 'Origins' that have become referential milestones are those of the human species (Hominisation), agricultural production (the Neolithic Revolution), Civilisation, State and Social Classes (the Urban Revolution of Childe) or Society today (the Industrial Revolution).

The background of an Evolutionist idea of Origins can be found in the acceptance of a path of no return, the start of something that heads right on. Its development, in terms of Progress or Process, follows the appropriate path in the appropriate direction (these days, it is often said, towards complexity). The appropriate final destination is our own society, taking for granted the fact that we have arrived at the end of a path of Progress - the "end of history itself" in the words of Fukuyama. "There once was history, but not any longer", because the dominant class today, the one that understands Progress as "economic history", revokes the threat of any other irreversible employment of time (Debord 1967:143).

With this unilateral and univocal vision of historical paths, the concept of the Origins turns into an unquestionable landmark in pushing out the boundaries. Going beyond Origins involves an apathetic contemplation of all of what have not reached similar breakthroughs. The collectives or societies that have not managed to overcome one barrier or another no longer form part of the "History of Their Time". They remain "Backward" or from "Other Periods in Time". We frequently hear of one community or other being "prehistoric" or "medieval", as if its reality did not form part of a common present, or of a determined historical situation. Consequently, they are silenced or hidden away.

In practice, social interpretations of Prehistory also tend to follow the same lead. All the attention is fixed preferentially on "advanced" societies, and there is a certain admiration for the accomplishments of Civilisations in detriment to the "backwardness" of other societies. Who

could not but admire the Pyramids as a masterpiece of humanity (forgetting, of course, the toil and misery that accompanied their construction)?

The notion of Origins leaves historical reality waiting in the wings which demonstrates, through its dogged presence, how what "started" came to an "end". Moreover, it offers the information necessary to avoid overlooking the fact that, often, the beginnings of something cannot be extrapolated from one historical situation to another.

The concept of Origins is also part of the conceptual foundations of Historical-Cultural issues. Peoples, ethnic groups and nations also have origins, those *roots* that are submerged in the past, and from which emerge the 'being' in search of his/her destiny. A destiny that, moving away from the foci of Evolution and Process, will not be eternal but, in contrast, will suffer a life and a series of cycles that take on the assumption of its finiteness.

The concept of Development also concurs with ideas of Progress. The very same conception of Economic Development takes into account the technological dimension and growth of production, but in detriment of an appropriate evaluation of the quality of life that accompanies it. As such, the notion of Underdevelopment displaces the communities subjected to expropriation, looting and colonial extortion from History itself. Those who have fallen from the train of Progress are placed in the realms of the "Ahistoric"

Situations of Advanced Development or Underdevelopment are conceived as Social Inequalities, and are explained rather more as fruits of chance and History than as the reality of colonial, imperial or capitalist global relations. Of course, it has been some times now since the dependence of the underdeveloped and the existence of "advanced countries" have been demonstrated. Not to mention the fallacy that the Undeveloped would attain more advanced "Levels" of development, forgetting that this development depends on the transfer of wealth from underdeveloped areas.

No doubt, the nostalgia for historical laws often leads to the search for necessary and adequate emergent conditions for the observed phenomena. However, social practices have been able to obfuscate the process, sketching out unsuspected paths.

In the light of these implications, it would be better to abandon notions of Origin and, for each individual situation, to pay particular attention to the real conditions of social relationships in each one of the individual situations, and to the specific paths that each community followed. The opposite would be to accept that the path has already been written, and that we already know how things have been and how things will turn out.

2.3.- The fallacy of equality: Identity and its consequences

The values of equality dominate current Western political thought. They lay the ideological foundations of the so-called democratic societies. The political principle is that the rights of the individual must be identical, the same, equal.

The basic principle is that all subjects, whether part of one or other collective, should have exactly the same rights when participating in political and social life. In our society, this assumes the right to compete for or attain certain determined objectives that will only differ depending on merit and ability. A useful metaphor in this case is sport, where all competitors are behind the same starting line, each with the same right as the next to obtain his/her personal goal. The philosophy of winning and losing, of winner and loser, will ascribe both breakthroughs and frustrations to each subject. However, this sporting metaphor, with its equalitarian principles, does not take into account the social or objective conditions under which each subject or collective have arrived at the starting line. The past, the context, and the circumstances are avoided. Only the principle of equality prevails.

For this very reason, explanations are always isolated or shifted into psychological spheres (in social archaeology, the foundations of 'prestige' support the majority of the social interpretations). However, these explanations tend to overlook the conditions in which an individual/collective has lived socially-speaking, and to which benefits of material production of a society he/it has access.

These explanations have even recalled a sectorialised historicism, one that explains unequal situations in historical roots and dismisses social relations. Therefore, when we talk about social inequality, it is never clear whether we are making a reference to unequal histories, historical contingency (chance and luck) or dissymmetric social relations of exploitation and domination.

The formal equality of Law at the level of the individual is the basis for real dissymmetric relations, exploitation at a social level. Legal equality for collective businesses plays the same role. Since the acceptance of the Declaration of Human Rights, reality has exposed an unrecognised accumulation of wealth and misery unknown for any other moment of History. Furthermore: the declaration of the UN, which proclaims the equality of nation-states, established the juridical framework for a new form of Empire (Hardt & Negri 2000).

The notion of Equality also implies assimilation, that is to say, the assimilation of a common identity, a homogeniz-ing normative. Commonly this homogenisation is carried out by using reference points that emanate from a hegemonic power that establishes the examples of what is "normal". Among its usual practices, the state (i.e. the institutionalisation of coercive forms of power for the benefit of one social group), includes the establishment of identity models (global or sector-orientated). However, homogenizing identities are a commonplace as long as the political-ideological practices impose standard patterns, even in stateless societies with dominant groups. The resulting assimilation entails a tendency to eliminate heterogeneities and differences. We will discuss sexual difference later on, affected in the same way as differences of whatever nature. And, of course, it can even affect situations of dissymmetry, which prejudice certain collectives in benefit of others, even in those cases under the guise of avoiding and standardising these differences as a fictitious unit (a fictitious unit that can be understood in the form of family, tribe, ethnic group or state).

These validations derived from the fallacy of equality occupy a counter position in politics, which validates them as inequalities. Inequalities (differences) between collectives exist, but the hegemonic power and the exploiting classes use them to justify realities that have nothing to do with them. Exploitation of labour certainly does take place, but there are also prevailing arguments that talk about natural differences between sexes or race (housewives and passive women, indigenous layabouts) or of unquestionable (religious) truisms, which defend the privileges of a sector or class. As such, we should point out that Social Differences/Inequalities do exist, but only when there is exploitation between groups with "unequal" attributes. This difference is used to (ideologically) legitimise imposition. With this aim in mind, it is even possible to invent "ethnic" differences. When Social Inequalities come to the fore, the most important thing is to pinpoint exactly which elements compose these inequalities and not just describe the differences.

Keeping this in mind, we believe that it would be better to cast adrift the concept of equality (and therefore inequality). We prefer (Castro, Escoriza & Sanahuja 2003) to extend the definition of symmetrical to societies that are based on reciprocity and lack coercive powers. Given that symmetry does not imply equality between parties, it does, however, represent the equilibrium between social subjects which make up these parties. Reciprocity demands, therefore, the inexistence of relationships based on the imposition of a hegemonic power and it is only possible when agreed-upon compensations are offered among the subjects. In another order of things, the only possibility to compensate the existence of unequal social conditions would be to establish unequal rights, in other words, to establish discriminations that re-establish the symmetry. Everything else passes into the realms of the fictitious ground rules and of the fallacy of equality.

2.4.- Inequality, Difference and Diversity: Rhetoric and Reality

The notions of Diversity and Difference lack conceptual correctness and a theory to back them up. They are far from any form of reality and we can only hope that the use of adjectives is useful in creating a reference context: diversity, with respect to what? What terms of difference? Where can we establish the relevance of the concept 'difference'?

Nonetheless, nuances derived from the Fallacy of Equality have been introduced in the context of its usage. When we use the term Unequal we are also making reference to egalitarian values which imply negative connotations. In contrast, when we use terms such as Difference and Diversity, these assimilate values of particular wealth or individual varieties that appear to portray a positive meaning. Yet here again, we are flirting with ambiguity. It seems that it is pure rhetoric that takes priority, and that unsubstantiated suggestions fall into the realms of semantics. In the meantime, what is left unsaid becomes so prominent that debates are denied. Their meanings are taken for granted.

The idea of the negative in terms of Inequality/Difference faces off against the positive in terms of Diversity/Difference. But this does not tell us exactly what we are talking about, nor can we even be sure that we are talking about the same criteria or opposing criteria (although apparently this does not seem to matter). The vindication of private/individual diversities/differences appears a more attractive concept, under a formal homogeneity/equality cover, than clarifying exactly what is intended. The directions in which the arguments attempt to follow seem to be headed towards establishing an outline of topics under discussion. The conditions of the differences are not mentioned and, at best, only formal inequalities or specific diversities are identified. These lack relevance as a result of the absence of objective content.

The positive values bestowed upon the Diversity/Difference concept (which are incorporated in arguments on "Multiculturalism") claim that a variety of perspectives enrich the debate. But the 'why' and the 'with what objective' are not explained, whether a difference is of the same nature and product of the same conditions, or if we are quite simply talking in aesthetic terms (multicoloured as opposed to black and white). If we follow the aesthetic path when we refer to the Diversity/Difference concept, we would be looking at a multicoloured spectacle, a colourful theatrical play, nothing more. The reality of life disappears behind the colouring of a fictitious spectacle (Debord 1967).

An ideal position of these foci could lead us to the conclusion that the "unsaid" includes diversities in terms of sex, age, disability, personality, habits, taste and hopes.

We could even believe that we are talking about description criteria of private individuals and not collectives, of psychological profiles and not social collectives. If it is really like this, then we should consider the irrelevance of diversity, and propose social mechanisms for compensation, applying the long arm of law to Social Inequality, for the positive. The inevitable reality of female labour in basic production, and biological reproduction of our species (Castro *et al.* 1998) means that not intervening with social compensation will sacralise (in favour of equality) a reality that will benefit the masculine collective. If we maintain the vindication of the particularities as a mere aesthetic/spectacular exercise, when diversity is linked to situations involving domination or material exploitation, the consequence is the legitimisation of dissymmetry.

A second perspective envisages Diversity in terms of explicitly self-defining collectives. This occurs in the area of naturalisation of diversity, backed-up in biological-demographic criteria: Sex or, in many cases, Race categories (still being used) are employed to define various (unequal and different) groups. These groups are understood to be essential, and immanent, for each individual (for his/her biology). So much so that the consequence is that diversity, yet again, is used to hide possible situations of exploitation or dominion.

From the point of view of these two types of rhetoric, the diversity/difference is accepted as a universal phenomenon that can be recognised, described and measured. Nevertheless, the idea that the Diversities/Differences can be the fruit of social efforts, formulated ideologies, forms of social domination or labour conditions and material lifestyles, is not on the agenda. If material realities capable of re-dimensioning the diversities, which are the product of social conditions (and not individual differences), do exist, then the need for the transparency of these conditions becomes a must for understanding the concept of diversity.

As such, before being able to deal with the phenomenology of characterisation, we would need to know the conditions that produced diversity. Diversities would have to be explained in the light of these conditions if they incorporate domination/exploitation.

2.5.- Formal inequality, materiality and social explanation

A basic principle for any archaeological approach is the analysis of the similarities and differences in documented social materiality. From this starting point we construct typologies and classify evidence. Moreover, looking at inequality is always a good starting point for any study.

We will not ponder the question further, but we cannot forget that it has been some time since the impossibility of establishing/identifying taxonomic classifications came to the fore as a valid theory. In other words, cases in which all the elements ascribed to a single type were identical, and equal (Clarke 1978). Reality has shown that taxonomic classification brings together different objects under the umbrella of certain classifying criteria, but when we bring other criteria into the equation the organisation of the group types varies.   The intractability in looking for types based on attributes set out in a closed list usually involves using reference models that are put into action through empirical generalisations (description of a typical object for example). Without exception, fractures appear in the model. But the creation of polithetic classifications is not a successful venture, especially when observing how typologies are being constructed.

However, once the taxons/types have been established, the problem lies in what to do with the normal guidelines and the heterogeneous tendencies. At this point the criteria that extrapolate equalities (proximities) – inequalities (distances) in the social materiality to the field of social inequalities enter into the fray.   It follows that if the products of society are unequal, social reality will also be so. The main problem will be to establish exactly what kind of inequality (material and social).

Frequently, mostly in the case of tools, typological approaches attempt to explain typological (and social) inequality in functional terms, confirming it through independent tests or recurring associations (microwear studies, associated residues etc.). Nevertheless, the moment always arrives when the typological varieties do not have a functional explanation. Therefore, certain tools or building types or (why not?) sepulchres have the same functional meaning, but they are unequal. So, what happens then?

Relativist historical-cultural approaches attribute differences to specific "Cultures" or "Traditions" and the typological classification is replaced by a "cultural" classification. Documenting this course of action (which substitutes explanation with essences) does not solve the question, as it confuses social traditions with socially immanent beings. As a result, it remains to be clarified which social differences/inequalities explain cultures/traditions.

In contrast, a Social Archaeological approach provides the taxonomic differences of materiality with a specific meaning. Be it large or small, central or peripheral, standardised or heterogeneous, the approaches have to go as far as to refer to the guidelines in order to understand that inequalities have an explanation elsewhere. This principle carries the possibility of explaining material inequalities. The formal and descriptive approaches that aim to detect inequality cannot be the final object. Inequality in materiality can be explained in sociological terms (social traditions, diverse functionalities, readily available techniques, imposed politics of standardisation, etc).

The aim of pointing all of this out is precisely to recapture the question of Social Inequalities. Archaeology also allows us to detect Social Inequalities at a descriptive level in formal analysis. In other words, collectives that are not equal. In the same fashion as in social materiality, its explanation cannot be found in the description of Inequality itself. In order to root this out, we have to refer to certain key points in the reading. These should set forth which material or social objective conditions, and which economic or political relations are behind these social inequalities/differences.

We are therefore confronted with the necessity of abandoning a course of action that would place the approaches to Inequality in society in a formal, descriptive category which is badly lacking in substantial content. If we input the content, we should call things by their proper name. If the social inequalities involve exploitation between classes or oppression of one sex by another, then we will not beat about the bush in identifying it. If they involve autonomous environments of social organisation, then that is what we will unveil. If they entail traditions of socialisation within the framework of certain working environments, then this will be the explanation.

If we do not move in this direction, and we continue to talk in aseptic terms (aesthetics?) about Social Inequalities, we will not be offering relevant sociological content and will be allowing our social interpretation to dwell in the limbo of imprecision.

2.6.- Labour and Inequality

Faced with formal formulas, or formulas led by the linearity of procedure, we feel that it is imperative to get as close as possible to the social realities of the past (and present). We consider that the key factors for this are Labour and the objective living conditions of the subjects and collectives.

Labour, as well as the action of transforming material and social conditions, qualifies reality and creates social life. As social subjects, we work in such a way that we socialise matter and generate social life in objects and other members of society with whom we interact, as well as in economic or political-ideological activities (Castro et al. 2002). Labour represents the expenditure of time and energy on material production and on social reproduction, but also the contribution of all subjects, women and men, which is carried out for the benefit of the continuity of any social reality. Without labour, society falls apart at the seams.

However, labour is also an individual/collective effort that, although resulting in materiality and a social reality, is only truly compensated if the contributing subjects share in the produce. Although in terms of production/reproduction labour is always social, consumption/use of the produce, at the end of the day, always benefits the individual (Castro et al. 1998). If we do not establish this principle, and we only look at the benefits that work yields for the functioning of a society, we would not have one criterion available for discovering if material privileges exist socially or not. In short, if labour always goes in favour of a dominant group, which benefits from the exploitation of work carried out by other collectives, and our focus is on the social benefit, we should conclude that the dissymmetric appropriation on the part of the privileged collective is beneficial for the society as a whole. In other words, relationships based on domination and exploitation allow the fine functioning of society.

We have already put forward the argument elsewhere that in order to dismiss the existence of relationships based on exploitation, we need to ratify the existence of some sort of compensation or a social reality based on reciprocity. According to Marx, exploitation can be identified when the consumption, use, enjoyment or benefit of a product is affected, either entirely or in part, by outside agents who take charge of its production and/or maintenance, without offering counterparts (Castro *et al.* 1998). It is important to point out that the appropriation of work by a dominant group and the absence of reciprocal compensation are not always established with the same intensity and scope, and that it is therefore important to distinguish between relative, partial or extensive exploitation (Castro *et al.* 2003). In this way, we can find situations in which an "egalitarian" consumption hides (relative) exploitation, where one collective works to a lower degree than another, something which is very common in dissymmetry between sexes. We can also identify situations where there is an inverse participation in the work and in the access to the produce, in such a way that exploitation is based around lower work loads and greater material benefits for the dominant, privileged group (partial exploitation). Finally, the level of exploitation is increased when the dominant class imposes its dominion on the collectives that take on most of the work loads (and receive less of the produce) thanks to the support offered by associated social sectors. This is an example of extensive exploitation, where one sector benefits from one part of the appropriated product (for example, via its employment in state institutions or thanks to political privileges) instead of upholding the overall benefits that the dominant class receives.

As far as social symmetry and reciprocity is concerned, we must not forget that equality can never take place. Exact, calculated compensation for the work invested to obtain products of equal value (more precisely, of similar labour value, in terms of duration and intensity, according to Marx [1875]) can never form the basis of a symmetrical society, due to the fact that the actively working subjects will always have to compensate for the pluslabour caused by subjects who, for whatever reason (accidents, illnesses or invalidities) cannot offer similar contributions, in terms of quantity, to social production and reproduction. This being the case, by rights, there will always be inconsistencies in the quantity of labour invested with regards to the value of the produce. Another symmetrical

constant is deferred reciprocity, in which the work carried out by one generation for the benefit of the next and that will only be fully compensated when the sons and daughters of that particular period invest similar work into the subsequent period. And it will only be partially remanifested, in relative terms, if close attention and care is paid to situations of old age or invalidity.

None of this has anything to do with the existence of collective exploitation and appropriation of one part of the labour value of one group or another, whose contribution to social production and reproduction is lower than the value of the products that benefit them. But we could apply the concept of inequality to each and every case. Therefore, if by social inequality we mean social exploitation, it is important to employ this term in order to avoid confusions.

2.7.- Specialisation of labour and Inequality

To wait until work is carried out in conditions of equality is, without doubt, an unrealistic expectation, due to the fact that the training conditions of each subject as well as the abilities, qualities and limitations are not identical. Thus, at the level of the individual, we can already perceive marked differences.

In fact, the crucial difference can be found in the biological make-up of our species, in such a way that sex determines different capabilities in the production of social life (Castro *et al.* 1998). The capacity that women have to manage and give life, to carry out the most basic production that is the production of our bodies, entails work in which men cannot participate. This is a universal reality, fruit of the very sexuation of our species, and means that in all societies there is at least this specialisation of tasks, and the balance of work would need to be redressed in order to maintain the symmetry.

Therefore, as a universal characteristic, all human societies have specialised tasks to perform, at the very least in basic production or biological reproduction. It follows then, that in accordance with this universal principle, labour is unequal within human society. To maintain reciprocity based on a reality that consists of unequal productive labour, we must consider that this is possible and even that it is indispensable. We cannot rest on our laurels and assume that this was not possible in societies in the past, even when specialisation of labour was extended to diverse productive activities, even to the extent that it encompassed wide social collectives (Castro *et al.* 2003).

Sexual differences and unequal labour with regards to basic production, as well as the division of tasks in other areas, can be compensated for if politics that favour reciprocity come into the fray. Obviously, the male collective will have to compensate for the work carried out by the female section of society in biological reproduction through work in other areas. Undoubtedly, if we take reproduction for granted and we exclude it from the economic sphere, we are starting off on the wrong foot in attempting to attain a situation of symmetry between collectives. In fact, if we exclude any other type of work from the economy, the result will also be a dissymmetry that will prejudice those who carry out the work, as is the case of many tasks such as the care and upkeep of individuals, ranging from looking after infants to the care of ill people, victims of accidents or the aged. In order to ensure a symmetrical, balanced and reciprocal situation, the material evaluation of each task and its compensation in terms of the level of access to the produce will always be imperative.

The arguments put forward in regard of basic sexual division of labour and other unequal sharing of duties can be extended to any specialised labour activity. Whatever the specialisation, its extent, intensity or area, politics of compensation for work carried out will always be necessary through balanced access to the produce. It is only when this is not the case that we should start to make references to exploitation (Castro *et al.* 2003).

The inequality of tasks that the specialisation of labour entails should not necessarily imply other inequalities (such as, for example, the access to the product). In other words, specialisation of labour is not the same thing as exploitation of labour. Although, when examining the other side of the coin, social exploitation cannot survive without a division of labour that facilitates dissymmetry. If we were to establish as a general rule that the division of labour between collectives entails the inexorable existence of social dissymmetry and exploitation, we would be reconfirming the universal character of the male exploitation of women.

2.8.- Inequality and Sexual Difference

We need to reflect on the concept of Inequality when we attempt to explain the relationships between past gender collectives. In order to do so, we would have to agree on its significance in relation to the material evidence collected, using the already mentioned aspects. In playing with the idea of equality, we are entering into a minefield of ambiguity, risking to compromise the meaning of explanations.

It is therefore necessary to focus attention on the circumstances that have generally passed unnoticed, or on those that have not been explored sufficiently. Firstly, it is necessary to distinguish between inequality and sexual difference (Castro *et al.* 2002). Secondly, there is no reason why social inequality should be interpreted exclusively with regards to the exploitation that takes place between men and women if there are no mechanisms in place with this aim in mind. Finally, the conviction of what we have referred to as "the Fallacy of Equality" has

its more obvious merits in the existence of a fundamental material difference between sexes. We should insist that the sexuation of the past becomes a crucial question in archaeological studies (Escoriza & Sanahuja 2001).

We have already stressed the obvious of biological differences between sexes and their implications on the labour involved in social production. The existence/recognition of sexual difference has no reason to lead into situations of domination, coercion, subordination and exploitation between men and women, as generally happens nowadays. The "idea of sexual difference" meaningfully advocates the necessity for new "rules of the game" (Irigaray 1995). We are actually dealing with an idea that leads to definitive knowledge and not negation (Bocchetti 1996: 62).

The legitimisation of the exploitation of women and of patriarchal dominion has reached the difference in nature of the two sexes. Of course, if this was the explanation, the patriarchy would be, in itself, "natural". Therefore, the concept of "difference" cannot be considered synonymous with domination or exploitation, nor can it be confused in any way with inequality. It is actually the current dominant patriarchal ideology that tends to oppress, propose and organise precise contents, generate hierarchies, nullify, suppress and even degrade whatever may be different, and to homogenise for the sake of a chimerical common social good. Categorising rules are imposed over those not encompassed by the "exclusive norms" of the dominant social group. The concept of the 'different' is marginalised, silenced and devalued. If this occurs in the activities carried out by women, and they are no longer considered to be socially necessary, then sexual difference is converted, at the hands of the patriarchy, in a vehicle of discrimination, insolidarity and the seed of exploitation between sexes.

On too many occasions female difference has been portrayed as a threat to "democratic equality" (Castro *et al.* 2003), despite the fact that it is impossible to obtain reciprocal relations without taking into account the difference between sexes. The only viable purport of the equality between sexes can be found in the elimination of privilege, although with this comes the introduction of (positive) discrimination. To oppose and confront difference in an irreconcilable manner, vindicating the equality of mankind, is a fundamental theoretical inconsistency in which the female collective is the aggrieved party.

On the contrary, it is necessary to re-evaluate differences. If this is not the case, impositions and colonisations that homogenise everything are produced. These impositions appear to equal everything out, but what they do not manage is to legitimise the norms that normality reinforces. Symmetry between sexes has to be a necessary condition in the political arena; this is a good starting point, but it is not the be-all and end-all (Sendón 2002). In short, the comparison between men and women is permissible, but not the equality between sexes. If this is the case, it would be a triumph for the male paradigm.

In its usage, the concept of equality has been distorted, and has been distanced from the comparison between sexual collectives without privileges. Attention has been focused on one segment of society, in accordance with an androcentric vision which only deals with male adults, and where the world only seems to be a projection of the male subject. Let us not forget that in Anglo-American Anthropology, with many examples in Social Archaeology, those societies in which any adult male is capable of obtaining a determined leadership thanks to his own abilities have been labelled as "equalitarian", despite the fact that in many of these societies exploitation between sexes is evident (Meillassoux 1975).

On the other hand, it is necessary to reflect on the veracity of many perspectives which are based on a recent rational logic which deploys universal models of relationships between the sexes in societies gone-by. We are evermore conscious of the fact that female difference has suffered a narrow interpretation, resulting in the breakage and fragmentation of the overall image of the female. This fragmentation has led to the bestowing of specific functions on women throughout history (and prehistory) and has also meant assuming the impossibility of realising other tasks due exclusively to their sex. The existence of sexual difference, a duality of bodies, should not convey any notion of exclusion: it was the patriarchy that loaded it with such nuance. It has been the patriarchy that has insistently sought to hide/diminish the sexual difference, both in a symbolic and material sense (in the material sense, presenting the production of new individuals as something natural). In the symbolic sense, through political-ideological practices that structure the contents of that which is represented and the forms of representation that are employed. Affirming the existence of sexual difference means breaking with the universalist stereotype of the human being as neutral (a stereotype that regards all human beings as equal) and, consequently, stating the sexuation of the past (Sanahuja 2002).

All in all, in analysing the concepts of Difference and Inequality, we are led to evaluate under which premises the history of social groups of the past has been constructed together with the relationships that took place between sexes. We should also stop for a moment to consider the consequences of falling into the trap of using universal models to explain societies from the past, and of using concepts of substantial material in concrete historical situations. If we overcome these perspectives, we would also be favouring arguments of notable essentialist character which embrace the invariability of historical evolution and postulate concepts such as that of the patriarchy throughout history as nonchalant (Guerra 1994:157). This can only come into effect when dealing with the material conditions of the different groups and of the social and gender collectives. This also would entail tackling the true conditions of production and of social reproduction (conditions that, although particular in nature, are subject to specific historical situations).

Equality is an ideological attempt at the validation of subjects, whilst difference is an existential principle which is not necessarily essentialist in nature, and which views women as social and sexual subjects allowing them to express the true meaning of their existence and the reality that surrounds them (material conditions and social subjects). The dissymmetry between the two sexes (patriarchal dominion, exploitation of labour) needs to be reinforced beyond the actual biological differences and (or) the carrying out of different activities. At this level, we talk about the exploitation of the female collective when one or more of the following two situations is present: 1) when the major part of the work-load falls on the shoulders of women, while the produce benefits the group as a whole; 2) when the amount of time invested in work is unequal or burdensome for the female but beneficial for the men (who hold a privileged position in terms of access to the product). In situations such as this, the consequence is the denial of the work carried out by women. This is cemented on the systematic omission (invisibilisation) of the contribution of women's participation to the production of social life and maintenance of life itself, subtracting the importance of their work, and finally, considering it irrelevant.

2.9.- Conclusion

At his point, we feel that it is necessary to consolidate our arguments with some clarifying points. Our intention is to highlight the reality of social inequality (caused by both individual and social differences) as well as the need of unequal politics in order to afford the dignity of social conditions for unequal collectives. This can only happen if the main objective consists in eradicating dissymmetry. Therefore, the only relevant interpretation of the notion of Inequality lies in the reality of dissymmetry (exploitation and dominion). As a consequence, in place of ambiguous, formal, empty terminologies (Inequality), we prefer to call things by their proper name and speak frankly of oppression and exploitation. If the need arises to tackle other diversities, it will also be necessary to turn to clear content (formal variability, stylistic divergence, diversified production, specialisation of labour, functional segmentation, sexual difference and so on).

In order to offer a definitive meaning to a vindication of reality that, from the point of view of Inequality, must be understood materially and that, as such, must explain in terms of objective labour conditions and access to the end produce, another quotation from Marx comes to mind - *From each according to his abilities, to each according to his needs!* (Marx 1875). If this vindication of Inequality is not put into practice, social relationships can only be submitted to conditions of appropriation of labour, or they can only be the result of agreements between equals that calculate the benefits of their actions, to the exclusion of those who cannot fall in line with the rules of the game, even when this is with the aegis of a defence of equality.

2.10.- References

BOCCHETTI, A. 1996: *Lo que quiere una mujer*. Feminismos, 36. Cátedra. Madrid.

CASTRO MARTÍNEZ, P.V.; ESCORIZA MATEU, T. & SANAHUJA YLL, E. 2002: "Trabajo y Espacios Sociales en el ámbito doméstico. Producción y prácticas sociales en una unidad doméstica de la prehistoria de Mallorca", *Geocrítica. Scripta Nova*, VI, 119 (10), URL: http://www.ub.es/geocrit/sn/sn119-10.htm.

- 2003: "Trabajo, Reciprocidad y Explotación. Prácticas Sociales, Sujetos Sexuados y Condiciones Materiales". In: *Cultura & Política. IX Congreso de Antropología* (Barcelona, 2002). Institut Català d'Antropologia. CD-rom edition. Barcelona.

CASTRO MARTÍNEZ, P.V.; ESCORIZA, T.; OLTRA, J.; OTERO, M. & SANAHUJA, E. 2003: "¿Qué es una Ciudad? Aportaciones para su definición desde la Prehistoria". *Geocrítica. Scripta Nova*, VII, 146 (10). URL: http://www.ub.es/geocrit/sn/sn-146(010).htm.

CASTRO MARTÍNEZ, P.V.; GILI, S.; LULL, V.; MICÓ, R.; RIHUETE, C.; RISCH, R. & SANAHUJA, E. 1998: "Towards a Theory of Social Production and Social Practice". In S. Milliken & M. Vidale (eds): *Craft Specialization: Operational Sequences and Beyong. Papers from the EAA Third Annual Meeting at Ravenna 1997 (volume IV)*. British Archaeological Reports International Series, 720. Oxford: 173-177.

CLARKE, D.L. 1978: *Analytical Archaeology*. Methuen. London.

DEBORD, G. 1967: *La Societé du Spectacle*. Editions du Champ Libre. Paris.

ESCORIZA MATEU, T. 2002: *La Representación del Cuerpo Femenino. Mujeres y Arte Rupestre Levantino del Arco Mediterráneo de la Península Ibérica*. British Archaeological Reports International Series, 1082. Oxford.

ESCORIZA MATEU, T. & SANAHUJA YLL, E. 2002: "El pasado no es neutro: el cuerpo femenino como materialidad y forma de representación social". *III Congreso de Historia de Andalucía* (Cordoba, 2001). Volume II. Cajasur. Córdoba: 243-258.

FRIED, M.H. 1960: "On the Evolution of Social Stratification and the State". In S. Diamond (ed): *Culture in History*. Columbia University Press. New York: 713-731.

GUERRA, L. 1994: *La mujer fragmentada: Historias de un signo*. Colección Arte de Nuestra América. Casa de Las Américas. La Habana.

HARDT, M. & NEGRI, T. 2000: *Empire*. Harvard University Press. Cambridge.

IRIGARAY, L. 1995: "La diferencia sexual como fundamento de la democracia", *DUODA Revista d'Estudis Feministes*, 8: 121-134.

MARX, K. 1875: "Critique of the Gotha Programme (*Die Neue Zeit*, I, 18, 1890-1891)". In K. Marx & F. Engels: *Selected Works*. Progess Publishers, 1970: v. 3. Moscow: 13-30.

MEILLASSOUX, C. 1975: *Femmes, greniers, capitaux*. Masperó. Paris.

SANAHUJA YLL, E. 2002: *Cuerpos sexuados. Objetos y Prehistoria*, Feminismos 69. Cátedra. Madrid.

SEDÓN, V. 2002: "¿Qué es el feminismo de la diferencia?. (Una visión muy personal). Tertulia". URL: http://www.geocities.com/quatertulia (2002).

CHAPTER 3

Selection of data, determinism and scientific relevance in interpretations of social development in the Late Prehistory of the Iberian Southeast

Juan Antonio Cámara Serrano
Fernando Molina González
Universidad de Granada

Abstract

We believe that it is necessary to address four fundamental aspects when evaluating different hypotheses about social development in the late prehistory of the Iberian southeast: 1) the factors considered to be the driving forces behind social change, and their external (*e.g.* climate) or internal nature with respect to the society in question; 2) the elements whose control and appropriation are considered to be the key dynamic elements in the process of accumulation (products, labour force, means of labour, natural conditions of production, etc.); 3) the use of the available empirical base; and 4) the characterisation of the degree of social development and temporary changes (tribe, chiefdom, state, etc.). All these aspects are linked to the theoretical orientation of researchers, and are emphasised to a greater or lesser extent in their work over time. For this reason we have developed an analytical perspective that bears this evolution in mind by specially focusing on the different treatment of the second of these aspects.

Keywords: Iberian Peninsula; Late Prehistory; Social Hierarchisation; Labour Force; Means of Labour; Natural Conditions of Production; Social Classes; State.

Resumen

A la hora de valorar las diferentes hipótesis planteadas sobre el desarrollo social en la Prehistoria Reciente del Sureste de la Península Ibérica creemos que es necesario acometer la discusión de cuatro aspectos fundamentales: 1) el factor que se considera como impulsor del cambio social y su carácter externo (por ejemplo clima) o interno respecto a la sociedad en cuestión; 2) los elementos cuyo control y apropiación se consideran como dinamizadores del proceso de acumulación (productos, fuerza de trabajo, medios de trabajo, condiciones naturales de la producción, etc.); 3) la utilización de la base empírica disponible; 4) la caracterización del grado de desarrollo social y sus cambios temporales (tribu, jefatura, estado, etc.). Naturalmente todos estos aspectos están vinculados a la orientación teórica de los investigadores pero son remarcados en mayor o menor grado en sus obras a lo largo del tiempo por lo que desarrollamos una perspectiva de análisis que tenga en cuenta esa evolución a partir, sobre todo, de las diferencias en el tratamiento del segundo aspecto.

Palabras clave: Península Ibérica; Prehistoria Reciente; Jerarquización Social; Fuerza de Trabajo; Medios de Trabajo; Condiciones Naturales de la Producción; Clases Sociales; Estado.

3.1.- Social development in the Southeast

The sequence of transformations that led to class societies began in southern Iberia during the Late Neolithic (*c.* 4000 BC), although the process acquired greater depth near 3000 BC, when the exceptional settlement of Los Millares (Santa Fe de Mondújar, Almería) (Molina *et al.* 2004:155-156) was already occupied (Table 3.1, Fig. 3.1).

Until a few years ago, data on the occupation of the lowlands of the Southeast between the 6th millennium BC and 3500 BC was limited and reduced to the presence of Neolithic materials in some caves in the mountains that encircle the lowlands, with the possible chronological addition of some cave paintings and materials located in shelters and caves throughout the areas intensely investi-

gated by Louis Siret. Recently, more data has been supplied thanks to excavations at Cabecicos Negros-El Pajarraco (Cuevas del Almanzora, Almería) (Cámalich *et al.* 2004a: 94-97) and to systematic surveys carried out within the framework of the Los Millares Project (Alcaraz *et al.* 1994). Despite stratigraphic problems, the oldest findings at Cerro Virtud (Cuevas del Almanzora, Almería) correspond to this same time period (Ruiz & Montero 1999:209). This set of data has demonstrated the fallacy of a population vacuum. Among the classical sites, El Garcel (Antas, Almería) (Siret & Siret 1890: 6-7, 14 plate I; Siret 2001: 84, 89) shows the beginning of a process of sedentarisation that led to the formation of permanent and stable settlements in certain areas of the Southeast (Fig. 3.2).

In the second half of the 4th millennium the territory was

SITE NAME	KIND OF CONTEXT	DATE B.P.	DATES B.C. (1 σ)	DATES B.C. (2 σ)	LABORATORY REFERENCE	REFERENCE
LOS MILLARES (2)	FORTIFICATION LINE IV. PHASE 1	4410 ± 60	3095-2920	3325-2900	Beta124532	MOLINA et al., 2004
LOS MILLARES (2)	FORTIFICATION LINE IV. PHASE 6	4200 ± 60	2890-2665	2910-2590	Beta124531	MOLINA et al., 2004
LOS MILLARES (2)	FORTIFICATION LINE IV. PHASE 7a	4020 ± 60	2590-2465	2855-2400	Beta124529	MOLINA et al., 2004
LOS MILLARES (1)	FORTIFICATION LINE IV. PHASE 9	3900 ± 60	2465-2290	2555-2190	Beta124530	MOLINA et al., 2004
LOS MILLARES (1)	FORTIFICATION LINE III. PHASE 2	4220 ± 70	2900-2680	2920-2590	Beta124527	MOLINA et al., 2004
LOS MILLARES (1)	FORTIFICATION LINE III	4030 ± 130	2865-2400	2900-2175	Beta124528	MOLINA et al., 2004
LOS MILLARES (1)	FORTIFICATION LINE II. PHASE 2d	4460 ± 70	3325-2935	3355-2910	Beta124523	MOLINA et al., 2004
LOS MILLARES (1)	FORTIFICATION LINE II. PHASE 1g	4420 ± 70	3285-2920	3340-2895	Beta124524	MOLINA et al., 2004
LOS MILLARES (1)	FORTIFICATION LINE II	4150 ± 40	2871-2640	2879-2589	BM2343	MOLINA et al., 2004
LOS MILLARES (1)	FORTIFICATION LINE II. PHASE 4c	3990 ± 60	2575-2455	2610-2325	Beta124522	MOLINA et al., 2004
LOS MILLARES (1)	FORTIFICATION LINE I	4295 ± 85	3085-2710	3322-2625	H204-247	ARRIBAS, 1976.
LOS MILLARES (1)	FORTIFICATION LINE I	4220 ± 70	2900-2680	2920-2590	Beta124526	MOLINA et al., 2004
LOS MILLARES (1)	FORTIFICATION LINE I	4110 ± 110	2871-2504	2917-2347	BM2344	MOLINA et al., 2004
LOS MILLARES (1)	FORTIFICATION LINE I	4040 ± 70	2610-2470	2870-2400	Beta124525	MOLINA et al., 2004
LOS MILLARES (1)	FORTÍN I	4000 ± 70	2585-2455	2855-2310	Beta125862	MOLINA et al., 2004
LOS MILLARES (1)	FORTÍN I	3980 ± 40	2575-2440	2845-2290	Beta125861	MOLINA et al., 2004
LOS MILLARES (2)	FORTÍN I	3950 ± 40	2480-2440	2560-2325	Beta125860	MOLINA et al., 2004
LOS MILLARES (1)	FORTÍN I	3920 ± 50	2474-2310	2568-2212	BM2536	MOLINA et al., 2004
LOS MILLARES (1)	FORTÍN I	3880 ± 50	2458-2299	2473-2204	BM2537	MOLINA et al., 2004
LOS MILLARES (1)	FORTÍN I	3880 ± 60	2460-2270	2485-2145	Beta125859	MOLINA et al., 2004
LOS MILLARES (1)	FORTÍN I	3820 ± 40	2340-2155	2457-2141	BM2345	MOLINA et al., 2004
LOS MILLARES (1)	FORTÍN IV	3830 ± 70	2430-2150	2475-2040	Beta135669	MOLINA et al., 2004
LOS MILLARES (1)	FORTÍN V	3840 ± 50	2395-2205	2460-2140	Beta135670	MOLINA et al., 2004
LOS MILLARES (1)	FORTÍN V	3840 ± 70	2445-2195	2475-2050	Beta135671	MOLINA et al., 2004
LOS MILLARES (1)	NECRÓPOLIS, THOLOS XIX	3380 ± 120	3325-2893	3482-2677	KN72	ALMAGRO, 1959; ARRIBAS, 1976.

Table 3.1. Dates from Los Millares (Santa Fe de Mondújar, Almería). (1) Samples analysed by Standard radiometric, (2) Samples analysed by AMS. The stratigraphical phases are only referred to the belonging area.

occupied by open air settlements, some permanent, although the majority was still short-term (Molina 1988; Cámalich et al. 2004b:167-168). The material culture of these settlements reflects middle Neolithic traditions (less decorated ceramics, small flint blades and geometrics, etc.) but also a clear trend towards an increasing amount of open pottery vessels. Most of the necropolis classified by the Leisner's in Phase I of the Almeria Culture must be ascribed to this time period, with round sepulchres (rundgräber) in areas like Purchena or quadrangular tombs in Vélez. Both types lack passages and are defined by the presence of few individuals (Guilaine 1976:163). However, as the Tabernas case shows, their erection, which also took place in subsequent periods, was integrated into the progressive formation of a Copper Age ritual landscape next to more complex sepulchres (Cámara 2001).

The site of Los Millares (Santa Fe de Mondújar, Almería) was founded by the end of the 4th millennium. It is composed by three lines of walls and an interior citadel, two external lines of small forts and an immediate cemetery of large sepulchres with circular chambers, often covered with corbelled vaults (tholoi). It is the best example of the transformations that took place between the Late Neolithic and Chalcolithic in the Iberian Southeast (Molina et al. 2004:152) (Fig. 3.3). Built at a slightly later stage, the surrounding small forts constitute internal guard posts of a territory that was previously assimilated through an increasing pressure on certain movable resources, a continued threat of force, and an integration of elites into a centralized control system. This is suggested by the presence of circular sepulchres and perforated stone slabs (doors) in some of the megalithic cemeteries like Huéchar, or by the presence of at least 3 megaliths

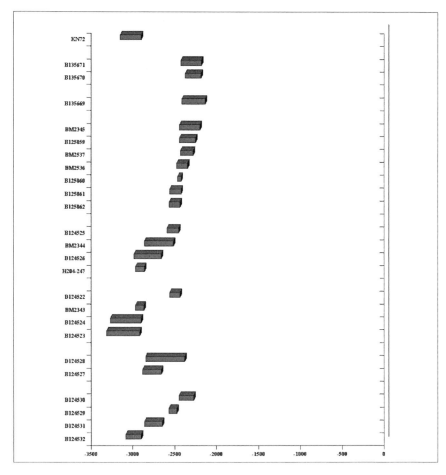

Fig. 3.1. Calibrated dates (1 σ) of different areas from Los Millares (following Molina *et al.* 2004).

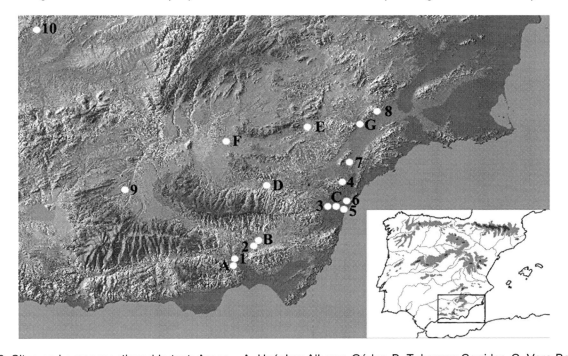

Fig. 3.2. Sites and areas mentioned in text: Areas – A. Huéchar-Alhama-Gádor, B. Tabernas Corridor, C. Vera Basin, D. Purchena, E. Vélez, F. Cúllar-Chirivel Corridor, G. Lorca; Sites – 1. Los Millares, 2. Terrera Ventura, 3. El Gárcel, 4. Fuente Álamo, 5. Cabecicos Negros, 6. Cerro Virtud, 7. El Rincón de Almendricos, 8. La Bastida, 9. La Cuesta del Negro, 10. Peñalosa.

23

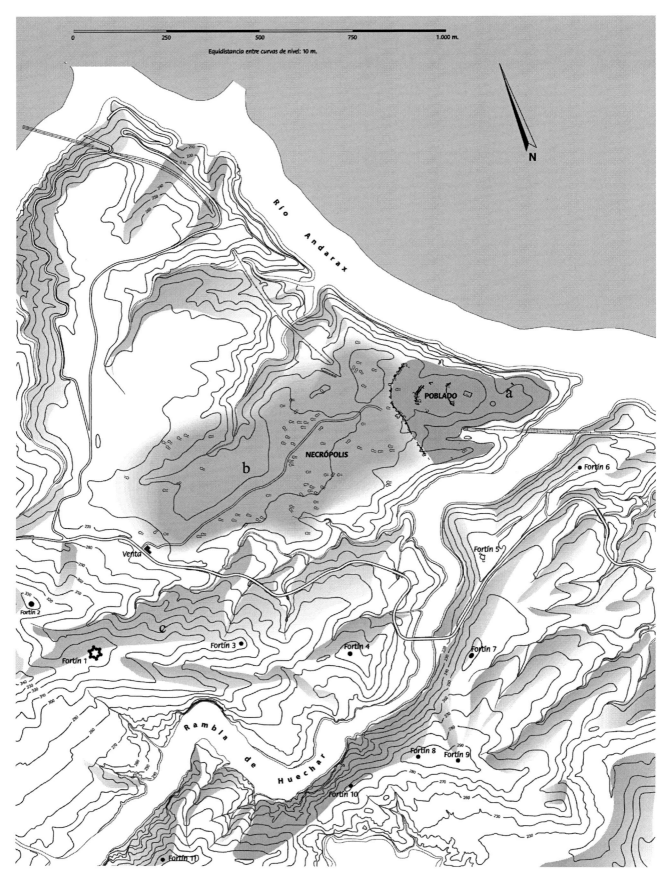

Fig. 3.3. Archaeological complex of Los Millares (Santa Fe de Mondújar, Almería) including:
a) fortified village, b) necropolis and c) hill-forts.

at Los Millares with certain funerary offerings that can be linked to the neighbouring dolmenic cemeteries of Gádor and Alhama. In any case, social differentiation between settlements has been argued for other areas like the Vera basin (Cámalich *et al.* 2004b), the surroundings of Lorca (Lomba 1999), Pasillo de Cúllar-Chirivel (Moreno *et al.* 1997) and Pasillo de Tabernas. In the last of these sites, a study of the distribution and position of the megaliths, together with an analysis of the settlement pattern has shown (Maldonado *et al.* 1992-93; Cámara 2001) the importance of the populations located next to the main waterways such as Terrera Ventura (Tabernas, Almería) (Gusi & Olaria 1991) during the 4th and 3rd millennia BC, in addition to an east-west opposition in settlement patterns or megalithic intervisibility. Some tholoi cemeteries are located next to these settlements, while more dispersed ones signal routes from valleys to mountains, with some small and possibly seasonal sites along them. There is a general lack of data concerning internal settlement differentiation, although meat consumption at Los Millares shows differences between the main settlement and the surrounding forts (Navas 2004). Moreover, some specialised arrowhead flint knapping and metallurgical activity areas have been located at Los Millares (Molina *et al.* 2004).

The Bronze Age extends between 2200/2100 and 800/600 BC (Castro *et al.* 1996). During the first part (2200-1450 BC), the El Argar culture developed in the Southeast, between the Vinalopó River in the northeast, Sierra Morena to the north and the western flank of the depressions of Jaén and Granada to the west (Molina & Cámara 2004: 455-458). In this time period, the process of consolidation of social hierarchies can be observed through the following evidence: (1) the articulation between walled settlements normally located on steep hills, although exceptions like El Rincón de Almendricos (Lorca, Murcia) do exist (Ayala 1986); (2) the internal differentiation of certain settlements with acropolis (Fuente Álamo, Gatas, El Oficio, Castellón Alto, etc.) and differential consumption patterns of certain products between dwellings (Sanz and Morales 2000); (3) the homogenisation of part of the portable material culture (Castro *et al.* 1999:69) that suggests the existence of a generalized measurement unit (Castro *et al.* 1999:65, 68; 2001: 202, 206); (4) differences between individual burial patterns generally located below dwellings (funerary offerings, living conditions, characteristics of the tombs, etc.) (Lull & Estévez 1986; Contreras *et al.* 1987-88; Jiménez & García 1989-90) (Fig. 3.4), suggesting the existence of aristocracies with attached servants at certain sites such as La Cuesta del Negro (Purullena, Granada), La Bastida (Totana, Murcia) or Peñalosa (Baños de la Encina, Jaén), where burials belonging to different social levels are associated to the same living space (Cámara 2001; Molina & Cámara 2004).

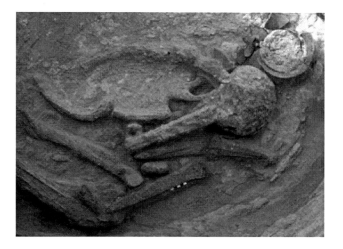

Fig. 3.4. Grave nº 109 from Castellón Alto (Galera, Granada) with metal grave goods.

3.2.- The historiography of hypotheses concerning the beginnings of social hierarchisation in the Southeast

3.2.a.- Introduction

When hypotheses on social development are expounded, they are usually presented (Hernando 1987-88; Chapman 1991; 2003; Arteaga 2002) as fully finished, as though the work of an author were homogenous from start to finish. It seems as if once a model has been set forth, it needs no change. Only the data that fits the model is sought. However, this is not an indisputable reality. On the contrary, the trajectories of many authors contain substantial changes, while certain models appear to be immutable (Gilman 1999; 2001). Time seems to have stopped in the year 1990 or earlier when presenting models of social change in southeast Iberia (Chapman 2003), especially when targeting anglo-american public. The main dilemma still seems to be the functionalist-diffusionist debate (Gilman 2001). These simplifications, connected with the delay that the latest Andalusian publications suffer in reaching international distributors (even in reaching authors who are familiar with our area of study), may serve as a sufficient excuse to undertake a review of our own perspective on the panorama put forward by these models (Cámara 2001). However, it may be convenient to elude a linear exposition of authors and proposals, offering our own point of view on three subject matters: (1) the importance given to certain components of social structure in the different models (means of labour, labour force, natural conditions of production and products); (2) the localisation and nature of the motors of social change; and (3) the definition of the resulting change.

This kind of perspective has two advantages: (a) it can allow us to appreciate not only the determinism (environmental, demographic, economic) of many approaches, but also the reductionism when characterising the production of a prehistoric society; (b) we can trace the influence of certain authors in the trajectories of others that present themselves as radically opposed. From this perspective, the greatest reductionism can be found not in authors that are or have been considered functionalists, but in the hasty adoption of "theoretical models" that try to fit isolated hypotheses together. Demonstrating this could alone be motive enough to justify the inclusion of not only complex models, widely cited in the literature, but also partial perspectives and views that are hidden in syntheses and articles on concrete topics. Furthermore, we believe to have an additional justification: the length of a theoretical exposition and the abundance of citations do not necessarily correspond to deeper perspectives. There are perfect examples for both extremes: the broad exposition of A. Ramos (1981) which hides a reductionist/deterministic model, and the excellent synthesis developed by F. Nocete (1989; 2001), integrating all social functioning into a perspective that brings together temporal and spatial variations.

3.2.b.- Driving forces in social development

Although some approaches lack almost any definition of the factor of social change, we have tried to limit the exposition to two large sets of factors: (1) external factors, mostly diffusionist models put forward by classical research and (2) internal factors, those integrated in the society under analysis. Most recent authors who emphasise the first set of factors do so on the basis of the idea that societies will remain under a stable equilibrium (result of their perfect adaptation to the environment) unless affected by external pressures or catastrophes. Almost all researchers who emphasise this factor must turn to two recurring causes in this type of interpretation: environmental pressure, in the form of ecological crises, climatic or edaphological constrictions, or demographic growth (being specific or general). This factor, although socially determined, is often placed as a constant given that, in the opposite case, it could not possibly explain why populations decide to occupy marginal lands (Chapman 1982; Mathers 1984). Anyhow, at times authors suggest that prehistoric groups do so when they have acquired the adequate technological level (Gilman 1976), without contextualising the technical advances in the framework of the society that produced them.

Other authors emphasise the demographic factor alone and, although referring to the need for an increasing food production, they separate this from any other social manifestation. Consequently, they reduce production to subsistence, and view trade as an autonomous sphere (Ramos 2004). They fall within the framework errors of substantivism, appropriately and often criticised (Carandini 1984). Additionally, part of the demographic factor presents important problems for empirical verification. In the

first place, it is difficult to determine, especially from data gathered from surface surveys, the number and the significance of the settlements, as well as their contemporaneity. Secondly, neither the extension nor the amount of dwellings produce a clear correlation to the number of inhabitants. Finally, once growth has been determined, it is difficult to evaluate with the time scale that we use for Late Prehistory, whether it preceded or succeeded change, or both. These aspects are even under discussion for periods as recent as the Industrial Revolution. Inseparably linked to this factor is conflict between communities (Díaz-del-Río 2004: 91).

Finally, environmental changes can be of some importance, although the quick, seasonal ones that might have had more catastrophic effects (e.g. droughts that produce famines) are difficult to detect in the archaeological record except in exceptional cases. But we also must bear in mind that societies are not found in isolation from other human groups. For this reason, contact must be important not only in relation to the adoption of certain elements (whose influence in recipient societies must be evaluated in the first place by the fact that they had already generated the necessity [Afonso 1998; Risch 1998]), but also to the pressures, frequently violent, between societies. Nevertheless, these must be characterised attending to the internal contradictions in each specific society.

In this respect, it must be made clear that the last factor that drives transformation is conflict, that is, the accentuation of the control of certain elements in the productive system in order to direct the results in one specific direction (often not completely conscious) (Nocete 1989; 1994a; 2001; Lull 1983; Martínez & Afonso 1998; Castro et al. 1999). This conflict, whether overt or hidden, as shown in fights for the control of labour force, takes place not only between men and women (Lizcano et al. 1997; Castro et al. 1999; Castro & Escoriza in this volume), dominant and dominated classes, but also between members of the dominant group (Nocete 1989; 1994a; Cámara 2001).

3.2.c.- Elements of critical access

A large part of the interpretations of the development of social hierarchisation in the Iberian southeast have considered that the control of the natural conditions of production is the key factor for the consolidation of inequality and the development of elites. Independently of the fact that, as G. Lukacs (1985) showed so well, control of men in pre-capitalist societies was not exercised via control of things, but rather control of things was exercised through control of men, it is difficult to sustain that control of certain resources (e.g. water and land), or elements susceptible of being used as raw materials (e.g. minerals), could have been fundamental before their conversion into means of production by human work. In any case, at times it is difficult to know if the authors are suggesting that there was competition for resources (e.g. land) before its conversion into a mean of labour (Gilman 1976; Vicent 1993) or afterwards (Arteaga 1993; 2001). In other cases, this factor becomes diluted in interpretations suggesting competition for a wide variety of resources (Pérez 2004: 234).

In the same way, the control of products, whether metal or flint tools, all of which share many of the problems referred to above, emphasize the role of products (Ramos 1998) especially as prestige elements (Shennan 1982; Mathers 1984; Molina 1988; Moreno 1993) or as means of labour (Lull 1983; Risch 1998; Castro *et al.* 1999). Some authors underestimate Iberian prehistoric production (Gilman 1987b: 31-33; 2001: 68-70; Montero 1993: 54-56; Müller *et al.* 2004: 51-52), overlooking the evidence for spatial concentration (Moreno *et al.* 2003; Nocete *et al.* 2001; Bayona *et al.* 2003), selection of raw material (Keesmann *et al.* 1997) and the implication of all of the processes that require cutting or puncturing tools (especially during the Bronze Age), except harvesting and threshing (Lull 2000: 589; Sanz & Morales 2000). Other means of labour such as domestic flocks have only received a secondary treatment (Gilman 1976; 1997; Molina 1983), occasionally reducing them to simple products (Harrison 1993). Only recently have they been emphasised for their role in the accumulation of wealth (Cámara & Lizcano 1996; Martínez & Afonso 1998; Cámara 2001).

Nevertheless, most complex approaches have accentuated the fundamental role of labour force control in the beginning of the process of hierarchisation (Nocete 1989; 1994a; 2001; Díaz-del-Río 2004: 85-86, 91). Some have stressed the initial importance of the control of women, both as labour force and as means of production in terms of the source of future labour (Castro *et al.* 1999; Cámara 2001; Afonso & Cámara in this volume). Others have considered women to be important in other moments of social development (Mathers 1984; Vicent 1993).

3.3.- Limitations and advances in the proposals

3.3.a.- Control of the natural conditions of production

R.W. Chapman (Fig. 3.5) has suggested that the lowlands of southeast Iberia were occupied as a consequence of demographic pressure only at the end of the Neolithic. These areas were previously unoccupied because of their excessive dryness. Processes of intensification (irrigation) were put into practice in areas with sufficient water (Chapman 1982: 46-48; 1991: 156-161), transforming land from a natural condition of production to a means of labour. The economic success led to the reproduction of demographic tensions, forcing new changes under limited technological conditions (Chapman 1991: 297). Copper metallurgy is only considered in relation to prestige objects (Chapman 1991: 232-233, 225-227).

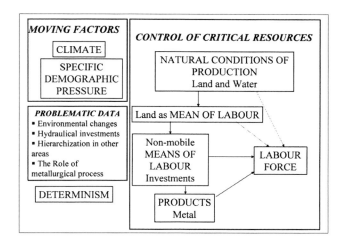

Fig. 3.5. Schematic diagram on R.W. Chapman's model.

The empirical limits of these approaches are particularly clear, especially because they overlook the processes of hierarchisation that occurred in wet areas of Iberia (Chapman 1991: 306-311), although at times they are linked to the interregional exchange of prestige goods (Chapman 1982; 1991; Gilman 1987c) and especially because they do not take into account the environmental data provided by Copper Age wildlife remains (e.g. Peters & Driesch 1990), anthracological data (Rodríguez & Vernet 1991) or lowland Neolithic settlement patterns (Cámalich *et al.* 2004a). One of the main theoretical limitations is their economic-environmental reductionism and their consideration of the beneficial role of elites (Gilman 1987b: 33; Hernando 1987-88: 59). R.W. Chapman has recently abandoned his model, more because of the data he recovered (including paleoenvironmental remains) than because of a recognition of its theoretical inconsistency (Chapman 2003: 156).

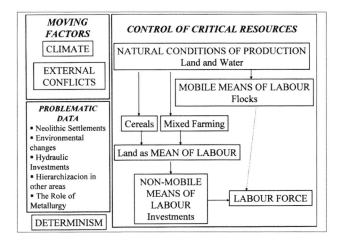

Fig. 3.6. Schematic diagram on A. Gilman's model.

A. Gilman (Fig. 3.6) also assumes that there were no stable settlements in the Neolithic since communities lacked the adequate technological level to subsist under a supposedly hostile environment (Gilman 1987a: 60-63; 1999: 79, 82-83; 2001: 61-62). Other authors emphasise that the critical factor was not so much climatic conditions as the scarcity of arable lands throughout the Southeast (Hernando & Vicent 1987). According to Gilman, agricultural intensification based on mixed farming and irrigation, and the exploitation of herds in new forms occurred during the Copper Age because further development would have been impossible under the conditions of extensive rain fed agriculture (Gilman 1976: 314; 1987a: 60-63; 1987b: 33; 1997: 88; 1999: 84; 2001: 67, 70-74). However, he does not grant any role to livestock as an independent means of accumulation. According to the author, pastoral communities are at no time class based (Gilman 1997: 89). Other authors have extended the importance of irrigation to other areas where natural conditions did not require this kind of intensified production (Zafra *et al.* 1999: 89-90).

According to his hypotheses, farmers could not abandon their infrastructural investments, whether public works for intensive irrigation or cultigens with deferred yields (olive trees, grape vines, etc.). They were thus bound to their land (Gilman 1976: 315-316; 1997: 88; 1987a: 66; 1999: 84-87; 2001: 72-74, 81). Under these conditions, exploitation as labour force became easier, through mechanisms that he termed as *protection blackmail* (Gilman 1991: 141), also referred to by others as the *mafia model* (Shennan 1989: 93). Other authors consider these public works (and therefore investments), along with participation in ritual activities, as mechanisms preventing the flight of the labour force (Díaz-del-Río 2004: 86). Gilman, although stressing the interest of those who have made a heavy investment in a resource when appropriating it against the community (Gilman 1997: 84), has never suggested its importance as the base for differential accumulation. He does not determine how elites arrive to their position of power, or why - bearing in mind the low population density in the Southeast during Late Prehistory - people decided to occupy areas that were allegedly marginal.

The difference between Chapman and Gilman's approaches lies not only in the absence of any demographic-technological role as a basis for explaining initial colonisation in the latter (considered by some authors as a *teleology* [Hernando 1987-88: 69]), or in the emphasis placed on public works that could be small in size (Gilman 1976: 314), but in the repeatedly reiterated affirmation that elites did not favour public works or propel them, but only benefited from them (Gilman 1987a: 65-66; 1987b: 33; 1991: 140; 2001: 74-77). However, Gilman's criticism of the administrative interpretation is reduced to the lack of data on central administrations. The basic defect of this proposal is the fact that beneficial systems do not exist for any society as a group under conditions of exploitation. In this respect, Gilman does not accept the existence of the State, but does consider the presence of both social classes and tribute (Gilman 1987b: 33; 1997: 83-84; 1997: 83; 2001: 77 n. 27, 77-81). He accepts an evolutionist succession of stages (Gilman 1987a: 31; 1993: 106, 109; 1997: 83-84; 2001: 77-81), but does not

use the term State for the Iberian southeast in order to avoid confusion with contemporary societies of the Aegean, to which the same term is applied (Gilman 1991: 142 n.2; 1999: 87-88). There is only one type of state according to him, a concept already criticised (Gailey & Patterson 1988: 79-80) even by previously functionalist authors such as Chapman (2003: 162-163). What they do not understand is that the State is simply the instrument of power of the dominant class (Marx & Engels 1987: 48).

Gilman tends to overlook various pieces of evidence that do not support his thesis: a) the presence of hierarchisation in humid regions; b) the size of settlements in the Guadalquivir valley; c) the existence of models of prehistoric states different to those from the Near East; d) the Neolithic settlements in Almería e) paleopathological evidence; f) the concentration of elements of production (lithic, metal, etc.) in certain places; g) the recycling of metal; and h) the common production of grains in dry areas.

Other theories link the appearance of a class society to the progressive territorialisation resulting from intergroup competition for land (Vicent 1993: 49, 53-58; Hernando 1993; Román 1999: 200, 204), although at times the causes for this competition are not made explicit (Díaz-del-Río 2004: 91). Starting with the circulation of adults, and later with the exchange of women for reproductive purposes as a way of controlling future labour force, the phenomenon provokes the adoption of a "peasant way of life" (Vicent 1993: 51-52). Permanent villages and megalithic tombs (or other collective burials) reinforce the community's right over the land as a means of labour, although other symbolic systems of cohesion, representation of social position, and exterior relationships are maintained (Vicent 1993: 46-51, 55-59).

The main problem with this hypothesis is that it underscores the cause of the phenomenon as its effect. Sedentarisation was the necessary condition for agricultural success, and the conversion of the land into a true means of labour, subsequently leading towards a true accumulation of capital. Other authors have emphasised competition over natural conditions of production within the framework of strong demographic determinism (Monks 1999:129, 132; Aranda & Sánchez 2004: 265).

Arteaga (Fig. 3.7) has shown the importance of the rise of "family" ties in relation to sedentarisation, with regards to the need to form tribal societies that claim a specific territory since the early Neolithic (Arteaga 2002: 259-260) and the progressive importance that land acquires as a means of labour as a result of frequentation (Arteaga 1993: 194; 2002: 271). The driving factor here is external conflict, which increases internal contradictions. Focusing exploitation on the circulation of labour force from dependent communities, he considers that the ownership of land, herds and instruments of work were still communal (Arteaga 2001: 130). Social differentiation increased because of the differing productivity of the land, requir-

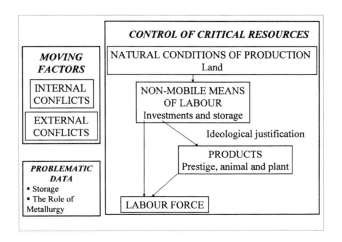

Fig. 3.7. Schematic diagram on O. Arteaga's model.

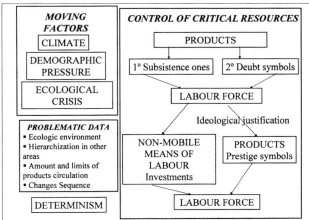

Fig. 3.8. Schematic diagram on C. Mathers's model.

ing new regulating mechanisms in order to avoid conflicts (Arteaga 1993: 193; 2002: 259). Thus, collective dependence has been suggested for the Copper Age (Arteaga 2001: 125, 129), described as a step from "communitary" to "collective", that is, the conversion from a communitary ideology to a masked ideology of inequality (Arteaga 1993: 193, 198; 2002: 258, 279-280). Influence is produced, via family relationships, in the possession of the means of production to control the labour force (Arteaga 1993: 196; 2002: 260). In this context, the production of arsenic copper is conceived as one more element integrated in a context of the circulation of prestige goods, which accentuated and displayed social inequality (Arteaga 2001: 125, 129, 133; 2002: 274, 278).

For El Argar, Arteaga suggests "private" appropriation, a specific and not unmasked form of private ownership of labour force, natural conditions and means of production (Arteaga 2001: 132, 141, 143, 173, 184). In this context, he defends both the existence of temple-palace-warehouses for the dominant classes and the mobility of the peasants as forms of social control (Arteaga 2001: 146-147).

3.3.b.- Control of the products

For Mathers (Fig. 3.8), high population density and technological limitations had propelled agricultural colonization towards high-risk marginal areas. Administration became fundamental to maintain economic stability, and systems of product circulation were organized to guarantee subsistence via zonal complementarity. Settlements located in the driest lowlands specialised in the production of prestige goods, among which metal. As indicators of a food debt with respect to the highlands, they were transformed into an ideological element of control during bad years (Mathers 1984).

The fundamental objections concerning the empirical base are shared with other determinist visions, although in this case, demographic pressure acquires a special

importance as a key factor in the process. When placing emphasis on competition for products and prestige, exploitation is hidden, and cooperation and administration are emphasised as results and motors of social change, tending to indicate that rulers *were and are inescapable* (Moscoso 1986: 109, 386; Gailey & Patterson 1987: 5).

A. Ramos has investigated the importance of the control of products and their trade. In his early works he pointed to demographic pressure as the motor of social change, leading to an increasing number of settlements and the occupation of new lands for intensified extensive grain agriculture. In turn, all these led to competition between communities. However, he does not consider that this would give rise to a rigid social organization (Ramos 1981: 250-251, 256) because the differences between settlements derived only from the number of their inhabitants (Ramos 1998: 32). This minimises the role of practically all objects as means of labour, both metal and lithic ones, attempting to separate production of instruments from specialised production of prestige goods designed for trade, the collapse of which would explain the final Copper Age crisis (Ramos 1998: 13-18, 22, 26-36; 2004: 420). This is a process similar to that used by other authors to eliminate the role of herds as means of production, limiting their role to that of products (Harrison 1993: 294). The main miscalculation in this approach is that it separates "trade" from the overall social production through a substantivist approximation. This perspective has much in common with formalism (Carandini 1984: 290-292) since it masks exploitation by placing the emphasis on the forms of distribution and not on the relationships surrounding overall production, suggesting the existence of social differentiation only according to the control of distribution (trade) by *Big Men* (Ramos 1981: 249, 253; 1998: 33-34, 36). Neither does this approach penetrate the meaning of goods that the ringleader gives and receives. This theory does not admit the exploitative character of this society. It does not accept social conflict, even in contexts of accumulation of wealth, certain specialisation and its possible institutionalisation (Ramos 1981: 247-248, 253; 1997: 674-679; 1998: 25-31, 33-34, 36; 1999: 601; 2004: 414-418).

In fact, new hypotheses developed by the author entail such an accentuation of the unilineal evolutionist perspective that one only has to ascribe the archaeological record to each one of the different stages in order to obtain a social explanation (Ramos 2004: 404, 414-415). Here, the reality of the archaeological record is secondary: interpretations are in no way based on proper archaeological evidence, whether with respect to the fortifications of the southeast or the chronology given to the sites themselves (Ramos *et al.* 1991: 129; Ramos 1997: 674-679; 1998: 17; 1999: 601; 2004: 414-418).

S. Shennan (1982: 159-160) has conceded an important role to metallurgy in the process of social hierarchisation. He notes that metal production can in some cases explain the differential degree of hierarchisation reached between certain areas. Also, metals associated to Bell-Beakers are used by aristocracies of different areas in Europe as a way of justifying their position. Prestige metal objects are presented as items acquired personally, not dependent on the dominated masses. Their deposition in tombs reinforces the timelessness of social inequality.

3.3.c.- Control of the labour force

From similar approaches that emphasise the control of products (Lull 1983: 457-458) with a catastrophist vision (ecological crisis) of the end of the Argaric world, the team of the Universidad Autónoma de Barcelona (Fig. 3.9) has recently underscored the importance of control of the labour force as a basic requirement for social development in the absence of technological advances (Castro *et al.* 1999: 31; 2001: 184-185, 203). However, the rigid separation between labour force and means of production, and the emphasis on the role of the social division of labour in the development of hierarchisation (Risch 1998: 107; Castro *et al.* 1999: 32-35, 26-30), create certain difficulties when explaining the first moments of the process (Late Neolithic). These regard limitations in the movements of people included in a specific group, their opposition to the exterior, and their connection to forms of earlier exploitation such as the exploitation of women.

They also point to the growing importance of increasingly specialised rain fed agriculture, in combination with valley horticulture, and non-transhumant herding patterns. The fact that the large Chalcolithic settlements were not especially located near the best lands suggests their dependence on smaller settlements that supplied them with agricultural products. Nevertheless, and according to the authors, there was no dissymmetry in consumption. Dissymetries can be found in the suprafamiliar organization of certain jobs, especially in larger sites (Castro *et al.* 1999: 44-46, 48-49, 52, 54). Control was not exercised through means of production that could be easily substituted (Castro *et al.* 1999: 55) but arose from control of

labour force, usable territory and movable means of production such as herds.

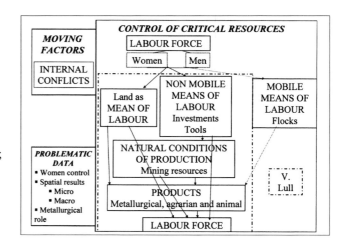

Fig. 3.9. Schematic diagram on UAB team's (Gatas Project) model.

The authors have suggested that a strong demographic increase took place during the Bronze Age. This was made possible by a greater emphasis on the control of labour force and of basic production through an increasing pressure on women. According to them, the process was accompanied by an increase in child mortality, reflected in a greater number of infant inhumations (Castro *et al.* 1999: 57-58; 2001: 192). The level of hierarchisation reached is expressed through funerary offerings, the increase of life expectancy among the dominant classes, and the inclusion of funerary offerings in children burials since at least 1800 BC onward (Castro *et al.* 1999: 69; 2001: 207).

Specialized extensive agriculture, mainly barley-based, would be most directly related to social change. In relation to demographic growth and degradation by deforestation, this agriculture entails an increase in the costs of production because of the growing distance and the use of worse lands, which must be left fallow for 1-2 years. On the plains, near the rivers where small settlements can be found, legumes and linen were cultivated in a limited horticulture (Castro *et al.* 1999: 59-61, 67-68; 2001: 195-196, 206-207; Lull 2000: 588).

Certain technological advances are also seen with *the elimination of production that demands a high level of preparation, reduction of the costs of production and transportation, improvement of the raw materials being used and greater specialisation and diversification of the instruments of work* (Castro *et al.* 1999: 63). Only specific raw materials such as minerals and volcanic rocks come from distant areas, as opposed to the majority during the Copper Age, something that the authors relate to a more restricted access to exotic elements (Risch 1998: 128-129; Lull 2000: 589-590; Castro *et al.* 1999: 61; 2001: 198, 208). Control of production and storage, especially in the central settlements, are forms of controlling people (Castro *et al.* 1999: 59-61; 2001: 195-197, 206; Lull 2000: 588).

While works from other researchers initially emphasise that the control of groups according to age or gender guarantees access to products (Aguayo *et al.* 1993: 342), they disconnect this from the later processes and, although territorial deterrence is already mentioned for the Chalcolithic era, internal conflicts are denied and change is justified as a consequence of ecological, demographic and intercommunity competition (Carrilero & Suárez 1997: 87, 106-107). Despite this, the difference between owners and non-owners is discussed (Carrilero & Suárez 1997:108), suggesting that the only relations of production were the forms of surplus extraction, considered as extraeconomic (in an absolute sense) personal relationships (based on dependency in the majority of the cases) mediated by legal relationships such as the ownership of means of production (Aguayo *et al.* 1993: 342-344). This conception supposes a double error: 1) the separation of income or salary from the relationships of control and 2) the denial of any possibility of extracting income in Prehistory.

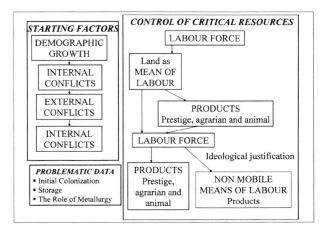

Fig. 3.10. Schematic diagram on F. Nocete's model.

F. Nocete's model (Fig. 3.10) is, without doubt, the most satisfactory of those offered to explain southern Iberia's late Prehistory. The main criticism (Lizcano *et al.* 1997) has focused on his view of the origins of the sedentarisation process in the Higher Guadalquivir valley as a result of a demographic growth. This impeded the reproduction of a *swidden* model of exploitation of the territory above the Guadalquivir river basin, forcing a colonising expansion (Nocete 1989: 154; 1994a: 277-279, 283-288). The importance of demographic pressure has also been maintained by other authors who emphasise control of the labour force (Jover & López 2004: 295-296).

Independently of this initial impulse, Nocete accentuates the role that control of the labour force has in social development, whether because of its simple increase or because of overexploitation (Nocete 1989: 183, 217). Here, development of social hierarchisation is two-fold: 1) an increase in the production space above that exercised

by those in control; and 2) the increase in work hours by the dependent population, initially foreign, deriving from conflicts between the settlements in addition to concentration, although the slight control between some villages and others ought to have quickly led to stressing control of the labour force linked to each of them (Nocete 1989: 179, 183, 190). The incapacity to apply direct violence within the lines of relationship (Nocete 2001: 45-46) produced the following phenomenology: 1) the ideological apparatus develops; 2) circulation of the products on a supraregional scale is guaranteed and driven, these being scarce and distant products that entail significant compensation and whose control justifies and drives the inequality; 3) constant expansion of the system is sought, whether because of colonization or because of absorption/conquest, even producing transformation of the societies around them (Nocete 2001: 21, 26, 89), until reaching its limits around 2200 BC because of their resistance and because of the overexploitation on the periphery (Nocete 1994a: 360-361; 2001: 96-97, 139-140). Facing a technological block and the incapacity to free labour in the centre, especially in the system's extreme (central periphery), new mechanisms are generated to exercise violent control over the subordinated labour force (Nocete 2001: 96, 142, 152), expressed on a microspatial level in the development of settlements that specialise in coercion, like Cerro de la Coronilla (Cazalilla, Jaén) (Nocete 1994a: 39-40, 336-338; 2001: 96, 150, 152).

A triple conflict develops over the base of competition for the agricultural surplus. This is expressed by different forms of class conflict (Nocete 1989: 217-220, 242; 1994a: 334-338, 360-361, 1994b: 188, 191-195): 1) internal settlement conflict between the theoretical representatives of the community and those who truly carry the development on their own shoulders; 2) differentiation between settlements as a result of the justification of the subordinate position of the inhabitants in the conquered areas or integrated by other coercive means or, simply, placed in a precarious position because of debts, manifested in their cultural material; 3) contradictions between the elites in the centre and those in the periphery, the latter of which are necessary for the reproduction of the system but are also a burden for the tributary systems of the periphery.

We finally present our own model in a separate paper (Afonso & Cámara, this volume). It condenses previous published syntheses (Cámara 2001; Martínez & Afonso 1998; Molina & Cámara 2004).

Concluding, we believe that the most interesting studies on the social development of southern Iberia are those that have interpreted with greater or lesser success the social evolution of a specific area from a Marxist perspective (Nocete 1989; 1994a; 2001a; Arteaga 1993; 2001; 2002; Castro *et al.* 1999), especially when they have emphasized the control of the labour force as the key factor.

3.4.- References

AFONSO, J.A. 1998: *Aspectos técnicos de la producción lítica de la Alta Andalucía y el Sureste*. Doctoral Dissertation in Microfilm. Universidad de Granada. Granada.

AGUAYO, P.; CARRILERO, M.; CABELLO, N.; GARRIDO, O.; MORALES, R.; MORENO, F.; PADIAL, B. & SEMINARIO PERMANENTE "MANDRÁGORA" DE RONDA 1993: "La Prehistoria Reciente en la Depresión Natural de Ronda 1985-1991". In J.M. Campos & F. Nocete (Dirs.): *Investigaciones arqueológicas en Andalucía. 1985-1992. Proyectos (Huelva, 1993)*. Junta de Andalucía. Huelva: 341-351.

ALCARAZ HERNÁNDEZ, F.M.; CASTILLA, J.; HITOS, M.A.; MALDONADO, G.; MÉRIDA, V.; RODRÍGUEZ, F.J. & RUIZ, Mª.V. 1994: "Prospección arqueológica superficial en el Pasillo de Tabernas. Primeros resultados y perspectivas metodológicas". In M. Kunst (Coord.): *Origens, estruturas e relaçôes das Culturas calcolíticas da Península Ibérica (Actas das I Jornadas Arqueológicas de Torres Vedras 3-5 Abril 1987)*. *Trabalhos de Arqueologia* 7. Lisboa: 217-223.

ALMAGRO, M. 1959: "La primera fecha absoluta para la cultura de Los Millares a base de C14". *Ampurias* XXI: 249-251.

ARANDA, G. & SÁNCHEZ, M. 2004: "El aumento de la conflictividad durante el III Milenio B.C. en el Sureste de la Península Ibérica". *Simposios de Prehistoria Cueva de Nerja. II. La problemática del Neolítico en Andalucía. III. Las primeras sociedades metalúrgicas en Andalucía*. Fundación Cueva de Nerja. Nerja: 261-271.

ARRIBAS, A. 1976: "Las bases actuales para el estudio del Eneolítico y la Edad del Bronce en el Sureste de la Península Ibérica". *Cuadernos de Prehistoria de la Universidad de Granada* 1:139-155.

ARTEAGA, O. 1993: "Tribalización, jerarquización y Estado en el territorio de El Argar". *Spal* 1 (1992):179-208.

- 2001: "La sociedad clasista inicial y el origen del estado en el territorio de El Argar". *Revista Atlántica-Mediterránea de Prehistoria y Arqueología Social* 3 (2000): 121-219.

- 2002: "Las teorías explicativas de los "cambios culturales" durante la Prehistoria en Andalucía: nuevas alternativas de investigación". *Actas del III Congreso de Historia de Andalucía (Córdoba, 2001). Vol. 3. Prehistoria*. Cajasur Publcaciones. Córdoba: 247-311.

AYALA, Mª.M. 1986: "La Cultura de El Argar en Murcia. Datos actuales. Un avance para su estudio". *Homenaje a Luis Siret (1934-1984)*. Consejería de Cultura. Sevilla: 329-340.

BAYONA, M.R.; NOCETE, F.; SÁEZ, R.; NIETO, J.M.; ALEX, E. & ROVIRA, S. 2003: "The prehistoric meallurgy of Cabezo Juré (Alosno, Huelva, Spain): the metal objects production". *Archaeometallurgy in Europe 2003 (Milán, 24-26 Septiembre 2003). Proceedings. Vol. 2*. Associazione Italiana di Metallurgia/Fondazione Museo Nazionale della Scienza e della Tecnologia "Leonardo da Vinci"/Archeologia Viva. Milano: 175-184.

CÁMALICH, Mª.D.; MARTÍN, D.; GONZÁLEZ, P. & GOÑI, A. 2004a: "Panorama actual de los inicios de la producción en la Depresión de Vera y valle del Río Almanzora (Almería)". *Simposios de Prehistoria Cueva de Nerja. II. La problemática del Neolítico en Andalucía. III. Las primeras sociedades metalúrgicas en Andalucía*. Fundación Cueva de Nerja. Nerja: 90-101.

- 2004b: "Análisis diacrónico del poblamiento en la Depresión de Vera y valle del Río Almanzora entre el VI y el III Milenio A.N.E.". *Sociedades recolectoras y primeros productores. Actas de las Jornadas Temáticas Andaluzas de Arqueología (Ronda, 2003)*. Junta de Andalucía. Sevilla:163-176.

CÁMARA, J.A. 2001: *El ritual funerario en la Prehistoria Reciente en el Sur de la Península Ibérica*. British Archaeological Reports International Series, 913. Oxford.

CÁMARA, J.A. & LIZCANO, R. 1996: "Ritual y sedentarización en el yacimiento del Polideportivo de Martos (Jaén)". *I Congrés del Neolític a la Península Ibérica. Formació e implantació de les comunitats agrícoles (Gavà-Bellaterra, 1995). Vol. 1., Rubricatum* 1. Museu de Gavà. Gavà: 313-322.

CARANDINI, A. 1984: *Arqueología y Cultura Material*. Mitre. Barcelona.

CARRILERO, M. & SUÁREZ, A. 1997: *El territorio almeriense en la Prehistoria*. Historia de Almería 1. Instituto de Estudios Almerienses-Diputación Provincial de Almería. Almería.

CASTRO, P.V.; LULL, V. & MICÓ, R.1996: *Cronología de la Prehistoria Reciente de la Península Ibérica y Baleares (c. 2800-900 cal ANE)*. British Archaeological Reports International Series, 652. Oxford.

CASTRO, P.V.; GILI, S.; LULL, V.; MICÓ, R.; RIHUETE, C.; RISCH, R. & SANAHUJA, Mª.E. 1999: "Teoría de la producción de la vida social. Mecanismos de explotación en el Sureste ibérico". *Boletín de Antropología Americana* 33 (1998):25-77.

CASTRO, P.V.; CHAPMAN, R.W.; GILI, S.; LULL, V.; MICÓ, R.; RIHUETE, C.; RISCH, R. & SANAHUJA, Mª.E. 2001: "La sociedad argárica". In Mª.L. Ruiz-Gálvez (coord): *La Edad del Bronce, ¿Primera Edad de Oro de España? Sociedad, economía e ideología*. Crítica. Barcelona: 181-216.

CHAPMAN, R.W. 1982: "Autonomy, ranking and resources in Iberian prehistory". In C. Renfrew & S. Shennan (eds.): *Ranking, resources and exchange. Aspects of Archeology of Early European Society*. New Directions in Archaeology. Cambridge University Press. Cambridge: 46-51.

- 1991: *La formación de las sociedades complejas. La Península Ibérica en el marco del Mediterráneo Occidental*. Crítica. Barcelona.

- 2003: *Archeologies of complexity*. Routledge. London.

CONTRERAS, F.; CAPEL, J.; ESQUIVEL, J.A.; MOLINA, F. & TORRE, F. de la. 1987-88: "Los ajuares cerámicos de la necrópolis argárica de la Cuesta del Negro (Purullena, Granada). Avance al estudio analítico y estadístico". *Cuadernos de Prehistoria de la Universidad de Granada* 12-13: 135-156.

DÍAZ DEL RÍO, P. 2004: "Factionalism and collective labor in Copper Age Iberia". *Trabajos de Prehistoria* 61 (2): 85-98.

GAILEY, C.W. & PATTERSON, T.C. 1987: "Power relations and state formation". In T.C. Patterson & C.W. Gailey (eds.): *Power relations and state formation*. American Association of Anthropology. Washington: 1-26.

- 1988: "State formation and uneven development". In J. Gledhill, B. Bender & M.T. Larsen (eds.): *State and Society. The emergence and development of social hierarchy and political centralization*. One World Archaeology 4. Routledge. London: 77-90.

GILMAN, A. 1976: "Bronze Age dynamics in South-east Spain". *Dialectical Anthropology* 1: 307-319.

- 1987a: "Regadío y conflicto en sociedades acéfalas". *Boletín del Seminario de Arte y Arqueología* LIII:59-72.

- 1987b: "El análisis de clase en la Prehistoria del Sureste". *Trabajos de Prehistoria* 44: 27-34.

- 1987c: "Unequal development in Copper Age Iberia". In E.M. Brumfiel, & T.K. Earle (eds.): *Specialization, exchange and complex societies*. New Directions in Archaeology. Cambridge University Press. Cambridge: 22-29.

- 1991: "Desenvolupoment agrícola i evolució social al Sud-Est espanyol". *Cota Zero* 7: 136-143.

- 1993: "Cambio cultural y contacto en la Prehistoria de la Europa Mediterránea". *Trabajos de Prehistoria* 50: 103-111.

- 1997: "Cómo valorar los sistemas de propiedad a partir de datos arqueológicos". *Trabajos de Prehistoria* 54 (2): 81-92.

- 1999: "Veinte años de prehistoria funcionalista en el sureste de España". *Boletín del Seminario de Arte y Arqueología* LXV: 73-98.

- 2001: "Assessing Political Development in Copper and Bronze Age Southeast Spain". In J. Haas (ed.): *From Leaders to Rulers*. Fundamental Issues in Archaeology. Kluwer Academic/Plenum Publishers. New York : 59-81.

GUILAINE, J. 1976: *Premiers bergers et paysans de l'Occident méditerranéen*. Mouton. Paris.

GUSI, F. & OLARIA, C. 1991: *El poblado neoeneolítico de Terrera Ventura (Tabernas, Almería)*. Excavaciones Arqueológicas en España 160. Ministerio de Cultura. Madrid.

HARRISON, R.J. 1993: "La intensificación económica y la integración del modo pastoril durante la Edad del Bronce". In V.O. Jorge (coord.): *1º Congresso de Arqueologia Peninsular* (Porto, 1993). *Actas II. Trabalhos de Antropologia e Etnologia* 33. Universidade do Porto. Porto: 293-299.

HERNANDO, A. 1987-88: "Interpretaciones culturales del Calcolítico del Sureste español". *Cuadernos de Prehistoria de la Universidad de Granada* 12-13:35-80.

- 1993: "Campesinos y ritos funerarios: el desarrollo de la complejidad en el Mediterráneo Occidental (IV-II Milenio A.C.)". In V.O. Jorge (coord.): *1º Congresso de Arqueologia Peninsular* (Porto 1993). *Actas II. Trabalhos de Antropologia e Etnologia*, 33. Universidade do Porto. Porto: 91-98.

HERNANDO, A. & VICENT, J.M. 1987: "Una aproximación cuantitativa al problema de la intensificación económica en el Calcolítico del Sureste de la Península Ibérica". In M. Fernández-Miranda (dir.): *El origen de la metalurgia en la Península Ibérica (Seminario organizado por la Fundación Ortega y Gasset, Oviedo, 1987)*. Papeles de Trabajo Arqueología. Universidad Complutense. Madrid: 23-29.

JIMÉNEZ, S.A. & GARCÍA, M. (1989-90): "Estudio de los restos humanos de la Edad del Bronce del Cerro de la Encina (Monachil, Granada)". *Cuadernos de Prehistoria de la Universidad de Granada* 14-15: 157-180.

JOVER, F.J. & LÓPEZ, J.A. 2004: "2200-1200 B.C. Aportaciones al proceso histórico en la cuenca del Vinalopó." In L. Hernández & M.S. Hernández (eds.): *La Edad del Bronce en tierras valencianas y zonas limítrofes*. Ayuntamiento de Villena/Instituto Alicantino de Cultura Juan Gil-Albert. Villena: 285-302.

KEESMANN, I., MORENO, Mª.A. & KRONZ, A. 1997: "Investigaciones científicas de la metalurgia de El Malagón y Los Millares en el Sureste de España." *Cuadernos de Prehistoria de la Universidad de Granada* 16-17 (1991-92): 247-302.

LIZCANO, R.; CÁMARA, J.A.; RIQUELME, J.A.; CAÑABATE, Mª.L.; SÁNCHEZ, A. & AFONSO, J.A. 1997: "El Polideportivo de Martos. Estrategias económicas y símbolos de cohesión en un asentamiento del Neolítico Final del Alto Guadalquivir". *Cuadernos de Prehistoria de la Universidad de Granada* 16-17 (1991-92): 5-101.

LOMBA, J. 1999: "El megalitismo en Murcia. Aspectos de su distribución y significado". *Quaderns de Prehistòria i Arqueologia de Castelló* 20: 55-82.

LUKACS, G. 1985: *Historia y conciencia de clase*. Planeta. Barcelona.

LULL, V. 1983: *La "Cultura" del Argar. Un modelo para el estudio de las formaciones económico-sociales prehistóricas*. Akal. Madrid.

- 2000: "Argaric society: death at home". *Antiquity* 74: 581-590.

LULL, V. & ESTÉVEZ, J. 1986: "Propuesta metodológica para el estudio de las necrópolis argáricas". *Homenaje a Luis Siret (1934-1984)*. Junta de Andalucía. Sevilla: 441-452.

MALDONADO, G.; MOLINA, F.; ALCARAZ, F.; CAMARA, J.A.; MERIDA, V. & RUIZ, V. 1992-93: "El papel social del Megalitismo en el Sureste de la Península Ibérica. Las comunidades megalíticas del Pasillo de Tabernas". *Cuadernos de Prehistoria de la Universidad de Granada* 16-17: 167-190.

MARTÍNEZ, G. & AFONSO, J.A. 1998: "Las sociedades prehistóricas: de la Comunidad al Estado". In Peinado, R. (Ed.): *De Ilurco a Pinos Puente. Poblamiento, economía y sociedad de un pueblo de la Vega de Granada*. Diputación Provincial de Granada. Granada: 21-68.

MARX, K. & ENGELS, F. 1987 (orig. 1848): *El manifiesto del Partido Comunista*. Eudymion. Madrid.

MATHERS, C. 1984: "Beyond the grave: the context and wider implications of mortuary practices in south- east Spain". In T.F.C.Blagg, R.F.J. Joves & S.J. Keay (eds.): *Papers in Iberian*

Archaeology I. British Archaeological Reports International Series 193 (I). Oxford: 13-46.

MOLINA, F. 1983: "La Prehistoria". In F. Molina & J.M. Roldán: *Historia de Granada I. De las primeras culturas al Islam*. Don Quijote. Granada: 11-131.

- 1988: "El Sureste". In G. Delibes, M. Fernández-Miranda, A. Martín & F. Molina: El Calcolítico de la Península Ibérica. *Congresso Internazionale L'Età del Rame in Europa* (Viareggio, 15-18 Ottobre, 1987). *Rassegna di Archeologia* 7. Firenze: 256-262.

MOLINA, F. & CÁMARA, J.A. 2004: "La Cultura del Argar en el área occidental del Sureste". In L. Hernández & M.S. Hernández (eds.): *La Edad del Bronce en tierras valencianas y zonas limítrofes*. Ayuntamiento de Villena/Instituto Alicantino de Cultura Juan Gil-Albert. Villena: 455-470.

MOLINA, F.; CÁMARA, J. A.; CAPEL, J.; NÁJERA, T. & SÁEZ, L. 2004: "Los Millares y la periodización de la Prehistoria Reciente del Sureste". *Simposios de Prehistoria Cueva de Nerja. II. La problemática del Neolítico en Andalucía. III.Las primeras sociedades metalúrgicas en Andalucía*. Fundación Cueva de Nerja. Nerja: 142-158.

MONKS, S.J. 1999: "Patterns of warfare and settlement in southeast Spain". *Journal of Iberian Archaeology* 1: 127-171.

MONTERO, I. 1993: "Bronze Age metallurgy in southeast Spain". *Antiquity* 67: 46-57.

MORENO, Mª.A. 1993: *El Malagón: un asentamiento de la Edad del Cobre en el Altiplano de Cúllar-Chirivel*. Doctoral Dissertation in Microfilm. Universidad de Granada. Granada.

MORENO, Mª.A.; CONTRERAS, F. & CÁMARA, J.A. 1997: "Patrones de asentamiento, poblamiento y dinámica cultural. Las tierras altas del sureste peninsular. El pasillo de Cúllar-Chirivel durante la Prehistoria Reciente". *Cuadernos de Prehistoria de la Universidad de Granada* 16-17 (1991-92): 191-245.

MOSCOSO, J. 1986: *Tribus y clases en el Caribe Antiguo*. Universidad Central del Este. San Pedro de Macorís.

MÜLLER, R.; REHREN, T. & ROVIRA, S. 2004: "Almizaraque and the Early Koper Metallurgy of Southeast Spain: New data". *Madrider Mitteilungen* 45: 34-56.

NOCETE, F. 1989: *El espacio de la coerción. La transición al Estado en las Campiñas del Alto Guadalquivir (España). 3000-1500 A.C.* British Archaeological Reports International Series, 492. Oxford.

- 1994a: *La formación del Estado en Las Campiñas del Alto Guadalquivir (3000-1500 a.n.e.)*. Monográfica Arte y Arqueología 23. Universidad de Granada. Granada.

- 1994b: "Space as coercion: the transition to the state in the social formations of La Campiña, Upper Guadalquivir Valley, Spain, ca. 1900-1600 B.C.". *Journal of Anthropological Archaeology* 13: 171-200.

- 2001: *Tercer milenio antes de nuestra era. Relaciones y contradicciones centro/periferia en el Valle del Guadalquivir*. Bellaterra. Barcelona.

NOCETE, F.; LIZCANO, R.; LINARES, J.A.; ESCALERA, P.; ORIHUELA, A.; PÉREZ, J.M.; RODRÍGUEZ, M.; GARRIDO, N.; AQUINO, N.; ALCÁZAR, J.M. & ALEX, E. 2001: "Segunda campaña de excavación arqueológica sistemática en el yacimiento de Cabezo Juré (Alosno, Huelva)". *Anuario Arqueológico de Andalucía* 1997-II. Junta de Andalucía. Sevilla: 107-111.

PÉREZ, M. 2004: "Hipótesis de trabajo para el estudio de la sociedad tribal en Andalucía". *Revista Atlántica-Mediterránea de Prehistoria y Arqueología Social* V (2002): 201-245.

PETERS, J. & DRIESCH, A. von den 1990: "Archäozoologische untersuchung der tierreste aus der kupperzeitlichen siedlung von Los Millares (Prov. Almería)". *Studien über frühe Tierknochenfunde von der Iberischen Halbinsel* 12: 49-110.

RAMOS, A. 1981: "Interpretaciones secuenciales y culturales de la Edad del Cobre en la zona meridional de la Península Ibérica. La alternativa del materialismo cultural". *Cuadernos de Prehistoria de la Universidad de Granada* 6: 242-256.

- 1997: "Flint Political Economy in a Tribal Society. A Material-Culture Study in the Malagón Settlement (Iberian Southeast)". In A.Ramos & Mª.A. Bustillo (eds.): *Siliceous rocks and Culture*. Monográfica Arte y Arqueología 42. Universidad de Granada. Granada: 671-711.

- 1998: "La minería, la artesanía y el intercambio de sílex durante la Edad del Cobre en el Sureste de la Península Ibérica". In G. Delibes (coord.): *Minerales y metales en la prehistoria reciente. Algunos testimonios de su explotación y laboreo en la península ibérica*. Studia Archaeologica 88. Universidad de Valladolid/Fundación Duques de Soria. Valladolid: 13-40.

- 1999: "Culturas neolíticas, sociedades tribales: economía política y proceso histórico en la Península Ibérica". In J. Bernabeu & T. Orozco (eds.): *Actes del II Congrés del Neolític a la Península Ibérica* (València, 1999). *Saguntum Extra 2*: 597-608.

- 2004: "La evolución urbanística del asentamiento millarense. Un texto de Historia social y política en la cultura tribal". *Simposios de Prehistoria Cueva de Nerja. II. La problemática del Neolítico en Andalucía. III. Las primeras sociedades metalúrgicas en Andalucía*. Fundación Cueva de Nerja. Nerja: 404-424.

RISCH, R. 1998: "Análisis paleoeconómico y medios de producción líticos: el caso de Fuente Álamo". In G. Delibes (coord.): *Minerales y metales en la prehistoria reciente. Algunos testimonios de su explotación y laboreo en la península ibérica*. Studia Archaeologica 88. Universidad de Valladolid/Fundación Duques de Soria. Valladolid: 105-154.

RODRÍGUEZ, Mª.O. & VERNET, J.L. 1991: "Premiers résultats paléocarpologiques de l'établissement Chalcolithique de Los Millares, Almería, d'après l'analyse anthracologique de l'établissement". In W.H.Waldren, J.A. Ensenyat & R.C. Kennard (eds.): *IInd Deya International Conference of Prehistory. Recent developments in Western Mediterranean Prehistory: Archaeological techniques, technology and theory. Vol. I. Archaeological techniques and technology*. British Archaeological Reports International Series 573. Oxford: 1-16.

ROMÁN, Mª. de la P. 1999: "Primeras aldeas con almacenamiento en el Sureste de la Península Ibérica". In J. Bernabeu & T. Orozco (eds.): *Actes del II Congrés del Neolític a la Península Ibérica* (València, 1999). *Saguntum Extra 2*: 199-206.

RUIZ, A. & MONTERO, I. 1999: "Ocupaciones neolíticas en Cerro Virtud (Cuevas de Almanzora, Almería): estratigrafía y dataciones". In J. Bernabeu & T. Orozco (eds.): *Actes del II Congrés del Neolític a la Península Ibérica* (València, 1999). *Saguntum Extra 2*: 207-211.

SANZ, J.L. & MORALES, A. (2000): "Los restos faunísticos". In F. Contreras (coord.): *Análisis Histórico de las Comunidades de la Edad del Bronce del piedemonte meridional de Sierra Morena y Depresión Linares-Bailen. Proyecto Peñalosa.* Arqueología. Monografías 10. Junta de Andalucía. Sevilla: 223-235.

SHENNAN, S. 1982: "Ideology, change and the European Bronze Age". In I. Hodder (ed.): *Symbolic and structural archaeology*. New Directions in Archaeology. Cambridge University Press. Cambridge: 155-161.

- 1989: "Tendencies en l'Etudi de la Prehistòria Europea Recent". *Cota Zero* 5: 91-101.

SIRET, L. 2001: *España prehistórica*. Junta de Andalucía/Arráez Editores. Almería.

SIRET, H. & SIRET, L. 1890: *Las primeras edades del metal en el Sureste de España. Resultados obtenidos en las excavaciones hechas por los autores de 1881 a 1887.* Barcelona.

VICENT, J.M. 1991: "El Neolítico. Transformaciones sociales y económicas". *Boletín de Antropología Americana* 24: 31-62.

ZAFRA, N.; HORNOS, F. & CASTRO, M. 1999: "Una macro-aldea en el origen del modo de vida campesino: Marroquíes Bajos (Jaén) c. 2500-2000 cal ANE". *Trabajos de Prehistoria* 56: 77-102.

CHAPTER 4

Between power and mythology. Evidence of social inequality and hierarchisation in Iberian megalithic art.

Primitiva Bueno Ramírez
Rodrigo de Balbín Behrmann
Universidad de Alcalá de Henares

Abstract

The study of megalithic art, its spatial distribution and its techniques, reveals the complexity of the megalithic ritual from the times of the very earliest constructions, making use of both the interior and exterior of the monuments. The presence of human figures, occupying the most distinguished spaces and displaying a wide variability of forms among which "armed" figures are particularly remarkable, is a valuable element in the analysis of evidence of hierarchical social organisation. Such evidence can be gathered from the sphere of collective burials and is the basis of the large scale ideological implementation taking place in the course of the III millennium cal BC The powerful armed figures which presided over dwelling and funerary spaces thus used references to the ancestors to justify their social position, in turn reinventing traditions.

Key words: Megaliths; Symbolism; Anthropomorphic Representations; Weapons; Bell Beaker; Hierarchical Organisation.

Resumen

El estudio del arte megalítico, su posición espacial y sus técnicas, revela la complejidad del ritual megalítico desde los tiempos de las primeras construcciones, haciendo uso tanto del interior como del exterior de los monumentos. La presencia de figuras humanas, ocupando los espacios más distinguidos y mostrando una amplia variabilidad de formas entre las cuales las figuras "armadas" son especialmente destacables, constituye un valioso elemento en el análisis de las evidencias relativas a la organización jerárquica de la sociedad. Tales evidencias pueden ser obtenidas de la esfera de los enterramientos colectivos y son la base de la implementación ideológica a gran escala que tiene lugar en el curso del III milenio cal BC. Las poderosas figuras armadas que presiden los espacios funerarios y de habitación invocan a los ancestros para justificar su posición social, reinventando así las tradiciones.

Palabras Clave: Megalitos; Simbolismo; Representaciones Antropomorfas; Armas; Campaniforme; Organización Jerárquica.

4.1.- Distribution and chronology of Iberian megalithic art. Ideological implications.

The perception of megalithic art as a funerary code specific to north-western megaliths emerged in early studies (Vasconcelos 1907). Among them, the work of R. de Serpa Pinto stands out particularly, given that the analytical parameters that he formulated were the basis of a hypothesis (Serpa Pinto 1929), whose main argument has been widely followed almost up until the present day. Serpa Pinto reflected the feeling of many Portuguese and Galician intellectuals who considered the past as the best argument to appreciate the Atlantic relationships which separated the Northwest from the rest of the Iberian Peninsula, a view in which the Atlantic was valued above any other type of cultural relationship.

Within this conceptual framework, megaliths and their productions united the whole of the Atlantic regions and supported a perception in which romantic mythologies had encouraged a successful mixture between Druids and Celts and Arthurian legends (De la Peña & Rey 1997: 308). A wishful prehistory was thus written, in which megaliths and their "cultural" details only existed in the Iberian Northwest. In parallel, the formulation of the oriental paradigm was being forged in all of European Prehistory, the Southeast being considered the focus of arrival of colonizers who introduced a new religion.

The position of the Galician and Portuguese prehistorians under consideration can hence be considered a response to the globalizing pressure of the orientalist hypothesis, attempting to point towards differentiation as an argument in favour of the cultural independence of the above mentioned civilizing foci. The vision of the Northwest as an unredeemed redoubt, foreign to the peninsular cultural movements, was not exclusive to megalithism, given that it was applied in a similar way to most prehistoric issues, the reason being that these appeared to be the clearest origin of ethnicity (Fernández-Posse 1998: 73). The Iberian Northwest and Southeast thus turned their backs to one another during a long period of time, and only very recently have the research interactions between both areas begun to take on a previously unsuspected importance (Fábregas 1991; Jorge 1986).

Within this framework, an implicit dichotomy was established between the megalithism of the Northwest and the rest of the peninsula. In the North, the walls of the megaliths were decorated with paintings, whilst in the South, idols formed part of the grave-goods but parietal decoration was not practiced. As a result, it was understood that the Northwest had its own ideology that was independent from the "oriental religion" characterised by the portable material representations known as "idols".

The suggestion of an ideological division developed alongside the parallel hypothesis of an architectural evolution following the 19th century tradition that was applied to the discussion of all cultural products: the progressive transition from simple to complex, and the subsequent disappearance of the phenomenon in a restitution of the simple, whether the analysis be artistic, historical or architectural. The megaliths would have started out as small tombs and later turned into larger constructions, the latter with parietal decorations. Thus the architectural peak coincided with the artistic, together forming the peak of funeral rituality in the Iberian northwest.

Megalithic art in 1929 thus appeared to be restricted geographically to the Northwest and architecturally to passage graves (Bueno & Balbín 2003: 295). Evidence falling outside this conceptual framework was either considered marginal, late or a result of de-structured cases. One of the most spectacular Iberian megaliths, the dolmen of Soto in Huelva (Southwest Spain), was identified at the beginning of the 20th century (Balbín & Bueno 1986; Obermaier 1924).

The concentration of finds in the North of Portugal between the 1930's and 1970's, including the sites of Antelas (Alburquerque et al. 1957; Girao 1921), Pedralta (Correa 1924) and many others (Shee 1981), contributed to reinforce the hypothesis formulated by Serpa Pinto. Similar data from Galicia (Leisner 1934a; 1934b) were interpreted by Galician prehistorians (López 1943) as evidence that megalithic art originated in the North of Portugal, along with the architectures, which from there spread to Galicia, reaching the South only in much later times.

The only author who went beyond the north-western proposal was Breuil (1935), who considered Megalithic Art as part of the sphere of Schematic Art in a hypothesis which would later be contrasted in various studies (Acosta 1968; 1984; Bueno & Balbín 1992). Paintings and open air and dolmenic engravings were perceived as part of the same expressive system which included sculpted anthropomorphic representations. In the fourth volume of the catalogue of schematic wall paintings in Spain, Breuil recorded the megalithic decorations of the dolmens of Soto and Menga, and those of the Catalan galleries. It was precisely the decoration of the latter

(those of Barranc de l'Espolla in particular), that was used by Bosch Gimpera (1965) to suggest the continuity of megalithic art into the phase coetaneous with Bell Beaker pottery. We shall return to this argument below.

The work of E. Shee (1981) is the only case since Serpa Pinto that supports a global consideration of Iberian Megalithic Art, this time within the framework of the Atlantic sphere defended by the early researchers. We will not however insist on themes that we have already developed in other studies. E. Shee built upon the hypothesis of Serpa Pinto, distinguishing the Viseu group as an example of a pristine nucleus of north-western art, and characterizing it according to the typology of the figures and their organisation upon the uprights. The marginality of the South was converted into a "miscellaneous group", while the idea of a later chronology than in the Northwest and the absence of pictorial techniques are maintained, precisely in the geographical area with the largest development of open air contexts in the same chronological framework as the construction of dolmens (Fig. 4.1).

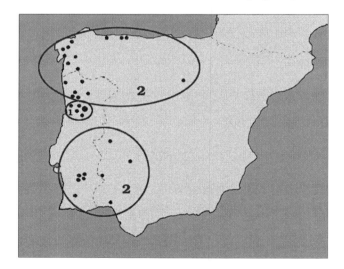

Fig. 4.1- Graphical representation of groups defined by E. Shee (1981).

In accord with Serpa Pinto, E. Shee placed the decorations in passage graves, dated precisely to 3000 BC, in relationship with the peak of megalithism. The dates of Iberian megalithic art would thus be later than Breton megalithic art. The repercussion of the work of the Irish professor was limited in the peninsula, given that the early 1980's were subject to strong debate over the contemporaneous nature of dolmens and decorations (Acosta 1984; Beltrán 1986), and over the diachronic relationship between paintings and engravings (Beltrán 1986; Jorge 1983), a position which has received recent support (Devignes 1993; 1997). The paintings and engravings could even have been made at any later date if the tombs were re-used in subsequent periods after their initial use, and in any case the "naturalism" of the paintings was considered a valid argument in terms of establishing its greater antiquity compared with the schematic nature of the engravings.

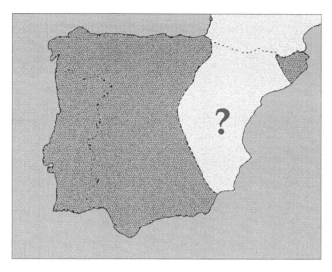

Fig. 4.2- Present day distribution of Iberian Megalithic Art. The question mark attempts to reflect the potential of areas which have so far been poorly studied.

But in the 1980's and the 1990's, a new generation of archaeologists demonstrated different concerns regarding the conception of megalithism, its regional evolution, its dates and, how not, the role of the decoration of the monuments (Balbín 1989; Bueno *et al.* 1983; Bueno & Balbín 1994b; Bueno & Piñón 1985; Cunha 1995; Lacalle 1999; Larsson 2001; Piñón & Bueno 1983; Rodríguez 1990; Silva 1993; Vázquez 1997), as well as the techniques employed in supposedly marginal sectors (Bueno & Balbín 2003: 297). Among these new concerns, not least was the need to reassess the many expressive facets of the megaliths (Bueno *et al.* 2003), one of which is obviously the symbolic component expressed through the painted, engraved or sculpted images within the monuments and their immediate surroundings.

The first critiques emerged from the same geographical area which had previously led the main interpretations: the North. Asturian (De Blas 1979) and Galician (Bello 1994) prehistorians argued in favour of the recognition of a factual reality further spread than the nucleus of Viseu and delimited at least by the so-called "north-western group" defined by Bello on the basis of pictorial and architectural productions. Our research in supposedly marginal areas, in particular the Southwest (Bueno 1988; Bueno & Balbín 1997c) and the centre of the Iberian Peninsula (Bueno 1991), led us to suggest an analysis of Megalithic Art from a different perspective from that of the mainstream framework (Bueno & Balbín 1992). Paintings were found to be present in megalithic monuments all over Iberia, and not only in those of the Northwest. Thus, previous geographical interpretations were not considered convincing (Fig. 4.2). Moreover, megalithic art appeared to be a funerary code strongly related with the graphical system of Iberian schematic art and was susceptible to be identified in any part of Iberia (Bueno & Balbín 2000d).

The identification of decorations in architectures of various types was another archaeological reality which made the exclusive relationship between megalithic art and passage graves no longer sustainable. Moreover, the radiocarbon dates available for passage graves from the centre of the peninsula (Bueno 1991; Bueno *et al.* 2004a; Cruz & Canha 1997; Cruz & Gonçalves 1995; Cruz & Vilaça 1994; Gomes 1996; Gomes *et al.* 1998) placed them among the oldest examples of peninsular megalithism, thus the complexity of their internal and external spaces could not either be explained by the relative modernity of the monuments (Bueno 1991; 1994; 2000).

We thus rejected the exceptional character of the Northwest by recognising the idiosyncrasy and early dates of the megalithic manifestations of the Iberian southern and central regions, and of course reassessing the complexity of Iberian megalithism based on the polymorphism of the architecture, which includes the presence of open spaces with evidence of ritual since the times of the earliest constructions. As is the case of Palaeolithic art or megalithic architecture, megalithic art must reflect a basic ideology shared throughout Europe and a very strong regional reinterpretation of this code (Bueno & Balbín 2002).

Once it had been established that graphical representations are associated with all types of megaliths throughout Iberia, the interpretative arguments regarding megalithic art necessarily had to be re-assessed. We thus channelled our thoughts in several directions. The chronology of the two iconographical schemes constituted a starting point for the formulation of a hypothesis regarding ritual complexity, as well as constituting a basis for the chronological attribution of open-air art (Table 4.1). We thus demonstrated the relationship of the graphical representations with the earliest megaliths (Bueno & Balbín 1992; 1998; 2000c; 2000e; 2003b; in press), as a means of analysing the complexity of the mechanisms associated with ancestor rituals (Bueno *et al.* 2001) since their origin in the V millennium cal BC (Fig. 4.3).

The concretion of these mythologies dated to the Middle Neolithic (with clear associations and a wide distribution) as well as an understanding of the conceptual basis of the system, point towards an earlier origin of the phenomenon, associated with early farmers (Bueno & Balbín 1997a; 2002). The symbolic development of architectures, engravings, paintings and sculptures during the V millennium cal BC all over Europe implies strongly rooted ideologies which can difficultly be defended as oriental, thus in turn supporting the hypotheses which highlight the role of the European groups in the emergence of producer societies.

The relationship between megalithic and schematic graphical systems also led us to suggest the symbolic contextualization and elements of the chronology of their development, with special focus on the interpretations of

NAME	ARCHITECTURE	DIRECT C14	INDIRECT C14	PAINTING	CARVING	REFERENCE
DOMBATE	CC		4918±46 BP	X	X	BELLO 1994
CASOTA DO PARAMO	CS	4740± 120 BP		X	X	CARRERA Y FÁBREGAS 2002
PEDRA CUBERTA	CC	5010±60 BP		X		CARRERA Y FÁBREGAS 2002
MONTE DOS MARXOS	?	4920±60BP		X	X	CARRERA Y FÁBREGAS 2002
		5330±80 BP				
PEDRA DA MOURA 1	CC	4980±70 BP		X		CARRERA Y FÁBREGAS 2002
ANTELAS	CC	4655±65 BP	5070±65 BP	X		DA CRUZ 1995
PORTELA DO PAU 2	CS		5131+40 BP	X	X	JORGE Y ALONSO 1996
			5087±31 BP			
			5435±44 BP			
PICOTO DO VASCO	CC		5140±40 BP	X	X	DA CRUZ Y CANHA 1997
MADORRAS 1	CC		4790±60 BP			GONÇALVES Y CRUZ 1994
			4540±65 BP	X	X	
CHA DE PARADA	CC		4820±40 BP		X	DA CRUZ 1995
			4610±45 BP			
CARAPITO 1	CS		4850±40 BP		X	LEISNER Y RIBEIRO 1968
			4590±65 BP			CRUZ Y VILAÇA 1994
			5125±70 BP			
			5120±40 BP			
AREITA	CC		5629+38 BP		X	GOMES ET ALII 1998
			5699+31 BP			
AZUTAN	CC		5250±40 BP	X	X	BUENO 1991
			5750±130 BP			BUENO ET ALII 2002
			5060±90 BP			
			4620±40 BP			
			4590±90 BP			
ALBERITE 1	G		5320 ±90 BP	X	X	RAMOS Y GILES 1996
			5110±140 BP			
			5020±70 BP			
SALA DE LA FUENTE	CUEVA	3880±50 BP		X	X	GOMEZ BARRERA ET ELII 2002
		3920±50 BP				
		4920±50 BP				
CASINHA DERRIBADA 3	CS		3056±42 BP		X	DA CRUZ ET ALII 1998
			3115±65 BP			
			3120±110 BP			

Table 4.1- Direct and indirect radiocarbon references for Iberian Megalithic Art (Bueno & Balbín in press).

the open air sites (Bueno & Balbín 2000a; 2000b; 2002; Bueno et al. 2004a). The strongest argument against the discrimination established between paintings and engravings was provided by the detailed analysis of the techniques employed in megalithic art. Thanks to megalithic art, we can affirm that painting, engraving and sculpting were all known and used techniques from at least the V millennium cal BC An even earlier date could be advanced if we are to consider the ever growing body of data relative to the VI millennium cal BC, associated with the erection of standing stones (Calado 1997). The possibility of confirming the early chronology of schematic art using the radiocarbon dates associated with megalithic art (Bueno & Balbín in press) would contribute to the redefinition of the ideological framework of the Neolithic and would certainly raise a lot of debate.

Constructions belonging to the III millennium cal BC display a funerary graphical code (Bueno & Balbín 1997b) including emblematic examples such as Los Millares. Moreover, evidence has been observed of repainting (Da Cruz 1995) and reviving, (Carrera & Fábregas 2002) which illustrate the diachronic discourse of the symbolic system of marking megalithic ritual spaces and their coexistence with the "Beaker ritual" (Bosch Gimpera 1965; Bueno et al. 2000).

In terms of typological considerations, we have argued against the groups suggested by E. Shee based on the absence of certain techniques and graphical representations (Bueno & Balbín 1997c; Bueno et al. 1999a; 1999b). The main difference in the treatment of the figures was observed in the case of anthropomorphic elements (Balbín & Bueno 1989; 1993; Bueno & Balbín 1994a; 1996a; 1997a; 2004) which display great variation attributed to both regional interpretations and intentions of individualization (Bueno 1990; 1992; 1995), the latter being understood as authentic images of power.

The incidence of very repetitive associations, particularly anthropomorph/sun, can be observed in both the interior of the monuments and open-air sites. In addition, the presence of snake patterns is mostly associated with the funerary sphere (Bueno & Balbín 1995), thus including in the megalithic repertoire an animal of clear oriental reminiscence whose presence in European symbology was not valued until the Iron Age (Bouza 1953). The central place of hunting themes coincides with the presence of arrowheads and microliths among the grave-goods, supporting the symbolic interpretation of the deposits accompanying the dead, within the framework of the mythologies expressed through the funerary code (Bueno 2000: 63). Genealogical scenes (Bueno et al. 2001) are another interesting thematic aspect which reveals the role of tradi-

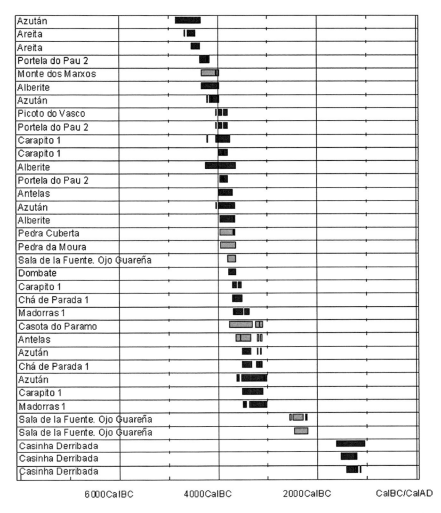

Fig. 4.3- Calibrated dates for Iberian Megalithic Art (Bueno & Balbín in press).

tion and the claim of belonging to a particular social whole, as a justification of the individuals buried within the monument, or of its builders.

The characterisation that we have briefly presented implies the existence of iconographic programs developed alongside the megalith (Bueno & Balbín 1996b; Bueno *et al.*1999a; 1999b; Bueno *et al.* in press) and the need for individuals able to put them into practice. Architecture and decoration are part of the same organization, thoughtful of the position of the graphical representations within the funerary space and thus an additional element in the selection and preparation of the stones prior to the construction of the monument.

Up until the 1980's, interpretations reduced megalithic art to a regionally defined expression, placed within a late chronological framework with respect to the development of megalithism, and characterised by particular techniques and architectures. Over the past years, megalithic art has been reconsidered as evidence of the ideological wealth of early agrarian societies and metallurgic groups,

as well as a new parameter of analysis for the assessment of social inequality in the context of European Prehistory.

At the same time as the preconceptions regarding Iberian megalithism, mostly focusing on the existence of foci, be they North or South, with sporadic and late entry into the interior, have evolved thus opening new lines of analysis for megalithic art. We are only beginning a research process which will lead towards substantial changes in many of the hypotheses regarding the megalith builders, just as the study of Palaeolithic art once changed our perception of the European Palaeolithic cultures.

4.2. Paintings and engravings for the dead?

The argument that we wish to develop in the following pages regarding the evidence of hierarchical organisation that can be gained from the analysis of the images within Iberian megaliths must begin with their assessment within the framework of schematic art. Megalithic paint-

41

ings, engravings and sculptures would thus be deeply rooted in the origins of the Neolithic, and would broaden the perspectives of possible inferences of (functionally speaking) specialized representations.

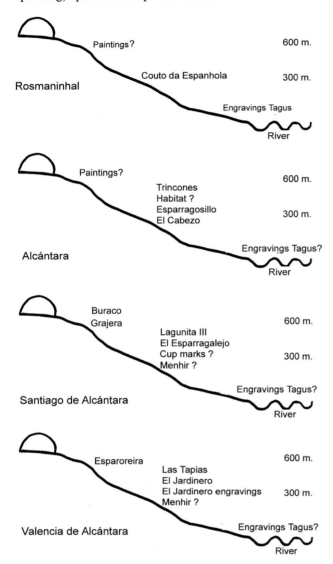

Fig. 4.4- Application of the "Tejo model" to the location of open air engravings, paintings, and dolmens in the international Tejo (Bueno *et al.* 2004).

This argument is most clearly supported by the analysis of particular regions that enable the development of models of images, megaliths and settlements, thus suggesting a global symbolic framework in which to integrate the territories of the producer and metallurgic groups throughout Europe (Bueno & Balbín 2000a; 2000b; 2003b; Bueno *et al.* 1998). Such models are supported by their empirical nature and their predictive potential (Bueno *et al.* 2004), as systems of analysis of megalithic territories (Fig. 4.4). For instance, the presence of engravings close to water ways suggests the possibility of inferring the presence of dolmens and dwellings on the high grounds immediately above the rivers, which could in

turn be used as a new reference to guide field surveys. Similarly, territorial organizations like those that we have analysed (Bueno & Balbín 2000a; 2000b; 2000e) justify the exhaustive field walking carried out in the hill ranges and foothills which have led us to locate paintings (Bueno *et al.* 2004). We are thus dealing with a theoretical hypothesis applicable to the spatial relationship between megaliths and other elements of the landscape, based on the role of graphical markers as indicators of ownership of territories and their acceptance by the people circulating throughout them.

The suggestion of the integration of open air paintings and engravings within the megalithic landscape for which we have evidence from the V millennium cal BC, refutes the view of dissociated paintings and engravings that considers the latter as necessarily later. The interpretation of Galician petrographs and their spatial relationship with megaliths (with a marked tendency to isolate cultural productions as foreign elements, or at least their exclusive association with simple themes such as cup-marks) has been a common tendency (Villoch 1995).

Petrogliphic themes in open air places were already pointed out by Breuil (1935) and P. Acosta (1968). Their identification in the tombs of Mota Grande (Baptista 1997) and Azután (Bueno *et al.* in press) (Fig. 4.5) dated by radiocarbon to the V millennium cal BC, as well as in other more recent sites such as Dolmen de Arroyo de las Sileras (Santos 1948) in the province of Córdoba and the cave of Haza del Trillo (Fernández 1951) in the province of Jaén, are strong enough argument for their coexistence with similar themes at open air sites.

Our argument is supported by an ever growing body of data and, most of all, opens up new lines of enquiry for future analysis, focusing on the hypothesis of a network of images and symbols in which each element introduced in the landscape by the megalith builders carried a "traditional" meaning. There are the symbols of the ancestors, deeply rooted in the mythology of the first farmers, which mark and define the functionality of the different spaces which were in use.

The comparison between open air representations (engravings and paintings) and those recorded within megaliths leads to a series of interesting observations. The predominant themes are generally those recorded by Breuil (1935) and Acosta (1968) as typical of schematic art: geometric elements (in particular circles), solar motifs, anthropomorphic figures and animals (mostly deer, but also some canines and snakes). These themes are dealt with differently in the Galician area, although we do not believe that this reflects essential differences compared with the open air engravings of the Tagus or the Guadiana basins, nor that this implies necessarily any difference in chronology. The surfaces normally used must play a part in these supposed differences and deserve further and more detailed analysis, alongside regional interpretations (Bradley & Fábregas 1999).

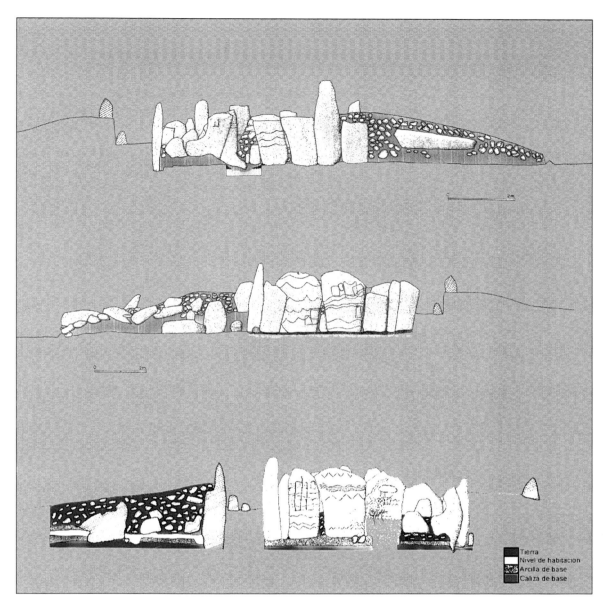

Fig. 4.5- Sides of the dolmen of Azután (Bueno et al. in press a).

The comparison of open air graphics with those from within the megaliths underlines two tendencies which are not observed in equal frequencies: the organization of the surfaces using geometric symbols and the presence of human figures, many of which are at the margins of the classical forms recorded in the repertoire of schematic art.

In other aspects however, the themes and their treatment are identical to those observed in open air engravings and paintings. The differences that we have pointed out deserve specific commentary. The organization of the decoration on the surfaces is an element already observed by G. Leisner (1934a; 1934b) in his magnificent study of Pedra Cuberta and recorded by E. Shee (1981) as one of the defining characteristics of the Viseu group. Both authors refer to the presence of sinuous or broken lines which draw a vertical and horizontal frame on the sur-

faces. In many cases, this decoration is found alone. A good example of this can be found in the uprights of the dolmen of Santa Cruz in Asturias (De Blas 1979). In this particular case, another defining characteristic of this decorative system is also present: painting and engravings are complementary in highlighting particular themes.

The interpretation of the surfaces of the megaliths as true *stelae* has been argued on more than one occasion (L'Helgouach 1996; 1998). Megalithic art provides strong arguments: for instance the widespread presence of dresses with geometric decorations which are identical to those found on other objects such as decorated plaques or larger anthropomorphic representations (Bueno 1992; 1995) (Fig. 4.6). The wide distribution of these motifs along the Atlantic coast (Bueno & Balbín 2002) and our understanding of the basic elements of megalithic anthropomorphic representations suggest that these could have been dressed with wool blankets, given that the dates of construction and decoration of the megaliths coincide with those of the use of secondary products throughout the whole of Europe (Bueno *et al.* 2002; Lichardus *et al.*1987).

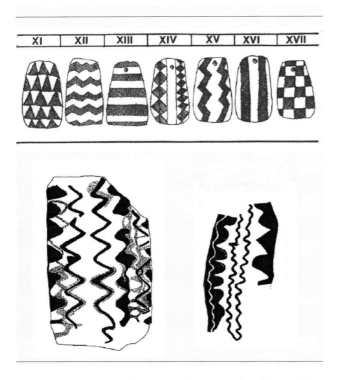

Fig. 4.6- Decorated plaques and engraved uprights of the dolmen of Santa Cruz (Bueno & Balbín in press).

The robed representations reflect the "megalithic type" *par excellence*, and engravings and/or paintings cover and accompany the predominant themes which usually occupy the head of the chamber. In this part of the tomb, we can observe the most explicit anthropomorphic representations, including hierarchical, hunting and genealogical scenes, alongside suns and snakes. Many of them present traits that can be traced to particular areas (Bueno & Balbín 1996b)and that can even lead them to be convincingly considered as "ethnic markers" as defined by Leroi-Gourhan (1971) in the case of regional symbols of Palaeolithic art.

More obvious still are the differences in the sculpted pieces found in the entrances of the chamber or of the passage, or the access area (Bueno & Balbín 1994; 1997a; 2004). They display individualising attributes, among which objects -staffs or axes- which are undoubtedly representative symbols (Bueno *et al.* in press a & b) (Fig. 4.7). The selection implied in the burials lodged within the megalithic architectures, the existence of items of prestige associated with particular individuals, the presence of children and women with rich grave goods and the appropriation of the collective code by some of them, are elements which reveal the extent of inequality within megalith-building communities. If we are to add the proliferation of anthropomorphic representations with a marked tendency towards individualization, then this hypothesis would thus be confirmed.

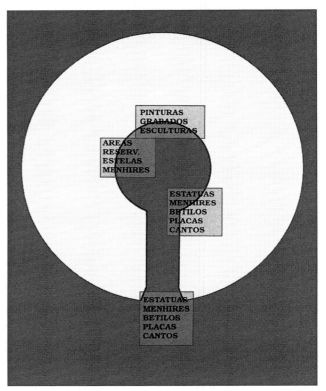

Fig. 4.7- Position and typology of megalithic anthropomorphic representations (Bueno & Balbín 2004).

As we mentioned at the beginning of this section, paintings and engravings at open air sites transcribe the symbolism of the farmers and metalworkers, thus establishing a complex territorial organization which implies visible and less visible or less accessible markers as are megalithic decorations (Bradley 1997). The difference between the graphical representations shared by the whole community and those used only by a segment of the community is perhaps the strongest evidence of inequality. Part of the group ostentatiously manipulated the shared symbols as a means of justifying their prestige position which was emphasised through the symbolic use of architectures, grave-goods and funerals. And this since the earliest dates of megalith construction. Evidence that the decorations focus in distinguished tombs, as is the case in some of the necropolis that we have excavated: Soto (Balbín & Bueno 1996), Alberite (Bueno & Balbín 1996b, Bueno *et al.* 1999), Alcántara (Bueno *et al.* 1999; 2000), Santiago de Alcántara (Bueno *et al.* 2004), etc. is another indication of inequality which further studies would need to assess in greater depth (Fig.4.8).

Along with other practices accompanying the ancestors, the decorations were made in such a way as to show the rest of the group the status of the individuals buried in distinguished tombs, and so that the inheritors of the

Fig. 4.8- North side of the dolmen of Alberite, Cádiz (Bueno et al. in press).

ancestors could legitimise their social position by means of the rituals which help to build irreversible ties between them, thus reuniting the past with the present and with the future.

4.3. The basis of tradition

The observation that engravings and paintings, as well as occupying standardised spaces inside and outside of the monuments, have been subjected to a series of processes of selection, leads to another observation regarding the hierarchical structure which we are discussing. This observation is that representations would have experienced the same social mechanism as the surrounding prestige objects introduced in the chambers as grave-good assemblages.

This mechanism of selection is well illustrated at open air sites, whose location in the landscape obeys some specific parameters (places of transit, economic or strategic interest, places of shared symbology), although the movement or prior working of difficulty obtained raw materials is not observed. However, it is noteworthy that surfaces which offer contrasts between the engraving and the background are preferred, such as the ferrous slates of the panels of the Tagus basin (Bueno & Balbín 2000b: 453), or large flat surfaces oriented predominantly towards the East and East-Southeast. Other factors in the selection of surfaces point towards the use of naturally outstanding surfaces, particularly visible as is the case of Peña Tú (Bueno & Fernandez-Miranda 1981) and of many other sites that we shall not list here.

In contrast, and in addition to the interpretations of techniques and the monumental enterprise, we suggest the assessment of the distinction between everyday and funerary art in relation with the importance of the cult of the ancestors and with the exaltation of hereditary factors which justify the position of specific sectors of the population that are buried in the megaliths.

The analysis of Iberian megalithic art has demonstrated the use of polychromatic images and various types of engravings (as well as sculpture), which are complemen-

tary in the technical development and that, so far, have not been identified at coetaneous open air sites (Bueno & Balbín 1992; 2003). In this sense, megalithic art is a "major art", as was that of the caves within Palaeolithic art, compared with other less technically-achieved forms of art.

The presence in many monuments of a range of different raw materials constituting the uprights and decorative surfaces takes on new importance when considering that the selection of the materials can be explained in part by an intention to contribute to the general design of the decoration. At times, spaces of transit, doorways, entrances to the chamber and passage, are marked by decorated pieces which have also been carried out in raw materials different to those of the rest of the monument. A good example is the slate slab with cup-marks which presides over the entrance of the passage of the dolmen of La Estrella (Bueno 1991: 89). In other cases, different materials are selected to produce visual contrasts that favour the engravings and paintings. An example of this is the chamber of the corbelled roofed tomb of Granja de Toniñuelo (Bueno & Balbín 1997b: 111).

The use of stones which naturally displayed a rough texture and grooves which imitated geometric themes has already been observed by Alburquerque and Castro (1961) in Portuguese dolmens, and we have confirmed this tendency in some fossil limestone pieces from the dolmen of Soto (Balbín & Bueno 1996) and dolmen of Alberite (Bueno & Balbín 1996b; Bueno et al. 1999). Many of these stones imply the investment of some effort in their movement over remarkable distances, as is known in other regions of European megalithism (O'Sullivan 1997). In addition, the sculpted materials, as well as displaying a selection of raw materials known from the most workable pieces such as idols, also show a clear preference for showy materials whose surfaces give play to the images carried out.

The tendency to use in the entrance of the tombs raw materials from the important aquiferous environments, quartzite in particular, is another element to consider in areas such as those of our main research area -the Tejo Basin- where evidence has been found of the production of decorated plaques in the immediate surroundings of rivers (Calado 2004: 256) which are also marked with profuse engravings.

We have no doubt that shelters and ensembles of engravings have an internal organization that affects each panel and the complete decorated area, although it is true that the organization of funerary spaces is more easily detectable. We have dealt with this theme on various other occasions (Bueno & Balbín 1994a; 1996a; 1997a; 2004) and so as not to repeat ourselves, we shall insist on defining the anthropomorphic representations which delimit internal and external spaces and distinguish areas of greater ritual significance.

The contrast between visible and less visible decoration, such as that of the megaliths, needs to be addressed here briefly. The megaliths have visible access areas where in many cases a series of deposits were made and were marked by sculptural elements of different scale. From small sculpted pieces (Bueno *et al.* 2003), to significantly shaped standing stones (Bueno & Balbín 2004; Bueno *et al.* 2004), without forgetting objects made from raw materials which have not survived.

The visibility of the funerary decorations is thus two fold and lies in contrast with their generally hidden nature, in the same way that not all megalithic mounds would have been originally visible if we are to consider the vegetation, the location of the mound and other factors which we shall not expand upon here. Standing stones, sculpted stones and possibly wood were most probably the references which made visible the location of the monuments. Again, the anthropomorphic representations, as well as belonging to the interior of the tombs, also benefited from a strong presence in the external spaces of the monuments.

When data are available, as is the case from the very interesting standing stone complex of Reguengos de Monsaraz (Gonçalves *et al.* 1997; Calado 1997), they point towards the existence of relationships of intervisibility setting up visual networks that connect one site with another. The evidence suggests that the visibility of the megalithic territory implied a great investment of work and social cohesion. This in turn supports the symbolic development which the megalith builders deployed around the human images and which was part of the basis of the ideology expressed in their graphics. The visibility in the surrounding area marked with engravings is also relative. Indeed, many engravings are located on surfaces on the ground which are barely appreciable unless their position is already known.

The importance of the knowledge of the terrain that is marked by the symbols of the tradition is therefore essential in understanding the global situation and value of the graphical markers that identify the territories of the megalith builders. It would thus be tradition which revealed the location of the markers and insured that it was safe to transit through the land belonging to the group (Bradley 2002; Bueno & Balbín 1997a; 2000b: 452; Edmonds 1999; Richards 1996; Thomas 2000; Tilley 1993).

The selection of surfaces, the deliberate visibility and the technical effort invested in the decorations are evidence of the symbolic repertoire which was developed in the context of the ancestral tombs, in addition to the well studied construction and maintenance of the architectures and so many other factors that defined megaliths as one of the most distinguishable expressions of ancestor cult documented in European Prehistory.

4.4.- The symbols of the producer groups and the Beaker culture

The strong tendency in European historiography to establish notorious ruptures based upon ergological evidence, the famous "type fossils", still has particular weight despite having been overthrown by broader visions of prehistoric cultures. This is most notable in the assessment of Palaeolithic groups, emphasising each one of its stages of development, -defined by its scholars to help in its analysis-, as drastic changes that span from the introduction of techniques of domestication to the arrival of colonizing groups, not to mention the evidence of strong ideological continuity that is displayed by the wide distribution of Palaeolithic images across all of Europe. The same situation occurs in the assessments of Late Prehistory. The new techniques of domestication and metallurgy imply drastic convulsions in the societies whose progressive impulses arrive from outside without taking into account the deep roots of a shared graphical code that had it clearest expression in the ancestor cults.

The images, their enormous connection with all of the spheres in which the social and economic activities of the prehistoric societies are carried out (Bueno & Balbín 2001) and their strength throughout several millennia during which the ergology was adapting to new circumstances (almost always derived from the growing economic intensification), suggest more continuities than discontinuities. We understand these images within a framework of persistence of values established through tradition, and not as their stagnancy. The meanings would have been changed over this time-span, as can be inferred from the development observed in the case of Palaeolithic art over its 20.000 years of existence. This process can be defined as a constant reinvention of tradition (Barrett 1988; Garwood 1991) that would act in favour of the legitimisation of the social situation of the newly emerging classes.

Megalithic art enables us to suggest some thoughts upon the directions that these changes appear to take, given that it offers evidence of individualization from the outset and a growing intensification in the later phases of the use and construction of megaliths.

The idea that megalithic ritual is opposed to Beaker ritual, given the collective and individual nature of each one, has been defended by many researchers over the past years (Sherrat 1997) who have drawn on the hypothesis which connects Beakers with an alcoholic ritual in the context of funerary feasting paid for by the elites, supported by the evidence provided from ceramic vessels deposited within megaliths since the V millennium cal BC The Beaker vessels did indeed contain alcoholic beverages, as did the coetaneous smooth vessels, as we have demonstrated in our work on the artificial caves of Valle de las Higueras in the province of Toledo (Bueno *et al.* 2000; 2004b). Earlier vessels, recovered from dolmenic deposits, also contained alcoholic beverages (Bueno *et al.* 2002; 2004a) and food.

The ancestor ritual implied the introduction of food and drink in ceramic vessels from its earliest emergence (Bueno 2000: 64), which over time would evolve into increasingly ostentatious funerary feasts that emphasised the power of particular social groups. Within the context of the symbolic and ostentatious development, images play a key role.

However, the consideration of Beaker pottery as neat evidence of inequality and the extension of individual burials appear to be only a partial truth if the larger European megalithic record is examined. It can be observed that collective burials built in early phases continue to be used at a later date (Delibes & Santonja 1987) and that many of them were maintained or rebuilt (Bueno *et al.* 2000 a & b; Bueno *et al.* 2004b), suggesting that the social values of the III millennium cal BC acknowledged earlier funerary contexts as representing a tradition of ancestor cult.

Moreover, some evidence from the Southwest (Bueno *et al.* in press) indicates that from the turn of the IV and III millennia cal BC megalithic necropolis were notably expanded, receiving more burials, and thus in turn reflecting some degree of "democratisation" (Tarrús 1987) of the burial practice alongside the investment of additional effort in differentiating each tomb. Among these efforts, the profuse decoration of tombs distinguished by their size, position within the necropolis, grave-goods and the number of anthropomorphic representations reveals that "tradition" plays a very important role in the Beaker ritual.

The dolmen of Lagunita III near Santiago de Alcántara (Cáceres) which we excavated during a project focused on the relationship between graphical markers and funerary and living areas in the Tagus region, provided juicy evidence. Of particular interest is the existence of a well-defined built area in front of the monument, in which abundant offerings of food and drink (currently under study by the team led by Juan Treserras) were deposited and accompanied by anthropomorphic references. The parallelism between this area and the "dados" described by Pedro Flores in his excavations of the necropolis of Los Millares (Almagro & Arribas 1963) is of extreme

interest in understanding the effort invested in the intensification of ritual areas presided over by anthropomorphic references throughout the III millennium cal BC.

Fig. 4.9- Photograph and rubbing of the armed stela of Soalar (Bueno *et al.* in press b).

In these tombs, chambers with or without passages, of different dimensions, corbelled roofed tombs and artificial caves, Beaker pottery is one of the most prestigious items within the individualized grave-goods, thus emphasising the inequality of the offerings since the earliest megaliths deposits (Delibes 1995; Bueno *et al.* 2000 a & b; Ramos & Giles 1996). Alongside the symbolic intensification of the III millennium tombs, open-air art, both engravings (De la Peña & Rey 2001) and paintings (Martínez 2004) also displays one of its highest points. If we are also to add the emergence of power relationships implied by the generally armed anthropomorphic representations, Beakers represent the greatest moment of symbolic development of ancestor imagery in all of Europe, above any other phenomenon, and perhaps as a legitimisation of the position of groups in territories in which there was increasing demographic pressure.

The process that we have been able to reconstruct tends to define ideological resources as the most solid basis for the justification of the privileged position of particular individuals or groups over the rest. The inkling of perceivable individualization since the first megaliths throughout the Atlantic façade can thus be neatly visualized in the presence of anthropomorphic figures that represent armed leaders.

The repeated association of these armed figures and megalithic spheres is notorious. Cases such as Peña Tú (Bueno & Fernandez-Miranda 1981), Sejos (Bueno *et al.* 1995), Monte da Laje (Silva & Cunha 1987), Garabandal (Saro & Teira 1992) or Soalar (Bueno *et al.* in press) (Fig. 4.9), presiding over the megalithic necropolis of the North of the peninsula and adding those of Hernán Pérez (Bueno 1995; Bueno & González Cordero 1995) and many others, demonstrate the close formal and symbolic connection between the armed *stelae* of the Copper Age and Bronze Age and the graphical references of a long-standing tradition.

The formal variability of these armed statues and *stelae* offer greater interest compared with that observed in the anthropomorphic specializations of the earliest megaliths. The spectacular nature and volume of some of these armed figures, their distinguished position within the megalithic landscapes of the III millennium cal BC and their association with metal weapons of Beaker date, reflect the long process leading towards hierarchical structures. Its roots are bound to megalithic mythology, adapted and "reinvented", as we mentioned above, to justify the progressive individualization of the grave-goods and megalithic decorations since the earliest moments of their existence.

4.5.- Power and ideology

We have assessed the position of decorated megaliths within the framework of symbolically codified landscapes, their role in particular necropolis, their relationship with numerous buried individuals and the richness of their grave-goods, but perhaps the clearest evidence of symbolic hierarchies is that suggested by the central place of the anthropomorphic representations. The symbols of the ancestors are those that legitimise the ownership of the goods to which only few had access, thus defining these individuals as the heirs of the mythological qualities and powers of the ancestors by means of the use of the symbols associated with them.

The armed statues that we can trace to the mid-III millennium cal BC are the best example of what Lull and Estévez called the "institutionalisation of power" (Lull & Estévez 1986: 451). The fact that these symbolic demonstrations of power can be traced to the earliest anthropomorphic representations suggests that the ancestor rituals reveal, from the symbolic sphere, the tensions generated within the producer groups due to their progressive sedentarisation, dolmens being one of the first expressions of "visual strength". Their position, associated with moral strength, provided the group with the arguments necessary for the justification of their ownership of the land. The progressive social complexity observable in the existence of the craftsmanship necessary to the creation of some of the symbolic productions, such as the decorated plaques of the early megalithic phase (Bueno 1992: 596), encouraged the use of these symbols by family groups who played the role of the heirs of the ancestors, defenders of tradition and guardians of social order.

Megaliths and the graphical symbols associated with them constitute the clearest evidence of the strong tendency towards a hierarchical organization, including production in so far as the system sought to create surplus. Their administration and their exchange against other raw materials was the basis of social differentiation. Inheritance and prestige were shaped to support the ideology of the leading classes, as is clearly indicated by the increasingly individualized armed figures of the Late Neolithic. The warfaring leaders of the early Bronze Age insured their symbolic value through mythological references to the ancestors, in the same way as the chiefs of the class societies of the Late Bronze Age, as well as by showing off exotic objects in their *stelae* and maintaining references to the old ancestors in order to claim back their status as heirs of the old social order.

Acknowledgments

We would like to thank Drs. L. García Sanjuán and P. Díaz-del-Río for their invitation to contribute on this theme. The development of our research on Megalithic art in the Iberian Peninsula has benefited from several consecutive DGCYT projects granted by the Spanish Ministry of Education and Science. The collaboration in these projects of other members of the Area de Prehistoria of the University of Alcalá de Henares (Madrid) has been essential. Our thanks also go to R. Barroso Bermejo who participated in the direction of the research in the Interior Tagus basin mentioned above as well as in the ongoing elaboration of the data from the dolmen de Alberite. J. J. Alcolea has copied the majority of the rubbings used in this study.

4.6.- References

ACOSTA, P. 1968: *La Pintura Esquemática en España*. Memorias del Seminario de Prehistoria y Arqueología 1. Universidad de Salamanca. Salamanca.

- 1984: "El arte rupestre esquemático ibérico: problemas de cronología preliminares". *Francisco Jordá oblata: scripta praehistorica*. Acta Salmanticensia 156. Salamanca: 31-61.

ALBURQUERQUE E CASTRO, L. 1961: "Um novo aspecto interpretativo da ornamentaçâo dos monumentos megalíticos". *Revista de Guimarâes* 71 (3-4): 255-260.

ALBURQUERQUE E CASTRO. L.; VEIGA FERREIRA, O. da & VIANA, A. 1957: "O dolmen pintado de Antelas (Oliveira de Frades)". *Comunicaçoes dos Serviços Geológicos de Portugal* 38: 325-345.

ALMAGRO BASCH, M. & ARRIBAS PALAU, A. 1963: *El Poblado y la Necrópolis Megalítica de Los Millares (Santa Fé de Mondújar,Almería)*. Bibliotheca Praehistórica Hispana 3. Madrid.

BALBÍN, R. de. 1989: "Arte megalítico y esquemático en el Norte de la Península Ibérica". *Sautuola 100 años después*. Diputación Regional de Cantabria. Santander: 237-247.

BALBÍN, R. de. & BUENO, P. 1986: "Soto, un ejemplo de arte megalítico en el Suroeste de la Península". In A. Moure (ed): *El Hombre Fósil, 80 Años Después*. Universidad de Cantabria. Santander: 467-505.

- 1989: "Arte megalítico en el Suroeste: el grabado del dolmen de Huerta de las Monjas (Valencia de Alcántara)". *XIX Congreso Nacional de Arqueología* vol. II (Castellón 1987). Zaragoza: 237-247.

- 1993: "Représentations anthropomorphes mégalithiques au Centre de la Péninsule Ibérique". *115 Congrés des Societés Savantes* (Avignon 1990). París: 45-56.

BAPTISTA, A.M. 1997: "Arte megalítica no planalto de Castro Laboreiro (Melgaço.Portugal e Ourense,Galiza)".*Brigantium* 10:191-216.

BARRET, J.C. 1988: "The living, the dead and the ancestors: neolithic and early Bronze age mortuary practices".In J.C. Barret & I.A. Kinnes (eds): *The Archaeology of Context in the Neolithic and Bronze Age: Recent Trends*. University of Sheffield. Sheffield :30-41.

BELLO DIEGUEZ, J.M. 1994: "Grabados, pinturas e ídolos en Dombate (Cabana, La Coruña). ¿Grupo de Viseu o grupo noroccidental?. Aspectos taxonómicos y cronológicos". *O Megalitismo no Centro de Portugal*. Viseu: 287-304.

BELTRÁN MARTÍNEZ, A. 1986: "Megalitismo y arte rupestre esquemático: problemas y planteamientos". *Actas de la Mesa Redonda sobre Megalitismo Peninsular*. Madrid: 21-32.

BLAS, M. A. de 1979: "La decoración parietal del dolmen de la Santa Cruz". *Boletín del Instituto de Estudios Asturianos* 98: 715-757.

BOSCH GIMPERA, P. 1965 : "La chronologie de l'art rupestre séminaturaliste et schémathique et la culture mégalithique portugaise". *In memoriam do abade Breuil,* vol. I. Lisboa.

BOUZA BREY, F. 1953:"Dólmenes con grabados serpentiformes y hachas rompecabezas nórdicos de la Galicia central". *Archivo Español de Arte y Arqueología* 26: 143-153.

BRADLEY, R. 1997: *Rock art and the Prehistory of Atlantic Europe: Signing the Land*. Routledge. London.

- 2002: *The past in the Prehistoric societies*. Routledge. London.

BRADLEY, R. & FÁBREGAS VALCARCE, R. 1999: "La 'ley de la frontera': grupos rupestres galaico y esquemático y prehistoria del Noroeste de la Península Ibérica". *Trabajos de Prehistoria* 56 (1): 103-114.

BREUIL, H. 1933-1935: *Les Peintures Rupestres Schémathiques de la Péninsule Ibérique*. 4 volumes. Lagny. París.

BUENO, P. 1988 : *Los dólmenes de Valencia de Alcántara*. Excavaciones Arqueológica en España 155. Subdirección General de Arqueología y Etnografía. Madrid.

- 1990: "Statues-menhirs et stèles anthropomorphes de la Péninsule Ibérique". *L' Anthropologie* 94 (1): 85-11.

- 1991: *Megalitos en la Meseta Sur:los dólmenes de Azután y la Estrella (Toledo).*Excavaciones Arqueológicas en España 159. Madrid.

- 1992: "Les plaques décorées aléntejaines: approche de leur étude et analyse". *L'Anthropologie* 96: 573-604.

- 1994: "La necrópolis de Santiago de Alcántara (Cáceres). Una hipótesis de interpretación para los sepulcros de pequeño tamaño del megalitismo occidental". *Boletín del Seminario de Arte y Arqueología* LIX: 25-100.

- 1995: "Megalitismo, estatuas y estelas en España". *Statuestele e massi incisi nell'Europ dell'età del Rame. Notizie Archeologiche Bergomensi* 3: 77-130.

- 2000: "El espacio de la muerte en los grupos neolíticos y calcolíticos de la Extremadura española". El Megalitismo en Extremadura. Homenaje a Elìas Diéguez Luengo. *Extremadura Arqueológica* VIII.:35-80.

BUENO RAMIREZ, P. & BALBIN BEHRMANN, R. de 1992: "L' Art mégalithique dans la Péninsule Ibérique. Une vue d' ensemble". *L' Anthropologie* 96: 499-570.

- 1994a: "Estatuas-menhir y estelas antropomorfas en megalitos ibéricos. Una hipótesis de interpretación del espacio funerario". *Homenaje al profesor. Echegaray. Museo y Centro de Altamira. Monografías* 17. Santander: 337-347.

- 1994b: "El arte megalítico como factor de análisis arqueológico: el caso de la Meseta española". *VI Congreso Hispano-Ruso de Historia.*Fundación Banesto-CSIC. Madrid: 20-29.

- 1995: "La graphie du serpent dans la culture mégalithique péninsulaire :représentations à plein air et représentations megalithiques". *L'Anthropologie* 99 (2/3): 357-381.

- 1996a: "El papel del antropomorfo en el arte megalítico ibérico". *Révue Archéologique de l' Ouest* 8 :97-102.

- de 1996b: "La decoración del dolmen de Alberite". In: J. Ramos, F. Giles (eds): *El dolmen de Alberite (Villamartín). Aportaciones a las formas económicas y sociales de las comunidades neolíticas del Noroeste de Cádiz*. Universidad de Cádiz. Cádiz: 285-313.

- 1997a: "Ambiente funerario en la sociedad megalítica ibérica: arte megalítico peninsular". In A. Rodríguez Casal (ed): *O Neolítico atlántico e as orixes do megalitismo. Actas do Coloquio Internacional* (Santiago de Compostela 1996). Consello da Cultura Galega. Santiago de Compostela: 693-718.

- de 1997b: "Arte megalítico en sepulcros de falsa cúpula. A propósito del monumento de Granja de Toniñuelo (Badajoz)". III Congreso Internacional de Arte megalítico. *Brigantium* 10: 91-121.

- 1997c: "Arte megalítico en el Suroeste de la Península Ibérica. ¿Grupos en el arte megalítico ibérico?". *Saguntum* 30 (II):163-161.

- 1998: "The origin of the megalithic decorative system: graphics versus architecture". *Journal of Iberian Archaeology* 0: 53-68.

- 2000a: "Art mégalithique et art en plein air. Approches de la définition du territoire pour les groupes producteurs de la péninsule ibérique". *L' Anthropologie* 104: 427-458.

- 2000b: "La grafía megalítica como factor para la definición del territorio". *Arkeos* 10: 129-178.

- 2000c: "Arte megalítico en la Extremadura española". Homenaje a Elías Diéguez Luengo. *Extremadura Arqueológica*, VIII: 345-379.

- 2000d: "Tecniques ,extensió geogràfica i cronología de l'art megalitic ibéric. El cas de Catalunya". *Cota Zero* 16: 47-64.

- 2000e: "Arte megalítico versus megalitismo: origen del sistema decorativo megalítico". In V.S.Gonçalves (ed.): Muitas antas, pouca gente. *Trabalhos de Arqueología* 16: 283-302.

- 2001: "Le sacré et le profane:notes pour l'interprétation des graphies préhistoriques péninsulaires". *Révue Archéologique de l'Ouest* 9: 141-148.

- 2002: "L'art mégalithique péninsulaire et l'art mégalithique de la façade atlantique: un modèle de capillarité appliqué à l'art post-paléolithique européen". *L'Anthropologie* 106: 603-646.

- 2003a: "Una geografía cultural del arte megalítico ibérico: las supuestas áreas marginales". In R. de Balbín & P. Bueno (eds): *Primer Symposium internacional de Arte Prehistórico de Ribadesella. El arte prehistórico desde los inicios del siglo XXI*. Asociación Cultural Amigos de Ribadesella. Ribadesella: 291-313.

- 2003b: "Grafías y territorios en Extremadura. Muita gente, poucas antas?". Origens, espaços e contextos do megalitismo. *Trabalhos de Arqueología* 25: 407-448.

- 2004: "Imágenes antropomorfas al interior de los megalitos: las representaciones escultóricas". M. Calado (ed): *Sinais de pedra. I Coloquio Internacional sobre Megalitismo e Arte Rupestre*. Evora. CD-rom.

- in press: "Arte megalítico en la Península Ibérica: contextos materiales y simbólicos para el Arte esquemático". *I Congreso Internacional de Arte Esquemático*. Los Vélez 2004.

BUENO, P.; BALBÍN, R. & ALCOLEA, J.J., 2003: "Prehistoria del lenguaje en las sociedades cazadoras y productoras del sur de Europa". In R. de Balbín & P. Bueno (eds): *Primer Symposium internacional de Arte Prehistórico de Ribadesella. El arte prehistórico desde los inicios del siglo XXI*. Ribadesella:13-22.

BUENO, P.; BALBIN, R. & BARROSO, R. 2004: "Application d'une méthode d'analyse du territoire à partir de la situation des marqueurs graphiques à l'intérieur de la Péninsule Ibérique: le Tage International". *L'Anthropologie* 108: 653-710.

- In press: *El dolmen de Azután (Toledo): áreas de habitación y áreas funerarias en la cuenca interior del Tajo*. Diputación de Toledo. Toledo.

- In press a: "La estela armada de Soalar, Valle de Baztán. Navarra". *Trabajos de Arqueología Navarra*.

- In press b: "Hierarchisation et métallurgie. Les statues armées de la Péninsule Ibérique". *L 'Anthropologie*.

BUENO, P.; BALBÍN, R.; BARROSO, R.; ALCOLEA, J.; VILLA, R. & MORALEDA, A. 1999a: *El dolmen de Navalcán. El poblamiento megalítico en el Guadyerbas*. Diputación de Toledo. Toledo.

BUENO, P.; BALBÍN, R. de; BARROSO, R.; ALDECOA, A. & CASADO, A. 2000: "Arte megalítico en el Tajo: los dólmenes de Alcántara.Cáceres.España". *Pré-historia Recente da Península Ibérica*. Porto: 481-496.

BUENO, P.; BALBÍN, R.; BARROSO, R.; ALDECOA, A.; CASADO, A.; GILES, F.; GUTIÉRREZ, J. M. & CARRERA, F. 1999b: "Estudios de arte megalítico en la necrópolis de Alberite". *Papeles de Historia* (Ubrique) 4: 35-60.

BUENO, P.; BALBÍN, R. de.; DÍAZ-ANDREU, M. & ALDECOA, A. 1998: "Espacio habitacional/espacio gráfico. Grabados al aire libre en el término de la Hinojosa (Cuenca)". *Trabajos de Prehistoria* 55 (1): 101-120.

BUENO, P.; BALBÍN, R. de & GONZALEZ, A. 2001: "El arte megalítico como evidencia del culto a los antepasados.A propósito del dolmen de La Coraja (Cáceres)".*Quaderns de Prehistória i Arqueología de Castelló* 22: 47-72.

BUENO,P.; BARROSO,R. & BALBÍN R.de 2004a: "El dolmen de Azután a la luz de las últimas investigaciones". *Investigaciones Arqueológicas en Castilla-La Mancha 1996-2002*. Junta de Comunidades de Castilla-La Mancha. Toledo: 25-34.

- 2004b: "Prehistoria reciente en la cuenca interior del Tajo: los yacimientos neolíticos y calcolíticos de Huecas (Toledo)". *Investigaciones Arqueológicas en Castilla-la-Mancha 1996-2002*. Junta de Comunidades de Castilla-La Mancha. Toledo: 13-24.

- In press: "Construcciones megalíticas avanzadas de la cuenca interior del Tajo.La provincia de Cáceres".*Spal*.

BUENO, P.; BARROSO, R.; BALBÍN R. de; CAMPO, M.; ETXEBERRÍA, F.; GONZÁLEZ, A.; HERRASTI, L.; JUAN, J.; LÓPEZ, P.; LÓPEZ, J.A. & SÁNCHEZ, B. 2002: "Áreas habitacionales y funerarias en el Neolítico de la cuenca interior del Tajo: la provincia de Toledo". *Trabajos de Prehistoria* 59 (2): 65-79.

BUENO, P.; FÁBREGAS, R. & BARCIELA, P. 2003: "Placas, estatuas, ídolos. Representaciones antropomorfas megalíticas en Galicia. A Carballeira (Pontevedra)". *Brigantium* 14: 47-61.

BUENO, P. & FERNÁNDEZ MIRANDA, M. 1981: "El Peñatú de Vidiago (Llanes, Asturias)". *Altamira Symposium*. Ministerio de Cultura. Madrid: 441-458.

BUENO RAMIREZ, P. & GONZALEZ CORDERO, A. 1995: "Nuevos datos para la contextualización arqueológica de estatuas-menhir y estelas antropomorfas en Extremadura". *Trabalhos de Antropologia e Etnología* 35 (I): 95-106.

BUENO, P. & PIÑÓN, F. 1985: "Los grabados del sepulcro megalítico de Magacela (Badajoz)". *Series de Arqueología Extremeña* 1: 65-82.

BUENO, P.; PIÑON, F. & PEREIRA, J. 1983: "Los grabados megalíticos del dolmen de Azután (Toledo)". *Zephyrus* XXXVI: 159-165.

BUENO, P.; PIÑÓN, F. & PRADOS, L. 1985: "Excavaciones arqueológicas en el Collado de Sejos. Valle Polaciones. Santander". *Noticiario Arqueológico Hispánico*, 22: 25-53.

CALADO, M. 1997: "Cromlechs alentejanos e a arte megalítica". *Brigantium* 10: 289-297.

- 2004: *Menires do Alentejo Central genese e evoluçâo da paisagem megalítica regional*. Unpublished Doctoral Dissertation. Lisboa.

CARRERA RAMIREZ,F. & FÁBREGAS VALCARCE, R. 2002: "Datación radiocarbónica de pinturas megalíticas del Noroeste peninsular". *Trabajos de Prehistoria* 59 (1):157-166.

CORREA, A.A.M. 1924: "Pinturas e insculturas megalíticas". *Revista de Estudos Históricos* 1: 65-66.

CRUZ, D. da 1995: "Cronología dos monumentos com 'tumulus' do Noroeste peninsular e da Beira Alta". *Estudos Préhistóricos* 3: 81-120.

CRUZ, D. da & CANHA, A.J.F. 1997: "Escavaçao arqueológica da Mámoa 4 do 'Rapadouro' (Pendilhe, Vila Nova de Paiva.Viseu)". *Conimbriga* 36: 5-26.

CRUZ, D. & GONÇALVES, H. de B. 1995: "Mamoa 1 de Madorras (Sabrosa, Vila Real): dataçoes radiocarbónicas". *Estudos Pré-históricos* 3: 151-159.

CRUZ, D. da & VILAÇA, R. 1994: "O dolmen I do Carapito (Aguiar da Beira,Guarda).Novas dataçoes de C14". *Estudos Prehistóricos* 2: 63-68.

CUNHA, A.L. da. 1995: "Anta da Arquinha da Moura (Tondela)". *Trabalhos de Antropología e Etnología* 35 (3): 133-151.

DELIBES, G. 1995: "Ritos funerarios, demografía y estructura social entre las comunidades neolíticas de la submeseta norte". In R. Fàbregas Valcarce, F. Pérez Losada & C. Fernández Ibáñez (eds.): *Arqueoloxia da Morte*. Excmo. Concello de Xinzo de Limia. Xinzo de Limia: 63-95.

DELIBES, G. & SANTONJA, M. 1987: "Sobre la dualidad megalitismo/campaniforme en la Meseta Superior española". In W.H. Waldren & R.C. Kennard (eds.): *Bell Beakers of the Western Mediterranean*.British Archaeological Reports International Series 331(i): 173-206.

DEVIGNES, M. 1993: "Contribution à l'étude de l'art mégalithique peinte ibérique". *Actas do 1º Congresso de Arqueología peninsular,* vol.1.Porto : 69-91.

- 1997: "Au sujet de la présence de peintures mégalithiques en Péninsule Ibérique" In A. Rodriguez Casal (ed.): *O Neolítico Atlántico e as orixes do megalitismo. Actas do Coloquio Internacional* (Santiago de Compostela 1996). Consello da Cultura Galega. Santiago de Compostela: 809-817.

EDMONDS, M. 1999: *Ancestral Geographies of the Neolithic. Landscape, Monuments and Memory*. Routledge. London.

FÁBREGAS VALCARCE, R. 1991: *Estudio de los ajuares líticos de las sepulturas megalítias de Galicia y Norte de Portugal*. Doctoral Dissertation. Universidad Nacional de Educación a Distancia. Madrid.

FERNANDEZ OXEA, J.R. 1951: "Lápidas sepulcrales de la Edad del Bronce en Extremadura".*Archivo Español de Arqueología* XXIV: 293-318.

FERNANDEZ-POSSE, Mª.D. 1998: *La investigación protohistórica en La Meseta y Galicia*. Arqueológica Prehistórica 1.Editorial Síntesis. Madrid.

GARWOOD, P. 1991: "Ritual tradition and the reconstitution of Society". In P. Garwood, D. Jennings, R. Skeates & J. Toms (eds.): *Sacred and Profane.Proceedings of a Conference on archeology, ritual and religion*. Oxford Committee for Archaeology. Oxford:10-32.

GIRAO, A.A. 1921: *Antiguedades préhistóricas de Lafôes*. Coimbra.

GOMES, L.F.C. 1996: *A necrópole megalítica da Lameira de Cima (Penedono-Viseu)*.Estudos Pré-históricos 4. Centro de Estudos Pré-históricos da Beira Alta. Viseu.

GOMES, L.F.C.; CARVALHO, P.S.; PERPETUO, J.M.A. & MARRAFA, C. 1998: "O dolmen de Areita (S. Joao de Pesqueira, Viseu)". A Pré-historia da Beira interior. *Estudos Pré-históricos* 6: 33-93.

GONÇALVES, V.; BALBÍN R. de & BUENO, P. 1997: "A estela-menir de Monte da Ribeira (Reguengos de Monsaraz, Alentejo. Portugal)". *Brigantium* 10: 235-254.

JORGE, S.O. 1986: *Povoados da Pré-história Recente (III. inícios do II. Milénios a. C.) da Região de Chaves -Vila Pouca de Aguiar (Trás-os-Montes Ocidental)*. Instituto de Arqueologia da Faculdade de Letras. Porto.

JORGE, V.O. 1983: "Gravuras portuguesas". *Zephyrus* XXXVI: 53-61.

LACALLE RODRIGUEZ, R. 1999: "Relaciones entre el arte y la mitología megalítica". *Gallaecia* 18: 37-52.

LARSSON, L. 2001: "Decorated façade?. A stone with carvings from the megalithic tomb Vale Rodrigo, monument 2, Alentejo, southern Portugal". *Journal of Iberian Archaeology* 3: 35-46.

LEISNER, G. 1934a: "Nuevas pinturas megalíticas en España". *Investigación y Progreso* VIII: 146-152.

- 1934b: "Die Malerein des dolmen Pedra Coberta". *Jahrbuch für Prähistoriche und Etnographische Kunst* 9: 23-44.

L'HELGOUACH, J. 1996: "De la lumière aux ténèbres". *Révue Archéologique de l'Ouest* 8: 107-123.

- 1998: "L'art mégalithique en Europe.Présentation générale". *Dossiers d'Archéologie* 230: 4-13.

EDINBURGH UNIVERSITY LIBRARY
EX BIBL. UNIV. EDINBURGH
WITHDRAWN

LICHARDUS, J.; LICHARDUS-ITTEN, M.; BAILLOUD, G. & CAUVIN, J. 1987: *La Protohistoria de Europa.El neolítico y el Calcolítico*. Labor.Madrid.

LEROI-GOURAHN, A.1971: *Prehistoire de l'Art occidentale*. Mazenod. Paris.

LÓPEZ CUEVILLAS, F.1943: "El Noroeste de Portugal y el arte megalítico". *Archivo Español de Arqueología* XXI: 245-254.

LULL, V. & ESTEVEZ, J. 1986: "Propuesta metodológica para el estudio de las necrópolis argáricas". *Homenaje a Luis Siret (1934-1984)*. Consejería de Cultura de la Junta de Andalucía. Dirección General de Bellas Artes. Sevilla: 441-452.

MARTÍNEZ GARCÍA, J. 2004: "Pintura rupestre esquemática: una aproximación al modelo antiguo (neolitización) en el sur de la Península Ibérica". *II Simposio de Prehistoria.Cueva de Nerja*. Fundacion Cueva de Nerja. Nerja: 102-114.

OBERMAIER, H. 1924 : "El dolmen de Soto (Trigeros, Huelva)". *Boletín de la Sociedad Española de Excursiones*. Año XXXII. Madrid: 1-31.

O'SULLIVAN M. 1997: "On the mining of megalithic art". *Brigantium* 10: 23-35.

PEÑA SANTOS, A. de la & REY GARCÍA, J.M. 1997: "Arte parietal megalítico y grupo galaico de arte rupestre: una revisión crítica de sus encuentros y desencuentros en la bibliografía arqueológica". *Brigantium* 10: 301-331.

- 2001: *Petroglifos de Galicia*. Via Láctea. A Coruña.

PIÑÓN, F. & BUENO, P. 1983: "Grabados megalíticos en el conjunto de Los Gabrieles, Valverde del Camino (Huelva)". *Homenaje al Prof. D. Martín Almagro Basch*. Vol. 1. Ministerio de Cultura. Madrid: 446-455.

PINTO, R. de S. 1929: *Petroglifos de Sabroso e a arte rupestre em Portugal*. Publicaçâo do Seminario de Estudos Galegos. A Coruña.

RAMOS MUÑOZ, J. & GILES PACHECO, F. (coord.) 1996: *El dolmen de Alberite (Villamartin). Aportación a las formas económicas y sociales de las comunidades neolíticas en el noreste de Cádiz*. Universidad de Cádiz. Cádiz.

RICHARDS, C.C. 1996: "Monuments as landscape. Creating the centre of the world in late neolithic Orkney". In R. Bradley (ed.): Sacred Geography. *World Archaeology* 28 (2): 190-208.

RODRÍGUEZ FERNANDEZ, R. 1990: "El arte grabado megalítico en la provincia de Cádiz: galería cubierta de 'El Toconal 1' (Olvera, Cádiz)". *Gades* 19: 25-40.

SANTOS GENER, S 1948: "Dolmen con insculturas en Arroyo de las Sileras (Córdoba, Espejo)". *Crónica del IV Congreso Arqueológico del Sudeste Español*. Elche.

SARO, J.A. & TEIRA, L. 1992: "El ídolo de Hoyo de la Gándara (Rionansa) y la cronología de los ídolos antropomorfos en la cornisa cantábrica". *Trabajos de Prehistoria* 49: 347-355.

SHEE TWOHIG, E. 1981: *The megalithic art of Western Europe*. Clarendon Press. Oxford.

SHERRAT, A. 1997: *Economy and society in Prehistoric Europe. Changing perspectives*. Edinburgh University Press. Edinburgh.

SILVA, E.J.L. 1993: "Représentations humaines sur deux monuments mégalithiques de la région du Nord de Portugal". In J. Briard & A. Duval (dir.): *Les représentations humaines du néolithique à l'âge du fer: actes du 115e congrès des sociétes savantes* (Avignon, 1990). Éditions du Comité des Travaux Historiques et Scientifiques. París: 21-27.

SILVA, E.J.L. & CUNHA, A.L. 1987: "As gravuras do Monte Laje (Valença)". *Trabalhos do grupo de investigaçao arqueológica do Norte* 2: 143-158.

TARRÚS I GALTER, J. 1987: "El megalitisme de l'Alt Empordá (Girona). Els constructors de dolmens entre el Neolitic Mitjá i el Calcolitic à serra de l'Albera, Serra de Roda i Cap de Creus". *Cota Zero. Revista de Arqueologia i Ciencia* 3: 35-54.

THOMAS, J. 2000: "Death, identity and the body in Neolithic Britain". *The Journal of the Royal Anthropological Institute* 6 (4): 653-668.

TILLEY, C. 1993: "Art, architecture, landscape (neolithic Sweden)". In B. Bender (ed.): *Landscape: politics and perspectives*. Explorations in anthropology. Berg. Providence: 49-84.

VASCONCELOS, J. de L. 1907: "Peintures dans les dolmens de Portugal". *Homme Préhistorique* 5.

VÁZQUEZ VARELA, J.M. 1997: "La ideología en el arte megalítico de la Península Ibérica". *Brigantium* 10:15-22.

VILLOCH VAZQUEZ, V. 1995: "Monumentos y petroglifos: la construcción del espacio en las sociedades constructoras de túmulos en el NO peninsular". *Trabajos de Prehistoria* 52 (1): 39-55.

CHAPTER 5
Early Social Inequality in Cantabrian Spain
(IV-III millennia BC)

Roberto Ontañón-Peredo
Universidad de Cantabria

Abstract

The archaeological record for Cantabrian Spain in the IV and III millennia cal BC offers certain indications of the development of profound economic and social transformations in the local communities. These transformations affect technology, the bases for subsistence, the organisation of work, the inter-group interaction as well as the symbolic world. An intensification and specialisation in production, an activation of interaction, changes in the symbolic world - in the funerary customs and schematic art - work together in a context of apparent climatic deterioration to complete the transition from the first Neolithic groups to fully-blown farming communities. It may be concluded that during this period the processes of neolithisation in the region were completed, giving origin to the configuration of a socio-economic structure in which tendencies developed leading towards social inequality. This paper discusses the available data and, after analysing a series of variables that are considered relevant for the explanation, proposes an interpretation for this part of the regional record, guided by explicit methodological assumptions.

Keywords: Social Inequality; Cantabrian region; Late Neolithic; Chalcolithic; Early Bronze Age.

Resumen

El registro arqueológico de la región cantábrica en el IV y III milenios cal A.N.E. ofrece algunos indicios que apuntan al desarrollo de profundas transformaciones económicas y sociales en las comunidades responsables de su formación: en el ámbito tecnológico, en las bases de subsistencia, en la organización del trabajo, en la interacción y en la esfera simbólica. Intensificación y especialización productiva, activación de la interacción, cambios en la esfera simbólica –en los modos funerarios y en el arte esquemático- se conjugan en un marco de aparente deterioro climático para culminar el tránsito desde los primeros grupos neolíticos hasta las comunidades con un modo de vida plenamente campesino. Puede concluirse que en este periodo se consuman en la región los procesos de neolitización, que dan lugar a la configuración de una formación económico-social en cuyo seno se desarrollan tendencias conducentes hacia la desigualdad social. En este artículo se exponen los datos disponibles y, tras el análisis de una serie de variables que se consideran relevantes para la explicación, se propone una interpretación de esa parte del registro regional, guiada por unos presupuestos metodológicos explícitos.

Palabras clave: Desigualdad Social; Región Cantábrica; Neolítico Avanzado; Calcolítico; Primera Edad del Bronce.

5.1.- Aims

The problem tackled in this paper is situated in a historical process with a long duration (IV and III millennia cal BC). Throughout this time period, phenomena can be detected in the Western European archaeological record that are generally interpreted as evidence of socioeconomic development, from an apparently communitarian phase in the first Neolithic communities, towards the creation of permanent structures of social inequality in the hierarchical societies of the Bronze Age. The main working hypothesis that is used in this article is the possible applicability of this socioeconomic dynamic in the geographical area of Cantabrian Spain. The following pages aim to verify this point.

The chosen framework of the study is justified by the use of a unit and scale of analysis that are relevant, coherent and feasible for solving the proposed historical problem, and further more, because of two reasons. First, the phenomena we aim to analyse appear to form at a local level, within self-sufficient units of production. However, in their own development they carry implicit a capacity for expansion which tends to increase the level of economic and social aggregation, which integrates these units in a much wider sphere of relationships, perceptible through multiple signs of interaction. Second, the very insufficiencies of the regional archaeological record impede an approach to this topic at a local or small scale. The scarcity of available information at a micro- or semi microspatial scale for this segment of the record in Cantabrian Spain does not allow more detailed approaches and therefore forces us to widen the field of the research aims.

The unit of analysis is assimilated to a natural or physiogeographical region, namely the so-called "Cantabrian Cornice", a narrow and long strip of mountainous land, about 350 kilometres in length and with an average width of 50 kilometres, which stretches between the Bay of Biscay to the North, and the Cantabrian Cordillera, an orographical barrier of considerable height which marks the southern limit, separating it from the mainland of the Iberian Peninsula.

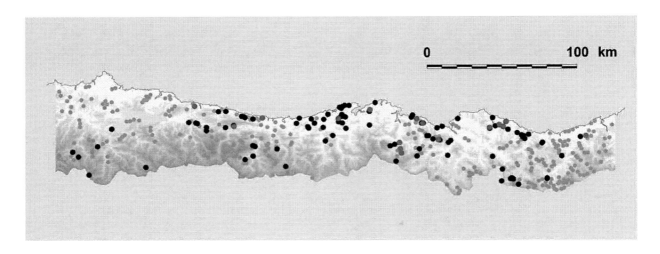

0   100 km

Fig. 5.1. Map of Cantabrian Iberia, locating Neolithic and Chalcolithic sites (Big grey dots = Neolithic cave sites; small grey dots = megaliths, some reutilised in later times; black dots = Chalcolithic cave sites).

Considering that in the same territorial unit, human societies are conditioned in an analogous way by a similar environment, this methodological option allows us to analyse the evolution of the economic and social processes in a homogeneous environmental framework. In the case of this northern-most zone of the Peninsula, the validity of this proposal is sufficiently supported by History and Ethnography. The "people of the north", living along the Cantabrian Coast in the Pre-Roman period (and, in a wider sense, those occupying the whole geographical area of "Wet Spain", from Galicia to the Pyrenees), display profound cultural analogies, described by Strabo and of which some traces have survived until contemporary times. In several features of the relict "traditional culture", this area can still by clearly differentiated from neighbouring regions (Caro Baroja 1977; Lisón Tolosana 1991). The choice of the study area is, in this sense, fully justified, as Cantabrian Spain is a perfectly differentiated region and well-defined geographical entity, both in the marked contrast with neighbouring regions of the Northern Meseta and the Ebro Valley - and to a lesser extent, with Galicia - and in its relatively clearly defined boundaries (Fig. 5.1).

5.2.- History of research

There has been no publication about the topic of this paper in the history of research in the region. However,

there are relatively common references to elements of the regional archaeological record (sites, stratigraphic units, collections of materials or isolated artefacts) and even technological, economic or ideological phenomena (such as the appearance of agriculture and stock-rearing, megaliths, the technique of flat retouching and metalworking), that are attributed in a more or less vague way to the "Late Neolithic", "Eneolithic" or "Chalcolithic". Some generalised proposals may also be found, integrating all or part of these aspects in diachronic schemes or "cultural sequences" (Ortiz Tudanca 1990; Alday Ruiz 1992). They are normally ascriptions made uncritically regarding the theoretical and methodological reference framework on which they are based.

Some studies about questions linked to the topic of this paper are found in syntheses of provincial areas, chapters of books on General or Late Prehistory in Asturias, Cantabria and the Basque Country, including very general interpretations of aspects such as the megaliths, the appearance of metallurgy, or the "bell beaker complex" (Apellániz 1975; Blas Cortina 1983; Rincón Vila 1985; González Sáinz & González Morales 1986; Blas Cortina & Fernández-Tresguerres 1989); they are also found in books or papers applied to the local or regional analysis of phenomena like the ones mentioned above, that are partly developed within the same chronological period as this study (Armendariz & Etxeberria 1983; Teira Mayolini 1994).

The factors intervening in the configuration of this research panorama are basically two. First, the insufficiency of empirical data (of qualitative nature more than quantitative), derived from the scarcity of recent works with exhaustive techniques of information gathering, hinders the posing of "ambitious" questions about this poor regional archaeological record. Secondly, and no less important, there is the persistence in regional research of meta-theoretical assumptions and methodological principles that are completely out-of-date, expressed with considerable conceptual indetermination, and the uncritical use of a conventional period scheme based on technology and typology, that has led to the establishment (explicit or, usually, implicit) of a "sequence" of chronocultural entities, to which groups of "features" are attributed, without going sufficiently into questions of processual nor, of course, social types. It may still be said that the dominant subject tendency in regional prehistoric research is what Vicent (1982) calls "modified positivism" or "pragmatic reformism", which is no other than a methodological *aggiornamento* - not theoretical - of the most traditional positivist research. In this sense, the idea of the Cantabrian Cornice as an "island", *i.e.* as an isolated and deeply retarded zone in comparison with neighbouring regions and their historical development, has had a strong influence.

Finally, the provincial compartmentation of research should be mentioned, as this has affected archaeological research in all of its phases, from field work to the publication of results, with the consequence of a fragmented and fragmentary knowledge of past reality, hindering approaches such as that of the present paper.

5.3.- Questions of method

First, it is appropriate to make the epistemological stand of this paper explicit, in order to avoid the traditional interpretative eclecticism, and to make our explicative proposals coherent with our starting points as well as with the working method we design. This epistemological stand is framed within what Fernández Buey (1991) has called "temperate rationalism", a "centred" or intermediate posture between the extremes of scientism and relativism, rigorous in its conception of science and method, but critical with neopositivist simplifications and dogmatisms, and with a focus that can be situated within the coordinates of a modern historical materialism, free of dogmatisms, within what has been called "social archaeology".

It is now necessary to define the parameters that are going to be considered in the assessment of the regional record to determine whether or not evidence exists that can be interpreted as an indication of the existence of some form of social inequality (Renfrew 1972; Chapman 1991; Wason 1994; Earle 1991). By social inequality we understand the existence in a socio-economic formation of asymmetrical and institutionalised social relationships

of production. That is, an inequality that goes beyond the interpersonal differences based on the status of age or sex that are present in all human societies. In fact, differences in rank or status alone are insufficient evidence of "social complexity", as they can equally be detected in societies that are apparently "egalitarian", but which in reality are also structured unequally on power relationships, although on a much smaller scale, restricted to the family or domestic community. It is consequently necessary for this social factor to be accompanied by others that can effectively show the existence of true socio-political stratification.

These potential archaeological indicators of social inequality refer to the different instances of the socio-economic structure, related both with the economic base and the ideological superstructure. In the case of the productive forces, these include questions such as the spatial and functional organisation of production, like settlement patterns, intensification of production, degree of specialisation or the distribution of singular materials. In the case of the superstructure, expressed in transcendent or symbolical behaviour, funerary practices and the iconography of schematic art are taken into consideration.

Within a Marxist theoretical framework, instruments of prestige such as those mentioned above, funerary rituals and the iconography of the new art, can together be interpreted, paraphrasing Gilman (1991), as material evidence of the effort by the emerging elites to maintain their adhesion against the expected resistance of the dominated. In this sense, therefore, we have an excellent opportunity to reconstruct the appearance of social stratification, studying the evidence of the "class awareness" of the first dominant class.

5.4.- General lines in the process of cultural change

In relation to land-use patterns, in the studied period we can see a considerable increase of the socio-economic system, (which now reaches, for the first time, practically the whole region), from the coastline itself to the peaks of the Cordillera. However, no hierarchisation can be observed neither in the network of settlements, nor in their internal organisation. The habitat in fact displays markedly archaic features, such as the use of habitats in caves until late in the 3rd millennium cal BC, as well as the appearance at this time of an extremely simple open air habitat: These mainly consist of the so-called "flint working areas", which include a limited number of built structures that may be isolated or forming small groups. The total absence of hierarchisation in the settlement pattern (both at micro and macro spatial scale), marks the limits of this process.

Regarding the technological transformations, there is a process tending towards cultural homogenisation throughout the region, which is expressed in the appearance and spread of elements of the material culture, like the technique of flat retouching, or in the structural similarity of industrial sets documented at sites located in different parts of the region (Ontañón 2001). Another form of evidence to be mentioned is the full integration of technical traditions and innovations in the socio-economic dynamics: use of geometric microliths in projectiles and also for harvesting; specific manufacture of sickle blades to harvest cereals; use of millstones to grind the products of the harvest; introduction of mining tools for the extraction of copper.

One of the most patent phenomena in the economic basis is the intense development of the subsistence bases, shown in the dual process of specialisation in the productive methods accompanied by a trend towards intensification. The process observed appears to lead to the formation of a true farming economy of self-subsistence. In this way, the animal remains found show an important increase of domesticated species in comparison with wild animals, and the little data available about the minimum number of individuals and their division in sex and age suggests a progressive use of secondary products (Castaños 1983; 1984; 1995; Mariezkurrrena 1990) (Fig. 5.2).

know that the predominant plants are cereals, especially naked wheat. Other summer cereals are known (millet and Italian millet), with growth cycles that are complementary to that of wheat (Zapata 1996; 1997). So it may be inferred that the local populations used primitive techniques of crop rotation, which would mean a continuous use of the limited agricultural land in Cantabrian Spain throughout the annual cycle. This would mean that, towards the end of the studied period, the agricultural system, which included other cereals like barley and complementary crops (pulses), would have become highly developed.

As regards the specialisation or functional division of labour, the only progress seen is linked to metallurgy, in the last phase of the process that we are studying here (see below).

Fig. 5.3. Flint dagger with notches from level S1 in Cueva de La Garma A (Cantabria).

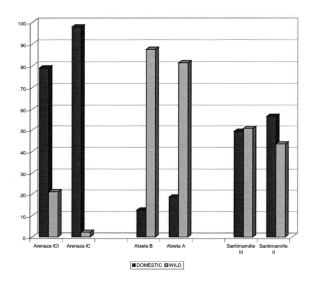

Fig. 5.2. Domestic and wild mammals in Neolithic and Chalcolithic levels in the Province of Vizcaya (No. of remains). Levels IC1/IC at Arenaza, B/A at Atxeta and III/II at Santimamiñe.

In view of this palaeo-economic information, it may be advisable in the Cantabrian region to talk of "processes of neolithisation" and not of a single development towards the installation of a productive economy, as appreciable differences can be seen among sites whose stratigraphic records appear to express the particular "course" taken by each one (although the dominant trends noted above are the same).

Concerning the exploitation of plants, the available data are rather patchy, although by the end of the process we

One of the most visible features of the period being analysed is the considerable expansion of interaction, shown by the vast diffusion of a wide material catalogue and the associated ideology, mainly in the symbolic world. Apart from the industrial homogenisation alluded to above, (which includes aspects such as the exchange of high quality raw stone material for the manufacture of blades, geometric microliths or arrow-heads, the technique of flat retouching or metallurgy, or certain decorative patterns on pottery), other clear evidence of this interaction is the rapid spread of manufactured products and ideas such as the form of burial in megalithic structures or, later, iconographic models seen in the regional schematic art (Fig. 5.3).

The one factor intervening in this process of cultural change that must be stressed is, undoubtedly, the profound transformation detected in the burial patterns. These variations should be understood rather as trends that develop along several parallel lines, overlapping for much of their existence. They affect practically all the variables encompassed by the so-called "archaeology of death" (Chapman *et al.* 1981), including, (1) the location and type of funeral context (from megalithic monuments to underground spaces), (2) the form of deposit of the bodies (reduction in the number of people buried in each sepulchral unit), and (3) the material culture associated with the burials, involving a qualitative and quantitative transformation of the material repertoire and a "condensation" of the ascribed intrinsic value (Renfrew 1986) of the grave goods.

These funerary trends seem to point in the same direction, which can be described, in a very simple way, as a process of transferring the symbolic content from the collective to the individual, and an intensification in the accumulation of wealth ascribed to the dead. Thus, in Cantabrian Spain there is a development of the funerary rites, similar to those seen in the whole of Western Europe. This begins with the "collective" burials of the Late Neolithic, followed by the introduction of funerary practices that will spread at the start of the Bronze Age such as the custom of individual, or at most double, inhumations, in tombs or cists, accompanied by more or less opulent and

highly variable goods, normally located in the living areas themselves or very near to them. This represents a truly radical symbolic change, which implies a significant move from the funerary structures of successive multiple inhumations, in which the human remains were elements that could be successively handled (deposited, moved or withdrawn), to simple burial contexts, products of a single burial act, in which the symbolic centre becomes the human body itself, which thus maintains its identity intact in perpetuity (Thomas 1991).

This evolution is coloured in the region by the appearance of what we can call a "transitional phase", formed by individualised burials that are the last phase of the use of successive multiple inhumation deposits, and which are commonly accompanied by grave goods including some of the components of the "bell beaker" complex (Fig. 5.4).

This is, perhaps, the most interesting funerary episode, as it represents a moment of transition between the burial practices of the Late Neolithic and the Bronze Age in which, at the same time, secular uses persist while other new ones appear, apparently in contradiction with the previous ones. It also seems to be the most difficult one to explain. Possibly, the maintenance during a time of the atavistic burial spaces for individualised inhumations is an affirmation (or, more correctly, the fundamentation) of the "new status" within the same spaces in which Neolithic groups expressed precisely their communality

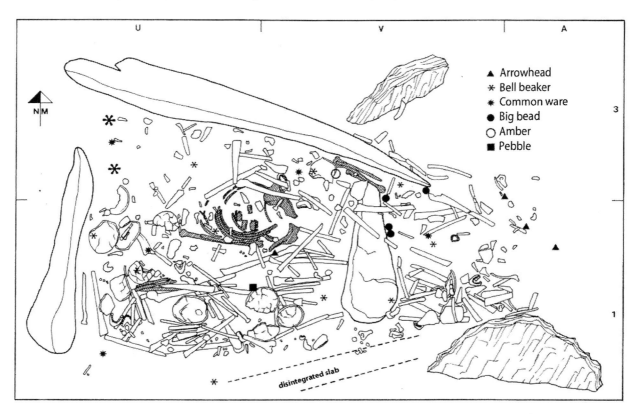

Fig. 5.4. Plan of the chamber (Dolmen of Larrarte, Guipúzcoa).
The striped bones correspond to an individual bell-beaker burial (following Mujika and Armendariz 1991).

through the collective burial of their dead. We would have, therefore, a phenomenon of the survival of ancestral traditions and their existence together - only temporarily - with those new hierarchised organisation patterns that would finally bring down the old social structure. In conclusion, we would be in a phase that represents the first explicit evidence of the development of social inequality within communities that are more or less homogeneous or, at most, differentiated to a minimal degree. This hierarchisation would still require, in its first impulse (and only then), its social legitimisation, sanction or backing in the common ritual framework. These communitarian ritual forms would finally lose their relevance - in a development not necessarily at a regional scale - as the consequence of their clear incompatibility with a flourishing process of social stratification (Ontañón 2003a). In a Marxist interpretation similar to the one proposed by Gilman (1976) for the process in the Bronze Age in the southeast of the Iberian Peninsula, the phenomena would form a symbolic manifestation of dialectical surmounting of conflicts or internal contradictions in the socio-economic order.

5.5.- Main features of the socio-economic formations in the late 3rd millennium cal BC

The process roughly outlined above results in the configuration of a socio-economic formation with the general characteristics summarised below. Regarding the economic base, it is defined by an organised and intensive use of natural resources, specialised in production and complemented by predatory strategies. In this instance, it is also seen that the pattern of settlement / intervention is perfectly adapted to the area's complicated relief and the requirements of the productive agricultural cycle (Fig. 5.5).

Concerning exchange of goods, a dense network of intra and extra regional contacts is seen to be in function. It has four main focuses of relationships: the Northwest, the Northern Meseta, the Ebro Valley and the South of France. The clearest expression of this system of interaction is the establishment of extensive circuits of exchange of goods with a high ascribed intrinsic value (Fig. 5.6).

An example which perfectly defines the nature of this interaction is the "break-up" of the bell beaker complex in Cantabrian Spain (Ontañón 2003b). Thus, the scarce presence of this complex in the region is characterised by the exclusive appearance of the S-shaped beaker (and not any bowls), the absence of dotted types, the dissociation of the different components of the "complex", the peculiar form of specific objects such as the tanged daggers... This presence, in comparison with the neighbouring regions of the North Meseta and the Ebro Valley, can be defined as exiguous, sporadic and marginal, and it can be argued that Cantabrian Spain can be considered as the

Fig. 5.5. Characteristic interior landscape of Cantabrian Spain (Carmona in Cabuérniga, Cantabria). (Photo: L.C. Teira)

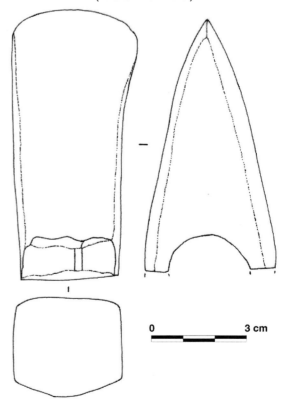

0   3 cm

Fig. 5.6. Polished stone axe with central perforation from the dolmen of Balenkaleku N (Guipúzcoa).

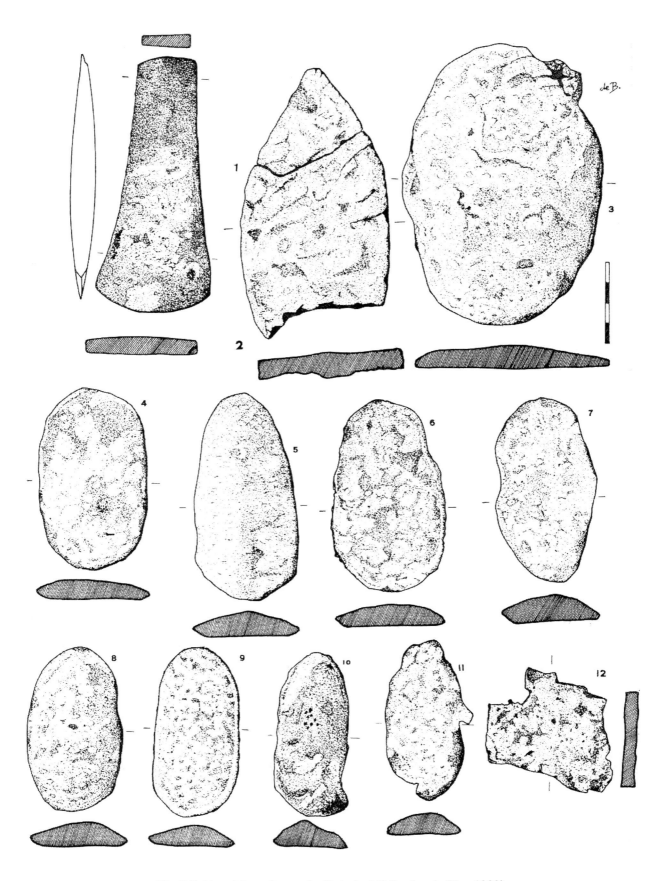

Fig. 5.7. Hoard from Gamonéu (Asturias) (following de Blas 1983).

"periphery" of a centre, at the end of the period being studied.

As regards productive specialisation, the existing evidence is limited to the metallurgical complex and, in consequence, the areas that have resources of copper that could be exploited with the available technology (centre and east of Asturias, eastern Basque Country). In the case of Asturias, by the end of the period studied, we can see the introduction of local mining and metallurgical activity on a certain scale, including all the phases in the process of production, exchange and amortisation of goods made in metal. Copper extraction from systems of pits and galleries, its reduction near the mine, the moulding of considerably standardised intermediate and finished products, as well as the storage in deposits, have been documented (Blas Cortina 1980; 1987; 1989; 1996; 1998) (Fig. 5.7).

In the superstructural instance, the high degree of variability in the mortuary rituals is very significant. This is observed in the funerary container, the number of people inhumed in each deposit, and the associated grave goods. The funerary variability documented between the late Neolithic and early Bronze Age in Cantabrian Spain can be systematised in a series of "burial classes" whose maintenance - as pointed out above – largely depends on chronological factors.

- Multiple inhumations with no apparent differentiating elements
- Individualised inhumation in multiple burial without grave goods
- Individualised inhumation in multiple burial with associated goods
- Individual sepulchre with no material accompaniment
- Individual sepulchre with grave goods

The list above follows a chronological order that indicates the general course of the evolution of funerary trends observed in the period of study, although several of them were functioning simultaneously and during a prolonged time. This variability in funerary practise should certainly be considered as an irrefutable sign of "social complexity", although it is necessary to point out that such variety has not been documented, strictly coetaneously, in a single necropolis.

As well as funerary practices, iconography is an important source of information for an approach such as the one being followed. There is a series of very characteristic depictions in Cantabrian Spain, making up a highly significant iconographic group in relation with the problem discussed here. It consists of armed idols that can be situated in a stage that conventional periodisation denominates Late Chalcolithic/Early Bronze Age. Two different groups can be differentiated, both of them without doubt transmitters of inter and intra group ideology (Fig. 5.8). The first of these, and the best known, is the

group of figures of the "Peña Tú" type, composed mainly of figures in the eponymous rock-shelter (Puertas de Vidiago, Asturias) (Bueno & Fernández-Miranda 1981), the orthostats at Sejos (Mancomunidad de Campoo-Cabuérniga, Cantabria) (Bueno 1982; Bueno et al. 1985; Teira & Ontañón 2000a), the rock at Hoyo de la Gándara (Garabandal, Cantabria) (Saro & Teira 1992), the stela at Tabuyo del Monte (León) (Almagro Basch 1972) and the recent find of the petrogliph at Outeiro do Corno (La Coruña) (Fábregas et al. 2004) (Fig. 5.9).

Fig. 5.8. Synthetic images of the "idoliforms" at Collado de Sejos (Cantabria) (following Teira and Ontañón 2000a).

If we exclude the possibility of a mere symbolic redundancy in the formation of this iconographic group, the vast space of ideographic identification that it defines proves the existence, if not of a total socio-cultural identity, at least of a certain conceptual community extended over a large area of northern Iberia. It appears reasonable, therefore, to propose the existence of a certain "universality" of meaning in the framework of a wide cultural community. A symbolic collectivity which goes well beyond the units of local population and which must imply the participation of a large number of primary cells of social organisation in a common and supracommunitarian situation of cultural and, certainly, social ascription. If proven, this hypothesis would make a good example of the definition of a geographical and social space in the late Prehistory of Cantabrian Spain, resulting from the culmination of a process of humanisation of the landscape - the conversion of space into territory. This process had its first clear manifestation in Neolithic megalithic structures and culminated with the consolidation of landmarks that indicated a new symbolic universe referring to the expansion of a new social order. Specifying further, this hypothesis could be accepted as an argument in favour of the recognition, at the end of the Chalcolithic,

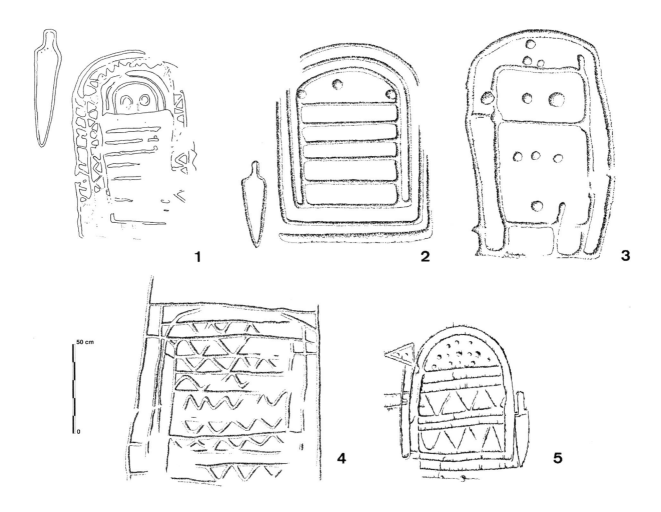

Fig. 5.9. "Idoliform" engravings in the north of the Iberian Peninsula. 1: Peña Tú (Asturias), 2: Sejos II (Cantabria), 3: Sejos I, 4: Hoyo de la Gándara (Cantabria), 5: Tabuyo del Monte (León)(from Saro y Teira 1992, following Bueno and Fernández-Miranda 1981 (1), Bueno, Piñón and Prados 1985 (2,3) and Almagro Basch 1972 (5).

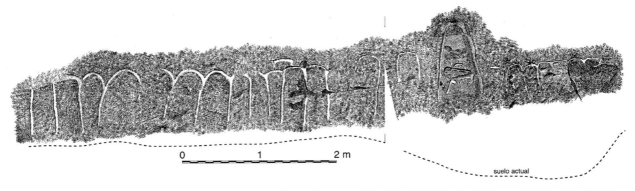

Fig. 5.10. Development of the engraved frieze at Peña Lostroso (Cantabria) (following Teira and Ontañón 1997).

of a level of cultural and social aggregation and organisation clearly more complex than that of the simple domestic community (Fig. 5.10).

The other group presents a much more restricted spatial distribution, as it is limited to the discoveries in the area of Monte Hijedo (Cantabria-Burgos) (Teira & Ontañón 1996; 1997; 2000b). It consists of three panels of deeply engraved rock art, whose central motif (the only one in two cases) is a very schematic anthropomorphic figure in the form of an arch. In the case of El Redular (Ruanales, Cantabria) the central part of this design contains a figure which at first is difficult to interpret, but which the discovery at Peña Lostroso (Las Rozas de Valdearroyo,

Cantabria) has finally clarified. Here, a large panel of rock art has a composition of idol-like motifs similar to the ones mentioned above, forming a long frieze in the centre of which, separated from the previous ones, appears a larger idol armed with a magnificent dagger. We have, therefore, a complex group formed by a row of unarmed anthropomorphs of identical height which flank another that displays the same form but a much larger size and which holds an attribute that clearly distinguishes it from the rest. This is, without doubt, a primitive example of hierarchical perspective, a representational convention further developed in later moments of the history of art, which consists of making the most important element larger in size. This, together with the personalisation of adding the weapon as a complement to a single anthropomorph, is no doubt an unmistakable depiction of social differentiation.

5.6.- Proposal of historical interpretation

Having described in the previous sections the main socio-economic changes inferred from the archaeological record in Cantabrian Spain for the 4th and 3rd millennia cal BC, and having defined general features of the social and economic formation that resulted from this process, we shall now outline an interpretative proposal that aims to explain, with a minimum of coherence and correspondence with the empirical data and our methodological assumptions, the historical development observed in the region during this period. This development is organised in two stages: the first "of formation" - or "epigenetic", following Friedman and Rowlands's terminology (1977) - and the second "of culmination or affirmation".

The "epigenetic" phase, which can be assimilated to the Late Neolithic in conventional periodisation, includes a progressive subordination of the economic base to productive forms, with the consequence of a sharp increase in the phenomena of spatial and temporal restriction inherent in the development of the agricultural cycle. This involves a profound modification in the relationship between communities and their environment, as well as among themselves, which is expressed in a greater attachment to the land and a strong rise in their mutual interdependence. As another consequence, this phase witnesses a considerable increase in the productivity of the economic system, which, to judge from the evidence of occupation of the territory, would be coupled to an increase in population size (without determining a causal priority between both phenomena). The demographic pressure would, in turn, have been the origin of certain social tension that could have been solved through mechanisms of segmentation or social fission, in a feedback process of population rise. This implies, therefore, a dynamic process of economic and demographic growth that is made feasible by its own scope for expansion, and would not necessarily involve a profound social transformation. The clearest superstructural evidence for this process would be the long duration of the use of mega-

lithic and hypogeum deposits for collective burials, which could be considered as expressions of the relative stability of the model.

The culmination phase for this process, which would be reached in the Chalcolithic, implies at the same time that the system enters a critical situation, derived from the impossibility of continuing the expansion of the socio-economic model. In other words, the basic reproduction mechanisms of the system would become inelastic. Any attempt at overcoming this situation would include intensifying production in the areas with the greatest potential for increased production: agriculture and stock-rearing. A total polarisation of the economic base would then be reached, in what can be called a true "peasant society", *i.e.* a population made up basically of primary producers, directly and permanently tied to the means of agricultural production (Vicent 1990). An essential corollary of this socio-economic model is the development of the possibilities for the accumulation of surpluses as an origin for inequality. This capacity, at first as reserves or provisions and directed towards the reproduction of the workforce (vital for the continuity of the agricultural cycle), would now be propitiatory for the appearance and maintenance, even if only part time, of specialists who do not work directly in subsistence tasks (mining and metallurgy). For the first time, the level of development of the productive forces would be sufficient to be able to act as a precondition in the formation of social relationships of production that imply true exploitation - that is, the extortion of overwork from primary producers. To put it another way, only in this phase of the process could the step be made from accumulation to monopolisation, a reflection of well-established social asymmetry. It must be pointed out, however, that this development does not determine by itself the specific form or nature of these relationships; *i.e.* it would form the necessary material basis allowing the existence for this kind of production relationships, but is not exactly their cause. In this sense, we may interpret the main long term economic transformations observed in the Cantabrian region between the start of neolithisation and the final establishment of peasantry as a transition from systems based on mobility and diversity to economies based on storage and exchange. This situation is often thought to be associated with - and strengthened by - a growing aggregation of the population, thus creating conditions that to a lesser or greater degree are favourable to an increase in conflicts, to the intensification of regional interaction, and to social stratification (O'Shea & Halstead 1989).

In this situation, several factors could concur in the development of "unequal growth" and intra and inter group conflicts:

- Potential control over primary resources or of subsistence: the land, the essential means for its cultivation (such as seeds), its products (mainly cereals) and the animals,

- Control over the metallurgical industry and its products,
- Inter group separation resulting from the permanent occupation or territorialisation of an area,
- An apparent climatic deterioration, with a constant tendency and critical in its evolution (Fábregas *et al.* 2003),
- The occasional incidence of natural setbacks or catastrophes (storms, draughts, plagues, epidemics, etc.).

This dialectical interaction between different aspects of the productive forces (environmental stress, evolution in the means of production) and production relationships (attempts at control over the new means of production), would lead to a process of economic and social differentiation that would end in the institutionalisation of true political power structures controlled by one sector of the community.

In the framework of an economic basis characterised by a considerable (although limited) development of the productive forces, highly specialised in terms of subsistence and progressively in other aspects of production, and which included a considerable new impulse to the circulation of goods and ideas, it can be proposed that important changes in the relationships of social production and reproduction were set in motion. These tended to concentrate economic, and then political, power in some family groups (at the expense of other members of the same community and, equally, in relation with other neighbouring groups) through the development of mechanisms of differential accumulation and control over the resources of production and social reproduction. This process would derive in the appearance of growing interfamily inequalities, a phenomenon that would finally lead to a radical social transformation. In this context, and following Meillassoux (1985), the reproduction of the whole society (the redistribution of subsistence and/or of human energy) would be exercised institutionally for the benefit of a specific sector at the expense of another, or, in other words, would be controlled by a fraction of the society and directed for its benefit. A permanent disassociation between the productive and the reproductive cycles would be reached, creating a social system based on organised relationships of the exploitation of some people by others. This process of social differentiation would begin with the adaptation of the preceding forms of power to the new types of domination, expressed in grades of ranks or statuses, in which the highest positions would be held by adult males, and would end in the institution of true political power structures.

Significant expressions of this process in the regional archaeological record are the model of long range circulation of goods with a high primary value, their hoarding and immobilisation in tombs and deposits, or the iconography of the new rock art. At a more specific level, some indications can be found about the nature of these new mechanisms of domination, such as the ubiquitous presence of weapons among these objects of "apparatus" and their individual ascription, either to real people (living or dead) or to anthropomorphic effigies, which indicates some form of personalised power qualified through a link with a very specific range of activities, including hunting and war. The eminent role of weapons as the ideological means of legitimising the new forms of power is certainly clear. From this derives the possibility of giving certain importance to coercion - direct or indirect - among the new methods of domination.

5.7.- General conclusions

The discussion formulated above has been aimed at characterising the social and economic structures of the communities that lived in Cantabrian Spain between the 4th and 3rd millennia cal BC. If we understand this as the final stage in a long term process of cultural change, it is in this period and not before when the process of neolithisation culminates in the region, with a polarisation of the economic base towards forms of production, which means that a true "peasant society" is established in the area.

In the socio-economic formation that results from this process, tendencies of change can be noted that lead towards social inequality. It is not suggested that there was a linear transition from egalitarian Neolithic societies to hierarchised societies of the Bronze Age, but profound transformations developed in social relationships which, subsuming the previous principles of sexual subordination and prelation restricted to the family structure, strengthen the mechanisms of power of a fully economic nature and which affect wider segments of the society.

The main reason in the process of historical transition is not the economic change seen in the basis of subsistence, although this is transcendental in other ways. This could also be interpreted, at least in part, as an accelerated progression of productive forces, as perfecting the means of production that, in the very long term, will lead to the final establishment of the traditional rural ways of life in the region; in other words, an "adaptive" development of economic strategies in a search of forms of land use which are more productive, more permanent and, therefore, more predictable and, at the same time, suited to the environment. The truly crucial point in the historical process outlined above is the profound transformation seen in the relationships of production and social reproduction, *i.e.* in the organisation of social relationships that control the economic mechanisms of production and circulation, both at the subsistence level and in the management of "prestigious" goods. Although this transformation is still insufficiently characterised, it can be said that it would lead from an apparently collective or communitarian system - although not exactly egalitarian - to another based on premises of social inequality, in which the surpluses obtained thanks to improvements in the forms of production are capitalised by a certain social sector for their own benefit, following a pattern of differential consumption introduced, obviously, in detriment of collectivity. So, paraphrasing Godelier (1990), the overwork previously destined for the satisfaction of common interests is now directed towards the maintenance of a minority holding control over the means (material, ritual or of other types) of ensuring the collective needs. An elite represented in material and artistic evidence expresses a desire of ideological monopoly with a view to the legitimisation or justification of a new social order based on permanent structures of inequality, although at a very primary stage of development.

5.8.- References

ALDAY RUIZ, A. 1992: "Síntesis sobre la secuencia cultural Neolítico - Edad del Bronce en el País Vasco". *Sancho el Sabio. Revista de cultura e investigación vasca* (2ª época) 2: 19-49.

ALMAGRO BASCH, M. 1972: "Los ídolos y la estela decorada de Hernán Pérez (Cáceres) y el ídolo estela de Tabuyo del Monte (León)". *Trabajos de Prehistoria* 29: 83-124.

APELLÁNIZ, J. M. 1975: "Neolítico y Bronce en la Cornisa Cantábrica". In M.A. García Guinea & M.A. Puente Sañudo (Prep.): *La Prehistoria en la Cornisa Cantábrica*. Institución Cultural de Cantabria - Instituto de Prehistoria y Arqueología "Sautuola". Santander: 199-218.

ARMENDARIZ, A. & ETXEBERRIA, F. 1983: "Las cuevas sepulcrales de la Edad del Bronce en Guipúzcoa". *Munibe* 35 (3-4): 247-354.

BLAS CORTINA, M.A. de 1980. "El depósito de materiales de la Edad del Bronce de Gamonedo (Asturias)". *Zhepyrus* XXX-XXXI: 268-276.

- 1983: *La Prehistoria Reciente en Asturias*. Estudios de Arqueología Asturiana 1. Fundación Pública de Cuevas y Yacimientos Prehistóricos de Asturias. Oviedo.

- 1987: "Los primeros testimonios metalúrgicos en la fachada atlántica septentrional de la Península Ibérica". In *El origen de la metalurgia en la Península Ibérica. II*. Seminario organizado por la Fundación José Ortega y Gasset (Oviedo 1987). Instituto Universitario José Ortega y Gasset-Universidad Complutense de Madrid. Madrid: 66-100.

- 1989: "La minería prehistórica del cobre en las montañas astur-leonesas". In C. Domergue (Coord.): *Minería y metalurgia en las antiguas civilizaciones mediterráneas y europeas* I. Ministerio de Cultura. Madrid: 143-152.

- 1996: "La minería prehistórica y el caso particular de las explotaciones cupríferas de la Sierra del Aramo". *Gallaecia* 14-15: 167-195.

- 1998: "Producción e intercambio de metal: la singularidad de las minas de cobre prehistóricas del Aramo y El Milagro (Asturias)". In G. Delibes de Castro (Coord.): *Minerales y metales en la prehistoria reciente: algunos testimonios de su explotación y laboreo en la Península Ibérica*. Studia archaeologica 88. Universidad de Valladolid - Fundación Duques de Soria. Valladolid: 71-103.

BLAS CORTINA, M.A. de & FERNÁNDEZ-TRESGUERRES, J. 1989: *Historia primitiva en Asturias. De los cazadores-recolectores a los primeros metalúrgicos*. Biblioteca Histórica Asturiana 11. Silverio Cañada Editor. Gijón.

BUENO RAMÍREZ, P. 1982: "La estela antropomorfa del Collado de Sejos (Valle de Polaciones, Santander)". *Trabajos de Prehistoria* 39: 343-348.

BUENO RAMÍREZ, P. & FERNÁNDEZ-MIRANDA, M. 1981: "El Peñatu de Vidiago (Llanes, Asturias)". *Altamira Symposium*. Dirección Gral. de Bellas Artes, Archivos y Bibliotecas. Ministerio de Cultura. Madrid: 451-467.

BUENO RAMÍREZ, P., PIÑÓN VARELA, F., & PRADOS TORREIRA, L. 1985: "Excavaciones en el collado de Sejos (Valle de Polaciones, Santander). Campaña de 1982". *Noticiario Arqueológico Hispánico* 22: 27-53.

CARO BAROJA, J. 1977: *Los pueblos del Norte* (3ª edición). Editorial Txertoa. San Sebastián.

CASTAÑOS UGARTE, P.M. 1983: "Estudio de los macromamíferos de la cueva de Atxeta (Guernica, Vizcaya)". *Kobie* 13: 251-259.

- 1984. "Estudio de los macromamíferos de la cueva de Santimamiñe". *Kobie* 14: 235-318.

- 1995. "Estudio de la fauna de mamíferos del yacimiento de Pico Ramos (Muskiz, Bizkaia)". *Munibe (Antropología-Arqueología)* 47: 177-182.

CHAPMAN, R. 1991: *La formación de las sociedades complejas. El sureste de la península ibérica en el marco del Mediterráneo occidental*. Editorial Crítica. Barcelona.

CHAPMAN, R., KINNES, I. & RANDSBORG, K. (eds.) 1981: *The Archaeology of Death*. Cambridge University Press. Cambridge.

EARLE, T.K. 1991: "The evolution of chiefdoms". In T.K. Earle (ed.): *Chiefdoms: power, economy, and ideology*. School of American Research Advanced Seminar Series. Cambridge University Press. Cambridge: 1-15.

FÁBREGAS VALCARCE, R., MARTÍNEZ CORTIZAS, A., BLANCO CHAO, R. & CHESWORTH, W. 2003: "Environmental change and social dynamics in the second–third millennium BC in NW Iberia". *Journal of Archaeological Science* 30: 859–871.

FÁBREGAS VALCARCE, R., GUITIÁN CASTROMIL, J., GUITIÁN RIVERA, J. & PEÑA SANTOS, A. de la 2004: "Petroglifo galaico con una representación de tipo Peña Tú". *Zephyrus* LVII: 183-193.

FERNÁNDEZ BUEY, F. 1991: *La ilusión del método. Ideas para un racionalismo bien temperado*. Editorial Crítica.Barcelona.

FRIEDMAN, J. & ROWLANDS, M.J. 1977: "Notes towards an epigenetic model of the evolution of "civilisation". In J. Friedman & M.J. Rowlands (eds.): *The Evolution of Social Systems*. Duckworth. London: 201-276.

GILMAN, A. 1976: "Bronze Age Dynamics in Southeast Spain". *Dialectical Anthropology* 1 (4): 307-319.

- 1991: "Trajectories towards social complexity in the later prehistory of the Mediterranean". In T.K. Earle (ed.): *Chiefdoms: power, economy, and ideology*. Cambridge University Press (School of American Research Advanced Seminar Series). Cambridge: 146-168.

GODELIER, M. 1990: *Lo ideal y lo material. Pensamiento, economías, sociedades*. Taurus. Madrid.

GONZÁLEZ SAINZ, C. & GONZÁLEZ MORALES, M.R. 1986: *La Prehistoria en Cantabria. Historia de Cantabria* I. Ediciones Tantín. Santander.

LISÓN TOLOSANA, C. (comp.) 1991: *Antropología de los Pueblos del Norte de España*. Universidad Complutense de Madrid - Universidad de Cantabria. Madrid.

MARIEZKURRENA, K. 1990: "Caza y domesticación durante el Neolítico y Edad de los Metales en el País Vasco". *Munibe (Antropología-Arqueología)* 42: 241-252.

MEILLASSOUX, C. 1985. *Mujeres, graneros y capitales. Economía doméstica y capitalismo*. Siglo Veintiuno Editores. México.

MUJIKA, J.A. & ARMENDARIZ, A. 1991: "Excavaciones en la estación megalítica de Murumendi (Beasain, Gipuzkoa)". *Munibe (Antropología-Arqueología)* 43: 105-165.

ONTAÑÓN PEREDO, R. 2001: *El Calcolítico en la Cornisa Cantábrica*. Edición en microforma. Servicio de Publicaciones de la Universidad de Cantabria. Santander.

- 2003a: *Caminos hacia la complejidad. El Calcolítico en la región cantábrica*. Servicio de Publicaciones de la Universidad de Cantabria – Fundación Marcelino Botín. Santander.

- 2003b: "El campaniforme en la región cantábrica: Un fenómeno arqueológico en el seno de las sociedades calcolíticas del norte de la Península Ibérica". *Trabajos de Prehistoria* 60 (1): 81-98.

ORTIZ TUDANCA, L. 1990: "Ordenación de la Secuencia Cultural del Calcolítico y la Edad del Bronce en el País Vasco". *Munibe (Antropología-Arqueología)* 42: 135-139.

O'SHEA, J. & HALSTEAD, P. 1989: "Conclusions: bad year economics". In P. Halstead & J. O'Shea (eds.): *Bad year economics: cultural responses to risk and uncertainity*. New Directions in Archaeology. Cambridge University Press. Cambridge: 123-126.

RENFREW, C. 1972: *The Emergence of Civilisation. The Cyclades and the Aegean in the Third Millenium B.C.* Methuen & Co Ltd. London.

- 1986: "Varna and the emergence of wealth in prehistoric Europe". In A. Appadurai (ed.): *The social life of things. Commodities in cultural perspective*. Cambridge University Press. Cambridge: 141-168.

RINCÓN VILA, R. 1985: "Las culturas del metal". In M.A. García Guinea (dir.): *Historia de Cantabria. Prehistoria. Eda-des Antigua y Media*. Ediciones de la librería Estvdio. Santander: 113-209.

SARO, J.A. & TEIRA, L.C. 1992. "El ídolo del Hoyo de la Gándara (Rionansa) y la cronología de los ídolos antropomorfos en la Cornisa Cantábrica". *Trabajos de Prehistoria* 49: 347-355.

TEIRA MAYOLINI, L.C. 1994: *El megalitismo en Cantabria. Aproximación a una realidad arqueológica olvidada*. Servicio de Publicaciones de la Universidad de Cantabria. Santander.

TEIRA MAYOLINI, L.C. & ONTAÑÓN PEREDO, R. 1996: "New Schematic Rock Art Finds in the Monte Hijedo Region (Cantabria-Burgos, Spain)". *International Newsletter on Rock Art* 15: 19-21.

- 1997: "Nuevas manifestaciones de arte esquemático en la comarca de Monte Hijedo (Burgos-Cantabria)". In R. de Balbín Berhmann & P. Bueno Ramírez (eds.): *II Congreso de Arqueología Peninsular. Tomo II Neolítico, Calcolítico y Bronce*. Fundación Rei Afonso Henriques. Zamora: 569-578.

- 2000a: "Revisión de los grabados rupestres del Collado de Sejos (Polaciones)". In R. Ontañón Peredo (coord.): *Actuaciones arqueológicas en Cantabria. 1984-1999*. Consejería de Cultura y Deporte del Gobierno de Cantabria. Santander: 285-287.

- 2000b: "Documentación de arte esquemático en la comarca de Monte Hijedo (Las Rozas de Valdearroyo, Cantabria – Alfoz de Santa Gadea, Burgos)". In R. Ontañón Peredo (coord.): *Actuaciones arqueológicas en Cantabria. 1984-1999*. Consejería de Cultura y Deporte del Gobierno de Cantabria. Santander: 241-243.

THOMAS, J. 1991: *Rethinking the Neolithic*. New Studies in Archaeology. Cambridge University Press. Cambridge.

VICENT GARCÍA, J.M. 1982: "Las tendencias metodológicas en Prehistoria". *Trabajos de Prehistoria* 39: 9-54.

- 1990: "El neolític: transformacions socials y econòmiques". In J. Anfruns & E. Llobet (eds.): *El canvi cultural a la prehistòria*. Columna. Barcelona: 241-293.

WASON, P.K. 1994: *The archaeology of rank*. Cambridge University Press. Cambridge.

ZAPATA, L. 1996: "Modos de subsistencia en el Cantábrico oriental durante el cuarto milenio B.C.". Actes del I Congrés del Neolític a la Península Ibèrica (Gavà-Bellaterra 1995). *Rubricatum* 1(1): 101-108.

- 1997: "El combustible y la agricultura prehistórica: estudio arqueobotánico de los yacimientos de Arenaza, Kanpanoste Goikoa y Kobaederra". *Isturitz, Cuadernos de Sección. Prehistoria - Arqueología* 7: 12-41.

CHAPTER 6

An appraisal of social inequalities in Central Iberia (*c.* 5300-1600 CAL BC)

Pedro Díaz-del-Río
Consejo Superior de Investigaciones Científicas

Abstract

The present paper is an overview of the available evidence for socioeconomic and political inequalities in Central Iberia, from the Neolithic to the Early Bronze Age. It focuses on mortuary practices, labour investments, craft production and settlement organization, disentangling the keys of prehistoric political economy. Following the evidence, I argue that the existence of permanent social inequalities would have been limited by three factors: a limited amount of surplus, the failure of small scale groups to increase the amount of labour force, and most important of all, the absolute absence of means of accumulation of value.

Keywords: Central Iberia; Neolithic; Copper Age; Early Bronze Age; Mortuary Practices; Labor Force; Surplus; Reproduction.

Resumen

El presente trabajo es una revisión de las evidencias actuales de desigualdad socioeconómica y política en el centro de la Península Ibérica, del Neolítico a los inicios de la Edad del Bronce. Evalua las evidencias de prácticas funerarias, inversión de trabajo, artesania y organización de los asentamientos, desenredando las claves de la economía política prehistórica. Atendiendo a la evidencia, argumento que la existencia de desigualdades sociales permanentes se encontraría limitada por tres factores: una limitada cantidad de excedente, la incapacidad para incrementar la cantidad de fuerza de trabajo por parte de grupos de pequeño tamaño y, sobre todo, la ausencia absoluta de medios de acumulación de valor.

Palabras Clave: Meseta Peninsular; Neolítico; Edad del Cobre; Bronce Antiguo; Prácticas funerarias; Fuerza de trabajo; Excedentes; Reproducción.

6.1.- Introduction

The aim of this paper is to present a comprehensive state-of-the-art survey of the economic and political nature of social relations in central Iberia during the III and II millennia BC. It highlights both the actual empirical limits to our inquiries, and what we understand as promising future research lines.

Southeastern Iberia has been the main laboratory for debates surrounding prehistoric social inequality since the seventies. The Los Millares and El Argar cultures offered abundant but poorly documented evidence. Processual models shared the optimistic view that the archaeological record contained information on social inequalities sufficient to orient field research programs that would assess their nature (e.g., Gilman & Thornes 1985; Chapman et al 1987). As Chapman (2003: 109-112) points out, fieldwork was not always oriented towards hypothesis testing, and the subsequent qualitative and quantitative increase of chronological, economic and environmental data has not resulted in a consensus over the interpretation (Chapman 2003; Gilman 2001). The political conditions of southeastern Chalcolithic and Bronze Age societies are currently under debate, but

scholars can now base their interpretations on evidence that is of reasonable quality.

This has not been the case for Central Iberia. The archaeological record did not offer enough clear evidence of social inequalities to attract processually-oriented scholars (with some remarkable exceptions such as R. Harrison 1977; 1985; 1993; 1994; 1995). Consequently, the construction of culture-historical frameworks remained the main object of archaeological inquiry. Spanish scholars have only recently undertaken the challenge of processual frameworks (Díaz-del-Río 2001; Garrido 2000; Muñoz 2000), and their search for social inequalities has afforded few and ambiguous results.

Throughout this paper I will argue that the existence of permanent social inequalities would have been limited by three key features: a limited amount of surplus, the failure of small scale groups to increase the size of the labour force, and most important of all, the absolute absence of means of accumulating wealth. In order to do so, I will present the archaeological evidence following the standard chronological order, from the Neolithic to the Early Bronze Age, the period known throughout Europe to have the first evidences for permanent social inequalities.

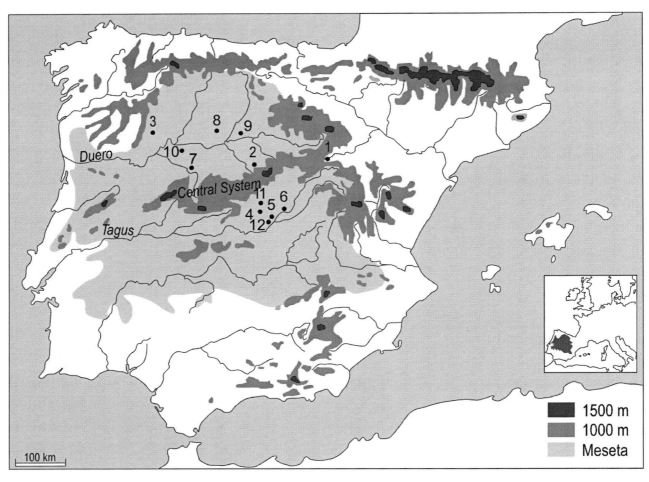

Fig. 6.1.- Iberian Meseta. Sites mentioned in text. 1. Valle de Ambrona; 2. La Vaquera; 3. El Pedroso; 4. Fuente de la Mora; 5. Gózquez; 6. Las Matillas; 7. Las Canteras; 8. Valle del Esgueva; 9. San Miguel; 10. Las Pozas; 11. El Ventorro; 12. Casa Montero

6.2.- Central Iberia

The Spanish Meseta is the largest geographical unit of Iberian Peninsula (Fig. 6.1). Located at the centre of Iberia, it is a 600 m high 181.000 Km² Tertiary plateau, partially surrounded by mountain chains, and divided in two by the mountains of the Central System, running northeast-southwest. With two of the Iberian Peninsula's main rivers, the Tagus and the Duero, crossing them, the vast plains on either side of the mountains have rich soils with frequent permanent pastures. Highlands are predominantly devoted to pasture and are rich in various raw materials used by prehistoric communities, particularly granite, amphibolite and copper. The interfluvial plateaus and the region of La Mancha to the southeast have dry-farmed lands of low agricultural potential, now put to extensive cereal crops, vines and olives. Both the north and south Mesetas have a continental climate, with dry and hot summers and cold and rainy winters, with a clear difference between the 1170 mm mean rainfall in peripheral highland areas and the 500 mm of the lowland river basins. This paper will focus on the northern Meseta and the central Tagus valley.

6.3.- Neolithic background

Traces of early Neolithic groups (5300-4700 cal BC) went almost unnoticed until the 1990s and are still scarce when compared to later phases of prehistory. Sites are frequently located in river valleys or bluffs, but also in caves. Settlements are defined by the presence of relatively small concentrations of underground features, some including primary burials. As in most western Europe, houses are circular when found. They all share the presence of impressed ware, curated lithic technologies, and occasional bone artefacts. The few published faunal analyses, such as those from the cave of La Vaquera, suggest that the role of domesticates was important only more than half a millennium after the initial presence of pottery in the sequence (Morales & Martín 2003; Morales 2003). This is also the case for cereal pollen, present only by the end of phase II (4600-3600 cal BC), and the minimal amount of cereal remains during the earliest occupation of the cave, especially when compared to subsequent phases (López et al 2003). Free-threshing wheat predominates throughout the sequence at Vaquera, while in the Ambrona valley, the rather poor samples available

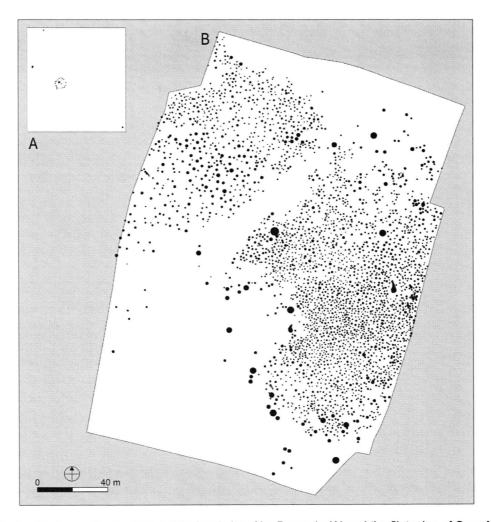

Fig. 6.2.- Contrast between the Neolithic habitational site of La Deseada (A) and the flint mine of Casa Montero (B) (following Díaz-del-Río & Consuegra 1999; Consuegra per. com.).

(Stika 1999) support the dominant role of hulled wheat, both einkorn and emmer (Peña-Chocarro in press).

Early Neolithic communities seem to have been very small, with probable short-term year-round settlement patterns, and variable dependence on domestics. Under these conditions, groups would have required permanent cooperative relations in order to maintain their basic reproduction, favoring the rapid spread of the 'Neolithic package'. Although this package was present in the Meseta by at least 5300 cal BC, the role of domestics varied through time and, most of all, regionally. This variability should be explained before accepting current hypothesis on the rapid colonization of central Iberia by peripheral Neolithic incomers (Kunst & Rojo 1999).

The almost 'invisible' settlement evidence contrasts with some recent discoveries, as the flint mine of Casa Montero (Consuegra et al 2004) (Fig. 6.2). Open-area excavations have documented over 4000 vertical shafts, measuring one meter mean wide and depths up to 7 meters. Located by a river bluff, where few and scattered Neolithic finds are known, it seems to be the result of reiterative short-term seasonal expeditions. Not one shaft cuts previous extracting pits, suggesting that the time-span of all mining activity may have been quite short, maybe less than a few centuries. Flint of variable quality was mined and knapped in order to obtain blades and occasionally flakes, products that would be finally transported off-site. All the remaining waste was dumped back into the shafts. This evidence opens promising lines of research. On the one hand, flint-tool production and use is probably the only complete craftwork we can track from procurement to final discard, something almost impossible to assess for other aspects of Neolithic economy. On the other, the study of extraction methods may shed some light on the manner and scale in which labour was mobilized. Considering the size of Neolithic groups, and the resulting population densities, one would again expect cooperative social mechanisms that would both mobilize work-groups and distribute the resulting products. As a matter of fact, any group wanting to exercise a monopoly over flint in the Madrid region would have had to confront the problem of an environment extremely rich in that resource.

The contrast between the scale of settlements, and the cumulative and finally monumental landscape created at the flint mine, can be also tracked when comparing settlements and funerary patterns. Although regionally variable, mounds and megaliths became part of funerary programs some centuries after the earliest Neolithic. Recent reviews (Delibes & Rojo 1997) suggest that monument construction went through at least two subsequent phases. During the last quarter of the fifth millennium cal BC megalithic and non-megalithic mounds were all constructed in such a way that access to the chamber was necessarily performed from the top. Passage graves increased in size and presence throughout the fourth millennium, and by its end, the biggest dolmens were erected. A similar trend has been suggested for Northwestern galician megaliths (Alonso & Bello 1997). These changes in monument design suggest that the increase in the amount of labour invested (and probably group size involved) ran parallel to the transformation in the way funerary rituals were performed. While smaller groups designed platforms that would have inevitably required staged acts, subsequent builders, probably incorporating more than one group, eventually limited ritual action to those who acceded into the funerary camera through the corridor. The increase in the scale of cooperative labour may have involved the renegotiation of social roles within and between groups.

Nevertheless, it is difficult to assess whether these changes were materialized in a differential treatment of the deceased. Although detailed burial disposal, paleoanthropological, and dietary analysis are scarce, recent research has revealed an aspect previously unknown that may shed some light on the political role of funerary programs: the increasing evidence for burning and ritual capping of charnel houses (Delibes & Etexberria 2002: 50). One such case is La Peña de la Abuela (Rojo et al 2002), a limestone charnel house constructed over a 10 cm platform built with soil that incorporated scattered pottery and lithic remains. These remains suggest some pre-constructive (domestic?) activity, although not necessarily in the immediate area. The interior had defined spaces, with some individualized burials associated with abundant offerings, and a remaining space containing fewer offerings and a mixture of human bones. Anthropological analysis has determined the existence of at least 11 individuals, including 2 children, and possibly equal numbers of adult men and women (Lohrke et al 2002). This pattern has been interpreted as a result of a social segregation of space, where the richest primary burials represent a "noble area" (Rojo et al 2002). An alternative view would suggest that the observed pattern is a characteristic archaeological result of a charnel house mortuary process. The recovered evidence would represent just "a phase in a program of mortuary treatment that included exhumation" (Brown 1995: 16). This of course would limit our expectations with respect to social differentiation (or inequalities) through the direct observation of this kind of burial practices. The physical disposal of the deceased would then be a consequence of the specific

moment when the final ritual act was performed. This involved the intense burning, boiling of quicklime through watering, and final capping of the charnel house remains, a mixture of water and fire not uncommon in western European Neolithic (Bradley 2005). Interestingly enough, in other charnel houses as La Sima (Rojo et al 2003), remains were subsequently monumentalized through a megalithic passage grave.

The overall picture suggests that funerary analysis has oversimplified its potential when evaluating social and political relations. Collective funerary rituals may offer one of the keys to understand Neolithic political economy. All in all, funerary patterns suggest the birth of emerging lineages that lacked the required *massing effect* (Sahlins 1961) to overcome social limitations for the establishment of regional polities. Cyclical involvement in labour investments and ritual performance, mainly but not only in funerary monuments, was one of the mechanisms by which small Neolithic communities assured their reproduction. It may have also been the channel through which tenure and a sense of community beyond individual groups was maintained.

Throughout the subsequent Copper Age communities grew in size, and increased their sedentariness. As in the rest of Iberia, labour investments mainly were transferred to the domestic sphere.

6.4.- The Copper Age (3050-2200 cal BC)

Chalcolithic sites (3050-2200 cal BC) have been defined by random distributions of pit structures. Clusters of hearths, underground storage or other functional domestic facilities are found horizontally distributed in areas up to two or three hectares. Until recent years, scarce evidence of circular wattle and daub dwellings, the absence of deep stratified deposits, and the broad distribution of sites were basic constituted the evidence upon which archaeologists argued for the pastoral semi-nomadic character of Copper Age groups.

Systematic extensive survey programs, like those already completed in the 7995 km^2 Madrid region, have documented a dense distribution of third millennium BC sites. Although settlement locations are varied (river flood plains, gullies, plateau bluff edges, knolls or hills), sites cluster throughout river basins, the areas with the richest soils and permanent pasture lands. Up to date, no scholar has argued for the existence of a settlement hierarchy, although the evidence suggests an increase in population densities when compared to previous phases.

Research on third millennium BC settlements has challenged commonly subscribed views about the homogeneous structure of all sites. Air photographs have documented the existence of up to 13 ditched enclosures in the northern Meseta (Ariño & Rodríguez 1997; Delibes 2001), all of them occupying fertile soils, while open area excavations in Madrid region have recovered evidence of three ditched enclosures ranging from 50 to 100 m in diameter (Fig. 6.3). Although they are all located in different settings such as river beds, hills and gullies, the evidence seems to suggest permanent habitation (Díaz-del-Río 2004a). All three had their ditches filled before any presence of Bell Beaker artefacts. At any rate, these villages were not abandoned by the second half of third millennium. On the contrary, two of them had scattered presence of Bell Beaker ceramic fragments and the three of them had Middle BA evidence on top or in the immediate surroundings. In addition to ditch enclosures, a very few cases of stone walled enclosured settlements are known, some of them peripheral to the Meseta (e.g., the village and rock art 'sanctuary' of El Pedroso [Delibes et al. 1995, Bradley 2005: 111]).

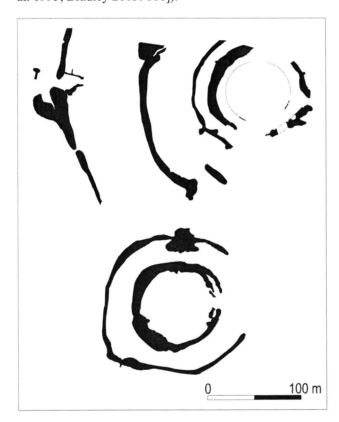

0   100 m

Fig. 6.3.- Copper Age ditched enclosures from Madrid region (following Díaz-del-Río 2004).

This new evidence is more complex than any scholar would have expected a few years ago. But one may notice that most of these habitational sites are just as small or even smaller in dimensions and labour investment than similar Neolithic and contemporary Chalcolithic sites in the rest of Europe. Although labour force and earthworks may be important components in the construction of monumental landscapes, as well as material expressions of the appropriation of land and surrounding resources, their relation to the existence of social inequalities does not seem to be straightforward. Central Iberian sites, and in fact most of fortified or enclosured settlements of Iberian Chalcolithic, can be reasonably explained through

the mobilization of immediate kin-groups. In any case, the extremely limited scale of labour investments in central Iberian sites stands out when compared to other regional developments, such as those documented in Andalusia (Díaz-del-Río 2004b). If the growth of labour force is a straightforward way to increase production, one would suggest that central Iberia Copper Age groups lacked the required surplus to sustain long-term sociopolitical inequalities.

Following the lead of other European scholars, some Portuguese and Spanish archaeologists have suggested a ritual role for Chalcolithic enclosures (Jorge 1998; 2002; Delibes 2001). Others have retained a more functionally-oriented interpretation (Monks 1997; Díaz-del-Río 2004a). Of course, that a reasonable functional interpretation can be argued for most prehistoric fortifications (Arkush & Stanish 2005), does not deny the role of ritual in or, better said, the possible *ritualization* of domestic life (Bradley 2005).

What seems clear when compared to the previous Neolithic is the *domesticity* of Chalcolithic evidence. Wattle and daub circular dwellings seem to be the most common type of buildings, some having stone foundations (Lopez Plaza 1991; Diaz-del-Rio 2001). Dwellings, with a diameter averaging about 5 m, generally including underground storage facilities, hearth, flint-knapping activities, and grinding stone tools, suggest a social organization of labour based on nuclear families. Most artefacts function to meet domestic needs, and were made, used and discarded in domestic spaces. Large amounts of pottery fragments are usually found when digging settlements. They mostly respond to simple spherical or semispherical non-decorated bowls, with extremely small percentages of carinated bowls, simple chevron-incised rim decorations and an absolute absence of big storage jars. Although lithic analyses have been frequently focused on fine flint tools, the most common and distinctive elements are non-retouched flakes, generally summing more than 95 percent of stone artefacts. This expedient technology seems to be a result of the basic need of cutting edges in domestic activities, and a predominant non-specialized or standardized industry. Flint resources are accessible in Tertiary formations, and frequently scattered along river valleys: they are generally available within the immediate vicinity of settlements or through down-the-line exchange mechanisms.

Evidence of small-scale and minimally specialized copper production is found in residential sites. Although other objects have been occasionally found, generally in early, uncontrolled archaeological excavations, awls are the most frequently recovered object. No more than a hundred metal artefacts are known scattered throughout Northern Meseta (Delibes et al 1999), most of them without any spatial relation to the primary source locations, situated in surrounding mountains, where granite and amphibolite are also accessible. All three have different but permanent presence in domestic contexts from Chalcolithic to LBA. Some objects provide clear evidence of a dynamical interregional exchange system, but with "essentially local patterns of procurement and distribution" (Harrison & Orozco 2001: 123).The low-frequency but widespread distribution of variscite beads, used from the fourth to the mid-third millennium BC (Blanco et al 1996; Harrison & Orozco 2001) are found together with granite grinding stones, anphibolite and other ground stones, most of them elements of regular domestic use.

Paleoeconomic evidence is still scarce. Systematic flotation techniques have not been used frequently, but when applied they show the presence of wheat and barley and various weeds related to abandoned or altered agricultural fields (Diaz-del-Rio et al 1997). Faunal analysis demonstrate the absolute predominance of domestic species: sheep/goat, cow, and pigs sum up more than 87 percent mean of total faunal remains. In terms of weight, cows and pigs are especially significant. Sites in northern Meseta, e.g. Las Pozas (3040-2217 cal BC), have strong evidence for evidence of draught cattle as well as butchery patterns related to seasonal consumption of young sheep, probable evidence of feasting activities (Morales 1992; Díaz-del-Río 2001). Most scholars agree on the existence of all components of the *secondary products revolution* (Sherratt 1981; Harrison & Moreno 1985). The up to date only trace elemental composition analysis of Chalcolithic burials shows the importance of vegetable sources and a middle/low ingest of animal proteins (Trancho et al 1996). Overall, palynological regional research programs (López 1997), have shown the existence of an open semi-steppe environment in the surroundings of settlements, usually related to the presence of a socially modified parkland landscape (*dehesa*) (Stevenson & Harrison 1992).

No regular funerary pattern has been determined (Fabian 1995). Chalcolithic funerary practices involved the reuse of megaliths, construction of small barrows, and use of caves for collective burials. They are mostly secondary burials that include small groups of individuals, frequently representing all genders and ages. Grave deposits, when documented and individually ascribed, are qualitative and quantitatively scarce, generally variscite beads, flint tools and occasional small non-decorated vessels. Single pit graves with primary and secondary burials are only occasionally found in habitational sites, although scattered human bones are not infrequent in settlements. All this suggests the existence of funerary programs that involve primary burials or exposure of dead bodies in the surroundings of settlements, and their final deposition as secondary burials in collective shrines. Although always studied as separate non-related burial practices, they may all represent stages in the *social life* of dead bodies. These secondary burial practices have been traditionally considered a result of egalitarian social relations, because of the apparent simplicity of the final collective and undifferentiated body disposal. The change from collective to the single burial bell-Beaker funerary program signalled the evolutionary shift from the simple to the complex. But

options for negotiating social and political relations are necessarily multiplied in secondary burial processes (Kuijt 2000), and the shift to primary burial practices need not necessarily be interpreted in terms of increasing complexity.

In sum, regional evaluation of first half of III millennium BC shows ubiquitous domestic evidence related to the first unambiguous village settlements. These are small, and probably based on nuclear families. The main social dynamic seems to relate to the increased permanence and territoriality of groups, something that would have contradicted their need for cooperative social mechanisms to assure their reproduction. This dynamic may well be a generalized phenomenon in most early agricultural societies. Differential consumption patterns inside settlements and asymmetrical exchange mechanisms may have been present, but are by no means obvious. Be that as it may, when compared to previous and latter phases, the Copper Age stands out because of its rich evidence for productive activities and labour organization. The limited concentration of labour force, surplus potential, and absolute lack of wealth finance, are all key to understand the conditions of the political economy in which bell-Beaker artefacts appeared.

6.5.- Beakers

Bell Beakers represent the second generalized pan-European phenomena after megalithism, and has been frequently associated with the rise of chiefdoms or big-man societies. As with megalithism, evidence suggests an important degree of temporal and regional variability, especially when incorporating quantitative regional data. In Central Iberia, known to be the origin of the Ciempozuelos style, Bell Beakers have always been a fuzzy 'phenomenon'. This situation relates to two main features of the traditional pan-European framework: its chronology and its assumed relation to emergent social complexity.

Although Chalcolithic has been traditionally divided into 'pre-Bell Beaker' and 'Bell Beaker' phases, actual radiocarbon dates and contextual studies show the existence of Beaker artefacts both in Chalcolithic (2700-2200 cal BC) and early Bronze Age contexts (2250-1630 cal BC). In fact, some of the richest Beaker burials, e.g.. Fuente Olmedo (2200-1880 cal BC), may be contemporaneous to the latter. As a result, and with a probable time span of 1000 years (2700-1700 cal BC), the traditional ascription of bell-Beaker style to a Chalcolithic 'culture' or 'phase' has not helped to clarify patterns of social change.

Beaker pottery fragments are extremely scarce in habitation sites. They always constitute less than 5% of total pottery fragments. Surprisingly enough, this highly patchy presence of Beaker assemblages has been frequently accepted as the earliest evidence of big-men or chiefdom societies in central Iberia. The argument is

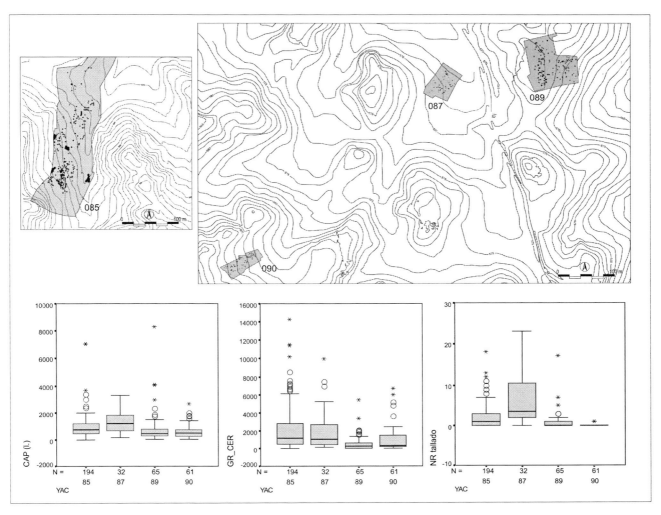

Fig. 6.4.- EBA site distribution at Gózquez (San Martín de la Vega, Madrid) and analysis of variance (storage capacity, pottery sherds and flint remains) (following Díaz-del-Río & Vicent in press).

mainly based on funerary evidence, by emphasizing some exceptionally 'rich' individual burials (Delibes et al 1999: Blasco et al 1998). But this evidence is also extremely patchy.

The fact that such variability has not been taken in account seems evident when revisiting El Ventorro, a site known since the seventies (Harrison et al 1975; Priego & Quero 1992). Contrary to the general low percentage of Bell Beakers in domestic contexts, El Ventorro has the highest accumulation of Chalcolithic 'garbage' per square meter of the whole Meseta (Díaz-del-Río 2001). Pithouse 013 (Priego & Quero 1992), a 44 square meter feature, contained an impressive collection of artefacts: 33595 ceramic fragments, 106 of them bell-Beakers, 2792 flint items, 3283 faunal remains with an important percentage of juvenile-adult pig consumption (Morales & Villegas 1994), 41 bone artefacts, 24 granite grinding stones, 7 ground stone tools, and sporadic human bones. An important amount of copper smelting refuse was also recovered.

The exceptionality of this midden stands out when com-

pared to other contemporary sites. It is the first outstanding evidence for differential accumulation of refuse recovered in a so-called dwelling. The evidence is not unambiguous though. Stratigraphic relations, concentration and disposition of artefacts, lack of structural features, and a windstopper associated to a hearth seems to suggest that the feature may not have been a building, but an open-air structure. I have recently interpreted it as a communal or supracommunal feasting area, maybe related to corporate groups (Díaz-del-Río 2001). The material results of feasting activities are also ambiguous by nature, but if I understand the evidence from this midden correctly, it suggests that by the end of the third millennium BC groups were occasionally consuming surplus collectively. Competitive or not, these kind of collective feasting would display the arena for the negotiation of social roles beyond the individual groups.

Extreme variability is also evident when evaluating funerary patterns. Individuals were buried in previously built megaliths, in small mounds, caves, or individual pit graves. Seventy six funerary sites are known for the Meseta, but only 18 are considered to have a "complete" Beaker set (Garrido 2000: 61). Out of these, the amount of burial goods range from a Beaker and a bowl to the unique Fuente Olmedo single burial, with a complete ceramic set (beaker, bowl and *cazuela*) and 18 metal objects, including a golden diadem. All the evidence suggests a limited capacity to accumulate wealth, although occasionally some outstanding burials did occur.

We may not be able to assess general standardization patterns in Beaker production. Statistical analysis of Beaker variability at local and regional scales may increase our knowledge of how Beaker artefacts were produced and eventually distributed. Artisans did share certain skills, aesthetic templates, and practical knowledge, but their production does not seem to be standardized. Of course, the multiplicity of production events and the extended time span of over which these occur frequently blur standardization signatures (Blackman et al 1993). When compared at a regional scale, coefficients of variation (CV) (Fig. 6.6) for all types of Beaker pottery heights and rim diameters are always higher than 15%. The only exception is the clearly standardized *cazuela* set from the burials at Ciempozuelos itself, which are nevertheless decorated following differentiated patterns. They were deposited in four single burials, probably two females (one young and one adult), a senile male with a double trepanation (Liesau & Pastor 2003), and an undetermined senile individual (Sampedro & Liesau 1998). The set suggests the work of a single artisan and the contemporaneity of the four burials, which may have been of kin-related individuals. If so, they may indicate that certain families or individuals obtained a differentiated status in life and thus a specific treatment when buried. Hosting of collective actions as those documented at El Ventorro could have been the means by which they acceded to higher status. But it is unclear if these individuals had the means to subordinate others outside the local group, as to assure the inheritance of their position in the long term. The rarity of Beaker burials over the millennium in which they occured, and their great variability in wealth suggests otherwise.

The actual archaeological record does not support the understanding of Bell Beaker assemblage as evidence of the first central Iberian chiefdoms. Settlement evidence is still too scarce to evaluate the role of these items in the domestic sphere, and changes from previous domestic patterns are not obvious except for some unique sites as El Ventorro. Funerary programs show minimal labour investment in graves and highly variable deposition of artefacts, some of them known to be involved in domestic production and consumption. Only metal objects as Palmela arrowheads, axes and daggers, all particularly associated with burials, seem to display a minimally *materialized* power (De Marrais et al 1996).

The long time span of Bell Beakers threatens any one-meaning explanation. A reasonable perspective should accept that the Bell Beaker *phenomenon* in central Iberia

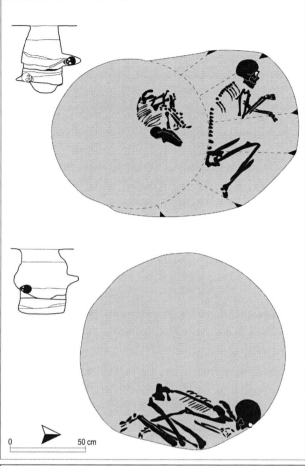

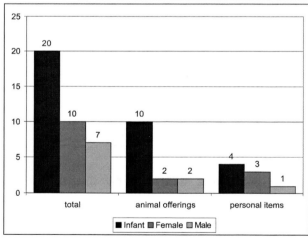

Fig. 6.5.- Characteristic EBA burials (following Díaz-del-Río et al 1997) and total number of BA burials from published sites of the Meseta (following Díaz-del-Río 2001: 361).

is made possible through a process of capital intensification developed throughout the first half of third millennium BC. All evidence seem to support the occasional presence of leaders with acquired status, who probably manipulated social relations in order to obtain small-scale and irregular prestige benefits. It would not seem that such leaders were capable of exercising or expanding their social position beyond the local group.

The limited evidence for wealth or prestige items disappears in the subsequent Bronze Age. Domesticity, and the critical need to maintain the reproduction of small-scale groups, becomes the main feature of the archaeological record.

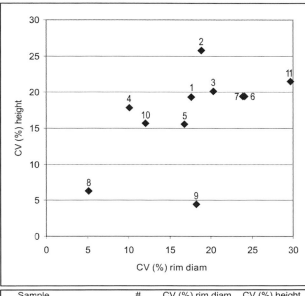

Sample	#	CV (%) rim diam	CV (%) height
1 Bell-beaker all types	61	17,58	19,38
2 Bell-Beaker nondec	12	18,87	25,74
3 Bell-Beaker puntillado	8	20,31	20,18
4 Bell-Beaker maritime	9	10,09	17,85
5 Bell-Beaker Ciempoz	32	16,76	15,57
6 Cazuela all types	29	24,09	19,5
7 Cazuela Ciempoz	26	23,89	19,5
8 Cazuela Cuesta Reina	4	5,12	6,26
9 Bell-beaker Cuesta Reina	2	18,28	4,52
10 Cuenco Cuesta Reina	3	12,11	15,73
11 Cazuelilla all types	12	29,7	21,52

Fig 6.6.- Coefficients of variation (CV) of bell beaker pottery heights and rim diameters (raw data obtained from Garrido 2000).

6.6.- The Early Bronze Age (2250-1630 cal BC)

The Early or 'Classic' Bronze Age in central Iberia (2250-1630 cal BC) contrasts with other areas of the Peninsula because of its lack of monumentality and the scarce evidence for social differentiation in burial practices. Sites are basically defined by the broad distributions of pit structures, frequently interpreted as underground storage and other domestic facilities. These appear in clusters of less than 1 to 2 hectares, occupying similar topographical positions as previous Copper Age settlements. Labour is no longer deployed in the construction of enclosures. Sites tend to look alike, and scholars

have frequently accepted the lack of clear discernible differentiation between them.

However, site variability does exist. This has been recently tested by analyzing the variance of pit volume, frequency of pottery and lithic refuse from four EBA sites in close proximity to one another (Díaz-del-Río & Vicent in press) (Fig. 6.4). Results show that, aside from chronological differences, functional diversification may be at work. Extensive use of landscape by small-scale groups in a semisteppe environment would explain the observed pattern, but intrasite asymmetries in for example the distribution of storage capacity cannot be assessed at present. Harrison (1985; 1993; 1994) has stressed the importance of mobile pastoralism as the means of production when interpreting central Iberian social dynamics. This is, of course, because in a relatively stable agricultural community, "raising animals is also the major way of converting surplus agricultural crops into [...] social and economic currencies" (Hayden, 2001: 577). Unfortunately, most central Iberian Bronze Age sites yield few faunal remains.

Changes in craftwork production suggest a sedentary lifestyle. Pottery types include for the first time in prehistory large (and often decorated) storage jars. The most evident transition to EBA happens to be observed through lithic tools, with a general simplification of flint industries and the predominance of serrated flint sickle teeth (Harrison, 1995: 69). This reduction in both the typological variety and quantity of flint production has been frequently considered as a result of the shift to metal tools. Nevertheless, copper and occasional bronze objects are infrequent and do not seem to substitute the function of previous stone industries.

Materialization of wealth is generally associated with the presence of durable objects, as for example metalwork. In Central Iberia, the ammount of metallurgy is minimal when compared to its contemporary Southeast (Montero, 1994; 1998) (Fig. 6.7). Scarce metal ornaments are known in the Meseta during Chalcolithic and EBA, something that contrasts with the dramatic inversion of metal production during the Millares-Argar transition. Copper production was a domestic semi-specialized activity, as the generalized distribution of smelting pots in settlements seem to demonstrate. With a simple technology that demanded no specialist craftsmen, scholars stress the unfeasibility of a specific metallurgical development associated to a new set of social relations (Rovira and Montero 1994). Although metal objects may have occasionally acted as status symbols, their role in the creation of exchange webs or alliance formation seems difficult to support.

A relevant aspect of the EBA archaeological record is the presence of human burials in almost all settlements. The most frequent pattern is the flexed fetal deposition inside underground storage pits, occasionally accompanied by complete or partial domestic animal offerings (Fig. 6.5).

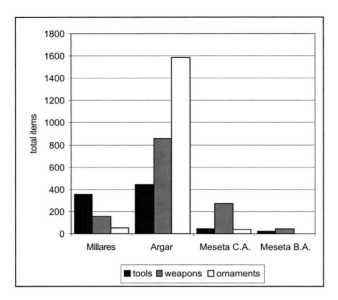

Fig. 6.7.- Comparative quantification of Southeastern (Millarian and Argaric) and Northern Meseta Chalcolithic and Bronze Age metallurgy (data obtained from Montero, 1994; Herrán, 1997). Gold objects from the Meseta following Garrido (2000: 197). Part of Bell-beaker phenomenon in the Meseta is contemporaneous to the early Argar phase, and is quantified as part of Copper Age metalwork. Multifunctional or ambiguous objects (weapons-tools) as daggers and axes have been included as weapons in all cases.

Burials generally lack metal objects, pots and other items frequently associated to bell-Beaker funerary patterns. Their main trend is the presence of an important number of infant burials, at least half of them associated to immature or subadult domestic animal offerings. Adult male and female burials have almost identical quantitative representation, and similar associated offerings or personal items, all extremely modest (bone pendant or awl, a few limestone beads). All this suggests that in these small-scale groups with high infant mortality, descendants became the key factor for the reproduction of labour force. The association of burials with underground storage facilities also highlights the importance given to life cycles, and may reflect the critical productive and reproductive conditions of these groups.

6.7.- Concluding remarks

Throughout the last ten years scholars have disagreed on the nature of prehistoric social relations in Central Iberia. Some have considered the existence of chiefdoms, especially during the bell-Beaker phenomenon, but their arguments should confront an undeniable lack of evidence to support their claims. Others have considered them to be transegalitarian (Garrido, in this volume). Clark and Blake (1994) and Hayden (1995; 2001) have used this term to define societies "with private ownership of resources and produce, low levels of sharing, and institutionalized hierarchies based ultimately on wealth (but also including ritual, kinship, and political dominance) [that are also] characterized by the production and transformation of food surpluses, economically based competition, the use of prestige goods, and a range of specific feasting patterns" (Hayden 2001: 232). If I understand Hayden's definition correctly, the presence of unequal distribution of a significant amount of wealth is the key feature to recognize 'transegalitarism', and up to date, this kind of evidence is mostly lacking in the discussed area. Of course, the definition is flexible enough to include a wide range of archaeological variability (Natufian, American Northwest Coast, Levant PPNB, Western European megalithic cultures, etc), and the generalization of such labeling may not always help us to understand the specific nature of social, economic, and/or political inequalities.

Finally, I have defended the existence of a kin-based mode of social organization (following Wolf 1982), with few evidences for social inequality, and a strong capacity to regenerate itself, limiting the options of potential leaders to transmit their power at their will (Díaz-del-Río 2001: 317). This has been wrongly interpreted as a statement favouring the existence of an egalitarian society (*e.g.* Garrido, in this volume), and thus requires some clarification.

Vicent (1995: 178) has stressed two limiting factors for socio-political change in prehistoric Iberia: "the resistance against the logic of accumulation of wealth and power by means of intra-community exploitation, and the absence of a means of accumulation of value due to the absolute predominance of use value". Both factors were at work in central Iberian Prehistory. The structural limits of any long-term political change were constrained by a modest surplus production, mostly oriented to assure the reproduction of small-scale groups, the failure to enforce socioeconomic or ideological mechanisms needed to increase the amount of labour force and, overall, no long term means of accumulation of value. Under these conditions, I see no way in which potential leaders could have perpetuated their power.

In order to refine the observed socioeconomic dynamics we will need to recover more and better data, oriented to increase our knowledge of both the productive and reproductive activities of these groups. Contrary to what was previously assumed, Central Iberian prehistoric groups did leave a rich and variable archaeological record, one that allows multiple lines of inquiry. One just has to pose good questions. And expect challenging answers.

Acknowledgements: This research has been funded by the Dirección General de Universidades e Investigación, Consejería de Educación, Comunidad del Madrid, Project title: "Paisajes Prehistóricos en la cuenca media del Jarama: indicadores tecnoeconómicos y ambientales a escala semimicro-local" Ref. n° 06/0081/2003. I am specially grateful to Antonio Gilman for his editing and comments on the draft. I am also in debt with my good friends Susana Consuegra, Tim Earle, Maribel Martínez

Navarrete and Juan M. Vicent for their comments on previous drafts, and for their permanent support.

6.8.- References

ALONSO, F. & BELLO, J.Mª. 1997: "Cronología y periodización del fenómeno megalítico en Galicia a la luz de las dataciones por carbono 14". In A. Rodríguez Casal (ed.): *O Neolítico atlántico e as orixes do megalitismo*. Universidad de Santiago de Compostela. Santiago de Compostela: 507-520.

ARIÑO, E. & RODRÍGUEZ, J. 1997: "El poblamiento romano y visigodo en el territorio de Salamanca. Datos de una prospección intensiva". *Zephyrus* 50: 225-245.

ARKUSH, E. & STANISH, C. 2005: "Interpreting Conflict in the Ancient Andes. Implications for the Archaeology of Warfare". *Current Anthropology* 46 (1): 3-28.

BLACKMAN, M.J.; STEIN, G.J. & VANDIVER, P.B. 1993: "The Standardization Hypothesis and Ceramic Mass Production: Technological, Compositional, and Metric Indexes of Craft Specialization at Tell Leilan, Syria". *American Antiquity* 58 (1): 60-80.

BLANCO, J.: LÓPEZ, M.A.: EDO, M. & FERNÁNDEZ, J.L. 1996: "Estudio analítico de determinación mineralógica y de composición química de las cuentas de collar de calaíta y otros materiales del yacimiento de Las Peñas (Quiruelas de Vidriales, Zamora)". *Rubricatum* 1 (1): 227-237.

BLASCO, Mª.C.; BAENA, J. & LIESAU, C. 1998: *La Prehistoria madrileña en el Gabinete de Antiguedades de la Real Academia de la Historia. Los yacimientos Cuesta de la Reina (Ciempozuelos) y Valdocarros (Arganda del Rey)*. Patrimonio Arqueológico del Bajo Jarama, 3. Universidad Autónoma de Madrid. Madrid.

BRADLEY, R. 2005: *Ritual and Domestic Life in Prehistoric Europe*. Routledge. London.

BROWN, J.A. 1995: "On Mortuary Analysis –with Special Reference to the Saxe-Binford Research Program". In L.A. Beck (ed.): *Regional Approaches to Mortuary Analysis*. Plenum Press, New York: 3-26.

CHAPMAN, R.W. 2003: *Archaeologies of complexity*. Routledge. London.

CHAPMAN, R.W.; LULL, V.; PICAZO, M. & SANAHUJA, Mª.e. eds. 1987: *Proyecto Gatas: sociedad y economía en el sudeste de España c. 2500-800 a.n.e. 1. La prospección arqueoecológica*. British Archaeological Reports International Series 348. Oxford.

CLARK, J. & BLAKE, M. 1994: "The Power of Prestige: Competitive Generosity and the Emergence of Rank Societies in Lower Mesoamerica". In E. Brumfiel and J. Fox (eds.): *Factional Competition and Political Development in the New World*. Cambridge University Press. Cambridge: 17-30.

CONSUEGRA, S.; GALLEGO, Mª.M. & CASTAÑEDA, N. 2004: "Minería neolítica de sílex de Casa Montero (Vicálvaro, Madrid). *Trabajos de Prehistoria* 61 (2): 127-140.

DE MARRAIS, E.; CASTILLO, L.J. & EARLE, T.K. 1996: "Ideology, materialization, and Power strategies". *Current Anthropology*, 37 (1): 15-31.

DELIBES, G. 2001: "Del Bronce al Hierro en el valle medio del Duero: una valoración del límite de Cogotas I-Soto de Medinilla a partir de las manifestaciones de culto". *Zephyrus* 53-54 (2000-2001): 293-309.

DELIBES, G. & ETXEBERRIA, F. 2002: "Fuego y cal en el sepulcro colectivo de 'El Miradero' (Valladolid): ¿accidente, ritual o burocracia de la muerte?". In M. Rojo & M. Kunst (eds.): *Sobre el significado del fuego en los rituales funerarios del Neolítico*. Studia Archaeologica 91. Universidad de Valladolid. Valladolid: 39-58.

DELIBES, G.; FERNÁNDEZ, J.; FONTANEDA, E. & ROVIRA, S. 1999: *Metalurgia de la Edad del Bronce en el piedemonte meridional de la Cordillera Cantabrica. La colección Fontaneda*. Monografías. Arqueología en Castilla y León, 3. Junta de Castilla y León. Zamora.

DELIBES, G.; HERRÁN, J.I.; SANTIAGO, J. de & VAL, J. 1995: "Evidence for social complexity in the Copper Age of the Northern Meseta". In K.T. Lillios (ed.): *The origins of complex societies in late prehistoric Iberia*. International Monographs in Prehistory, 8. Ann Arbor: 44-63.

DELIBES, G. & ROJO, M.A. 1997: "C^{14} y secuencia megalítica en La Lora burgalesa: acotaciones a la problemática de las dataciones absolutas referentes a yacimientos dolménicos". In A.A. Rodríguez Casal ed.: *O Neolítico Atlántico e as orixes do megalitismo*. Santiago de Compostela: 391-414.

DÍAZ-DEL-RÍO, P. 2001: *La formación del paisaje agrario. Madrid en el III y II milenios BC*. Arqueología, Paleontología y Etnografía, 9. Comunidad de Madrid. Madrid.

- 2004a: "Copper Age Ditched Enclosures in Central Iberia". *Oxford Journal of Archaeology* 23(2): 107-121.

- 2004b: "Factionalism and collective labor in Copper Age Iberia". *Trabajos de Prehistoria* 61(2): 85-98.

DÍAZ-DEL-RIO, P.; CONSUEGRA, S.; PEÑA-CHOCARRO, L.; MÁRQUEZ, B.; SAMPEDRO, C.; MORENO, R.; ALBERTINI, D. & PINO, B. 1997: "Paisajes agrarios prehistóricos en la Meseta Peninsular: el caso de 'Las Matillas' (Alcalá de Henares, Madrid)". *Trabajos de Prehistoria*, 54 (2): 93-111.

DÍAZ-DEL-RÍO, P. & VICENT, J.M. in press: "Movilidad, funcionalidad y usos del suelo en la Prehistoria Reciente". In A. Orejas ed.: *Paisajes Agrarios*. Arqueología *Espacial 26*.

FABIÁN, J.F. 1995: *El aspecto funerario durante el Calcolítico y los inicios de la Edad del Bronce en la Meseta Norte*. Acta Salmanticensia. Estudios Históricos y Geográficos, 93. Ediciones Universidad de Salamanca.

GARRIDO, R. 2000: *El Campaniforme en la Meseta Central de la Península Ibérica (c. 2500-2000 a.C.)*. British Archaeological Reports International Series 892. Oxford.

GILMAN, A. 2001: "Assessing Political Development in Copper and Bronze Age Southeast Spain". In Jonathan Haas (ed.): *From leaders to rulers*. Kluwer Academic / Plenum Publishers, New York: 59-81.

GILMAN, A. & THORNES, J.B. 1985: *Land-use and Prehistory in South-east Spain*. George Allen & Unwin. London.

HARRISON, R.J. 1977: *The Bell Beaker Cultures of Spain and Portugal*. American School of Prehistoric Reseach. Peabody Museum. Harvard University, bulletin 35. Cambridge.

- 1985: "The 'Policultivo Ganadero', or the Secondary Products Revolution in Spanish Agriculture, 5000-1000 bc". *Proceedings of the Prehistoric Society*, 51: 75-102.

- 1993: "La intensificación económica y la integración del modo pastoril durante la Edad del Bronce". *1º Congresso de Arqueologia Peninsular* (Oporto, 1993). II. *Trabalhos de Antropologia e Etnología*, 33 (3-4): 293-299.

- 1994: "New aspects of the 'Policultivo Ganadero' in Prehistoric Spain". *Origens, Estruturas e Relaçoes das Culturas Calcoliticas a Península Ibérica* (Torres Vedras, 1987). Trabalhos de Arqueologia, 7. IPPAR. Lisboa: 273-276.

- 1995: "Bronze Age Expansion 1750-1250 BC: The Cogotas I Phase in the Middle Ebro Valley". *Veleia*, 12: 67-77.

HARRISON, R.J. & MORENO, G. 1985: "El policultivo ganadero o la revolución de los productos secundarios". *Trabajos de Prehistoria* 42: 51-82.

HARRISON, R.J. & OROZCO KÖHLER, T. 2001: "Beyond Characterisation. Polished Stone Exchange in the Western Mediterranean 5500-2000 BC". *Oxford Journal of Archaeology*, 20 (2): 107-127.

HARRISON, R.J.; QUERO, S. & PRIEGO, M.A. 1975: "Beaker metalurgy in Spain". *Antiquity*, 44: 273-278.

HAYDEN, B. 1995: "Pathways to Power: Principles fort Creating Socioeconomic Inequalities". In T.D. Price and G.M. Feinman (eds.): *Foundations of Social Inequality*. Plenum Press. New York: 15-85.

- 2001a: "Richman, Poorman, Beggarman, Chief. The Dynamics of Social Inequality". In G. Feinman and T.D. Price (eds.): *Archaeology at the Millenium: A Sourcebook*. Kluwer Academic/Plenum Publishers. New York: 231-272.

- 2001b: "The dynamics of wealth and poverty in the transegalitarian societies of Southeast Asia". *Antiquity*, 75: 571-581.

JORGE, S.O. 1998: "Colónias, fortificações, lugares monumentalizados. Trajectória das concepções sobre um tema do Calcolítico peninsular". In S.O. Jorge and V.O. Jorge (eds): *Arqueologia. Percusos e interrogações*. Associação para o Desenvolvimento da Cooperação em Arqueologia Peninsular. Porto: 69-150.

- 2002: "From 'fortified settlement' to "monument": accounting for Castelo Velho de Numao (Portugal)". *Journal of Iberian Archaeology* 4: 75-82.

KUIJT, I. 2000: "Near Eastern Neolithic Research. Directions and Trends". In I. Kuijt ed.: *Life in Neolithic Farming Communities. Social Organization, Identity, and Differentiation*. Fundamental Issues in Archaeology. Kluwer Academic/Plenum Publishers. New York: 311-322.

KUNST, M. & ROJO, M. 1999: "El valle de Ambrona: un ejemplo de la primera colonización de las tierras del Interior Peninsular". Actes II Congrés del Neolític a la Península Ibèrica. *Saguntum* Extra, 2.Valencia: 259-270.

LIESAU, C. & PASTOR, I. 2003: "The Ciempozuelos Necropolis Skull: a Case of Double Trepanation?". *International Journal of Osteoarchaeology* 13: 213-221.

LOHRKE, B.; WIEDMANN, B. & ALT K.W. 2002: "Die anthropologische Bestimmung der menschlichen Skelettreste aus La Peña de la Abuela, Ambrona (Prov. Soria)". In M. Rojo & M. Kunst (eds.): *Sobre el significado del fuego en los rituales funerarios del Neolítico*. Studia Archaeologica 91. Universidad de Valladolid. Valladolid: 82-98.

LÓPEZ GARCÍA, P. ed. 1997: *El paisaje vegetal de la Comunidad de Madrid durante el Holoceno Final*. Arqueología, Paleontología y Etnografía, 5. Comunidad de Madrid. Madrid.

LÓPEZ, P. ARNANZ, A.M.; MACÍAS, R.; UZQUIANO, P. & GIL, P.M. 2003: "Arqueobotánica de la Cueva de la Vaquera". In Mª.S. Estremera: *Primeros agricultores y ganaderos en la Meseta Norte: el Neolítico de la Cueva de la Vaquera (Torreiglesias, Segovia)*. Arqueología en Castilla y León 11. Junta de Castilla y León. Zamora: 247-256.

LÓPEZ PLAZA, M.S. 1991: "Aproximación al poblamiento de la Prehistoria Reciente en la Provincia de Salamanca". In M. Santonja (coord.): *Del Paleolítico a la Historia*. Salamanca: 48-60.

MONKS, S.J. 1997: "Conflict and Competition in Spanish Prehistory: The Role of Warfare in Societal Development from the Late Fourth to Third Millennium BC". *Journal of Mediterranean Archaeology* 10(1): 3-32.

MONTERO, I. 1994: *El origen de la metalurgia en el sureste peninsular*. Historia, 19. Instituto de Estudios Almerienses. Almería.

- 1998: "Metallurgy and society: two spanish Bronze Age cases". In C. Mordant, M. Pernot and V. Rychner (eds.): *Látelier du broncier en Europe du XX au VII siecle avant notre ere*. (Neuchâtel and Dijón). Vol. 3: 273-282.

MORALES, A. 1992: "Estudio de la fauna del yacimiento calcolítico de 'Las Pozas' (Casaseca de las Chanas, Zamora)". *Boletín de la Sociedad de Arte y Arqueología*, LVIII: 65-96.

- 2003: "Informe sobre los mamíferos de la Fase III (Neolítico Final)". In Mª.S. Estremera: *Primeros agricultores y ganaderos en la Meseta Norte: el Neolítico de la Cueva de la Vaquera (Torreiglesias, Segovia)*. Arqueología en Castilla y León 11. Junta de Castilla y León. Zamora: 305-313.

MORALES, A. & MARTÍN, S. 2003: "Informe zooarqueológico". In Mª.S. Estremera: *Primeros agricultores y ganaderos en la Meseta Norte: el Neolítico de la Cueva de la Vaquera (Torreiglesias, Segovia)*. Arqueología en Castilla y León 11. Junta de Castilla y León. Zamora: 257-303.

MORALES, A. & VILLEGAS, C. 1994: "La fauna de mamíferos del yacimiento de 'El Ventorro': síntesis osteológica de la campaña de 1981". *Estudios de Prehistoria y Arqueología Madrileñas*, 9: 35-56.

MUÑOZ, K. 2000: "The Tagus middle basin (Iberian Peninsula) from the Neolithic to the Iron Age (V-I Millennium cal. BC): The long way to social complexity". *Oxford Journal of Archaeology* 19(3): 241-272.

PEÑA-CHOCARRO, L. in press: "Early agriculture in Central and Southern Spain". In J. Conolly and S. Colledge eds.: *Origins and Spread of Agriculture in SW Asia and Europe: Achaeobotanical Investigations of Neolithic Plant Economies.* UCL Press. London

PRIEGO, M.C. & QUERO, S. 1992: *El Ventorro, un poblado prehistórico de los albores de la metalurgia.* Estudios de Prehistoria y Arqueología Madrileñas, 8. Madrid.

ROJO, M.; KUNST, M. & PALOMINO, A.L. 2002: "El fuego como procedimiento de clausura en tres tumbas monumentales de la Submeseta Norte". In M. Rojo & M. Kunst (eds.): *Sobre el significado del fuego en los rituales funerarios del Neolítico.* Studia Archaeologica 91. Universidad de Valladolid. Valladolid: 21-38.

ROJO, M.A., MORÁN, G. & KUNST, M. 2003: "Un défi à l'éternité: genèse et réutilisations du tumulus de La Sima (Miño de Medinaceli, Soria, Espagne)". In J. Leclerc & C. Masset coord.: *Sens dessus dessous. La recherche du sens en Préhistoire.* Revue Archeologique de Picardie: 173-184.

ROVIRA, S. & MONTERO, I. 1994: "Metalurgia campaniforme y de la Edad del Bronce en la Comunidad de Madrid". In M.C. Blasco (ed.): *El horizonte campaniforme de la región de Madrid en el centenario de Ciempozuelos.* Patrimonio Arqueológico del Bajo Manzanares, 2. Universidad Autónoma de Madrid. Madrid: 137-171.

SAHLINS, M.D. 1961: "The Segmentary Lineage: An Organization of Predatory Expansion". *American Anthropologist* 63(2): 322-345.

SAMPEDRO, C. & LIESAU, C. 1998: "Los restos antropológicos". In C. Blasco, J. Baena, & C. Liesau: *La Prehistoria Madrileña en el Gabinete de Antigüedades de la Real Academia de la Historia. Los yacimientos de Cuesta de la Reina (Ciempozuelos) y Valdocarros (Arganda del Rey).* Patrimonio Arqueológico del Bajo Jarama 3. Universidad Autónoma de Madrid. Madrid: 55.

SHERRAT, A. 1981: "Plough and Pastoralism: aspects of the secondary products revolution". In I. Hodder, G. Issaac and N. Hammond (eds.): Patterns of the Past: Studies in honour of David Clarke. Cambridge: 261-305.

STEVENSON, A.C. & HARRISON, R.J. 1992: "Ancient forest in Spain: a model for land-use and dry forest management in south-west Spain from 4000 BC to 1900 AD". *Proceedings of the Prehistoric Society* 58: 227-247.

STIKA, H.P. 1999: "Erste Archäobotanische ergebnisse der ausgrabungen 1997 in Ambrona (Prov. Soria)". Madrider Mitteilungen 40: 61-65.

TRANCHO, G.J.; ROBLEDO, B.; LÓPEZ-BUEIS, I. & FABIÁN, F.J. 1996: "Reconstrucción del patrón alimenticio de dos poblaciones prehistóricas de la Meseta Norte". *Complutum*, 7: 73-90.

VICENT, J.M. 1995: "Early Social Complexity in Iberia: Some Theoretical Remarks". In K.T. Lillios ed.: *The Origins of Complex Societies in Late Prehistoric Iberia.* International Monographs in Prehistory, Archaeological Series 8. Ann Arbor. Michigan: 177-183.

WOLF, E.R. 1982: *Europe and the People Without History.* University of California Press. Berkeley.

CHAPTER 7

Transegalitarian societies: an ethnoarchaeological model for the analysis of Copper Age Bell Beaker using groups in Central Iberia

Rafael Garrido-Pena
Universidad de Valladolid

Abstract

Anthropologist Brian Hayden has coined the concept of "transegalitarian societies" for the various kinds of societies in which political leadership seems to surpass the boundaries of kinship, acting further afar than the strictly local sphere and extending beyond the life of the individual who exerts it, but in which there are neither institutionalised forms of power nor clear political centralisation. In this paper, I contend that this concept can be applied in the study of the Copper Age communities of the Iberian central plateau that were involved in the Bell-beaker networks of exchange. My aim is to suggest a more detailed interpretation of the societies that emerged from the collapse of the Neolithic communal structures and occupied the transition period that separates them from the Bronze Age chiefdoms. This interpretation seeks to carefully avoid simplistic conclusions either in terms of a prolonged egalitarianism or of an early social complexity.

Keywords: Transegalitarian Societies; Chalcolithic; Bell Beaker; Hayden; Social Ranking; Iberian Peninsula; Feasts.

Resumen

Se propone la aplicación al estudio de las sociedades calcolíticas de La Meseta implicadas en la red de intercambios campaniforme, del modelo que el antropólogo Brian Hayden ha elaborado para estudiar los variados tipos de sociedades en las que el liderazgo político parece rebasar los límites del parentesco, extiende su ámbito de acción más allá de la esfera estrictamente local y rebasa la vida de la persona que lo ejerce, pero en las que aún no existe la institucionalización del ejercicio del poder ni una clara centralización, y que este autor denomina "transigualitarias". Con ello se intenta realizar una interpretación más detallada y precisa de aquellas sociedades que surgen del colapso de las estructuras comunales neolíticas, ocupando el periodo de transición que las separa de las jefaturas de la Edad del Bronce, intentando no caer en atribuciones simplistas tanto de un pretendido igualitarismo prolongado como de una prematura complejidad.

Palabras clave: Sociedades Transigualitarias; Calcolítico; Campaniforme; Hayden; Jerarquización Social; Península Ibérica; Banquetes.

7.1.- Introduction

The study of the social and economic structure of Iberian prehistoric societies, especially of those occupying the Spanish central plateau (Meseta), is rather recent, because Spanish and Portuguese Prehistory has been largely dominated by the traditional culture-historical approach until the 1980's. Even today, this theoretical paradigm is still widely used by Iberian prehistorians. Works on this subject published in recent years (*e.g.* Delibes *et al.* 1995; Díaz-del-Río 1995; 2001; 2003; 2004; Garrido-Pena 1994; 1995; 1997; 2000; Garrido & Muñoz 2000; Muñoz 2000; Rojo *et al.* 2005) must therefore be regarded as tentative and preliminary steps of a line of research to be extended in the near future.

The topic itself has great complexity and is extremely demanding with what in fact is a rather complex archaeological record that often lacks enough detail to answer highly specific questions. At times, this ambiguity opens a wide territory for rather diverging or even diametrically opposed views. This is particularly true in a region like central Iberia, where the available data is still both quantitatively and qualitatively poor. Only the sustained application of new theoretical approaches which address the right questions to the archaeological record, and look for demonstration in the field, would change this situation. But this will take years of fieldwork. Therefore, it is now the high time for theoretical debate, looking for those models that could be tested at a later stage, and which could also help us to deal with the existing data in a fresh new way.

The state of the art of the research of social organisation during the Late Prehistory of central Iberia can be roughly characterised as follows. On one hand, the area is presented in many recent works (Díaz-del-Río 1995; 2001; 2004; Muñoz 1993; Bueno *et al.* 2000) as a paradigm of egalitarianism, without any major detectable economic or social changes before the Iron Age. It is, in a sense, an extension of the traditional view of the region as backwater land, isolated and remote from the mainstream processes of change taking place in other regions of Iberia and Western Europe at large. However, it is also true that some recent articles perhaps overestimate the degree of social change in the Late Prehistory of this region, even claiming the existence of established chiefdoms during the Bell Beaker Copper Age (Delibes *et al.* 1995: 61; Delibes 1995: 79-87). As Chapman (1997) has pointed out, complex societies are being seen almost everywhere in the archaeological record, something dangerous and confusing for the future of our studies.

The theoretical models that have prevailed in the study of social change in Iberian Late Prehistory were designed in the 70's and 80's to deal with the problem of the origins of complex societies in the Southeast (*cf.* Gilman 1976; 1987; Gilman & Thornes 1985). These were indeed pioneering studies of social change in Spanish Prehistory, and are still quite interesting in their case-study areas. However, the regions for which those approaches were implemented have rather peculiar ecological contexts, with strong resources stress, all of which make those approaches relatively limited for the analysis of other Iberian regions. This is the case of the interior plateau, an area without resource shortages such as arable land or water, and where signs of ecological stress are less obvious.

It is also hard to understand how it could be possible that social and economic changes did not take place in a region as large and varied as inner Iberia, and during such a long period (three or four thousand years). This is especially true when considering that this was not an isolated area: there is already plenty of evidence for the presence of all the major "paneuropean" archaeological phenomena like megalithism or Bell Beakers, which in many other regions of the old world were related with profound economic and social transformations.

There are also theoretical and methodological problems. One good example is the widely established clear-cut distinction between egalitarian and ranked societies, based on a particular set of archaeological indicators: rich children burials or signs of centralization in the settlement patterns, for instance. This set of indicators may be useful for the analysis of prehistoric social inequality in a broad perspective, but fails when faced with the study of specific societies which do not fit easily in those simplistic categories: the reality of the archaeological and ethnographical record is much more complex (Hayden 1995: 16-17). In addition, it is important to observe that the very notion of egalitarianism demands some explanation, since all societies contain "seeds of inequality". We cannot take equality for granted as a "natural" starting point. The term "egalitarian" is rather complex, usually more related to a sort of egalitarian *ethos* or ideology than a real *de facto* egalitarian social structure (Roscoe 2000: 96, 104).

Amongst the many methodological problems which seriously affect the research of prehistoric social inequality,

two deserve some preliminary consideration. Firstly, the ambiguity of the archaeological indicators, and secondly the extremely poor archaeological record that must be used as the empirical basis.

Regarding the first of these problems, two well known examples deserve some discussion:

a) Rich burials of infant or juvenile individuals are one of the supposed indicators of ranked societies, in which leadership is inherited. Leaders are no longer the most talented men of the group (as it happens in egalitarian societies, where leadership is unstable and also related with sex, age or kinship), but those individuals (and their descendants) who control political institutions. Now chiefs inherit their position and do not need to show their merits to gain power (Berreman 1981: 9; Feinman 1995: 262; Fried 1967; Hayden 1995: 63; Johnson & Earle 1987: 318; Service 1971; Wason 1994: 44; Roscoe 2000: 104). The problem with this line of argumentation is that rich infant grave-goods do exist in well documented egalitarian societies. Several ritual or symbolic factors, and not just inherited social status, can explain these funerary deposits (Hayden 1995: 16). In addition, as Wason (1994: 100) remarks, it is difficult to be sure whether these tombs indicate the status of the deceased or that of his/her family. Moreover, in egalitarian societies in transition to complexity, leadership can be also inherited. Even in the most egalitarian communities, an ideology of primogeniture sometimes occurs, something equally documented in transegalitarian groups, with hereditary political positions based on genealogical seniority (Roscoe 2000: 109). As Hayden (1995: 58) pointed out, nearly 75% of New Guinea big men leaders had fathers that were also big men. The difference is that in this sort of social context, leadership is unstable and can hardly last for more than one generation. It is also archaeologically difficult to assess.

b) Economic differences among domestic units within settlements. The main difficulty of testing those expected distinctions has even led some scholars to question the existence of real social complexity in contexts such as the Bronze Age Argaric groups (Gilman 1997), widely considered as chiefdoms or even primitive states (see Cámara & Molina in this volume). It is my opinion that this problem is closely related with the interpretative limits of the archaeological record. Far from the optimistic expectations of the first processual approaches, it has now become clear that site formation processes are much more complex than previously thought. Settlements suffer many additional disturbances of their original distribution patterns before they are finally abandoned (Cameron & Tomka 1993).

The only alternative to these problems is to try not to draw such abrupt and clear-cut distinctions, taking into account the great variety of factors defining a past social structure, and not forgetting the importance of widespread phenomena which simultaneously affect different regions. An excessive emphasis on the local perspective could lead to serious misunderstandings and confusions: local scale is obviously the basic scale of study; but it must be adequately framed within more general scales of analysis.

The second of the two main issues mentioned above is the poor quality of the archaeological record available for the Prehistory of central Spain. Only recently major research projects have been carried out. Among these, the Ambrona Valley (Soria) project has implemented extensive fieldwork in Neolithic and Copper Age settlement and tombs, uncovering a much more complex and rich landscape for central Iberian Late Prehistory than previously thought (Rojo & Kunst 1999a, 1999b; 1999c; Rojo *et al.* 2003; 2004; 2005). But we are still right at the beginning of research. The majority of information belongs to old dispersed traditional works, or modern rescue excavations, mostly unfortunately unpublished, although some remarkable exceptions do exist (Díaz-del-Río 1995; 2001; 2003; 2004).

7.2.- The "transegalitarian societies" model as an alternative

As we have previously mentioned, the theoretical models put forward for other Iberian contexts such as the South-east are not necessarily appropriate to explain the situation of prehistoric social inequality within the Spanish Meseta, a region with a rich and varied environment where no signs of resources stress have been documented. From the Late Neolithic to the Late Copper Age, different prehistoric social structures are found that cannot be properly described within the categories usually employed in this sort of studies. They are neither complex nor egalitarian societies.

To study this variety of societal contexts, widely recognized not only in the archaeological but also in the ethnographical record, Brian Hayden (1995) employed the useful concept of "transegalitarian societies", initially proposed by Clarke and Blake (1994). As Hayden (1995: 18) points out, the term is broad and involves much variability, including simple horticulturalists and complex hunter-gatherers. Because of this variability, Hayden made several further distinctions in a complex and detailed typology of social structures, supported by a huge *corpus* of ethnographic data from the American Northwest and New Guinea. However, it is also important to note that, in this last region, some recent critical accounts have questioned many of the (usually taken for granted) assumptions about leadership in big men societies present in the great majority of papers using New Guinea ethnographic analogies, which thus need to be carefully reconsidered (Roscoe 2000).

In transegalitarian societies, as Hayden (1995: 22) points out, individual or small group claims of special access to

resources must be negotiated with the rest of the community. Moreover, the only situation in which people will tolerate privileged access to basic subsistence resources is when the majority has their survival insured in normal times, that is to say in situations of abundance and wealth. This approach contrasts with other theoretical positions relating the origins of socioeconomic differences to situations of resources stress or demographic pressure, or to the need to manage risk.

Hunter-gatherers suppress economically-based competition over resources because it is destructive for their limited economies and dangerous for their survival. Economically based competition emerges only when subsistence surpluses become available on a regular basis (Hayden 1995: 24). To explain how ambitious individuals in egalitarian societies can transform production surpluses into personal power, in conditions in which everybody has their survival assured, the clue must be searched in an important social and economic institution: competitive feasts involving contractual debts (Hayden 1995).

Feast-organizing leaders can benefit greatly from establishing a wide contractual debt-relationship network, thus motivating people to produce and surrender surpluses that they control. Supporters hope to profit from their investments in feasts by promises from leaders of repayment with interests for their contributions, as well as increased influence in the affairs of the community (Hayden 1995: 25). As long as the potential for producing surplus increases, socioeconomic inequalities also progress. Among the different types of leaders and "transegalitarian" societies distinguished by Hayden, Copper Age Western European Bell Beaker ones could be classified in his third "stage", the closest to chiefdoms, with the kind of leader he calls "entrepreneur". Potlatch type systems will be the classic example of this sort of community and competitive feasts.

However, is this model appropriate to further understand inner Iberia Copper Age Bell Beaker societies? It is clear that we lack many of the necessary archaeological indicators, but, in my view, a significant bulk of evidence supports this new approach.

7.3.- A previous testing: archaeological indicators

Despite the contribution of recent and major research projects, such as that of the Ambrona Valley (Rojo & Kunst 1999 a, b and c; Rojo *et al.* 2005), which are showing the importance and early arrival of the farming way of life in central Iberia, information about the Early Neolithic in this region is still very scarce. Since my first works (Garrido-Pena 1994; 1995; 1997; 2000) I have stressed the importance of wide scale phenomena, especially the so called "secondary products revolution" (SPR) (Sherratt 1981; 1997), in the processes of socioeconomic change documented in this region during the IV and III millennia cal BC. This process would have probably affected inner Iberia since the beginning of the IV millennium cal BC, during the Late Neolithic, altering the economic systems and social structures by effectively generating an increase in the amounts of available surplus.

The ritual and social complexity of megalithic monuments, well documented in different parts of central Iberia, would perhaps be a first consequence of those large scale transformations. Another possible archaeological indicator of the arrival to the Spanish Meseta of some SPR elements is the spectacular increase in the number of sites from the Late Neolithic and the beginning of the Copper Age, according to observations made in many recent rescue excavations and surveys (Delibes *et al.* 1995: 46-49; Garrido-Pena 1994: 83; 1995: 143; 1997: 201; 2000: 193). The quantitative differences are still so striking that it is not unlikely that a certain demographic increase, a feature that characterises the evolution of "transegalitarian societies, especially those of "entrepreneur" type (Hayden 1995: 51), started during the Late Neolithic.

With the available data it is difficult to prove the supposed increase in economic surplus. Until the above-mentioned research projects (now in progress) provide more solid evidence, one can just look for possible evidences in, for example, a characteristic settlement type that arose during the Neolithic and more clearly since the Copper Age. This is the so-called "campos de hoyos" sites, or open air dwelling sites, with rock-cut structures of several forms (oval, circular) and sizes, filled up with domestic residues (pottery sherds, lithic industry and faunal remains). Of complex interpretation (see *e.g.* Márquez in this volume), very few of them can be safely identified as hut floors because of their small dimensions (less than 1 metre of diameter), and are more probably related (at least originally) with storage, although the great majority ended up as rubbish-pits.

Pollen analyses carried out in different sites (López 1997; Delibes *et al.* 1997: 795) suggest an intense deforestation and increased anthropic impact since the Copper Age. At the same time, different faunal assemblages, such as those of the Copper Age settlements of El Ventorro in Madrid (Morales & Villegas 1994), Viña de Esteban García in Salamanca (Delibes *et al.* 1997: 796), and Las Pozas in Zamora (Morales 1992) show a clear predominance of adult individuals in every recorded species (ovicaprines and pigs mainly), which suggests a secondary exploitation of animals, which prolongs their life to obtain for example milk or dairy products (the consumption of the latter is also suggested by the widespread appearance of the so called cheese-strainers in many Copper Age sites of the area). However, the results of some of these faunal studies must be carefully considered, because they are based on collections that are in a poor state of preservation (Morales & Liesau 1994). The recent extraordinary finding of wool textiles in a Bronze Age

argaric tomb in the Southeast (Molina *et al.* 2003) shows the importance of the SPR in Iberia. In addition, some recent settlement pattern analyses have documented the increasing importance of cattle-raising during the Copper Age in the central plateau area (Muñoz 1993; 2000; Rojo *et al.* in press a).

Those remarkable socioeconomic changes must be considered as a long process, which began in the first half of the IV millennium cal BC. When Bell Beakers appear in the Iberian plateau around the mid III millennium, they already were at an advanced stage of development. However, this process was significantly slower than in other areas of Iberia such as the Southeast. Thus, Bell Beakers would have occupied a transitional phase in the process of social change between mostly egalitarian Neolithic communities and the first chiefdoms of the Bronze Age. It is not until the Bronze Age that it is possible to see clear archaeological indicators of social complexity, for example in settlement patterns (Muñoz 1993; 2000).

Since Clarke (1976), Bell Beakers have been considered not as common domestic materials but as high value commodities that circulated through the fully developed exchange networks of the Western European Copper Age. Beakers must be understood as part of a crucial stage of social and economic change towards social complexity, in which emergent leaders consumed those special items in their legitimizing strategies.

In central Iberia, the expansion of long distance exchange systems since the Late Neolithic, and especially during the Copper Age, has been clearly attested by the characterisation of materials like copper (Delibes *et al.* 1995: 53; Montero *et al.* 1990), high quality flint (Delibes *et al.* 1995: 57), and luxury commodities used for ornaments such as callaite (Delibes *et al.* 1995: 59; Edo *et al.* 1997) or ivory (Espadas *et al.* 1987; Val & Herrán, 1995: 302). This earlier development of long distance exchanges could explain the fast and widespread adoption of Beakers when contact was made with a wider network (Garrido-Pena 1997: 202). In fact during Bell Beaker times those exchange systems clearly expand, as it is suggested by the general distribution of sites (Fig. 7.1), mostly related with the most important natural routes, mainly rivers, and also on visually-dominant emplacements (Garrido-Pena 2000: 46-47).

Those exchange systems must be understood not in the modern sense of a purely economic activity, but as a social strategy of the leaders. These social strategies are meant not to obtain basic resources or food, but special and exotic (*i.e.* rare and foreign) commodities to be used as part of strategies to reinforce their power and prestige. Among these strategies, alliances or political pacts, perhaps related with opportunistic marriages and competitive gift exchanges, in which large numbers of supporters and labour force could be obtained, are undoubtedly essential. In this view, Bell Beakers can be interpreted as symbols of status (Thomas 1987), and not just prestige items,

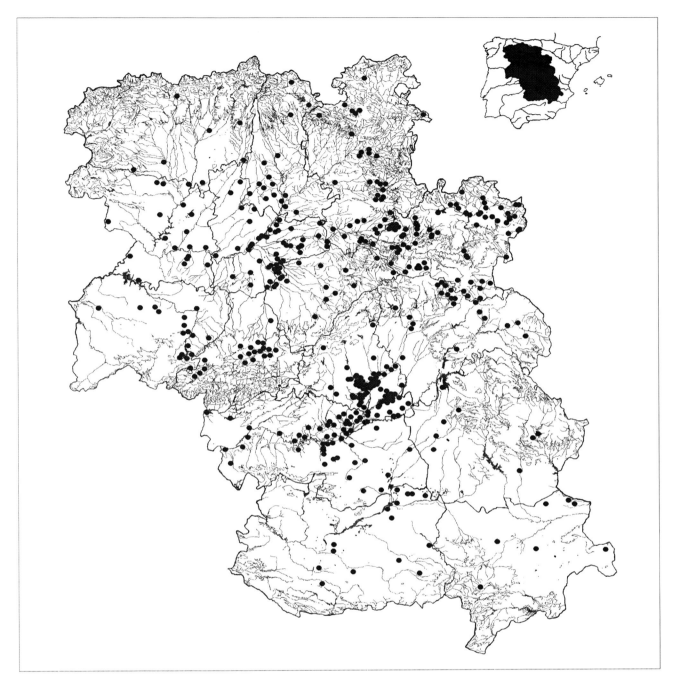

Fig. 7.1. Inner Iberia Beaker sites distribution (after Garrido-Pena 2000).

because they were used to display a powerful position previously obtained with the opportunistic manipulation of different strategies (marriage or competitive gift exchanges, for instance) upon which the whole system of inequalities was built.

Within the Beaker societies of central Iberia, leaders must have been constantly struggling to reinforce their still unstable position, and probably they just partly succeeded in doing so. It is likely that power was inherited during just one or two generations at most, as Hayden (1995: 58) suggests for New Guinea big men. They were not chief-

doms, and that would be the reason explaining the long duration of Bell Beakers in the interior of Iberia, contrasting with its short life in other regions such as the Southeast where the whole process was quicker and chiefdoms emerged soon in the Argaric Bronze Age, contemporaneously with Meseta Beakers. In fact, as the ethnographical record clearly shows, these sort of competitive exchange systems are characteristic of societies based upon unstable forms of leadership.

As it has been previously mentioned, it is extremely difficult to find true archaeological indicators of this sort of unstable inherited status in child graves. Even the existence of rich infantile burials is a complex matter to be easily interpreted in terms of inherited status (Wason 1994: 100; Hayden 1995: 16). In Iberia, the only documented case is an isolated example of a child burial from the Aldeagordillo mound in Ávila (Fabián 1992).

7.4.- Beaker competitive feasts

As Hayden (1995: 51-52; 1996; 2001) suggests, in transegalitarian societies, leaders looking for supporters try to increase their economic surplus through labour intensification and exchanges, in order to organize larger and more elaborate feasts. The greater the return profit that leaders could offer to their supporters as contributions to competitive feasts, the stronger their motivation to produce surpluses, thus indirectly increasing the total contractual debt in the community. Leaders compete with each other organizing larger feasts to attract supporters and exchanges, with contractual debts involving interest payments as the underlying economic logic behind it.

Following Sherratt (1987; 1991) the Bell Beaker package may be defined as a successful combination of copper weapons, ornaments and pottery to drink a very special substance. As it was proposed in previous hypothesis of European (Childe 1947: 218; Sherratt 1987; 1991) or Iberian scale (Garrido-Pena 1994; 1995; 1997; 2000), those singular decorated vessels, which were deposited in single graves accompanied by other luxurious paraphernalia, probably contained an alcoholic beverage. Recent chemical analyses of samples collected in Bell Beakers from different sites of Spain, like those from the Ambrona Valley, have demonstrated that they contained beer (Rojo *et al.* in press).

Alcoholic beverages are part of social relations. They facilitate and moderate social interaction. They are part of hospitality etiquette, and construct networks of reciprocal obligations among drinkers (Vencl 1994: 313). The importance of alcohol in social relations has been widely recognised, especially within the context of struggle and support of power in preindustrial societies lacking political institutions. This struggle involves the creation of a body of supporters, with instruments such as hospitality rituals or work feasts, where leaders invite community members to abundant food and alcoholic drinking in exchange for their labour (Sherratt 1987: 98; Dietler 1990).

Prestigious alcoholic beverage production is a potential way to obtain power and richness. Surplus investment by certain members of the community, like beer consumed in feasting, might create obligations or deferred reciprocity, serving as an important instrument by which to gain power. There are many ethnographic testimonies about the value of beer in "primitive" societies. As Arthur (2003: 516-517) shows in his study of many African beer drinking groups, alcoholic beverage was a valued luxuri-

ous food, an indicator of status and wealth that required an important amount of grain and labour investment. Amongst the Tanzanian Chagga, beer creates reciprocal political and economic links between leaders and the common people. Chiefs offer generous quantities of this drinking to fulfil their redistributive obligations, and to maintain warriors who will fight for them. The Cameroon Koma elaborate beer and sacrifice cattle to improve individual status, through livestock redistributive feasts, where large amounts of beer are consumed (490 litres equivalent to 100 kg. of cereals). In the Ethiopian Gamo, beer production is related to the richest households and highest castes. They are usually the ones that possess land and special places where beer was elaborated (Arthur 2003: 518-519, 523).

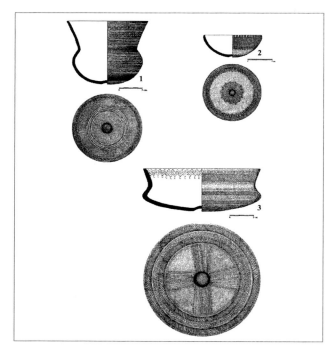

Fig.7.2. Bell Beaker vessels from the Ciempozuelos cemetery (Madrid): 1) Bell Beaker, 2) Bowl, 3) Carinated Bowl (after Garrido-Pena 2000).

In the Iberian Meseta, the analysis of the Beaker formal repertoire provides interesting clues about possible drinking rituals that could be displayed with that ceramic equipment (Garrido-Pena 1995; 1997: 204; 2000: 70-74). There are some pottery forms that could perfectly be classified within the range of measures typical of the individual drinking vessels, like the Bell Beaker itself. Nearly 70% of those documented throughout the region have capacities between 450-1250 cc. (Fig. 7.2: 1) (Garrido-Pena 2000: 84). Beaker cups, represented in the Spanish Meseta by the fragmented piece uncovered in the Madrid settlement of El Ventorro (Priego & Quero 1992), are clearly related with individual drinking, as predecessors of the famous Bronze Age Argaric ones. Open forms like the Beaker carinated bowl (the Spanish *cazuela*) are more likely to be related with solid foods (Figure 7.2: 3), as Harrison (1995) has pointed out for Late Bronze Age troncoconic carinated bowls, which he suggest would have been used for meat presentation.

Many central Iberia Beaker grave goods, especially those of Ciempozuelos pottery style (Late Beakers), were composed by the well-known set of Bell Beaker, carinated bowl and bowl (Fig. 7.1 and 7.4), the latter being usually placed inside the second (Delibes 1977: 89-90). In this context, a careful analysis of the existing proportions between vessels of complete sets with ceramic grave goods provides interesting evidence concerning the features of the rituals displayed with them. Bell Beakers and bowls have a remarkable volumetric control, with a clear predominance of nearly 1 litre cases in the former and 500 cc. in the latter. Carinated bowls have a much more irregular behaviour. Together with their overall shape, too open for a liquid content vessel, they may have played a complementary role in rituals. They could have been related to the consumption of different kind of materials such as meat or cereal porridge.

The smaller vessels (bowls and small carinated bowls) could have been used for individual consumption of the eventual content of Bell Beakers and large carinated bowls. Their documented deposition inside both types of recipients in several central Iberia Beaker single grave goods suggests so (at Villabuena del Puente, Zamora, for example). The bowl is also the most closely associated form to Bell Beakers (Garrido-Pena 2000: figure 15), and there are many examples of tombs with just these two kinds of vessels (Aldeagordillo, Valdeprados, or Los Pasos).

The proportion between their respective capacities is remarkably varied, with the Bell Beaker always overcoming the bowl in size. Pearson coefficients of complete containers show a strong negative correlation between these two beaker forms. Thus, there is a clear tendency in Beaker bowls to have less capacity whenever the Bell Beaker is bigger. It seems that the bowl plays a distributive role of the Bell Beaker content (beer) between the participants in the ritual. Taking into account the proportions already mentioned, groups would have been formed of three to eight individuals (Garrido-Pena 2000: 72-73).

The problem is much more complex when complete single grave goods with three vessels are studied, because the two already mentioned ceramic forms are accompanied by a rather different kind of recipient, the carinated bowl (larger and more open), probably used to manage solid foods. In some of those graves, the bowl was deposited inside the carinated bowl, as a distributive element of its possible content. Pearson coefficients of the three types of recipients in the single complete grave goods studied showed that Bell Beakers used to be significantly larger than bowls, and that there was a strong negative correlation between the capacities of both. The bigger the Bell Beakers, the bigger the accompanying bowls. Carinated bowls were always the largest of the ceramic trio equipment, and had no correlation with Bell Beaker vol-

ume, but displayed a low and positive one with bowls. This clearly shows that Bell Beakers and carinated bowls would have probably played different roles in the ritual, the first related with the consumption of beverages (beer) and the second with solid foodstuffs.

Could those rituals reflect feasting activities of Copper Age inner Iberia Bell Beaker leaders? Is the same sort of vessel combination found on high status "entrepreneurs" tombs present in settlements? In Beaker habitats this luxury decorated pottery usually represents around 5% of the total ceramic assemblage, which suggests that it was also occasionally used in everyday life. Would they have been used during special high social occasions such as hospitality rituals or competitive feasts? Interestingly, Hayden (1995: 62) stresses that in transegalitarian entrepreneur communities, ritual feasting paraphernalia like prestige food-serving containers are frequently documented and used in all investment transactions, between individual partners or communities.

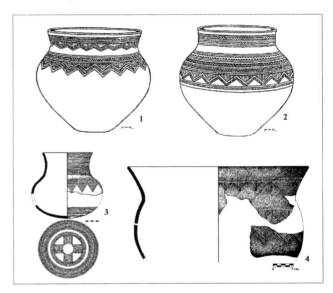

Fig.7.3. Inner Iberia Beaker Storage/Feasting vessels: 1-2) Molino de Garray (Soria) (after Schulten), 3) after Cajal (1981), 4) after Garrido-Pena (2000).

However, some scholars (Brodie 1997; Case 1995) have recently criticized the Beaker drinking model with different arguments. One of them is the widespread existence of large sized vessels with Beaker decoration throughout the European archaeological record, especially in settlements, which would prove the purely domestic and everyday use of this pottery, quite apart from elite rituals. Obviously, given their large size and volume (between 2 and 10 litres, and sometimes more than 20 litres), those large storage Beaker vessels (the Spanish Molino type) (Fig. 7.3) only found at settlements and widely documented in our case study area, were not used for individual drinking. It is unlikely that they would have participated in the exchange system (Garrido-Pena 2000: 126-129, figures 56-58).

However, those large Beaker vessels still only represent around 5% of the total ceramic storage recipients, with a clear predominance of the plain common ones. This is important because, along with their careful elaboration, it suggests they had a special role. Moreover, those vessels, likely to be related with storage or collective consumption, are strikingly similar to those employed in many African preindustrial societies to brew and serve beer in feasts (Arthur 2003: 522) (Fig. 7.3). Would those large Beaker recipients have been used in competitive feasts where the whole community drank beer celebrating the prestige and power of the host? This is an interesting hypothesis to be fully confirmed once the necessary chemical content analyses become available.

7.5.- Beaker entrepreneurs in Copper Age central Iberia

Another feature of typical transegalitarian leadership societies can be found within the archaeological record of Iberian Beakers. As Hayden remarks (1995: 56), entrepreneurs are ambitious individuals who try to concentrate all important roles of power in their hands, including economic, political, military and ritual. Recent approaches to the Beaker package stress the plural and flexible nature of the ideological meanings surrounding its components (Waldren 1995; Garrido-Pena 2000: 25-26). A "clash of symbols", according to Edmonds (1995): weapons, luxurious ornaments (golden jewellery), symbolic items (stone wrist guards), alcoholic beverages, and "magic" technologies like metallurgy (Brodie 1997: 309), many of them obtained through long distance exchange (Fig. 7.4). This flexibility would have been one of the reasons in explaining its success and wide geographical distribution.

It is also quite common in emergent leaders to use supernatural claims to legitimate their power, especially through the manipulation of ancestors in their own benefit (Parker Pearson 1993: 214-216; Wason 1994: 50; Hayden 1995: 56). In this sense, it is likely that the reuse of Neolithic megalithic monuments during the Copper Age to bury Beaker leaders was also a way of looking for the validation of newly emergent inequalities by the ancestors (Garrido-Pena 1994: 70; 1995: 127; 1997: 202; 2000: 55-58; Rojo et al. 2005).

As Hayden (1995: 57, 62) points out, leaders also tend to control access to both imported and locally crafted prestige goods through their regional connections. That is, a significant craft specialization should be present. Since Clark (1976), Bell Beaker pottery has been widely considered as a luxury commodity, a special craftsmanship product. Obviously, the careful and rich decoration of these vessels, sometimes affecting even the inner side, is not a functional or hygienic feature for a domestic cooking recipient. Dimple bases or sinuous profiles are hardly functional when cleaning them. They also provoke heating differences when used for cooking (Howard 1981: 9;

Rice 1987: 241-242). Inappropriate for cooking are also the characteristic extremely thin walls, as well as the lack of handles for serving hot foods (Rice 1987: 240). These are fragile recipients, easy to break. Consequently, and taking into account the specialised work behind their manufacture, it is unlikely that they were used in everyday domestic activities.

In prehistoric societies pottery decoration was not a simple ornament, but had a valuable intellectual and religious background (David et al. 1988) that our Western modern accounts frequently forget. My detailed study of the dimensions and complex decoration of central Iberia Beaker pottery shows that it was not a vulgar domestic ceramic, but a very special product, with a strong symbolic dimension and profound meanings. There was not only a reduced decorative vocabulary, with certain motifs used only in particular places of the vessels, but designs were also structured around a reduced set of organization patterns with a clear symmetrical logic (Garrido-Pena 2000: 136-167).

Clear differences in the quality of Beaker pottery productions between and within sites are likely to be attributed to an emulation phenomenon. This has been widely documented in prestige item exchange systems, where lower status individuals try to imitate high ranking symbols in their social ascension strategies (Hodder 1982b: 208; Miller 1982: 89-90).

Grave goods are normally abundant in entrepreneur burials and include ritual paraphernalia. Funerals are manipulated in transegalitarian societies in order to reassert the debt structure created by the prominent deceased person (Hayden 1995: 61, 65-66) and where descendants claim their rights to inherit his advantageous and endangered position. Beaker funerals were also extraordinarily important events in Copper Age societies: grave goods were carefully chosen (often even elaborated for that specific purpose - Garrido-Pena 2000: 34-35 and 66) to clearly transmit the desired message to the community, which could explain the remarkable standardization of burial offerings (Thomas 1991a: 129; 1991b: 34-35). In fact, the typological study of central Iberia Beakers shows strikingly high degrees of standardization, especially in pottery forms (Garrido-Pena 2000).

There is an overall and major change in burial customs between the Late Neolithic communal and monumental graves and the Copper Age Beaker ones, stressing the increasing importance of individual burials accompanied by rich grave goods (Rojo et al. 2005). If in megalithic graves the main focus of attention during burial rituals was the tomb (itself a permanent reference in cyclic ceremonies), with the appearance of Bell Beakers that focus seems to have shifted to the dead person's corpse and his selected accompanying objects (Sherratt 1991: 60). Beaker graves of the Spanish Meseta are single primary crouched inhumations, mostly of adults, with unfortunately scarce information about gender, accompanied

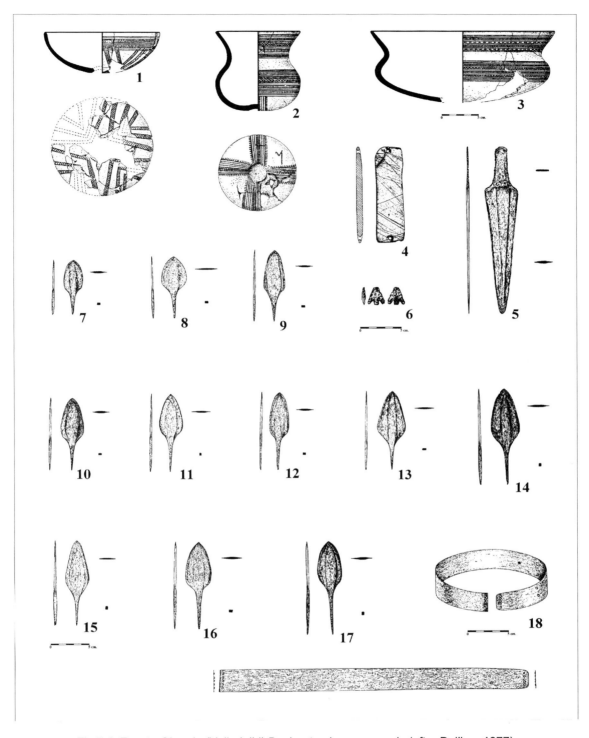

Fig.7.4. Fuente Olmedo (Valladolid) Beaker tomb grave goods (after Delibes 1977).

by rich grave goods (Fig. 7.1 and 7.4), usually arranged near the body or even in contact with it.

Those emergent Beaker leaders would have been interested in interregional exchange systems in their legitimating strategies. Not surprisingly, Hayden (1995: 62) notes that in entrepreneur communities, regional exchange networks should be the largest of all transegalitarian societies, involving generalized elite styles and values. In the absence of the necessary raw material source analysis, the exhaustive multivariate statistic analysis of the spectacular sample of central Iberia Beaker decorations gives important clues to study the different exchange spheres probably functioning during that period, at local, regional and interregional levels (Fig. 7.5, 7.6 and 7.7). The intense and sustained contact between neighbouring groups

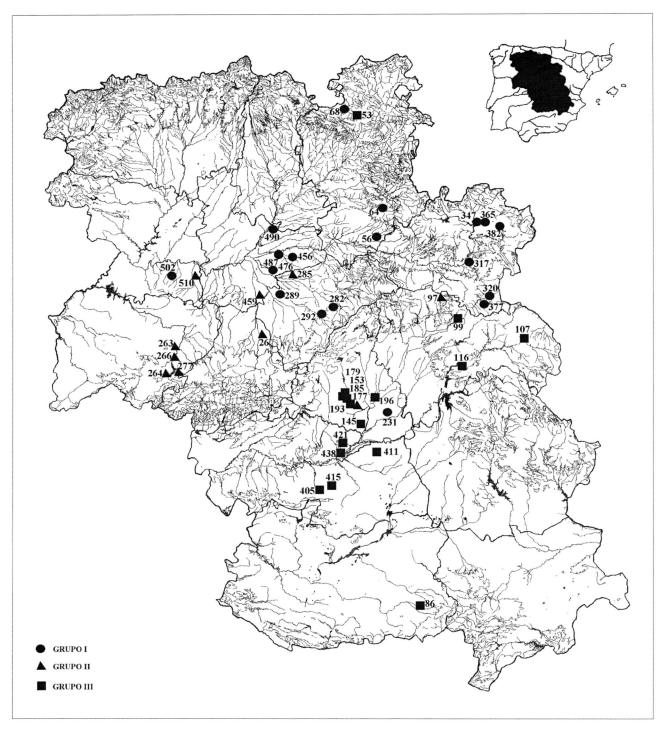

Fig.7.5. Stylistic areas of Ciempozuelos style Inner Iberia Beaker decorations (after Garrido-Pena 2000).

created local decorative patterns emerging from preferred use of some designs, but there was also an interregional continuous flux of exchanges which explains the widespread dispersion of some rare and specific motifs (Fig. 7.6) and schemes, as well as the overall similarities of Beaker decorations throughout so vast a region as central Iberia (Garrido-Pena 2000: 147-167).

Classic hypotheses arguing that the greater the intensity of contact amongst groups, the greater the resulting similarity of pottery designs, through mother-daughter learning designs and marriage exchanges, proposed by "new archaeologists" in the 70's (Plog 1978), have been extensively criticized during the last decade in postprocessual accounts (Hodder 1982a; 1990). This criticism has shown that, in fact, reality is much more complex than those pioneering studies thought, as became clear in diverse ethnoarchaeological observations. Those critiques

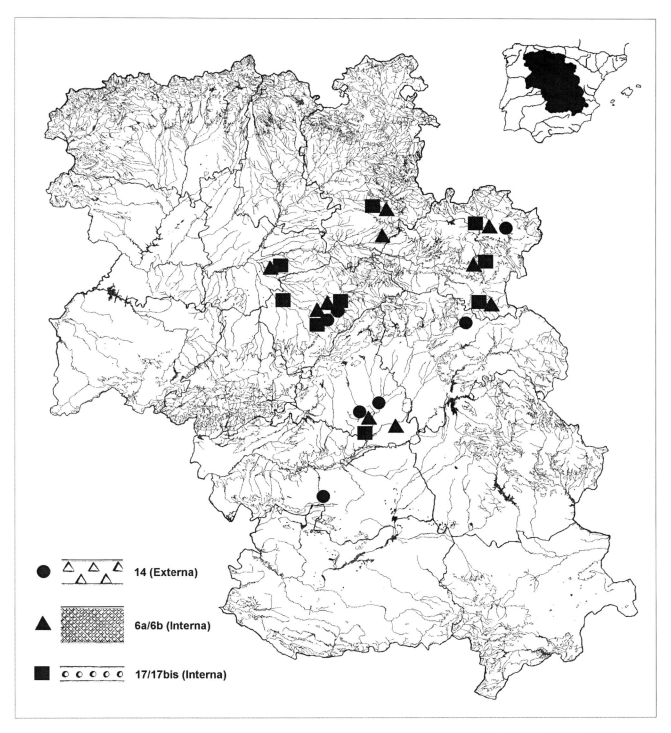

Fig.7.6. Wide geographic distribution of certain rare Inner Iberia Beaker designs (after Garrido-Pena 2000).

stressed the importance of material culture, not just as a passive reflection of past behaviours but as an active character in the social scenario. Style could function as an active communication instrument, and not just as a passive indicator of social contact intensity.

Style does structure people's thinking and approaches to reality (Shanks & Tilley 1987: 148; Hodder 1990: 46), and stylistic similarity is not a direct reflection of the degree of intensity of the interaction between groups. Instead, it is closely related to the sort of relationship that they hold with each other. When there is strong competition for resources and hostility, style tends to be strikingly different, actively marking that situation. When there is a cooperative and mutual economic benefit interaction, pottery designs, for example, tend to be rather similar, even among groups that are physically neighbouring (Hodder 1982a).

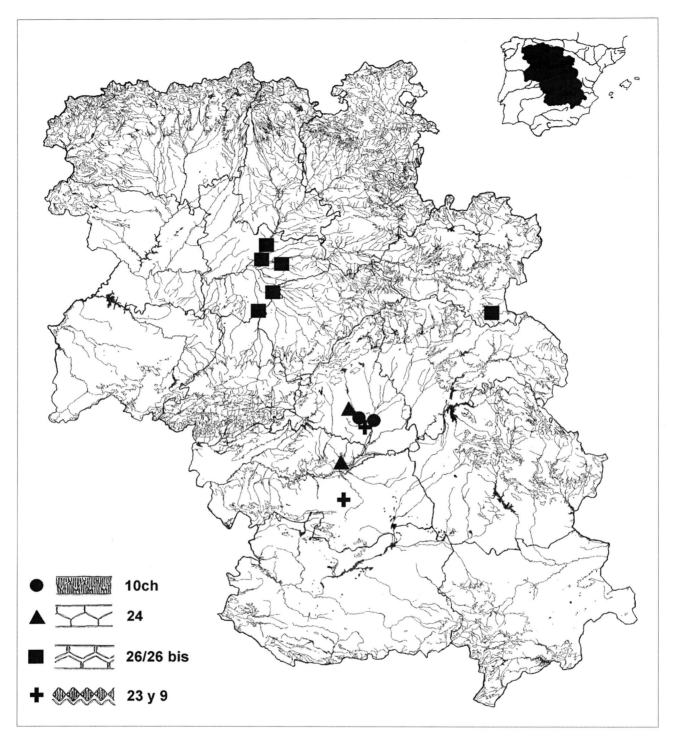

Fig.7.7. Regional and local geographic distribution of certain rare Inner Iberia Beaker designs (after Garrido-Pena 2000).

Perhaps, this is an interesting clue to analyse strong stylistic similarities documented in Copper Age central Iberia, where Bell Beakers exhibit surprising and profound regularities. Taking into account that they were probably luxury and high status commodities, only consumed by emergent leaders seeking to legitimate their unstable position, they may inform us not about interaction intensity between communities but about the kind of contact established between leaders. From this perspective, it is possible to assume that those stylistic similarities could reflect the entrepreneurial quest for mutual support, capable of manipulating those special symbols of power which distinguished the important people from the rest of the common ones, adhering to a successful interregional ideological complex.

Site	14C date	Calibration(2 σ) Ox-Cal v.3.9	Sample	Context and Beaker Style	References
Aldeagordillo (Ávila)	(GrN-19167) 3685±25 b.p.	2150-1970 cal BC	Charcoal	Tomb Ciempozuelos	Fabián (1992)
Cerro del Bu (Toledo)	(I-13.959) 3970±100 b.p.	2900-2100 cal BC	Charcoal	Habitat Maritime	De Álvaro and Pereira, (1990: 205)
Cerro del Bu (Toledo)	(I- 14.416) 3830±100 b.p.	2600-1950 cal BC	Charcoal	Habitat Maritime	De Álvaro and Pereira (1990: 205)
Fuente Olmedo	(CSIC-483) 3620±50 b.p.	2140-1820 cal BC	Human bones	Tomb Ciempozuelos	Martín and Delibes (1989: 81)
Fuente Olmedo	(OxA-2907) 3730±65 b.p.	2340-1930 cal BC	Human bones	Tomb Ciempozuelos	Hedges and others, (1992: 150)
Quintanilla de Arriba	3750±60 b.p.	2400-1960 cal BC	Charcoal	Habitat Ciempozuelos	Rodríguez and Herrán, (1988)
Pajares de Adaja	3870±50 b.p.	2470-2190 cal BC	Human bones	Tomb Ciempozuelos	Delibes and others, 1999: 162
La Sima III	(KIA 17999) 3860±30 b.p.	2460-2200 cal BC	Human bones	Tomb Maritime	Rojo and others, in press
La Sima III	(KIA 18000) 3862±28 b.p.	2460-2200 cal BC	Human bones	Tomb Maritime	Rojo and others, in press

Table 7.1 14C dates from Inner Iberia Beaker contexts.

7.6.- Concluding remarks

Although unfortunately the Copper Age central Iberian archaeological record is still scarce, and we lack many crucial data about socioeconomic changes, the available information seems to fit with the main features of the transegalitarian social model proposed by Hayden (1995), especially in the entrepreneur type. According to this model, emergent leaders use diverse means, such as marriage strategies, competitive feasts and gift exchanges, to reinforce their still weak and unstable position, increasing their economic base and also their personal prestige, with the help of ancestor cult manipulation as well as the control of exchange systems, in which high status and symbolic value items like Bell Beakers were circulating.

The process of social change towards complexity and more stable inequalities finally would have led to the establishment of the first Bronze Age chiefdoms of the Iberian Meseta, although there is still much research to carry out regarding this period. At least, Bell Beakers disappeared, and with them presumably the economic and social structure supporting and explaining them. Perhaps, there was no need for such constant and clear display of status, and competitive feasts and exchange gift systems seemingly faded away. In fact, as the ethnographical record shows, these ostentatious material displays become most pronounced when there is uncertainty in reckoning relative status and positions of power and competition for succession (Hayden 1995: 64).

In chiefdoms, the position of the chiefs tends to be strongly hereditary, competitive feasts no longer appear to serve as primary means of organizing the community and extending general control, and a high degree of eco-

nomic intensification and settlement pattern hierarchy, involving warfare, are documented (Hayden 1995: 63).

The social and economic structures of Bronze Age central Iberia have barely been studied. But once again the available data seems to fit the model. This is at least the case of certain areas with decreasing testimonies of stylistic behaviour, certain degree of ranking in settlement patterns (Muñoz 1993; 2000), warfare, and significant fortified settlements (especially clear in La Mancha Bronze Age "Motillas"). In this sense, the presence of Bell Beakers could be interpreted as a kind of social "thermometer", characteristic of the presumable transition between Neolithic egalitarian communities and Bronze Age chiefdoms. The chronological development of Beakers in a given region would then be reflecting the rhythm of socioeconomic changes. These were probably slow in central Iberia, judging by their long temporal extension (c. 2500-2000 cal BC) (Garrido-Pena 2000: 195-198) (Table 7.1), and rather fast (just one or two centuries – see Harrison 1988) in other areas such as the Southeast.

7.7.- References

ARTHUR, J.W. 2003: "Brewing beer: status, wealth and ceramic use alteration among the Gamo of south-western Ethiopia". *World Archaeology* 34 (3): 516-528.

BERREMAN, G.D. 1981: "Social Inequality: A Cross-Cultural Analysis". In G.D. Berreman (ed.): *Social Inequality. Comparative and Developmental Approaches*. Academic Press. New York: 3-40.

BRODIE, N. 1997: "New Perspectives on the Bell-Beaker Culture". *Oxford Journal of Archaeology* 16 (3): 297-314.

BUENO, P.; BALBÍN, R. de & BARROSO, R. 2000: "Valle de las Higueras (Huecas, Toledo, España). Una necrópolis Ciempozuelos con cuevas artificiales al interior de la Península". *Estudos Pré-Históricos* VIII: 49-80.

CAMERON, C.M. & TOMKA, S.A. 1993: *Abandonment of settlements and regions. Ethnoarchaeological and archaeological approaches.* New Directions in Archaeology. Cambridge University Press. Cambridge.

CASE, H.J. 1995: "Beakers: loosening a stereotype". In I. Kinnes y G. Varndell (eds.): *Unbaked Urns of Rudely Shape.* Oxbow Monographs 55. Oxford: 55-67.

CHAPMAN, R.W. 1997: "All Change? A commentary on Iberian archaeology". In M. Díaz-Andreu & S. Keay (eds.): *The Archaeology of Iberia. The Dynamics of Change.* Routledge. London: 279-292.

CLARKE, D. 1976: "The Beaker network-social and economic models". In J.N. Lanting & J.D. van der Waals (comps.): *Glockenbecher Symposium, Oberried, 1974.* Fibula-van Dishoeck. Bussum/Haarlem: 459-477.

CLARK, J. & BLAKE, M. 1994: "The Power of Prestige: Comparative Generosity and the emergence of Rank Societies in Lowland Mesoamerica". In E. Brumfiel & J. Fox (eds.): *Factional Competition and Political Development in the New World.* Cambridge University Press. Cambridge: 17-30.

DAVID, N., STERNER, J. & GAVUA K. 1988: "Why pots are decorated". *Current Anthropology* 29 (3): 365-379.

DE ÁLVARO, E. & PEREIRA, J. 1990: "El cerro del Bu (Toledo)". *Actas del Primer Congreso de Arqueología de la provincia de Toledo.* Diputación de Toledo. Toledo: 199-213.

DELIBES, G. 1977: *El Vaso Campaniforme en la Meseta Norte española.* Studia Archaeologica, 46. Universidad de Valladolid. Valladolid.

- 1995: "Neolítico y Edad del Bronce". In G. Delibes, S. Moreta, J.I. Gutiérrez & M.A. Mateos (coords.): *Historia de Zamora. Tomo I. De los orígenes al final del Medievo.* Diputación de Zamora, Instituto de Estudios Zamoranos "Florián de Ocampo", Caja España. Zamora: 49-100.

DELIBES, G.; FERNÁNDEZ, J., FONTANEDA, E. & ROVIRA. S. 1999: *Metalurgia de la Edad del Bronce en el piedemonte meridional de la Cordillera Cantábrica. La Colección Fontaneda.* Arqueología en Castilla y León, Monografías, 3. Junta de Castilla y León. Zamora.

DELIBES, G., HERRÁN, J.I., SANTIAGO, J. de & VAL, J. del. 1995: "Evidence for social complexity in the Copper Age of the Northern Meseta". In Lillios, K.T. (ed.): *The Origins of Complex Societies in Late Prehistoric Iberia.* International Monographs in Prehistory, 8. Ann Arbor: 44-63.

DÍAZ-DEL-RÍO, P. 1995: "Campesinado y gestión pluriactiva del ecosistema: Un marco teórico para el análisis del III y II milenios A.C. en la Meseta peninsular". *Trabajos de Prehistoria* 52 (2): 99-109.

- 2001: *La formación del paisaje agrario. Madrid en el III y II milenios BC.* Arqueología, Paleontología y Etnografía, 9. Comunidad de Madrid. Madrid.

- 2004: "Copper Age Ditched Enclosures In Central Iberia". *Oxford Journal of Archaeology* 23 (2): 107-121.

DIETLER, M. 1990: "Driven by Drink: The Role of Drinking in the Political Economy and the Case of Early Iron Age France". *Journal of Anthropological Archaeology* 9: 352-406.

EDMONDS, M. 1995: *Stone Tools and Society. Working Stone in Neolithic and Bronze Age Britain.* Batsford. London.

EDO, M.; FERNÁNDEZ, J.L.; VILLALBA, M.J. & BLASCO, A. 1997: "La calaíta en el cuadrante NW de la Península Ibérica". *II Congreso de Arqueología Peninsular (Zamora, 1996),* vol. II. Zamora: 99-121.

ESPADAS, J.J.; POYATO, M.C. & CABALLERO, A. 1987: "Memoria preliminar de las excavaciones del yacimiento calcolítico de El Castellón (Villanueva de los Infantes, Ciudad Real)". *Oretum* III: 41-78.

FABIÁN GARCÍA, J.F. 1992: "El enterramiento campaniforme Túmulo 1 de Aldeagordillo (Ávila)". *Boletín del Seminario de Estudios de Arte y Arqueología* LVIII: 97-132.

FEINMAN, G.M. 1995: "The Emergence of Inequality. A Focus on Strategies and Processes". In T.D. Price & G.M. Feinman (eds.): *Foundations of Social Inequality.* Plenum Press. New York: 255-279.

FRIED, M. 1967: *The Evolution of Political Society: An Essay in Political Archaeology.* Random House. New York.

GARRIDO-PENA, R. 1994: "El fenómeno campaniforme en la región de Madrid: actualización de la evidencia empírica y nuevas propuestas teóricas". *Estudios de Prehistoria y Arqueología Madrileñas* 9: 67-90.

- 1995: "El Campaniforme en la Meseta sur: nuevos datos y propuestas teóricas". *Complutum* 6: 123-151.

- 1997: "Bell Beakers in the Southern Meseta of the Iberian Peninsula: socioeconomic context and new data". *Oxford Journal of Archaeology* 16 (2): 187-209.

- 2000: *El Campaniforme en la Meseta Central de la Península Ibérica (c. 2500-2000 A.C.).* British Archaeological Reports International Series S892. Oxford.

GARRIDO, R. & MUÑOZ, K. 2000: "Visiones sagradas para los líderes". *Complutum* 11: 285-300.

GILMAN, A. 1976: "Bronze Age dynamics in southeast Spain". *Dialectical Anthropology* 1: 307-319.

- 1985: *Land-use and Prehistory in South-East Spain.* The London Research Series in Geography, 8. George Allen & Unwin. London.

- 1987: "Regadío y conflicto en sociedades acéfalas", *Boletín del Seminario de Estudios de Arte y Arqueología* 53: 59-72.

- 1997: "Cómo valorar los sistemas de propiedad a partir de datos arqueológicos". *Trabajos de Prehistoria* 54 (2): 81-92.

HARRISON, R.J. 1988: "Bell Beakers in Spain and Portugal: working with radiocarbon dates in the 3rd millenium B.C.". *Antiquity* 62: 464-472.

- 1995: "Bronze Age expansion 1750-1250 BC: The Cogotas I phase in the middle Ebro valley". *Veleia* 12: 67-77.

HAYDEN, B. 1995: "Pathways to Power. Principles for Creating Socioeconomic Inequalities". In T.D. Price.& G.M. Feinman (eds.): *Foundations of Social Inequality*. Plenum Press. New York: 15-86.

- 1996: "Feasting in prehistoric and traditional societies". In P. Wiessner and W. Schiefenhovel (eds.): *Food and the status quest*. Berghahn Books. Providence: 127-147.

- 2001: "Fabulous feasts: A prolegomenon to the importance of feasting". In M. Dietler and B. Hayden (eds.): *Feasts: Archaeological and Ethnographic Perspectives on Food, Politics, and Power*. Smithsonian Institution Press. Washington, DC: 23-64.

HEDGES, R.E.M.; HOUSLEY, R.A.; BRONK, C.R. & VAN KLINKEN, G.J. 1992: "Radiocarbon Dates from the Oxford AMS System: Archaeometry Datelist 14", *Archaeometry* 34 (1): 141-159.

HODDER, I. 1982a: "Society, economy and culture: an ethnographic case study amongst the Lozi". In I. Hodder; G. Isaac y N. Hammond (eds.): *Pattern of the Past: Studies in honour of David Clarke*. Cambridge University Press. Cambridge: 67-95.

- 1982b: "Towards a Contextual Approach to Prehistoric Exchange". In J.E. Ericson & T.K. Earle (eds.): *Contexts for prehistoric exchange*. Academic Press. New York: 199-211.

- 1990: "Style as historical quality". In M. Conkey and C. Hastorf (eds.): *The uses of style in archaeology*. Cambridge University Press. 44-51.

HOWARD, H. 1981: "In the wake of distribution: towards an integrated approach to ceramic studies in prehistoric Britain". In H. Howard & E.L. Morris (eds.): *Production and Distribution: a Ceramic Viewpoint*. British Archaeological Reports International Series 120: 1-30.

JOHNSON, A.W. & EARLE, T. 1987: *The Evolution of Human Societies: from foraging groups to agrarian state*. Stanford University Press. Stanford.

LÓPEZ, P. (coord.) 1997. *El paisaje vegetal de la Comunidad de Madrid durante el Holoceno final*. Arqueología, Paleontología y Etnografía, 5. Comunidad de Madrid. Madrid.

MARTÍN, R. & DELIBES, G. 1989: *La cultura del vaso campaniforme en las campiñas meridionales del Duero: el enterramiento de Fuente Olmedo (Valladolid)*. Monografía nº 1 del Museo Arqueológico de Valladolid. Valladolid.

MILLER, D. 1982: "Structures and strategies: an aspect of the relationship between social hierarchy and cultural change". In I. Hodder (ed.): *Symbolic and Structural Archaeology*. Cambridge University Press. Cambridge: 89-98.

MOLINA, F.; RODRÍGUEZ-ARIZA, M.O.; JIMÉNEZ, S. & BOTELLA, M. (2003): "La sepultura 121 del yacimiento argárico de El Castellón Alto (Galera, Granada)". *Trabajos de Prehistoria* 60 (1): 153-158.

MONTERO, I.; RODRÍGUEZ, S. & ROJAS, J.M. 1990: *Arqueometalurgia de la provincia de Toledo: Minería y recursos minerales de cobre*. Excma. Diputación Provincial de Toledo, Servicio de Arqueología. Toledo.

MORALES, A. 1992: "Estudio de la fauna del yacimiento calcolítico de Las Pozas (Casaseca de las Chanas, Zamora). Campaña 1979". *Boletín del Seminario de Estudios de Arte y Arqueología* LVIII: 65-96.

MORALES MUÑIZ, A. & LIESAU VON LETTOW-VORBECK, C. 1994: "Arqueozoología del Calcolítico en Madrid: Ensayo crítico de síntesis". In C. Blasco (ed.): *El Horizonte Campaniforme de la Región de Madrid en el centenario de Ciempozuelos*. Universidad Autónoma de Madrid. Madrid: 227-247.

MORALES MUÑIZ, A. & VILLEGAS BRONCANO, C. 1994: "La fauna de mamíferos del yacimiento de 'El Ventorro': síntesis osteológica de la campaña de 1981". *Estudios de Prehistoria y Arqueología Madrileñas* 9: 35-56.

MUÑOZ LÓPEZ-ASTILLEROS, K. 2000: "The Tagus Middle Basin (Iberian Peninsula) from the Neolithic to the Iron Age (V-I millennium Cal. B.C.): The Long Way to Social Complexity". *Oxford Journal of Archaeology* 19 (3): 241-272.

PARKER PEARSON, M. 1993: "The Powerful Dead: Archaeological Relationships between the Living and the Dead". *Cambridge Archaeological Journal* 3 (2): 203-229.

PLOG, S. 1978: "Social interaction and stylistic similarity: a reanalisis". In M.B. Schiffer (ed.): *Advances in Archaeological Method and Theory*, I: 144-182.

PRIEGO, M. C. & QUERO, S. 1992. *El Ventorro, un poblado prehistórico de los albores de la metalurgia*. Estudios de Prehistoria y Arqueología Madrileñas, 8. Madrid.

RICE, P.M. 1987: *Pottery Analysis. A Sourcebook*. University of Chicago Press. Chicago.

RODRÍGUEZ, J.A. & HERRÁN, J.I. 1988: "Informe sobre la excavación de urgencia realizada en el yacimiento de El Pico del Castro, Quintanilla de Arriba (Valladolid)". Unpublished Report. Servicio territorial de Cultura de Valladolid. Valladolid.

ROJO, M.A.; GARRIDO, R.; GARCÍA, I. & MORÁN, G. in press: "Tombs and settlements in the Landscape: The Ambrona Valley (Soria, Spain) Beaker sequence". *The "Beaker Days" in Bohemia and Moravia (*Prague-Brno 2004*)*. British Archaeological Reports International Series. Oxford.

ROJO, M.A.; GARRIDO, R.; MORÁN, G. & KUNST, M. 2004: "El Campaniforme en el Valle de Ambrona (Soria, España): dinámica de poblamiento y aproximación a su contexto social". In M. Besse & J. Desideri (eds.): *Graves and Funerary Rituals during the Late Neolithic and the Early Bronze Age in Europe (2700 – 2000 BC). Proceedings of the International Conference held at the Cantonal Archaeological Museum, Sion (Switzerland) October 4th - 7th 2001*. British Archaeological Reports International Series 1284. Oxford: 5-13.

ROJO, M.A. & KUNST, M. 1999a: "La Lámpara y La Peña de La Abuela. Propuesta secuencial del Neolítico Interior en el ámbito funerario". *II Congrés del Neolític a la Península Ibèrica* (Valencia 1999). *Saguntum Extra 2*: 503-512.

- 1999b: "Zur Neolithisierung des Inneren der Iberischen Halbinsen. Erste Ergebnisse des interdisziplinären, spanisch-deustchen Forschungsprojekts zur Entwicklung einer prähistorischen Siedlungskammer in der Umgebung von Ambrona (Soria, Spanien)". *Madrider Mitteilungen*, 40: 1-52.

- 1999c: "El Valle de Ambrona: un ejemplo de la primera colonización Neolítica de las tierras del Interior Peninsular". *II Congrés del Neolític a la Península Ibèrica* (Valencia 1999). *Saguntum Extra 2*: 259-270.

ROJO, M.; KUNST, M.; GARRIDO, R.; GARCÍA, I. & MORÁN, G. 2005: *Un Desafío a la Eternidad. Tumbas Monumentales del Valle de Ambrona*. Memorias. Arqueología en Castilla y León 14. Junta de Castilla y León. Soria.

ROJO, M. A.; MORÁN, G. & KUNST, M. 2003: "Un défi à L'Éternité: genèse et réutilisations du tumulus de La Sima (Miño de Medinaceli, Soria, Espagne). *Sens dessus dessous. La recherche en Préhistoire. Receuil d'études offert à Jean Leclerc et Claude Masset. Revue Archéologique de Picardie*, nº Special 21: 173-184.

ROSCOE, P. (2000): "New Guinea Leadership as Ethnographic Analogy: a critical review". *Journal of Archaeological Method and Theory*, 7 (2): 79-126.

SERVICE, E. 1971: *Primitive Social Organization*. 2nd edition. Random House. New York.

SHANKS, M. & TILLEY, C. 1987: *Reconstructing Archaeology. Theory and Practice*. New Studies in Archaeology, Cambridge University Press. Cambrigde.

SHERRATT, A. 1981: "Plough and pastoralism: aspects of the secondary products revolution". In I. Hodder, G. Isaac y N. Hammond (eds.): *Pattern of the past. Studies in Honour of David Clarke*. Cambridge University Press. Cambridge: 261-305.

- 1987: "Cups that Cheered". In W.H. Waldren y R.C. Kennard (comps.): *Bell Beakers of the Western Mediterranean. Definition, interpretation, theory and new site data. The Oxford International Conference 1986*. British Archaeological Reports International Series 331. Oxford: 81-114.

- 1991: "Sacred and profane substances: the ritual use of narcotics in Later Neolithic Europe". In P. Garwood, D. Jennings, R. Skeates and J. Toms (eds.): *Sacred and Profane: Proceedings of a conference on archaeology, ritual and religion*. Oxford University Committee for Archaeology Monographs 32. Oxford: 50-64.

- 1997: *Economy and Society in Prehistoric Europe. Changing perspectives*. Edinburgh University Press. Edinburgh.

THOMAS, J. 1987: "Relations of production and social change in the Neolithic of North-West Europe". *MAN* 22 (3): 405-430.

- 1991a: *Rethinking the Neolithic*. Cambridge University Press. Cambridge.

- 1991b: "Reading the Body: Beaker Funerary Practice in Britain". In P. Garwood, D. Jennings, R. Skeates and J. Toms (eds.): *Sacred and Profane: Proceedings of a Conference on Archaeology, Ritual and Religion*. Oxford University Committee for Archaeology Monographs 32. Oxford: 33-42.

VAL, J. del & HERRÁN, J.I. 1995: "El Calcolítico precampaniforme en el Duero Medio". In M. Kunst (coord.): *Origens, Estruturas e Relacoes das Culturas Calcolíticas da Península Ibérica*. Actas das I Jornadas Arqueológicas de Torres Vedras (3-5 Abril 1987). Trabalhos de Arqueologia 7. Lisboa : 293-304.

VENCL, S. 1994: "The Archaeology of Thirst". *Journal of European Archaeology* 2 (2): 299-326.

WALDREN, W.H. 1995: "The function of Balearic Bell Beaker pottery as a ceremonial and votive object". In W.H. Waldren, J.A. Ensenyat & R.C. Kennard (eds.): *Ritual, Rites and Religion in Prehistory*. IIIrd Deyá International Conference of Prehistory 2: 238-263.

WASON, P.K. 1994: *The archaeology of rank*. New Studies in Archaeology. Cambridge University Press. Cambridge.

CHAPTER 8

Inequalities and Power.
Three millennia of Prehistory in Mediterranean Spain
(5600 – 2000 cal BC)

Joan Bernabeu Aubán
Lluis Molina Balaguer
Agustín Diez Castillo
Teresa Orozco Köhler
Universidad de Valencia

Abstract

This paper focuses on recent discoveries made in the central valleys of the Spanish Mediterranean coast. Fresh evidence recovered from this area allows us to propose some alternative pathways in the development of power and social inequalities, using an approach based on non-linear systems and the so called chaos-complexity theory. In archaeological terms, non-linear systems can explain cycles of power and complexity in richer ways than classical Braudelian theories, thus giving more relevance to concepts such as conjuncture and historical contingency. This paper is an attempt to explain why, with the arrival of agriculturalist pioneers to the Mediterranean West, power and social inequalities rapidly emerged, showing how they were maintained and also why they collapsed.

Keywords: Spanish Mediterranean Valleys; Neolithic; Copper Age; Bronze Age; Monuments; Communal Feasts; Chaos Theory; Social Inequalities.

Resumen

Este artículo parte de descubrimientos hechos recientemente en los valles centrales de la costa mediterránea española para proponer rutas alternativas en la interpretación del desarrollo del poder y las desigualdades sociales, utilizando una aproximación basada en los sistemas no lineales y la denominada teoría del caos-complejidad. En términos arqueológicos, los sistemas no lineales pueden explicar ciclos de poder y complejidad de forma más elaborada que las teorías braudelianas sobre ciclos, dando así más relevancia a conceptos tales como la coyuntura y la contingencia histórica. Este artículo es un intento de explicar por qué, con la llegada de los pioneros agrícolas al Oeste mediterráneo, emergieron rápidamente formas de poder y desigualdad social, mostrando cómo fueron sostenidas y también por qué desaparecieron.

Palabras clave: Valles mediterráneos españoles; Neolítico; Edad del Cobre; Edad del Bronce; Monumentos; Banquetes Comunales; Teoría del Caos; Desigualdad Social.

8.1.- Change and evolution

As in most of Europe, Spanish research has traditionally centred the debate on the formation and development of "complex societies" around the Bronze Age. There are two aspects that have most influenced our understanding of social complexity in Spanish Prehistory: the enormous weight of the archaeological record from the Southeast, and the theoretical development of Spanish archaeology itself.

In the first case, the early research of the Siret brothers, at El Argar or Los Millares, has been a constant reference for the discussion of social inequality in Iberian Prehistory. Contributions by authors such as V. Lull (1983), C. Mathers (1984), R. Chapman (1991) and A. Gilman (1976; 1987), to mention but a few, have marked waypoints in the route of Spanish archaeology on this subject. In the second case, different theoretical approaches in recent decades share, in spite of their differences, two common relevant characteristics:

- A classic evolutionist approach that tends to present change as a series of linear and cumulative dynamic processes, in which every period has its roots in the previous phases, developing them.

- The considerable importance of materialist and Marxist positions, where inequality development is tied to class formation. As a consequence, the recognition of pristine state formations becomes a first order issue.

The combination of both perspectives has hindered the explanation of the persistent absence of class/state forms in diverse regions of the Iberian Peninsula. In other words, it has not been able to explain why most of the regions do not seem to evolve in accordance with the proposed model.

97

One consequence of both aspects has been that, in the search of the origins of social complexity within the communities of the second millennium BC, indicators of inequality have been found to be similar to those documented later on: villages with the size and constructive complexity of Marroquíes Bajos (Zafra *et al.* 1999) or La Pijotilla (Hurtado 1997) are no different from the Los Millares traditional references, expanding in both time and space the "inequality" stage of the Iberian archaeological record. As a result, in the first place, the term class society has been applied to periods previous to the Bronze Age (Nocete 1989; 2001), and, on the other hand, the debate about pristine states in most recent phases has been opened, launching the discussion of the value that must be given to different archaeological indicators (Nocete 1989; Lull & Risch 1995; Gilman 1997).

On the other hand, recent developments in diverse fields have remarked the importance of nonlinear systems. From Thermodynamics (Prygorine 1996) to Life Sciences (Kauffman 2003), there seems to be an increasing interest towards nonlinear dynamics, open and complex systems, emergency, responses to initial conditions, etc. These concepts are all handled and proposed from theoretical positions that could be summarized, following Bintliff (2003: 80), as the chaos-complexity theory (or theories). Its impact in Archaeology is more and more evident (Van der Leeuw & McGlade 1997; Bentley & Maschner 2003), even from diverse theoretical standpoints: neo-evolutionism (Shennan 2002), materialism (Rowlands & Gledhill 1998) or post-processualism (Shanks & Tilley 1987). In this view, human societies are conceived of as open systems, where energy and relations flow in every direction, following both centripetal and centrifugal forces that push them out of equilibrium. Such complexity makes the system unpredictable when asserting directional changes or, otherwise, makes it more sensitive to start point conditions. In this way, similar factors at different historical moments and places will have different consequences (Bentley & Maschner 2003: 2). Under this perspective, concepts like contingency and conjuncture gain more relevance.

All this takes us to a point where it becomes necessary to recognize situations of rupture, or blockade, as well as transformation or dissolution processes between different "social endeavours" set out by different human groups. A diachronic view would appear as twisted cycles without a precise direction: series of ruptures and discontinuities affecting periods of social reproduction of variable duration.

From the inside, communities are viewed as a complex of social networks where each of the involved agents (individuals, households, clans, villages, and so on) has different interests. From this frame of superposed social networks, power occurs (Mann 1986). Power must be interpreted as an emergent quality of certain social networks: it is not an objective in itself, but a means by which to obtain other ends. Inequality, on the other hand, must be

better understood as a consequence of power. Both concepts must be differentiated from stratification and state. As we will demonstrate, power and inequality developments - even impressive ones- did not achieve increasing stratification or states.

Power, as such, is twofold: one side is oriented towards the group, the sum of different interests improves individual results; the other side is restrictive, on the basis of the existence of agents (individuals, families, clans, villages...) with special functions when contributing to the collective or group. Resolution of this kind of contradiction between both sides will define the process of social hierarchisation: institutionalisation of redistributive power (a sort of "zero-sum game," where the amount of power that is gained by some will be lost by others) occurs parallel to stratification and state (Mann 1986: 6-10).

From this point of view, we can understand why in none of the cases of unequal development found in the Late Prehistory of Iberia (even the most paradigmatic ones), do we document indicators of state formations that are not subject to criticism or alternative interpretations (Díaz-del-Río 2004). Some works (Bernabeu *et al.* 2003; Gibaja 2003) even suggest that key aspects such as inheritance, greater capacity of mobilization of manual labour, or control of the circuits of exchange, can be documented in older phases, dating back, in some cases, to the sixth millennium BC where no indicator of either social stratification or state-like organization can be sustained.

It is our view that throughout the Holocene there were different consecutive cycles marked by the development of power networks. All of them produce some kind of inequality, which is rooted in different aspects of the social arena. A tendency to consolidate a determined power situation by the implied agents, along with the resistance of non-favoured agents, will influence its own development. But historical contingency demands to consider the influence of other external factors that we are not always able to consider in their full extent.

This paper attempts to create an initial approach to the development of power and inequality in Iberian Late Prehistory based upon a combination of diverse ways to confront social complex systems (Bentley & Maschner 2003) and power networks (Mann 1986).

8.2.- Geographical setting: central Mediterranean valleys of the Iberian Peninsula

We depart from the examination of two of the most traditional indicators of social inequality: the capacity to mobilize manual labour and the generation and appropriation of agricultural surpluses. Our study is centred in an area that is marginal with respect to the traditional south-

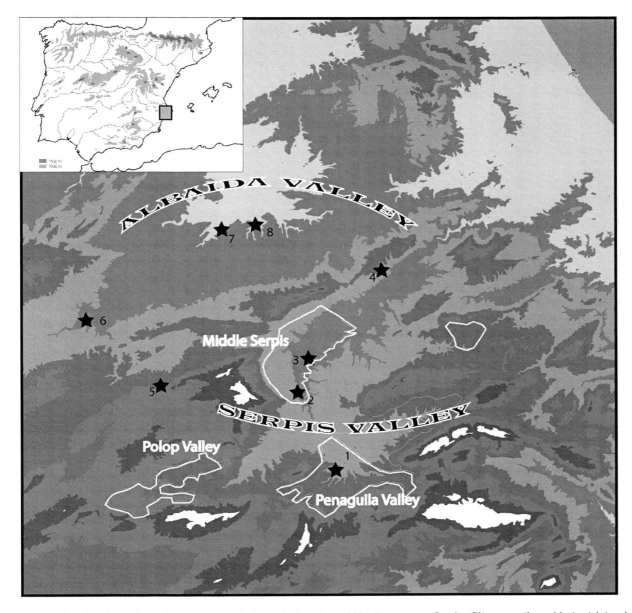

Fig. 8.1. The Serpis and the Albaida valleys the central region of Mediterranean Spain. Sites mentioned in text (stars) and systematic survey areas are indicated (highlighted). 1) Mas d'Is; 2) Jovades; 3) Niuet; 4) Cova de l'Or; 5) Cova de la Sarsa; 6) Arenal de la Costa; 7) Colata; 8) Missena

eastern contexts for which these themes have been discussed: the central section of the Iberian Mediterranean coast or, more precisely, the central valleys of the Valencia region (Fig. 8.1). In order to give some temporal depth to our analysis, we have chosen to examine the span between 5600 and 2000 BC, that is, from the establishment of the first Neolithic communities to the beginning of the Bronze Age.

This geographic area includes an extensive territory with a varied topography: from the coastal strip, with changing characteristics from the shore (littoral area, sandy beaches and cliffs), to the highland zones, where a series of valleys have been shaped following different directions. All these reliefs are located in the outer zone of the Béticas ranges, with ENE-WSW orientation. These axes mark the

direction of the main fluvial courses: the Serpis (or Riu d'Alcoi) and the Albaida rivers.

The high and middle Serpis basins are formed by a series of small convergent fluvial courses that usually adopt the name of the small valleys that they cross (Penàguila, Barxell-Polop, Agres, Alcalà, Ceta, etc.). Systematic surveys have been carried out on some of them and preliminary results have also been published (Barton *et al.* 2004; Bernabeu *et al.* 1999). Further North, the neighbouring Albaida basin, which is larger than the Serpis, is drained by the river of the same name. Both connect with the coastal plain through diverse carved valleys.

The diversity of ecological niches within this region has

Neolithic I A	Cardial Ware Horizon	(*c.* 5550-5200 BC). It could be divided in 2 moments (5550-5400 BC; 5400-5200 BC)
Neolithic I B.	Incised and no-cardial impressed Ware Horizon.	(*c.* 5200-5050 BC)
Neolithic I C.	Brushed Ware Horizon.	(*c.* 5050-4550 BC). It could be divided in 2 phases (5050-4900 BC; 4900-4550 BC).
Neolithic II A	Carved Ware Horizon.	(*c.* 4550-4200 BC). Lack of information *c.* 4200-3900 BC.
Neolithic II B.	Plain Pottery Horizon.	(*c.* 3900-2800 BC)
HCT.	Bell Beaker Horizon.	(*c.* 2800-2200 BC)
Bronze Age.		(*c.* 2200-1400 BC)

Table 8.1 Cultural sequence of the central Spanish Mediterranean Coast from Neolithic time to the Bronze Age

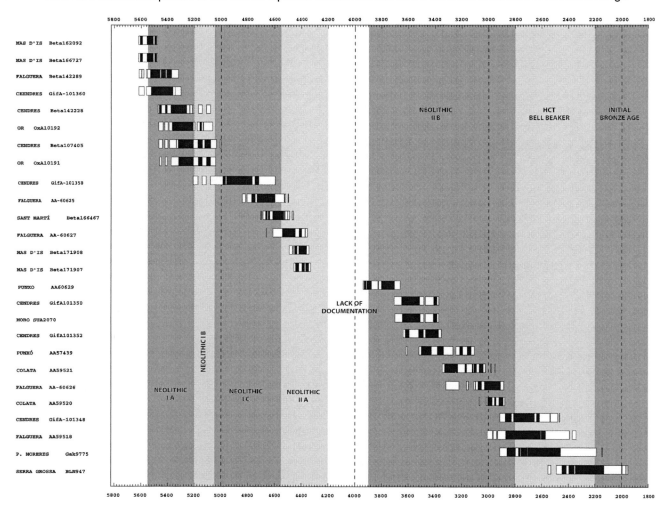

Fig.8.2. Datings on short life samples from the Early Neolithic to the Bronze Age, in the study area.

favoured human presence in Late Prehistory. Thus, archaeological investigations, beginning at the end of 19th century, have highlighted an important number of human deposits dated within the Holocene. In more recent dates, several excavations of Neolithic villages have completed the information available in both valleys.

Despite sample limitations, the available information allows us to approach the strategies and management of power. We will basically use data coming from the areas that have been subject to systematic survey, comple-

mented with other data from the Serpis and the Albaida valleys. In some cases, precise references to other Iberian zones will be provided as needed for comparative purposes.

8.2.1.- Chronology

Stratified assemblages coming from different excavations have allowed the proposal of a regional chronological sequence on the basis of ceramic evolution criteria (Bernabeu 1989). Table 1 synthesizes the well-established cultural sequence for this region. The oldest phase (Neolithic I) shows an iconographic and formal repertoire related to the cultural tradition of the Mediterranean impressed-ware ceramics, the so-called cardial decoration. In later phases (since the Neolithic II), there is a typological development of open vessels and a process of marginalization of decorations in ceramics. To date, a wide series of C-14 datings on short life samples (in order to avoid the old wood effect) have shed some light on the chronological framework, showing a clear hiatus between c. 4200 and c. 3900 BC (Fig. 8.2). Earlier Neolithic periods have proven more susceptible to detailed chronological subdivision than recent ones. The evolution of ceramic typology and decoration indicates phases of around 150-300 years for the period c. 5600-4200 BC. However, between 3900-1400 BC, the defined phases last between c. 600 and 1100 years.

8.2.2.- Dynamics of landscape occupation

The dynamics of landscape occupation can be used as a first approach to the study of social evolution. In order to obtain an acceptable reading of settlement occupation through time, the number of sites and the estimated extension occupied by each of them have been compared. In order to avoid irregularities in the samples, only information coming from valleys of the Serpis basin (which have been subject to systematic survey) is used. A more detailed picture will be obtained with data coming from non-surveyed areas in the Serpis basin, as well as from the Albaida drainage basin.

Figure 8.3 represents the relationship between both variables with periods of different duration. Quantification has been made for each phase, independently of how long they last.[1] In the graphics, the results are shown by centuries, each one being assigned the total amount obtained by period. Thus, all the 30 sites considered Neolithic IIB are also represented in each century of its span. Size is noted in hectares, with ranges of 0.5 ha. The scale in both cases is semi logarithmic to better visualize low values.

In the first case (Fig. 8.3-B), the periods are the real ones (that is to say, they reflect our present capacity to discern between phases). As can be observed, they are transposed in different time scales of representation in the same graph (150-300 year periods before c. 4200 BC; and larger ones, 600-1000 years, after 3900 BC). In order to avoid (or at least to evaluate) the effect of these changes in scale, Figure 8.3-A represents the same data but with a similar span for old phases, so time periods last as long as those of more recent phases. Thus, old phases have been grouped in only two periods: c. 5550-4900 BC and c. 4900-4200 BC.

In spite of their differences, both graphs reflect, first, that settlement dynamics are not so linear. The presence of cycles, with remarkable increases and decreases in both the number of sites and the total extension is evident. The difference between both graphs is that the larger periods

in the Figure 8.3-A give an image of more stability (continuity). This situation is a precise view of what is known about the kind of settlements in the area from the Neolithic to the Bronze Age. If Neolithic settlements are characterized by a low number of structures, reflecting an important and variable distance between different houses, during the Bronze Age settlements are much smaller with a larger number of houses (therefore denser) and are usually walled. We could be talking about true fortified settlements.

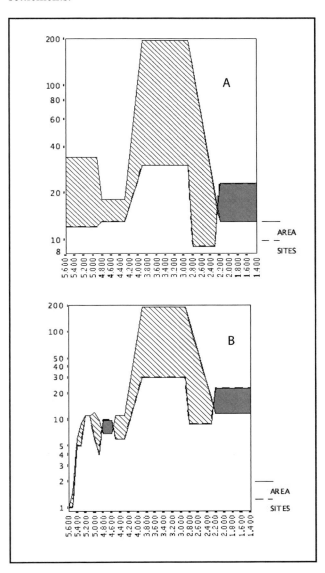

Fig.8.3. Number of surface collections and extension occupied by them (in Ha). A) information per similar periods of time. In this case old phases have been grouped to make them equivalent to recent recent ones; B) information per actual time periods. Further details in text.

The above description could correspond to the evidence of long cycles, and the persistence throughout time of certain ways of life, which are abruptly altered in certain occasions. Using a resemblance of the Chaos Theory, it could be thought that the tendency towards the occupation of the territory in a dispersed way constitutes the attractor that tends towards the primitive agricultural system. This tendency only seems to change between the Bell Beaker and the Bronze Age. Of course, within these great cycles of apparent stability, fluctuations occur. Such fluctuations seem to mark periods of greater or smaller population aggregation. This aspect is clearer when we descend to a greater chronological detail, as occurs in the period c. 5600-4200 BC (Fig. 8.3-B).

In effect, after an initial period of about 150 years in which settlements and occupied area increase in parallel, two successive periods (c. 5400-5300 BC and c. 5050-4900 BC) are observed in which the number of establishments is stable, or decreases. However, the total occupied extension increases. On the contrary, the middle period c. 5200-5050 BC supposes an increase of the number of establishments, but not of the total occupied area.

Previous dynamics could be understood as the repetition of aggregation-dispersion cycles where the changes that are introduced do not reach a rupture point to modify the system as a whole. Nevertheless, what happens after c. 4900 BC seems to exceed this logic. Between this date and c. 4550 BC there is a dispersion phenomenon of much greater importance. Here settlements are more numerous, but the extension occupied is smaller. The rupture is unambiguous and it suggests a collapse of the system, something that is very similar to what seems to happen during the Bronze Age.

Given the similarity between the early and recent periods (before and after the hiatus, when greater time scales are considered - see Fig. 8.3-A), we may suppose that these finer cycles also could be observed in recent phases if we were able to look at analogous time periods. As a consequence, a type of fractal geometry would be formed, in which it would not matter at what scale we look at the data since they seem to always behave in the same way, although the explanations can be different.

Yet, this does not mean that we can read the graphs as a repetition of the same cycles throughout 4000 years of Prehistory without any changes. The other option seems more accurate: changes are constant throughout time, although the cycles never are repeated in the same way. In other words, each cycle starts in the resolution of conflicts that characterize the previous conjuncture, constituting a new frame of relations. Therefore, what has happened previously leaves its track in the new social context, in such a way that each cycle does not return to the departure point. The graphical indication of this dynamic can be similar, to some extent, to the representation of the degree of organizational coherence in the exchange systems of the human groups of southern Papua (Van der Leeuw 1987; fig 7).

Recent proposals (Díaz-del-Río 2004) that have attempted to explain similar behaviour patterns in the Chal-

colithic of the Iberian Southeast as cycles of aggregation and conditional dispersion, basically responding to two variables - capacity to control labour (concentration) and presence of factions (superposed social networks and with non-coincident interests) – do not seem to fit with the data. Extended over time, it would only reach to describe the cyclical repetition but not changes that are introduced after their definition.

In the following sections we will try to expand on these questions by evaluating two different aspects: labour force mobilization and capacity to increase production.

8.3. Monuments and the mobilisation of work force

Investment in communal work by prehistoric groups is a variable that can explicitly serve as an indicator of the degree of power developed within them. But investment in collective works is not the only archaeological correlate of power, since aspects related to agricultural intensification can also be treated as an indicator of power. Regardless of the mechanisms that make those profits possible, both variables can be seen as indicators of the capacity of labour mobilisation and, therefore, of the power of some members of the society. In this section we will analyse the mobilisation of work force aimed at the construction of collective structures. Some of them usually could be considered monuments, but others cannot be considered as such.

Monumental architecture helps to structure and give sense to the social world in different ways. It plays an active role in the social construction of reality by local groups, and serves as a key piece for the definition of group identity. But social ties are also reinforced through special events, like banquets or feasts–communal consumption of food and/or drink–that offer the possibility of mobilising large amounts of manual labour. At the same time, they serve as aggregation arenas and as transformations of values and power relations (Dietler & Hayden 2001). The nature of these banquets can be diverse (sacred, profane), as well as their temporality (seasonal, exceptional, etc.).

According to our research, three different kinds of collective work can be found among the communities under research, namely: monumental enclosures, habitat enclosures and terraces and stonewalls. The two first categories fit quite well in what have been considered undefined communal work and where "work feasts" can be deployed. Nevertheless, there are remarkable differences among them. Monumental causewayed ditches in the Serpis valley are located close to the villages, but not in the inhabited space (Bernabeu et al. 2003). Their chronology goes from the beginnings of the Neolithic until c. 3800 BC -although with interruptions- after which time their construction stops. Habitat enclosures have been

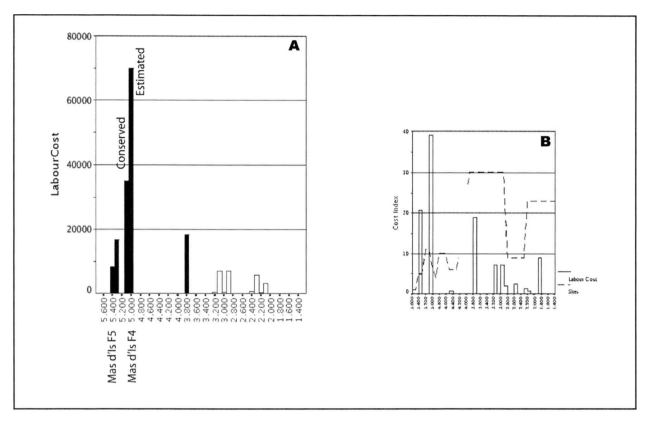

Fig.8.4. Comparison between total labor investment (hours per person) in segmented ditches.
A) comparison on the basis of actual costs of preserved enclosures (left) and inferred total extension (right);
B) Costs standardization for 1 m long segment. Overlayed appears a curve of the number of settlements per period.

documented from the end of the Neolithic IIB onwards. Available dates show that the oldest one would be Niuet (Bernabeu *et al.* 1994), whose date of construction is around c. 3200 BC. After this moment, the following dated enclosure corresponds to the end of the Bell Beaker phase (*c.* 2300 BC) at Arenal de la Costa, in the neighbouring Albaida valley (Bernabeu 1993).

Both kinds of enclosures seem to be formed by segmented ditches, but their resemblances stop there. The monumental enclosures are formed by great ditches of different dimensions, but with conserved transects longer than 40 m, and in some cases more than 80 m in each segment. Domestic structures have not been documented within them. Habitat enclosures, on the contrary, are of smaller dimensions, and their segments never reach 30 m. In two excavated cases, domestic spaces have been located in the interior. Despite being simple architectonic elements, the necessary investment of work for their construction must have been remarkable. There are numerous studies in which the quantification of labour investment has been treated, although there are less studies based on direct experimentation using prehistoric technology (and in most cases they refer to constructions of great dimensions such as temples or nuraghes, among others). In the case of excavated structures or ditches, the most frequently used estimation is of 10 working hours to excavate 1 m^3 (Andersen 1997: 296), although other

authors indicate 1.3 m^3 per person, leaving out earth transport (Erasmus 1965).

Stone terraces and walls only begin to be documented in the Bronze Age. In this case, quantification of the investment made is more complex inasmuch as a complete set of different tasks take part in the process: stone quarrying, transportation, preparation, wall construction, and even decoration (Abrams & Bolland 1999). A module used by different authors consists of a considered cost of 15 hours per cubic metre in the construction of walls or stonewalls, including extraction, transportation and construction (Gracia Alonso 1998; Nelson 1995). In sum, this is a kind of work that requires greater coordination and, at least some degree of specialisation among participants. Given that comparisons are not straightforward we have chosen to avoid them.

Transforming the volume of ditches into amount of work (hour per person), according to the modules discussed above, Figure 8.4 represents a redistribution of the workload through the considered time. There is a remarkable discrepancy between results obtained from the conserved known segments and those obtained from the total estimation of their plans (Figure 8.4-A). This may happen because these enclosures are located next to current gullies and rivers that could have deeply eroded them (Bernabeu *et al.* 1994; 2003).

In order to minimise these deviations, Figure 8.4-B presents transformed data, trying to standardise them in order to avoid the problems arising from different preservation conditions as well as from disparate documentation criteria. This transformation only consists of considering costs derived from excavation of a one metre long segment, variable in width and height. In this way, non-excavated ditches with known profiles can be included. In addition, this figure also presents the distribution of the number of settlements per period, which has been considered of interest for evaluating their relation with the previously described population cycles.

Although these calculations must be accepted as only estimations, they could shed some light on tendencies throughout long time periods.

8.3.1.- The age of monumental enclosures

Monumental enclosures occupy the oldest part of the Neolithic sequence and represent, by far, the most remarkable and expensive sum of work investment when considered individually. All of them are set apart from the inhabited area, which is developed in nearby open villages (without enclosures) of diverse size. Their evolution can only be followed to some extent in the oldest periods and along the course of the Penàguila River.

The Mas d'Is monumental ditches were first constructed around 5400 BC (Ditch 5) and once again around 5050 BC (Ditch 4) (Fig. 8.5). Their construction seems to be coetaneous to the beginning of habitat aggregation periods that were immediately followed by other periods of dispersal. This sequence can be linked to Díaz-del-Río's (2004) suggestion of the direct relation between labour force mobilisation, concentration of population and power consolidation, as well as its ephemeral development due to the existence of internal factions that competed with each other.

Yet again, there seems to be some difference in what happens after the construction of both structures. If with the first dispersal, after the construction of Ditch 5, the system not only recovers but seems to grow, as is suggested by the greater capacity of mobilisation of the manual labour involved in Ditch 4, yet after its excavation (5050-4900 BC) all constructive activity stops at Mas d'Is. Although during the Neolithic IIA (c. 4550-4200 BC), the excavation of a small structure (a kind of palisade?) is documented in Mas d'Is -parallel and surrounding Ditch 4- the amount of work required for its construction is very small when compared with the others. It seems as if the monumental enclosure is used once again, but without the summoning ability of previous moments. Neither in the Serpis, nor in the Albaida basins are there documented cases of the construction of other ditches at this time.

Towards 3900 BC another monumental ditch was constructed, this time in the middle Serpis. Since then onwards, a large settlement expansion occurs that affects, for the first time, all of the valleys of the main basin. Valuing this indication, we could conclude that the absence of data regarding the construction of monumental enclosures throughout the V millennium BC could be due to a lack of information. In any case, evidence of ditch construction is very scarce and is not documented again until the end of the IV millennium BC. Nevertheless, something had happened.

8.3.2.- The age of habitat enclosures

Ditches in the late horizon are much smaller. When individually considered, they imply the mobilisation of a smaller labour force and, in addition, they are clearly constructed to delimit the villages, thus starting a trend to allocate the biggest labour investments inside settlement areas that continues well into the Bronze Age. Nevertheless, it is also possible that they were a more common landscape element than before. We do not have enough information to follow their evolution with the necessary detail and to assess whether their construction dynamics are comparable to that described for the period 5600-4900 BC. Nevertheless, their use until the end of the Bell Beaker horizon could be asserted, as seems to be the case in Arenal de la Costa.

At a later stage, stone architecture is fully implemented within small villages (<0.25 ha) located on easily defensible slopes and hilltops. The necessary work involved in this domestic architecture, although difficult to quantify, is lesser than that demanded for the construction of the monumental ditches. It is possible that the current image of settlement patterns during the Bronze Age could be partial. Some data suggest the existence of some kind of lowland settlements, not well known and difficult to evaluate (Bernabeu et al. 2003).

Overall, greater mobilisation of the work force occurs during the earliest periods (c. 5400-5050 BC), systematically associated with phases of demographic aggregation (fewer but larger settlements). Investment focuses on loci aside the habitat zone, so that their appropriation by specific social agents (individual, family, clan, etc.) does not seem likely. Yet, the case of Mas d'Is (where the largest labour force investment within a single place for the whole sequence is documented) seems to indicate the preference and centrality of some places over others.

It is possible that the construction of these causewayed enclosures was made by means of the so-called "work feasts." These banquets make it possible to gather the precise amount of work force for a specific project. Such a work force would have been independent from the permanent structure of social relations. These gatherings are used to congregate groups of workers who carry out identical, non-specialized tasks, and therefore are useful in contexts where the simple multiplication of arms carrying out a task reduces notably the total working time. The repetition of feasts usually transforms certain people in

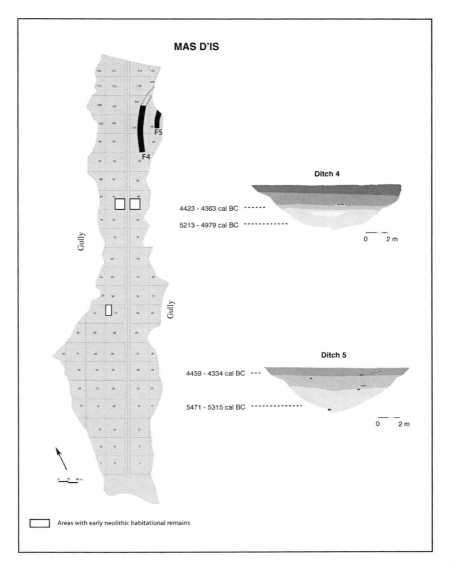

Fig.8.5. Monumental Mas d'Is (Penàguila valley) ditches *c.* 5400-5050 BC.

"guests-debtors," while others become "host-creditors," thus allowing for a continual and unidirectional mechanism for the supply of work force (Dietler & Herbich 2001).

These feasts set up the framework to trade economic capital with symbolic capital, in a cycle in which the host invests product to obtain another product, gaining at the same time symbolic capital (authority) to organise other celebrations and to continue the cycle, hence increasing his final profit. It is not easy to verify the presence of these communal food consumption events (which are not of a unique type) through the archaeological record. Nevertheless, some types of evidence can be used to build different interpretations.

Some habitat enclosures, such as Niuet, show rather fast filling patterns, with abundant food remains (especially fauna) and diverse archaeological objects. In turn, monumental ditches seem to experience comparatively slower filling processes with periods of no deposition at all, and consequently fewer archaeological remains deposited. Should the latter cases be interpreted in the sense that work mobilisation was not made through work feasts? Probably not. It seems more likely that monumental enclosure events were of variable nature. Perhaps the slow-filling patterns are a consequence of the absence of acute internal competition (itself derived from the characteristics of *older* patterns of social organisation). On the other hand, the increase of competition among those agents able to organise celebrations in the later horizon would have conveyed greater food consumption and disposal of residues, showing a recurrent pattern that has also been described in other areas (Perodie 2001:207-209).

It seems possible to relate these changes to an increase of negative intergroup reciprocity (increase of competition between local groups as archaeologically shown by external signs of violence), which would indicate a deep change in the system. How did such a change take place?

105

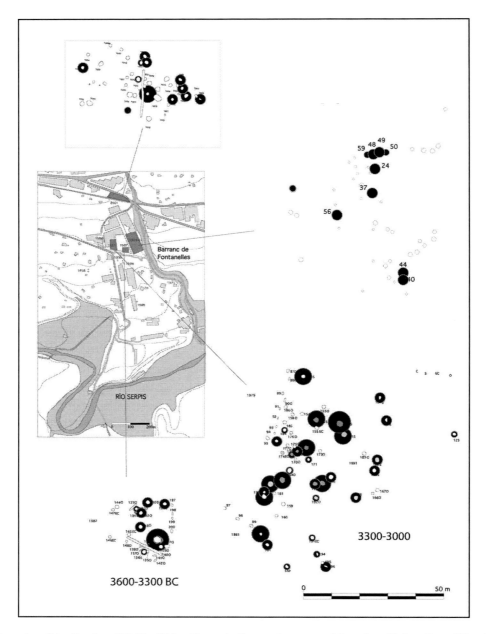

Fig.8.6. Les Jovades, IV millenium BC Neolithic village. In the center, map of the site with location of the different areas where archaeological intervention has been carried out; blank points indicate the presence of storage-pits in non-excavated zones. Storage-pits schematic in each sector, finer dots represent pits under 750 liters, medium dots a rank between 750 and 2500 l, and the coarse those bigger than 2500 l.

The information currently available is too coarse to approach this problem in detail, but some evidence suggests that intensification (increase of the production) associated to changes in subsistence and greater competition (within and between groups) should now be examined.

8.4. Intensification, change and competition

One of the most widely distributed kinds of feature in the Neolithic record are the "silos" (storage pits) which are an essential element in considering a possible economic intensification. These structures are common in the period c. 3900-2200 BC; earlier or later than this lack of data on their existence, although silos dated to both periods are known in other Spanish and Portuguese regions (Alonso 1999; Bordàs *et al.* 1996).

Assessing the volume of agricultural production during the Early Neolithic is difficult due to the lack of robust evidence which makes the evaluation of the intensification difficult, and not just indirectly. Certainly, the growth in the number and size of settlements that took place during the Neolithic IIB seems to suggest some parallel increase in production, although it is not possible to assume that this growth was constant in time.

Recent publications (Bernabeu 1995; Barton *et al.* 2004) have suggested that a major change in the subsistence system occurred during the Neolithic IIB, namely the appearance of dry land agriculture based on the introduction of the plough. Direct evidence proving plough use does not yet exist, but the presence of old bovid phalanxes with pathologies typically related to plough has been pointed out (two of these bones have been recovered in archaeological contexts of around 3200 BC) (Perez Ripoll 1999). The introduction of the plough would have certainly meant a greater capacity to cultivate the land.

In fact, we suggest that the introduction of the plough

(and the changes that it entailed in the organisation of the subsistence) is behind the seemingly huge volume of product stored in the silos. All these changes seem to be related to the construction of habitat enclosures. Examples such as Jovades or Niuet (Bernabeu 1993; Bernabeu *et al.* 1994) are suggestive in this sense.

Jovades is a large village (its minimum extension is not below 25 hectares, but the maximum dispersion of known structures reaches a total of 55 ha), where 4400 m² have been excavated in three different sectors (Pascual Benito 2003). No ditches have been documented in the excavated areas (Fig. 8.6). Two of these sectors have been dated (by charcoal samples) offering a more than probable chronology between c. 3600-3000 BC.

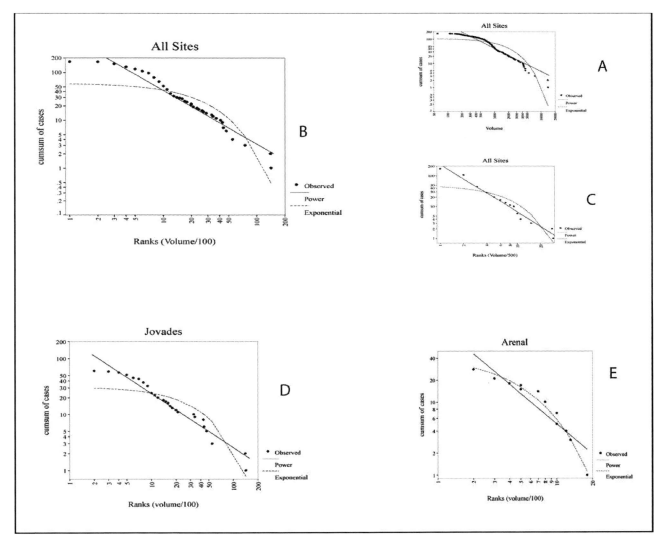

Fig.8.7. Comparison between Power-Law and Exponential accumulated distributions of storage-pits based on volume capacity. Graphics of bilogarithmic scale. A) all the storage-pits, with the original volume; B) and C) all the storage-pits, but grouped by ranks of 100 and 500 liters. As it can be observed, data fit better a power-law distribution in every case, but this is more clear when data are grouped by categories. On these basis, graphics D and E present the Jovades (3600-3000 BC) and Arenal de la Costa (2400-2200 BC) distributions, grouped by ranks of 100 liters. In the first case, it is clearly a power-law distribution type, whereas the second fits better to an exponential distribution.

r2	All Sites	All Sites 100	All Sites 500	Jovades	Missena	Colata	Arenal
Power	0.907	0.937	0.975	0.949	0.855	0.882	0.846
Exponential	0.749	0.758	0.705	0.785	0.617	0.97	0.98

Table 8.2 R square for volumes power and exponential distributions among pit-storage. As shown, for all silos communality and in Jovades case, the best fitted curve is the Power-Law one, this is also true in Missena case but with less definition. Colata and Arenal de la Costa are better explained by exponential distribution curves.

From the rest of the excavated and/or documented zones, radiocarbon dates do not exist, but the recovered materials suggest a very similar chronology (based on pottery). Within the excavated sectors, silos amounting to a total storage capacity of 98,000 litres were opened during that time span. Extrapolating this figure to the minimum extension of the site (25 ha), the total storage capacity would sum up to 5,575,000 litres, resulting in a density of 223,000 litres/ha. Taking into account time, the total duration of this sector (600 years), and considering that a silo lasts for an average of 10 years (Reynolds 1979), it is possible to work out that the storage capacity implemented per decade at Jovades was of 92,925 litres.

In order to interpret these figures it would be necessary to know, at least approximately, how many households were needed to store such quantities of crop, as well as what their total production was. Following preliminary calculations,[2] it turns out feasible to suppose that an average population of 152 inhabitants would be able to store nearly 93,000 litres, supposing a total production of 2031 litres per household per year.

Fluctuations in harvests and population size had to affect the stored volume of crops at any given time. Therefore it would be highly unreasonable to assume a constant production, storage and population for the 600 years under analysis. In other words, it is likely that most of the production and inhabitants were concentrated during some specific, shorter time spans. Is it possible that the introduction of the plough could have produced increasing crop yields, taking the system over its own limits and, as a consequence, transforming it? Perhaps, in order to better understand this aspect, it would be useful to evaluate whether distribution both between and within communities could show the existence of true inequality. To examine this, data (published or unpublished)[3] of some villages in the Serpis (Jovades and Niuet) and the Albaida (Colata, Missena and Arenal de la Costa) basins, with a chronology staggered between c. 3600 and 2200 BC, can be of help.

Considering all of the silos together, their volume resembles a power-law distribution, indicating that surplus accumulation is clearly unequal among different settlements (Fig. 8.7). The same observation can be deducted from the distribution of the total volume within the settlements (Figs. 8.7-D and E; Table 8.2). In this case, only Jovades clearly shows the presence of a power-law distribution; on the contrary in Arenal de la Costa (c. 2400-

2000 BC) and Colata (c. 3300-3000 BC) the distribution is exponential; Missena (c. 3600- 3000BC) also shows a distribution closer to the power-law than to the exponential one.

This aspect is of maximum interest since the distribution of the storage pits inside the settlements allows us to consider, for the first time, the possibility of appropriation of the volume stored by one part of the households: some of them seem to have stored considerably more resources than others.

Data suggest that the greatest capacity of accumulation, as well as the most unequal distribution of resources, occurred between the last centuries of the fourth millennium and the beginning of the third millennium BC. At this time, long lasting changes in the subsistence system (in the first place), and in the settlement pattern (later), triggered the appearance of villages delimited by enclosures. Presence of power-law distribution seems related to scale-free networks and the existence of inequalities (Bentley 2003). This aspect contains the crucial element to understand how some particular agents (households, clans or villages) became increasingly richer ("rich-get-richer"), as the network grew, as shall be discussed in the next section.

8.5. Social networks

Scale-free-networks are a special type of network, also known as "small-world-systems," whose characteristics combine high "clustering" in the local realm, necessary to maintain inner social cohesion, with an ease to reach the outer world. The latter is obtained by means of some well-connected agents who channel these relations. What characterises these networks (Bentley 2003) is that, in their growth, new agents tend to connect themselves, preferably, with those that previously enjoyed an outstanding degree of interconnection. In this way, along with system growth, differences of connectivity between agents are also accentuated. Another interesting characteristic of scale-free-networks, as is the case of social ones, is their assortativity: better located agents show a tendency to connect themselves to each other, unlike what happens in other physical world networks (or on the Internet, for instance).

This type of growth can explain wealth inequalities among agents of a particular system. The only thing needed, apparently, to trigger the process is the opportunity to do so. In this way, preferential connections would explain growth, inequalities and, consequently, power development. Meanwhile, assortativity will tend to produce exclusions or differentiations between agent groups with differentiated levels of power and wealth.

Nevertheless, this description does not fit reality in an absolute way. Preferential connections must be subjected to certain limits, allowing for the emergence of new well-connected agents. Otherwise, change could not take place. However, we should consider that these agents are diverse; they belong to (and, in some cases, represent) diverse collectiveness, and frequently compete with each other to attract followers who constitute the base of their power. This competition will tend to be higher when the network grows and, in more than one occasion, is in the origin of the recurrent failures of leaders trying to consolidate their power.

In previous pages we have presented some information that, while uneven, allows us to approach some aspects of power and inequality development. As shown, although the cyclical character of evolution is independent from the chronological scale observed, its reading is not. In fact, current data only allows for an approximation of two different moments with some likely degree of guarantee: one early horizon (c. 5600-4900 BC) and a recent one (c. 3600-2900 BC). In both cases, an expansive cycle seems to take the system to limits very close to bifurcation, but with different consequences. In both, power patterns of diverse nature were developed. It is now time to try to explain those differences.

8.5.1.- Development of collective power: Monumental causewayed enclosures

During the early horizon (5550-4900 BC), the great majority of known settlements were located in the Penàguila valley. The rest of the Serpis basin either does not present information, or there are some isolated and short-spanned sites (Fig. 8.8). It is possible that this could be the result of the lack of intensive surveys in other places of the region. But it also has been suggested (Barton *et al.* 2004) that the current image can be due to differential fluvial erosion, more acute here, so that older sites, located closer to the river, were destroyed. This would essentially affect the middle Serpis basin, where, in addition, some cave deposits of this period are known.

However, what seems to be deducted is the presence of local groups separated by very ample territories. Certainly, population increase occurred, but not as much as to overflow the Penàguila valley. Beyond the Serpis, both on-shore and inland, some evidence suggests the existence of other groups since at least the same date as in the Penàguila (in the shore case) or since c. 5400 (inland). All of them are located at a distance of 25 km or more as the crow flies (Fig. 8.9).

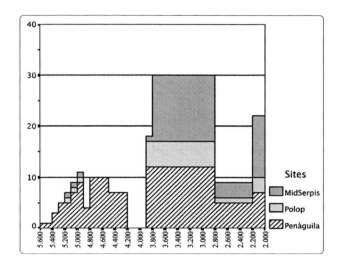

Fig.8.8. Settlement distribution, by valleys, in the Serpis river basin. Only information from regions where systematic survey has been carried out is considered.

Under these conditions, contacts between local groups would tend to be concentrated around few agents. Internal and external competition is limited by restricted opportunities for the development of new agents able to become as well connected as the previous ones. Networks of marriage exchange, for instance, could be controlled or directed by some individuals with some degree of authority based on their special position. At the same time, this position could derive in the control or monopolisation of such exchange networks. But, where does their position derive from? Going back to the Penàguila valley and to Mas d'Is we could find some indicators. As we have seen, in this monumental site the greatest work force mobilisation takes place.

Over a period of about 500 years, work investment in the construction of the two ditches could surpass 100,000 hours/person. How can we explain the ability to mobilise such an extraordinary labour force? Probably, the monumental enclosure worked as an aggregation centre of the Penàguila local group, formed by several villages dispersed throughout the valley. Therefore, we can suppose that its construction was basically a means of asserting identity and promoting the internal cohesion of the local group. The persistent attraction of work force towards this place, the continuous occupation of the surroundings (forming the most extensive cluster of the valley, for this period), as well as the presence of remains suggesting an episode previous to the construction of the first enclosure (Ditch 5), may suggest that the first occupation of the valley by agricultural pioneers took place here. Perhaps the pre-eminence of this locus, and the ascendance of some of its nearby dwellers, can be explained by the fact that it housed the founding clan or lineage.

Authority recognition of genealogical order is based upon ideological criteria. It allows an explanation of how some agents acquire initial pre-eminence and become privileged nodes of the system as it grows. An important part

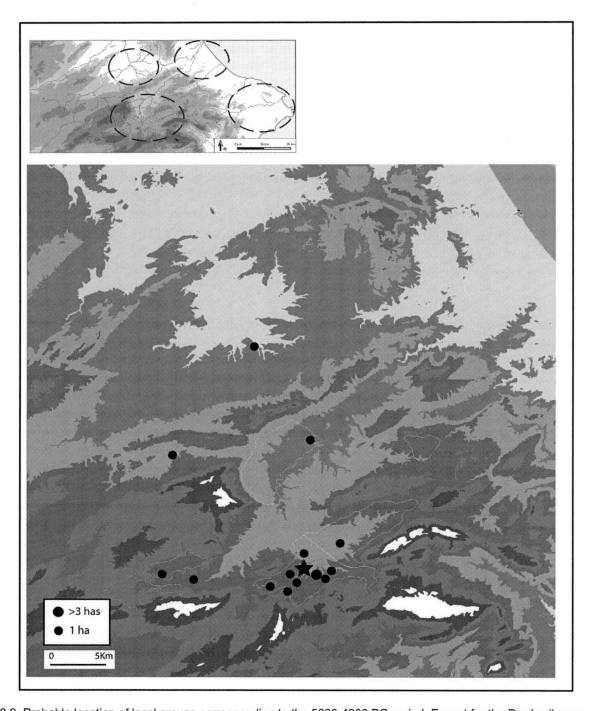

Fig.8.9. Probable location of local groups corresponding to the 5600-4900 BC period. Except for the Penàguila one, the rest is known either through cave deposits or scattered surface findings. In the Serpis basin location of the few points -dated in the same chronological frame- outside the Penàguila valley are included.

of the network's internal and external relations will pivot around them. Its sphere of influence is the local group and its power depends on its capacity to effectively mobilise the whole collectivity. Judging by its results, this possibility was achieved at a considerable scale but it was a collective power in the sense that Mann (1986) gives to the term. From his perspective, it does not matter who exerts the power (big men or heads of hereditary lineage) since it could be easily reverted. Also, it is possible to

dissociate heritage from power, admitting that hereditary systems of transmission not associated to stratified groups can exist, even if their presence can have some important connotations in the future.

A second class of aggregation centres has been documented in these groups. This is the case of some exceptional caves such as Cova de l'Or and Cova de la Sarsa, in the Serpis, where large quantities of symbolic and prestige items have been recovered (Bernabeu *et al.* 2003) including: slate bracelets - made with stones of southern peninsular provenance (Orozco 2000), ceramic vessels with symbolic styles (Martí & Hernández 1988), musical instruments (Juan-Cabanilles *et al.* 2001), ochre powder and bars stored and ready to be used as pigments (Garcia Borja *et al.* 2004), large amounts of stored cereals, as well as the remains of meat consumption where infantile caprinae represent an important amount of the total faunal remains (Perez Ripoll 1980). In Cova de la Sarsa, the existence of burials suggests its use as a funerary cave (Martí 1977:34). This extreme is not so obvious in the case of Cova de l'Or. However, around both caves there are some smaller natural cavities where much smaller concentrations of prestige items indicate their use as necropolis (Bernabeu *et al.* 2001).

The archaeological record of Cova de l'Or and Cova de la Sarsa suggests significant consumption of some special meals and the exhibition of enormous amounts of prestige elements, all within an atmosphere that, if only by its physical constraints, should haven been restricted to certain members of the community. This seems to be quite different from what happened within the monumental ditches or at other symbolic places that could be temporarily related to them, such as several rock art sanctuaries (Bernabeu *et al.* 2003) where ceremonial activities were more open, involving the participation of wider collectives (local, in the first case and intergroupal, coming from more than one clan, in the second).

In our view, this represents symbolic control of ritual performances and prestige elements, which are in some cases restricted to certain members of the group. Only the ideological nature of this power allows the appropriation of symbols when controlling ritual practices, as archaeologically shown by the appropriation of some items, and even in specific consumption practices. In other words, as we could expect, a large development of collective powers allowed the emergence of some inherent aspects of distributive powers (Mann 1986). And it is just at this moment when the system seems to arrive to a point of crisis. Its end comes marked by:

a) Population increase and disaggregation of prime local groups. In effect, at some vague point in time, another monumental ditch in the Penàguila was constructed, 1 km away of Mas d'Is (radiocarbon dates do not exist, and excavation has not been carried out). Scattered findings related to the ditch indicate a chronology of around 4500-4200 BC and, on the basis of data collected in Mas d'Is (Bernabeu *et al.* 2003), we know that usually ditches are filled up at a slow pace, or over long periods of time, so it is possible to suppose a construction date contemporary to Ditch 4 (Mas d'Is). This extreme should be verified in the near future, but it is a reliable indicator to understand reasons lying behind the system rupture that occurred after 4900 BC, mainly if we are looking at the possible generalisation of this process in other local groups.

b) Rupture of the control over the exchange networks. Since c. 5200 BC we begin to document polished stone tools made from exotic raw materials. At the beginning, this trade circuit is still centralised but soon new materials seem to be distributed in a broader way. The concentration of exchanged objects represented in Cova de l'Or and Cova de la Sarsa in the early horizons lost importance after 4900 BC. Simultaneously, slate bracelets and symbolic ceramic containers, characteristic of the previous moment, disappeared. At the same time, the places that concentrated most of these items, like Cova de l'Or and Cova de la Sarsa, ceased in their functionality and their occupation is discontinued around 5000 BC, showing the decline of the social networks that they sustained.

It is not possible to evaluate what happens after c. 4900 BC. Population seems to decline, since only evidence of some small and scattered villages are found in the Penàguila valley. This tendency seems to continue until the fourth millennium BC. Migration towards neighbouring valleys seems to be a plausible option, although it remains to be tested.

8.5.2.- Production and competition

This situation changed after 3900 BC. At this moment all the valleys of the Serpis basin had already been occupied, although with notable differences both in density and intensity. The case of the middle Serpis has shed some light on the process because, although the number of settlements does not differ significantly from that of the Penàguila, the occupied area was four times as big (140 ha. against 35 ha.). Moreover, sites were now larger. Thus, if in the early horizon, the largest recorded settlement was less than 6 hectares, now it is common to find 20-25 ha settlements that in some cases, such as Jovades, reached up to 50 ha. In short, this process involved, therefore, substantial demographic growth as well as the reduction of buffer territories between local groups. As a consequence, a greater level of interaction should be expected, as should be the degree of competition. Something similar seems to happen in the Polop and the Penàguila valleys, but at a smaller scale (Fig. 8.10).

Diverse data suggest that towards the end of the fourth millennium BC and beginnings of the third essential changes occurred, including demographic growth, bigger production capacity and the introduction of plough agriculture. Causewayed enclosure habitats seem to sequentially occur in only 400 years, or even less. Few radiocarbon dates are known and all of them come from charcoal, so we cannot exclude the old wood effect.

The analysis of storage-pits and their distribution shows uneven agricultural production and differential accumulation, both between groups and inside them. This implies a clearly unequal distribution of wealth between two classes of agents: households and villages. Storage capacity is remarkable in Jovades, where almost 60 storage pits

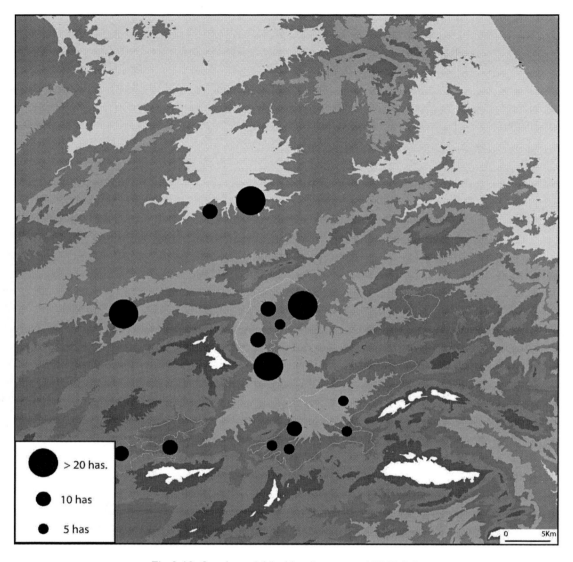

Fig.8.10. Serpis and Albaida sites around 3000 BC;
only sites whose size is known to be larger than 5 ha are represented. Further details in text.

have been documented in less than 0.5 ha. Some of them have a capacity superior to 10 cubic metres. This is also the case in Missena and in the Albaida valley. Both show a clearly unequal internal distribution of the stored volume.

We interpret these sites as places where accumulation of surpluses occurred. Around them, there was a mobilisation of work force used to expand the cultivated area, thus allowing local hierarchies to produce more surpluses. Storage of huge amounts of cereal triggered mechanisms of redistribution of wealth both at an intragroup level and throughout regional networks. But, what mechanisms are those?

Control over crop storage allows local hierarchies to develop; those wealthier hierarchies have an ever higher calling power and the capacity to lead a bigger work force. The mechanism making all of this possible could be work feasts, as previously happened around the ditch

constructions. However, in this case there is an important variation: the product of the work can be appropriated by the host, something that did not happen in ditch construction. The mechanism has been described in different ethnographic contexts (Dietler & Herbich 2001: 249). What we want to remark is that in this case a double appropriation takes place.

Work feasts are not only used to collect the harvest, but to expand the host fields over land disputed with neighbouring groups, the result being that if land is expanded at the expense of the neighbours, host production increases and, simultaneously, its capacity to attract new followers grows. The hosts systematically appropriate land and production. This would explain the unequal distribution of stored product in the interior of the village. It is likely that this situation happened prior to 3200 BC, as some data from Jovades seem to suggest (one of the largest storage pits has been dated to c. 3500-3400 BC).

The introduction of the plough, on the other hand, may have had a multiplying effect, allowing the cultivation of wider extensions of land. At the same time, naked wheat and barley varieties raised levels of production and hosts increased their wealth and properties to a point never reached before. Greater wealth of some could derive in greater a facility to hold and to feed the new basic instrument of work, oxen, therefore increasing social distances within the group. Some would be in the position of indebted-guests and others in the position of creditor-hosts. This cycle of increasing yields attracted more followers to some points, causing increased competition inside and outside the group. A more than noticeable growth of some places, like Jovades, can be the best archaeological correlate of the process.

Furthermore, development of local hierarchies may have had a negative impact in shared regional networks, which may have triggered episodes of intergroup violence. It is in this context that the appearance of enclosured villages delimited by ditches, such as Niuet (where the ditch enclosure seems to be dug and filled up between 3200 and 3000 BC) makes sense. Also, it is within this context that the emphasis on military equipment in burial grave-goods shown during the first Bell Beaker phase must be understood.

Nevertheless, it seems once again that the process was stopped. Not much evidence is available for the 600 years marked by the use of Bell Baker ceramics, and the existing evidence does not support the idea of greater social inequality and power institutionalisation. Arenal de la Costa, the only site known to some detail, is dated close to the end of this phase (2400-2300 BC). This settlement has an enclosure with a double ditch system encompassing 6 ha inside of which the recorded storage capacity (as shown in storage pits) is distributed in an exponential way, thus not suggesting the presence of major social inequalities.

The system certainly seems to change; settlement units are smaller, but aggregated, and enclosed by causewayed ditches. If funerary deposits of this moment are significant, exhibition of force and military apparatus –weapons and the like– are now attributes of leadership and they are associated with individuals as shown by individual burials. The ideological fracture with the previous cosmogony, where collective burials were the norm, is clear.

The new networks of power implemented at this time would have implied a more effective control over a considerably smaller number of individuals. As far as we can say, it is possible that they did not evolve in an unequal accumulation of wealth. This process was continued and increased throughout the Bronze Age. With the current data it is not possible to describe the form of the process between the beginning of the Beaker and the Bronze Age.

In summary, in at least in two occasions during the Late Prehistory of the Spanish Mediterranean valleys (c. 5000

BC and c. 3000 BC), networks of power capable of mobilising important amounts of labour force arose and developed. Although the means put in place may have been the same in both occasions, neither their origin nor their consequences may be the same. In both, the development of power does not seem to have been consolidated: in the words of Mann (1986: 39) "[…] human beings devoted a considerable part of their cultural and organisational capacities to ensure that further evolution did not occur. They seem not to have wanted to increase their collective powers because of the distributive powers involved."

Certainly, this quote could be considered more as a reflection, or better yet, a hypothesis. Available empirical evidence shows some gaps that should be filled in by future research projects in order to test our conclusions. For instance, the way in which settlement areas are estimated must be improved by taking into consideration means to weigh the relative importance of each chronological period. We need improvements in our estimations of agricultural production by looking into which species were truly stored, and in what proportion.

This is why our interpretation should be considered a previous and preliminary attempt to open new ways to understand the development of social inequalities in Iberian Prehistory. Even with current empirical constraints, we believe that this approach based on complex systems has shown us enough possibilities to deserve a follow-up within prospective projects.

Notes

[1] Quantification of both variables offers diverse problems. Number of settlements per phase is affected by the fact that not all located sites can be easily assigned to a particular period. Being that the case, we have chosen not to use them.
Total extension of each site, in turn, is affected by several problems when surface collections reflect large periods of time. In absence of any other information, we have chosen to manage them in the following way:

- when a particular collection can be assigned to 2 periods, its surface extension is divided in two halves.

- if represented periods are three, then the total surface has been distributed under the assumption that the first and the last the periods had less extension in a proportion of 25-50-25%. When phases are 4: 20-30-30-20%; and, finally, when dealing with 5: 10-30-30-30-10%.

This way of estimating size affects mainly to the oldest period (c. 5600-4900 BC), subdivided in 4 phases. Collections belonging to at least 3 of these subdivided phases are common, lasting in some cases until the period 4900-4550 BC.

This procedure constitutes a mere attempt to approach the problem of settlement extension, that should necessarily be improved in the future.

[2] Production estimation and demography in Jovades. Taking the minimum estimated extension of the site and the duration considered for this sector, we will have

(1) Known storage capacity = 98000 litres
(2) Excavated area = 4400 sq m
(3) Density x Ha = 223,022 litres
(4) Minimum Surface = 25 Hectares
(5) Total capacity (estimated) = 5,575,550 litres
(6) Considered site occupation = 600 years
(7) Pit-storage Average Life = 10 years
(8) Average Capacity each ten years = 92,925 litres

Furthermore, we know that household interannual consumption is stored inside the houses, in cooked mud containers, or at least this is the case at sites such as La Illeta del Banyets (Campello, Alicante; J. Soler pers. com.). Consequently our assumption is that the amounts kept in storage-pits basically correspond to seed stock for the following year and to risk reserve (bad years, celebrations, payment of specialists?...)
Establishing a formula for the total production as follows

A+B+C = P, where
A = interannual consumption of the families (between harvests)
B = seed stock
C = reserve against risk
P = Total Production

The equation can be solved if we take for granted that A it is a well-known parameter; B, is a proportion of P that depends on productivity; and C is a variable proportion of A. This way the formula would be as follows:

$A + \alpha P + \beta A = P$, then
$P = (1+\beta/1-a) * A$
Multiple proposals exist to establish values of A. Since we only try to have a reasonable estimation, we use interannual consumption proposed in the Greek Iron Age: 650 kg (~ 812.5 litres) for a family of 4 (Gallant, 1991).
Productivity is very unstable. We can use a productivity of 1:5 (then α=0.2) for wheat. This can be a little overestimated, but it could compensate productivity values for barley that more are a little more elevated; and we suppose that individual households would store the amount needed for 1 year of consumption and, therefore, $\beta = A$,
Thus (2/0,8) = 2.5 * 812.5 = 2.5 * 812.5 = 2031.25 l, and
B = 406,25 l
C = 812,5 l
B+C = 1218.75 l
If we divide the average density by this amount, we obtain a result of 76 households per decade. Certainly, this supposes to admit that pit-storage contents are totally renewed each year, which is not likely. Surely, the part corresponding to B (20% of the total) and, probably, a portion of C. Under these premises, to suppose that an amount equivalent to 50% is renewed annually does not seem preposterous. The remaining grain, once winded, would be stored again. Accepting that, the total number of households should also be reduced by half, totalling 38, or representing around 152 inhabitants.

[3]We would like to express our acknowledgment to J. Pascual Beneyto, A. Ribera y M. Barberà, for allowing us to use unpublished data from Missena.

8.6.- References

ABRAMS, E.M. & BOLLAND, T.W. 1999: "Architectural Energetics, Ancient Monuments, and Operation Management". *Journal of Archaeological Method and Theory*, 6 (4): 263-291.

ALONSO, N. 1999: *De la llavor a la farina. Els processos agrìcoles protohistúrics a la Catalunya occidental*. Monographies d'ArchÈologie Mediterranèenne, 4. Centre National de la Recherche Scientifique. Paris.

ANDERSEN, N.H. 1997: *The Sarup Enclosures. The Funnel Beaker Culture of the Sarup site including two causewayed camps compared to the contemporary settlements in the area and other European enclosures*. Jutland Archaeological Society Publications XXXIII, 1. Aarhus University Press. Aarhus.

BARTON, C.M.; BERNABEU, J.; AURA, J.E.; GARCÍA, O.; SCHMICH, S. & MOLINA, LL. 2004: "Long-Term Socioecology and Contingent Landscapes". *Journal of Archaeological Method and Theory* 11 (3): 253-295.

BENTLEY, R.A. 2003: "Scale-free-network Growth and Social Inequality". In R.A. Bentley and H.D.G. Maschner (eds): *Complex Systems and Archaeology. Empirical and Theoretical Application*. University of Utah Press. Utah: 27-46.

BENTLEY, R. A. & MASCHNER, H. D. G., 2003: "Preface: considering Complexity Theory in Archaeology". In R.A. Bentley & H.D.G. Maschner (eds): *Complex Systems and Archaeology. Empirical and Theoretical Applications*. University of Utah Press. Utah: 1-8.

BERNABEU AUBAN, J. 1989: *La tradición cultural de las cerámicas impresas en la zona oriental de la Península Ibérica*. Trabajos Varios del SIP 86. Diputación de Valencia. Valencia.

- 1995: "Origen y consolidación de las sociedades agrícolas. El País Valenciano entre el Neolítico y la Edad del Bronce". *Jornades d'Arqueologia. Alfís del Pi (1994)*. Valencia: 37-60.

- (dir.) 1993: "El III milenio a.C. en el País Valenciano. Los poblados de Jovades (Cocentaina, Alacant) y Arenal de la Costa (Ontinyent, Valencia)". *Saguntum PLAV* 26: 9-179.

BERNABEU, J.; PASCUAL-BENITO, J.LL.; OROZCO, T.; BADAL, E.; FUMANAL, M.P. & GARCÍA, O. 1994: "Niuet (L'Alqueria d'Asnar). Poblado del III milenio a.C.". *Recerques del Museu d'Alcoi* 3: 9-74.

BERNABEU, J.; BARTON, C.M. & GARCÍA, O. 1999: "Prospecciones sistemáticas en el valle del Alcoy (Alicante): primeros resultados". *Arqueología Espacial* 21: 29-64.

BERNABEU, J.; MOLINA, LL. & GARCÍA, O. 2001: "El mundo funerario en el Horizonte Cardial valenciano. Un registro oculto". *Saguntum PLAV* 33: 27-35.

BERNABEU AUBÁN, J.; OROZCO KOHLER, T.; DIEZ CASTILLO, A.; GOMEZ PUCHE, M. & MOLINA HERNANDEZ, F.J. 2003: "Mas d'Is (Penáguila, Alicante): Aldeas y recintos monumentales del Neolítico Inicial en el valle del Serpis". *Trabajos de Prehistoria* 60 (2): 39-59.

BINTLIFF, J. 2003: "Searching for Structure in the Past or Was It 'One Damm Thing afther Another'?". In R.A. Bentley and H.D.G. Maschner (eds) *Complex Systems and Archaeology. Empirical and Theoretical Application*. University of Utah Press. Utah: 79-84.

BORDAS, A.; MORA, R. & LOPEZ, V. 1996: "El asentamiento al aire libre del Neolítico Antiguo en la Font del Ros

(Berga, Bergadá)". I Congrès del Neolìtic a la Península Ibèrica. *Rubricatum* 1: 397-406.

CHAPMAN, R., 1991: *La formación de las sociedades complejas. El Sudeste de la Península Ibérica en el marco del Mediterraneo occidental*. Crítica. Barcelona.

DÍAZ-DEL-RÍO, P. 2004: "Factionalism and collective labor in Copper Age Iberia". *Trabajos de Prehistoria* 61 (2): 85-98.

DIETLER, M. & HAYDEN, B. (eds.) 2001: *Feasts. Archaeological and Ethnographic perspectives on Food, Politics and Power*. Smithsonian Institution Press. Washington.

DIETLER, M. & HERBICH, I. 2001: "Feast and labor mobilization. Dissecting a fundamental economic practice". In M. Dietler & B. Hayden (eds): *Feasts. Archaeological and Ethnographic perspectives on Food, Politics and Power*. Smithsonian Institution Press. Washington: 240-264.

ERASMUS, C.J. 1965: "Monument building. Some field experiments". *Southwestern Journal of Anthropology* 21 (4): 277-301.

GALLANT, T.W. 1991: *Risk and survival in Ancient Greece*. Polity Press. Cambridge.

GARCÍA BORJA, P.; DOMINGO, I.M. ROLDÁN GARCÍA, C.; VERDASCO CEBRIÁN, C.; FERRERO CALABUIG, J.; JARDÍN GINER, P. & BERNABEU AUBÁN, J. (2004): "Aproximación al uso de la materia colorante en Cova de l'Or". *Recerques del Museu d'Alcoi* 13: 35-52.

GIBAJA, J. F. 2003: *Comunidades neolíticas del Noreste de la Península Ibérica: una aproximación socio-económica a partir del estudio de la función de los útiles líticos*. British Archaeological Reports International Series, 1140. Oxford.

GILMAN, A. 1976: "Bronze Age dynamics in southern Spain". *Dialectical Anthropology* 1: 30-319.

- 1987: "Unequal developement in Copper Age Iberia". In E. M. Brumfiel & T. K. Earle (eds): *Specialization, exchange and complex societies*. Cambridge University Press. Cambridge: 22-29.

- 1997: "Como valorar los sistemas de propiedad a partir de datos arqueológicos". *Trabajos de Prehistoria* 54 (2): 81-92.

GRACIA ALONSO, F. 1998: "Arquitectura y poder en las estructuras de poblamiento ibéricas. Esfuerzo de trabajo y corveas". *Congreso Internacional Los Íberos, príncipes de Occidente. Saguntum Extra* 1: 99-113.

HURTADO, V. 1997: "The dynamics of the occupation of the middle basin of the river Guadiana between the fourth and second millenia BC". In M. Díaz-Andreu & S. Keay (eds.): *The Archaeology of Iberia. The Dynamics of Change*. Routledge. London: 98-127.

JUAN-CABANILLES, J.: MARTÍNEZ VALLE, R.; ARIAS GAGO-DEL MOLINO, A. & MARTÍ OLIVER, B. 2001: "Los tubos de hueso de la Cova de l'Or (Beniarrés, Alicante): instrumentos musicales en el Neolítico Antiguo de la Península Ibérica". *Trabajos de Prehistoria* 58 (2): 41-67.

KAUFFMAN, S.A. 2003: *Investigaciones. Complejidad, autoorganización y nuevas leyes para una biologÌa general*. Matemas 76. Tusquets. Barcelona.

LULL, V. 1983: *La Cultura de El Argar. Un modelo para el estudio de las formaciones económico-sociales prehistóricas*. Akal. Madrid.

LULL, V. & RISCH, R. 1995: El Estado Arg·rico. *Verdolay* 7: 97-109.

MANN, M. 1986: *The sources of social power. Volume I. A history of power from the beginnings to AD 1760*. Cambridge University Press. Cambridge.

MATHERS, C. 1984: "Beyond the grave: the context and wider implications of mortuary practices in south-east Spain". In T.F.C. Blagg, R.F.J. Jones & S.J. Keay (eds.): *Papers in Iberian Archaeology*. British Archaeological Reports International Series 193. Oxford: 13-46.

MARTÍ OLIVER, B. 1977: *Cova de l'Or (Beniarrés, Alicante). Vol.I.*. Trabajos Varios del SIP 51. Diputación de Valencia. Valencia.

MARTÍ OLIVER, B. & HERNANDEZ, M.S. 1988: *El neolític valenciá: art rupestre i cultura material*. Servei d'Investigació Prehistórica. Valencia.

NELSON, B.A. 1995: "Complexity, hierarchy and scale: A controlled comparison between Chaco Canyon, New Mexico, and La Quemada, Zacatecas". *American Antiquity* 60 (4): 597-618.

NOCETE, F. 1989: *El Espacio de la Coerción. La transición al estado en las campiñas del Alto Guadalquivir*. British Archaeological Reports International Series 492. Oxford.

- 2001: *Tercer milenio antes de nuestra era: relaciones y contradicciones centro-periferia en el valle del Guadalquivir*. Bellaterra. Barcelona.

OROZCO KOHLER, T. 2000: *Aprovisionamiento e Intercambio. Análisis petrológico del utillaje pulimentado en la Prehistoria Reciente del Pais Valenciano (España)*. British Archaeological Reports International Series 867. Oxford.

PASCUAL BENITO, J.LL. 2003: "Les Jovades". In Domenech, E.(eds.): *El Patrimoni historic i artìstic de Cocentaina i la seua recuperació: les intervencions arquitectóniques i arqueológiques*. Ajuntament de Cocentaina. Cocentaina.: 343-394.

PEREZ RIPOLL, M. 1980: "La fauna de vertebrados". In B. Martí, V. Pascual, M.D. Gallart, P. López, M. Pérez Ripoll, J.D. Acuña & F. Robles (eds.): *Cova de l'Or (Beniarrés, Alicante). Vol. II*. Trabajos Varios del SIP 65. Diputación de Valencia. Valencia: 193-255.

- 1999: "La explotación ganadera durante el III milenio a.C. en la Península Ibérica. *II Congrès del Neolític a la Península Ibérica. Saguntum Extra* 2: 95-103.

PERODIE, J.R. 2001: "Feasting for prosperity: a study of southern nothwest coast feasting". In M. Dietler & B. Hayden (eds.): *Feasts. Archaeological and Ethnographic perspectives on Food, Politics and Power*. Smithsonian Institution Press. Washington: 185-210.

PRYGORINE, I. 1996: *El fin de las certidumbres*. Taurus. Madrid.

REYNOLDS, P.J. 1979: "A general report of underground grain storage experiments at the Butser Ancient Farm Research Project". In M. Gast & F. Sigaut (dir.): *Les techniques de conservation des graines á long terme: leur role dans la dynamique des systemes de cultures et des societes*. Vol. 1. Centre National de la Recherche Scientifique. Paris: 70-80.

ROWLANDS, M. & GLEDHILL, J. 1998: "Materialism and multilinear evolution". In K. Kristiansen & M. Rowlands (eds.): *Social Transformations in Archaeology*. Routledge. London/New York: 40-48.

SHANKS, M., TILLEY, C.H. 1987: *Social Theory and Archaeology*. Polity Press. Cambridge.

SHENNAN, S. 2002: *Genes, Memes and Human History. Darwinian archaeology and cultural evolution*. Thames & Hudson. London.

VAN DER LEEUW, S.E. 1987: "Revolutions revisited". In L.Manzanilla (ed.): *Studies in the Neolithic and Urban Revolutions: the V. Gordon Childe Colloquium* (Mexico 1986). British Archaeological Reports International Series 349. Oxford: 217-243.

VAN DER LEEUW, S.E. & McGLADE, J. (eds.) 1997: *Time, Proceses and Structurated Transformation in Archaeology*. Routledge. London.

ZAFRA, N.; HORNOS, F. & CASTRO, M. 1999: "Una macro-aldea en el origen del modo de vida campesino: Marroquíes Bajos (Jaén) c. 2500-2000 cal ANE". *Trabajos de Prehistoria* 56 (1): 77-102.

CHAPTER 9

Sociological hypotheses for the communities of the Iberian Mediterranean basin (From the VIth to the IInd millennia BC)

Pedro V. Castro Martínez
Universidad Autónoma de Barcelona
Trinidad Escoriza Mateu
Universidad de Almería
Joaquím Oltra Puigdomenech
Universidad Autónoma de Barcelona

Abstract

This paper discusses the current sociological hypotheses for the communities of the Iberian Mediterranean basin between the VI and II millennia BC. Different types of evidence associated to various interpretations are critiqued. The sociology of the communities between the VI to IV millennium BC is based on the analysis of the Levantine rock art. For the period 3500-2300 BC, the existence of a possible state formation is assessed. The discussion of the phase between 2330 and 1500, once assumed the existence of the Argaric state, focuses on the mechanisms of social exploitation. Finally, for the period 1500-1300 BC, the conditions of social reproduction within the Villena horizon and, again, the issue of whether or not state-like societies existed, are dealt with. Differences between communities, inter-community networks and evidence pertaining gender relationships, are taken into account when dealing with the relationships of reciprocity or exploitation between social groups.

Keywords: Iberia; Production; Reciprocity; Exploitation; Neolithic; Los Millares; El Argar; Villena.

Resumen

Revisamos las hipótesis sociológicas vigentes para las comunidades del Arco Mediterráneo Ibérico durante 5 milenios. Exponemos y discutimos las evidencias asociadas a las explicaciones y señalamos las lecturas sociales que consideramos más adecuadas al registro empírico. La sociología de las comunidades del VI° al IV° milenios se apoya en lecturas sociales derivadas del Arte Rupestre *Levantino*. Para la etapa 3500 al 2300 se recoge el debate sobre la existencia o no de una formación estatal. La etapa 2300-1500, asumida la existencia del estado *argárico,* focaliza la atención del debate entorno a los mecanismos de explotación social. Finalmente, para la etapa de 1500-1300 se abordan las condiciones de reproducción social en el *Horizonte de Villena* y nuevamente la cuestión de la existencia o no de estado. Las diferencias entre comunidades, las redes intercomunitarias y las evidencias sobre la situación de mujeres y hombres en cada etapa, son tenidas en cuenta al abordar las relaciones de reciprocidad o explotación entre colectivos sociales.

Palabras clave: Iberia; Producción; Reciprocidad; Explotación; Neolítico; Los Millares; El Argar; Villena.

9.1.- Introduction to the problems. Facing sociology for five millennia.

The purpose of this paper is to set forth the current state of the reading matter for the Mediterranean regions of the Iberian peninsular (Fig. 9.1). We will focus on recent contributions that remain valid and that represent the current situation in terms of scientific debate. We shall also attempt to evaluate the empirical support that we are currently able to rely upon. We hope that research moves forward as a result of facing off hypotheses, not only in the field of coherence, reason and logic, but also by providing new tests that allow us to gradually dismiss any findings that prove to be inconsistent with the empirical information. We are aware that simple ideas may be necessary for their use in the social dissemination of knowledge, but stark reality cannot be reduced to obvious stereotypes, naïve preconceptions, logical estimates or empty trivialities. Simplifications only help to perpetuate an archaeology of the spectacle or to add value to cultural merchandise and can not make knowledge advance. For this very reason, we sometimes create more problems than we solve. We must prevent the spectacle from continuing at all costs.

The structuring of sociology into the prehistory of the Mediterranean coast is affected by a range of problems resulting from factors that are not exclusive to the scientific production of this region. They are part of the undercurrent of academic inertia and involve an enormous waste of energy in coming up with useless findings that do little to advance our historical and sociological knowledge of the past.

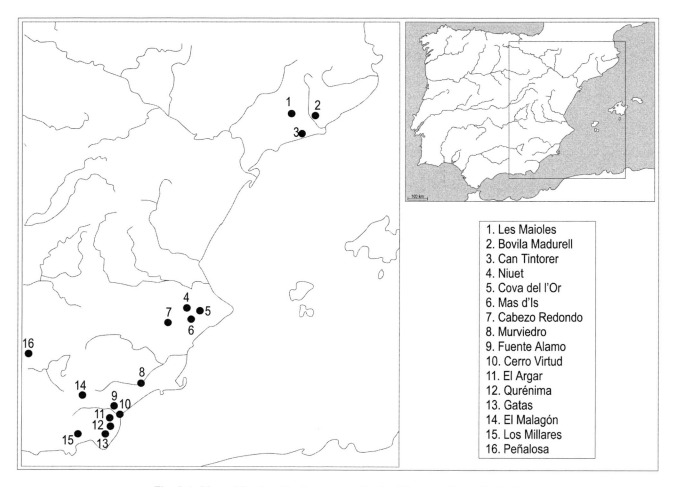

Fig. 9.1. Map of Iberian Mediterranean Basin. Sites mentioned in text.

a.- Visibility of sociological indicators. Although this poses problems in answering certain questions, it has benefited a number of scientific contributions. In terms of funerary rites, having individual graves (*Sepulcros de Fosa, El Argar*) has allowed a better understanding of both social relationships and early sociological readings, even in the absence of paleoanthropological studies. Yet when the tombs contain numerous individuals, applying the same analysis proves to be a much more complex process and it is often impossible even to accurately determine the chronological proximity of the burials, particularly if they lack broad dating series. In cases where the tomb is unaccompanied by "diagnostic types," it is only these datings that make tombs "visible" by positioning them in certain time horizons in which they previously passed unseen. In terms of the social spaces of daily life, the visibility of stone structures has given fortified settlements and stone buildings more protagonism. Yet vegetation or mud structures remain almost invisible, whilst the "negative structures" (pits, underground stores) proliferate any appearance of the spaces of activity. Visible stone structures are the determining factor in interpreting sedentarisation, war or centralisation, whilst invisible structures represent the social places of those lower down the hierarchy or in a dependent relationship.

Function tends to be forgotten (similar function with different base material) and appearance is given importance. Either that or anything visible is granted an all-embracing function (every place of work of consumption is "seen" as domestic, all daily life is "seen" as exclusively domestic). If all social spaces of every time horizon (funerary or daily life) could be recovered, we would be able to see the synchrony between recognisable places as well as to appreciate the functional heterogeneity of the social space of any human community.

b. Cultural assumptions. Although there are numerous theoretical standpoints, there is a general tendency for the space-time demarcation to have a historical-cultural outlook. The traditional or reformed "archaeological cultures" continue to lead the way in terms of analysis. It is easier to make social readings when one has a "culture" defined in terms according to Childe (recurrence of kinds of artefacts, tombs or architecture) than when one attempts to tackle the reality of the production of social life. With this, although uncertainty remains a factor (the anomalies in normative cultures are very "normal" statistically speaking), one can obtain the peace of pleasant inward-facing worlds. The result is that social readings are taken of only one part of the society; that which reproduces and respects certain guidelines and obeys the rules, whilst groups that do not do so remain hidden and in silence. So as to attend to all groups, we must study the realities of every historical situation in detail.

c. Fragmentation of the research. The research is broken down into sites. We know of only a few well-studied sites, together with countless points on the maps, classified by means of guiding fossils. It is one of the main fields for empirical generalisations. What a well-studied site has to offer is classified as normal in an age or region. Research is also broken down into administrative demarcations. Although Spanish provinces and autonomous communities are realities created by the prevailing conditions of archaeological financing and the professional groups that take part, as for history they are mere fiction. Their boundaries are only passed in the case of "traditional cultures." In all other cases, conventional regional periods predominate. It is frequently the case that those investigating an area are unaware of what is happening around it. As a paradigmatic case for the Iberian Mediterranean basin, we have the Southeast-Northeast rift. Research is also divided between specialists. Specialisation in specific periods is and has always been the most common division. We will talk of this towards the end of this essay. Yet even more dangerous is fragmentation of a scientific nature arising from an archaeological study based upon a range of analytics: sectorial visions limited to a single field produce decontextualised transhistorical perspectives.

d.- Evolutionary cycles. The diachronic knowledge of history (*Prehistory*) is split between two poles. A double evolutionary cycle has been accepted, based on a notion of increasing complexity: history would cover the same path twice (moving towards complexity): 1) From the *Neolithic* to the *Bronze Age*. 2) From the *Bronze Age* to the *Roman Empire*. We always appear to be on some point of the same path and we already know where everything comes from, where it is heading to and how it ends. The "Dark Ages" are excluded from the evolution, as are the "Dark Places" which do not meet the standard (speaking in evolutionary terms) of their time. Looking into Dark Ages and Places entails that they must be made visible. If we sidestep them, we will fail to come up with a complete social history, although already known (recognised) and we will therefore not advance our knowledge.

e.- Speculation and reason. The precarious nature of current prehistoric sociological research is such that hypotheses formulated with the freedom to do so without empirical evidence represent the majority. If we lack evidence concerning a large portion of social issues, we are free to say whatever we want. Only reason keeps speculation in check. The result is that the hypotheses are rational yet speculative. They are not the fruit of relevant findings but rather of subjective impressions or social acknowledgement of these subjectivities through repeating formulae accepted in academic circles. Speculation is

easy, but it is difficult and expensive to thoroughly look into the empirical implications of the hypotheses by means of methodical research projects. Moreover, speculation is repeated without any form of control, whereby criticisms of quotations in bibliographies outweigh comparisons of independent evidences.

f.- Theoretical force of habit. This routine involves an indiscriminate use of sociological notions that are cut off from a social theory to guide them. The professional routine (repeating what is repeated in the bibliography) does not help to build social studies as the concepts lack meaning and are disassociated from the empirical evidence. It is a problem that extends to all theoretical-methodological approaches currently used in scientific archaeological production. The banal use of concepts even results in the use of notions from a range of different theories (including contradictory ones). The interpretative rhetoric, which is barely regularised, moves to the academic-scientific circuit to be forgotten, or, depending on the reputation of the author, to be routinely cited.

From this point onwards, we will tackle the social hypotheses used over a series of stages into which we have grouped the historical time *horizons*. In light of our objective to deal with the social hypotheses, we have established these stages with preliminary political-ideological demarcated criteria instead of using the regional periodisations. We have of course paid suitable attention to the relevance of the changes in the material production and have placed the time in our calendar through the series of radiometric datings (C14 calibrated through dendrochronology) (Fig. 9.2). The aim is to demarcate the historical times of social life in which material production affected distinct entities (sexual collectives, domestic groups, communities, state institutions, social networks) by means of relationships, the nature of which must be determined in every case. Pinpointing the synchronic horizons allows us to analyse the reality of social relationships, which goes beyond the formal appearance of social aspects, beyond the established political limitations or the ideologies shared or imposed from time to time. The reproduction of the social life always breaks the mould that the institutions or perceptions would like to conserve.

9.2.- 5700/5500 - 3700/3500 CAL BC. Horizons of early agricultural practices

These two millennia correspond to horizons in which cattle-raising and farming techniques aimed at the production of food are introduced, that is to say, the time the Iberian Mediterranean communities live the "Neolithisation". They are the ages of *macroschematic* rock painting and *Levantine* rock painting.

Reflections on the implications of the Mediterranean "Neolithic" have led many of the studies into seeking out the primitive "origins" or into claiming indigenous fac-

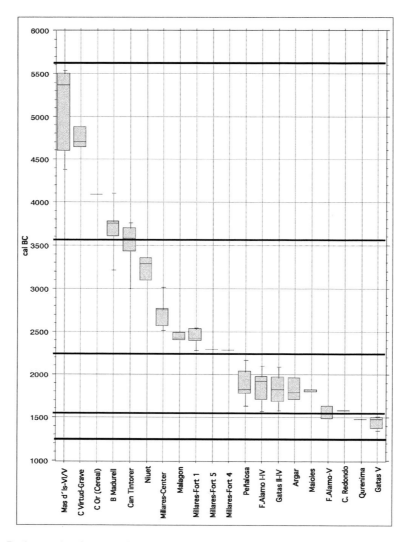

Fig. 9.2. Dating series from metioned sites. Box-plot of median dates (Castro *et al* 1996: 49).

tors, without going into the network of relationships in which the women and men were involved nor touching upon the production of social life (Castro *et al.* 2005). Talk of the "Neolithisation" has often been replaced by linear evolutionary processes (supposedly logical), which diminish our knowledge of the historical conditions and the concrete reality. Universals such as the stages of human progression (the technique) or the structures of thinking and being (the peasant life) displace history.

For this reason, work spent on the daily social reproduction (the numerous essential tasks of bringing up, feeding and taking care of the members of a society) is practically non-existent. Whilst technical innovations, demographic increases or apparent improvements continue to fascinate researchers, the realities of increases in workloads for some or all of a collective remain hidden. As a result, the growth in the population revealed by archaeological findings is described, but the central role of the women in the basic production of new social subjects and in the upkeep of the social life in general is forgotten (Escoriza 2002a).

The "Neolithic" concept itself takes for granted phenomena (demographic growth, sedentarisation, territorialisation, surplus) that are not always associated with agropastoral techniques, and that must be proved in each particular case (for example, in the Iberian Peninsula). We should become aware of the technologies for the production of food and the ways of organising labour, distributing products and possessing product, and this must be an objective more relevant than locating domestic animals and/or plants. For this reason, we have defended (Castro *et al.* 2005) the fact that it is necessary to abandon pairings such as the fictitious break between "Palaeolithic" and "Neolithic", the dichotomy between hunting-gathering and agropastoral groups, or the polarization between egalitarian-simple and civilised-complex societies (Chapman 2003). We must avoid valuing in positive terms agropastoral techniques which result in greater workloads for a important part of society and ask ourselves why these techniques were adopted and whether it may have been the result of group interests, of needs imposed due to a crisis surrounding other forms of production or of strategies of the groups that would stand to benefit from such techniques (Castro *et al.* 2005).

We will not enter into debate over the autochtonous or allochothonous nature of the agropastoral communities, as for this, we would require genetic tests that are not available at present. The "Dual Model" remains valid, in defence of the theory of the arrival by sea of communities that introduce domestic species and farming-herding techniques and who co-exist with the local hunter-gatherer communities (Bernabeu 2002). The same can be said of the percolative model, which emphasises the mechanisms for introducing agriculture and livestock-raising without the need for population migrations (Vicent 1991; Díaz-del-Río 2001). In this second model, conservation and storage techniques gain importance in evaluating the stabilisation of food reserves as a crucial factor in the adoption of new techniques (Vicent 1991; Román 1996).

The social spaces that we know of for the two millennia under consideration here are, in fact, quite minimal. There are storage caves (Cova de l'Or) and settlements that can reach a certain level of stability, even linked to ditched enclosures such as Mas d'Is (Bernabeu *et al.* 2003). The funerary sites vary significantly (burial caves, pit graves) and are spread around the Mediterranean regions, from the Northeast to the recent discoveries in Almería (Cerro de la Virtud) (Montero *et al.* 1999).

The Serpis basin (Alicante) is perhaps the best-known region, with a social study that highlights a coordination of community labour invested in political-ideological places as far back as 5000 cal BC (ditched enclosures, "sanctuaries" with *macroschematic* rock-art) (Bernabeu *et al.* 2003). This community structure of the territory cannot be extrapolated to other areas. To infer "accumulation of power" from it, would entail a proposal that we believe to be infeasible (supposedly, community labour is impossible without a social hierarchy). The regional ideology of the Serpis Basin lacked continuity and was replaced by another large territorial extension ideology, materialised in *Levantine* rock-art (Escoriza 2002a).

We should consider that the introduction of agropastoral techniques is not associated with territorial conflicts (Vicent 1991), but with dissymmetry of access to the production and to control over those that carry out the work (Cámara 2001). More importantly than domesticating the countryside, animals and plants, the domestication of social subjects generated substantial benefits for a certain sector of society. Therefore, the hypothesis of the patriarchal domination of the female collective (Escoriza 2002a; 2002b) allows us to understand the transformations between the VI and IV millennia in the Iberian Mediterranean. Or even provides the vital link for the explanation of the adoption of farming-herding techniques. Thanks to the patriarchal relations that were imposed, the pluslabour that these techniques entail would fall on the women, even though production would also benefit the male collective. Although consumption remained symmetrical, men exploited women in order to invest less labour (Castro, Escoriza & Sanahuja 2003). *Levantine* rock-art informs us of the conditions of social reproduction through the ideology of those communities.

Levantine art is dated by the superimposition of paintings and ceramic parallels during early times of agropastoral techniques (Martí Oliver & Hernández 1988), or in the period immediately after (Molina Balaguer *et al.* 2003). Representations of animals and archers (men) in hunting or fighting scenes, dominate the art form. This style remains consistent from Eastern Andalusia to North-eastern Catalonia, a span of hundreds of kilometres, suggesting a homogeneous ideology which legitimises hunting as a fundamental activity (Escoriza 2002a). The economic evidence shows that in the area of distribution of the *Levantine* art, not all the communities shared the same economic practices or in the same order of importance (Schuhmacher & Weniger 1995). Then, we must conclude that the existing thematic (artistic) uniformity entails a set of norms that is shared by communities with heterogeneous economic activities and that it is an ideology that portrays the false image that hunters are the most important economic contributors (Escoriza 2002a, 2002b). This would be a shared "ideology of patriarchs", notwithstanding how each group obtained its food. An alternative hypothesis would be that *Levantine* art captures the ideology of communities in which hunting is important in the (non exclusive) obtention of food and that they shared territories with other communities for whom agropastoral techniques were more important. It would express a "hunter ideology", giving too much importance to just one economy, male activity, in detriment to the other practices. This ideology subtracts relevance from the varied works that women carry out, which are barely represented.

An important conclusion emerges from these two hypotheses: that of a patriarchal ideology legitimised by the coercive power that generates figurative representations, which transcend the existing economic forms. The figurative representation of the division of labour depending on sex enables us to identify situations of social dissymmetry and exploitation among Mediterranean communities, independent of the techniques of food obtention implemented.

This social interpretation concurs with the evidence from the Northeast c. 5000-3700 cal BC (Molist, Ribé & Saña 1995). There, the *Sepulcros de Fosa* (Muñoz 1965) consist of individual burials, which allow us to jointly analyse paleoanthropological studies, associated grave goods and functional analyses. In this way, we have managed to establish a division of labour between men and women. Men tend to have bows and arrows and tools to cut meat and women are associated with tools for other activities (e.g. for working skin) (Gibaja 2002). Trace-element analysis of human bones from Bóvila Madurell indicates sex inequalities of diet (men have a meat diet, while women follow a vegetable diet) (Malgosa *et al.* 1996). The dissymmetric labour, that favours the male collective, is documented in the patriarchal ideology (*Levantine* art), in the funerary expression (grave goods) and in material reality (food consumption), confirming the male domination around the V millennium cal BC.

In the *Sepulcros de Fosa* some objects of remote origin as well as collections of materials in some male burials (including child tombs) have been discovered, which strongly suggest hereditary social dissymmetry (Gibaja 2002). This situation is detected at the moment of development of the mining activities of flint and variscite in Can Tintorer (Bosch & Estrada 1997), a system of planning and control of a considerable amount of specialised work. However, from 3000 cal BC onwards, the spreading collective funerary rites in Northeast Iberia suggest that the mechanisms of appropriation and individualisation that had been instigated were discontinued.

9.3.- 3700/3500 – 2300/2200 CAL BC. Horizons of duality

This stage can be defined by a new political-ideological reality, which is expressed in the "Chalcolithic idols" and in *Schematic* rock-art. Their datings are staggered over more than a millennium (Castro *et al.* 2004; Sanchidrian & Valladas, 2002). The dominant ideology is expressed through this iconographic world and through collective tombs, sequential burials and varied secondary treatments. The material expression of this ideology is distributed throughout a large part of the Iberian Peninsula, especially in the southern half. The funerary sites are natural caves or artificial hypogeum, and in the Southeast there is a funerary architecture with chamber tombs of various types (Leisner & Leisner 1943). *Tholoi* can be safely dated from 3100 cal BC onwards, although absolute dates are lacking for most of their variants (including Almerian circular tombs without corridor and megalithic tombs with corridor). Paleoanthropological studies, offering the key to social understanding and clearly sex-defined information, are almost completely lacking as well.

It is possible to distinguish three horizons, with turning points in 3100 and 2500 cal BC (Castro, Escoriza & Sanahuja 2004; Molina González *et al.* 2004). Right from the start new settlements appear in flat areas. Towards 3100 fortified settlements and *tholoi* appear (Los Millares). From 2500 onwards, there are new fortified sites (Los Millares "Forts" and mountainous settlements in the Iberian Levant) and *beaker* pottery.

The *Los Millares Horizon* has attracted international interest, as a reference point for the beginning of unequal societies. The singularity of the Los Millares site, where a large village with stone walls co-exists with a necropolis of *tholoi* and more than ten small forts, led to consider it as a central place, first as a colonial foundation (metallurgic prospectors from Eastern Mediterranean) and then as the centre of a hierarchical society. Many social interpretations presupposed arid conditions similar to those of today in Southeast Iberia (Chapman 1978; 1982; 1990; Gilman 1976, 1987; Gilman & Thornes 1985; Mathers 1984a, 1984b). Now, however, isotopic carbon analysis in plants (Araus *et al.* 1997) and oxygen isotopes in marine shells and carbonates (Castro *et al.* 1998b) show higher rainfall in the III millennium and a drop in temperature in the II millennium (Castro *et al.* 2000). Defenders of the first hypothesis have had to adjust their theories (Chapman 2003).

The social inferences regarding Los Millares are supported by the study of its necropolis. The analyses conducted by Chapman (1978, 1982) associated each tomb to one unit of kinship and concluded that we are dealing with a hierarchical society, with ranked lineages and economic management based on redistribution. The lineages (tombs) of high rank would be those of bearers of "prestige goods", identifiable by their exoticism (allochthonous materials such as ivory or ostrich eggs), their symbology (decorated pottery) and technical complexity (metal objects, right at the moment when copper metallurgy was beginning).

However, a revision of the evidence does not allow us to draw conclusions on the dissymmetric societies or to conclude anything about relationships of exploitation (Micó 1993, 1995; Castro *et al.* 1998a; Chapman 2003). The distribution of grave goods in tombs (quantity and quality of the materials) does not reflect appropriation of wealth. In those where there are individual elements or allochthonous materials, there is no accumulation, only unequal presence. These singular goods coincide with the larger tombs and with a larger number of burials, in other words, with larger groups and with a greater capacity of labour (Micó 1993; 1995). However, the dissymmetry at the heart of the lineages and domestic groups eludes us, in the light of the community ideology of the funerary rites.

Another argument employed in the inferences of social hierarchy is the so-called defensive architecture of the village and forts of Los Millares. This has attempted to perceive signs of military power and an encoding of prestige. A territory surrounded by forts that defend the frontier has even been suggested. Semi-nomadic communities and constructors of megalithic tombs (Arribas & Molina 1978) would have resided outside. These interpretations have been extrapolated to other fortified settlements, not only in the Southeast but also in other areas.

These proposals, however, are loaded with pitfalls. Firstly, the datings of the "forts" (Molina González *et al.* 2004) demonstrate that they only co-exist with the central settlement and necropolis for three centuries, c. 2500-2200 cal BC, the only horizon in which the frontier would fit. Secondly, the only agricultural land lies outside of this territory, which would mean that it would depend on other communities for food (Caro & Rodríguez 1989), a situation that also affects similar settlements in the Vera basin (Castro *et al.* 1998a). In short, if there was a frontier, it was political and not economic. Thirdly, there is a functional paradox here, as the fortification of a settlement does not correspond with its political position nor with its size, thus it may well be a mistake to compare a fortified village with a hierarchical one (Chapman 2003). A fourth problem can be found in the assumption that military architecture can only be understood in vertical relations and that there is no room for community coordination in order to go about setting up collective defence.

Recent research has proven that Los Millares is not the only case in point. There are other settlements with stone and adobe walling in the Southeast and in other regions, and there are also enclosed areas defended with ditches in other areas, even in earlier chronologies (Nocete 2001a; Díaz-del-Río 2004a). Although we may be able to trace these back to the VI millennium (Bernabeu *et al.* 2003), for now, the settlements defended by ditches are only dated to 3400 cal BC in Niuet (Bernabeu *et al.* 1994).

As such, greater heterogeneity is increasingly observed in the settlements (Castro *et al.* 2004). Right from the time of their appearance, walled places co-exist with open settlements, and hillside villages with villages on the planes (of varying size). The duality in settlement size was an argument used to consider two hierarchical levels and to defend a hierarchical society (Chapman 1990). But there are also arguments that question whether such a duality entails political hierarchy. There is nothing to say that a community that constructs defensive structures or is of greater size dominates the other open or smaller settlements, if no other information is forthcoming. To locate a central power from this argument simply is not possible, nor does it show vertical relations without other evidences. A community may decide to defend its living conditions, or there are objective conditions that allow demographic concentration (Castro *et al.* 1998a). It has also not been possible to demonstrate differences in wealth between domestic units, although knowledge of the records is lacking and despite the fact that an explanation has been provided for the collection of lithic materials in a dwelling (El Malagón) in terms of a "big man" type leadership (Ramos Millán 1998).

Places of specialised labour have been discovered (metallurgy, lithic carvings, bone work). These are located in specialised buildings or in domestic units, preferentially located in large and/or fortified villages. And location of numerous small open villages in the most fertile lands supports the hypothesis that these communities carried out agricultural and livestock farming (Castro *et al.* 1998b). With this evidence, current sociological debate is centred on the nature of the relationships within communities associated to fortified sites such as Los Millares and on their relations with other communities.

One hypothesis defends a class society with a tributary state. Farming and livestock-raising communities would pay taxes to certain elites that manage rituals (theocracy) and also allochthonous or singular materials (Cámara 2001). This "initial class society" is set in an *Atlantic-Mediterranean Civilisation of the Copper Age* (Arteaga 2000), being the Southeast a periphery of a system with its epicentre in the Guadalquivir valley (Nocete, 2001b). Empirical support can be found in the differences between settlements (fortified and/or large as opposed to open and/or small) and craft specialisation (metallurgy in particular) as an indicator of the control exercised by the elites.

In the light of this position, the analysis of conditions of production and appropriation has led us to negate the evidence of exploitation, at least among communities or lineages (Castro *et al.* 1998a). Division in tasks is accompanied by a non differential access to products. The only differences are due to the direct pluslabour of communities (defensive structures, tombs, singular products that are widely disseminated). A "Dual Production" did exist (Castro *et al.* 1998a; Risch 1995; 2002), with craft specialisation in large/fortified villages that distributed artefacts, and agropastoral activities in small communities that supplied food to the former. There were no restrictions on the distribution of production. This exemplified a situation of symmetry between communities and domestic units, which does not cast aside exploitation relationships in the domestic or relative-based sphere, or between sexes.

Following this line of thought, equalitarian and unequal social relationships could co-exist (Chapman 2003), or by incorporating models of competitive factionalism, inequalities between settlements may be explained in political terms, due to competition between leaders and domestic groups, and between social sectors (Díaz-del-Río 2004b).

More recently, we have proposed another discussion of the "urban" character of large nuclei with handicraft specialisation as is the case at Los Millares, posing the question of whether these settlements are meeting places that act as supra-community political epicentres (Castro *et al.* 2003). The alternative, in our hypothesis, would be closed communities, although they maintained the productive complementarity and the distribution networks. Investigating the first hypothesis would entail recognising the existence of cities and political centres in conditions of social symmetry and economic reciprocity, a remote possibility for ethnography and historiography, whilst accepting the lack of knowledge about the reality of prehistoric illiterate societies.

With regards to the distribution of products, we find ourselves with the same material models in remote regions and without territorial continuity. Therefore, architectural forms (surrounding walls, circular houses, megalithic tombs, *tholoi*), decorated ceramics (including *beaker* forms) or symbolic media (*idols, schematic* art) are present in an uneven way in synchronic, domestic or funerary places of the Iberian Peninsula. Different types with the same use-value demonstrate the juxtaposition and inconsistent distribution. From the perspective of an "initial class society", the "Chalcolithic idols" would be an expression of the ideology of the elite (Nocete 2001a; 2001b). In contrast, our explanation frames them in horizontal politics of links between collectives. The reciprocity and social symmetry would allow unobstructed mobility, thanks to the security that relationships (of whatever type) between "relatives" afford, and between geographically inconsistent places, as there are no ground rules imposed in the ideological expression, only an open and polymorphic style (Castro *et al.* 2004).

Between 2500-2200 cal BC, fortified and hilltop villages begin to appear in the Southeast and Levant, together with *beaker* pottery, in keeping with recurring models throughout Europe. Speculative explanations have proliferated about the significance of the *beaker* wares (new ethnic presence, matrimonial trousseau, vessels for prestige drinks), however their function remains to be clarified and their dissemination in the III millennium forms part of the aforementioned inter-communitarian networks. This stylistic tradition disappeared from the Southeast and the Levant (but not the Northeast) around c. 2000-1800 cal BC. The indicators of inter-community violence (sophisticated systems of defence, new types of weapons, destruction of settlements) do not have a concrete explanation to date. Perhaps the inter-community relations generally originated from inequalities in symmetric dissemination, maybe the communities of the Southeast attempted to defend their system of "Dual Production" in the light of the expansive politics of other production mechanisms (*Argaric* norms appeared), or perhaps remote violent groups arrived to disrupt previously stable social structures (evidence of which can be found in the tombs of warriors with *beaker* grave goods from other regions and later dates).

9.4.- 2300/2200 – 1550/1500 cal BC. Horizons of El Argar

The seven centuries that span this stage are dominated by what is known as the *El Argar Culture*. Its existence was first discovered in the 19th Century with the first excavations (Siret & Siret 1890) and was later systematised within a sociological framework two decades ago (Lull 1983).

To date, around 2000 tombs have been documented and are situated in areas within the settlements. They are individual, or at best triple. Grave good associations, indicators of sex and social category, have enabled a definition of the *Argaric* norm, an ideological expression possible in the conditions of social reproduction which benefit the dominant class and their political correlate,

the state (Lull & Risch 1995; Castro *et al.* 1998a; Lull 2000). The uneven distribution of social wealth in tombs and the possession of weapons by a restricted group enable us to distinguish burial categories, expression of social classes (Lull & Estévez 1986; Castro *et al.* 1993-94; Lull 2000). Physical anthropological studies show lower physical activity and lower occurrences of pathological diseases among the dominant class (Jiménez Brobeil & García 1989-90), or the benefit of better health care and a longer life expectancy (Castro *et al.* 1999a).

There are two main stages in the development of the *Argaric* society, with changes around 1800 cal BC (Castro *et al.* 1993-94). The first stage shows a dominant group in tombs of adult males with halberds, short swords and gold, and women with the female knife and awl association that we will find until the end of the *Argaric* society. From 1800 cal BC onwards, inheritance was consolidated, expressed in child tombs with normative associations. In this recent stage there is a graduation of wealth inside the dominant group, with a prominent sector of sword-bearers (men) or diadem-owners (women), and a second order in which men are entrusted with axes-adzes and women with knifes and awls.

Years ago, it was debated whether "chiefdom" or "gangster-elite" where appropriate descriptions for the *Argaric* political system. However, it is now generally accepted that there was a state system. The institutionalisation of violence and its control by the dominant class enables us to define the political structures as State type (Lull & Risch 1995). An "Argaric expansion" from the Southeast towards interior regions implies the imposition of their norms on other communities, where they organised the specialisation of labour on a regional scale and territorial political control, legitimised by an ideology which manifests itself in funerary rites. Even analysis of the political "complexity" of the territory indicated three hierarchical levels in settlements, which correspond to the State structures (Chapman 1990). Only those who associate the 'state' with governmental institutions, comparable with those of the Ancient Middle East, doubt the state nature of the system (Gilman 1997; 1998).

The scientific debate today is centred on the mechanisms of social exploitation, the existence of which cannot be doubted. One of these mechanisms would be the tax levied at a local level, to explain the movement of products towards the centre where they come under the control of the dominant class (Contreras & Cámara 2002). However, on another scale, taxation has been considered as the mechanism of dependence of a series of "*Argaric* principalities" on the state political centres (Arteaga 2000).

The importance of servitude linked to the dominant domestic groups is another mechanism of exploitation under discussion. It is recognisable by the coexistence in *Argaric* houses of graves of the dominant group and of individuals without grave goods, and who show signs of lower nutrition and higher work loads, arguments for talk about a "servile society" (Cámara 2001; Contreras 2001). However, these differences have been justified due to the fact that belonging to a social class would depend on extra-domestic circumstances and not on inter-familiar relations. The noteworthy absence of graves of adult males in secondary populations, such as Gatas, contrasts with their representation in central places such as El Argar, which entails an extra-community management of the funerary appointment of the men of the higher classes (Micó 1993). The child burials of the dominant class confirm that inheritance was strengthened from 1800 cal BC onwards (Castro et al. 1993-94), although precision is needed about the institutional area of the acquisition of rights.

On the other hand, the importance of the appropriation of means of labour by the *Argaric* aristocracy and of the productive conditions that are derived from them has been highlighted (Castro et al. 1998a; 1999a; Risch 1995; 2002). It has even been noted that ownership would not be in the hands of the families, but in those of extra-familiar state institutions (Lull 2000). In this way, they established a "system of vertical production" (Risch 1995; 2002; Castro et al. 1998a). This implies the existence of small communities dedicated to farming (presence of sickles) and cattle-raising, who work under the obligation to supply products and labour in fortified settlements equipped with mills, storage areas for grain and thermal process ovens (Lull & Risch 1995; Risch 1995; 2002). Patrons of measures in ceramics (capacities) would permit the control of grain. Imposition of extensive agriculture, based on the cultivation of barley, would ease management of this system in the final centuries of the *Argaric* state.

Furthermore, rigid production norms are imposed on crafts (metallurgy and pottery). In pottery production, specialised workshops managed at an extra-domestic scale and domestic industry co-existed, both subject to the standard models (Castro et al. 1999a: 195). In making reference to ethnographic cases in order to draw conclusions of a generalised domestic and exclusively feminine labour (Colomer 2005: 207), we distance ourselves from empirical evidence and fall into the realms of naturalised stereotypes of women's work.

In the mining-metallurgy works, regional organisation of labour was imposed, as the only places of transformation have been discovered in specialised settlements in mining areas (Peñalosa) or in few and far between political economic centres like El Argar. As the primary analysis of lead isotopes suggests, despite its wealth of copper minerals, allochthonous metals arrived to coastal Almería, possibly from Sierra Morena (Gale et al. 1999). Weapons, tools and copper and silver ornaments passed through the hands of the *Argaric* aristocracy who monopolised their use and circulation, and ended up in their tombs.

Unfortunately, very little is known of the *Argaric* domestic buildings and the activities that took place in them,

and even an estimation of their size has proved difficult to establish. The domestic groups linked to the dominant class could be grouped in concrete spaces within the settlements, as is indicated by distributions of burials in Fuente Alamo (Risch 2002: 274). However, the spatial coexistence with singular buildings ("towers") or buildings for communal use (cisterns), inform us about their coexistence with political ideological spaces or common services.

The idea of a society based on mono-parental nuclear families, which has arisen through the discovery of married couples in twin man/woman graves, has therefore to be rejected. Carbon-14 dating of these burial sites indicates that both individuals died decades apart (Castro et al. 1993-94), and as such the domestic group must have another make-up, perhaps of extended family (Lull 2000). Furthermore, osteometric variability studies indicate male mobility and practices of exogamy with matrilocality, to which it is also important to add the hypothesis of a matrilineal transmission of rights (Castro et al. 1993-94; 1998a; Lull 2000).

The social conditions of women, at least in the dominant class, and without ruling out patriarchal relationships, are without doubt more favourable in matrilocal and matrilineal lineages than when patrilineal and patrilocal lineages impose a forced female exogamy. Nevertheless, the demographic increase documented in the *Argaric* state, together with a high rate of infant mortality, placed enormous burdens on the women in order to sustain basic *Argaric* production (biological reproduction) and to assume the duties of the maintenance of subjects (Castro et al. 1998a; 1998b); despite the fact that these burdens could vary depending on social class.

Towards the Northern *Argaric* territories, in the Iberian Levant region, the synchronic stage of the *Argaric* world is associated with the *Valencian Bronze Age* (Tarradell 1963; Hernández Alcaraz & Hernández Pérez 2004). Small populations in fortified settlements have been discovered, with architecture of stone, almost inexistent up until that point in time, as well as heterogeneous funerary rites outside the settlements. Historical-cultural concerns have dominated the bibliography to date, and sociological proposals have only arisen in the past decade, beyond the hypothesis of the predominance of autarchic agricultural villages (Aparicio 1976).

It is this proposal that currently dominates the debate. In the light of the possibility of the political organisation of the territory into a hierarchy (centralisation) and of social hierarchy, depending on the size and on some of the documented crafts (Bernabeu et al. 1989), the hypothesis in force is that of a society based on small autonomous and autocratic communities which are formed by extended families who maintain reciprocal relations, given the inexistence of the appropriation of labour methods or final products (Jover 1999).

The relationship between these Levantine communities and the *Argaric* political systems has been largely overlooked (except in historical-cultural code). The only sound contribution suggests the transfer of the surplus of the communities of the southern Levant (Alicante) towards *Argaric* territories, thanks to the circulation of metal objects, whose manufacture is not documented in Levantine populations at the moment (Jover 1999). This point opens the way for investigating the inter-territorial relations that affect other regions (Mancha, Guadalquivir, and Southwest).

Information regarding the coastal/pre-littoral area of Northeast Iberia continues to be fragmented and heterogeneous. At this point, they use and construct megalithic tombs in the pre-Pyrenees regions (Les Maioles) (Castro *et al.* 1996; Clop & Faura 2003), whilst other funerary sites continue to be used (caves, hypogeum, graves). This situation does not seem to have changed substantially since 3500 cal BC. Imbalances between collectives have not been detected and for this reason a social atomisation with small semi-nomadic communities dedicated to the production of food and handicrafts for self-consumption has been generally accepted. However, some tombs with *beaker* grave goods suggest the existence of a privileged sector of society, and it remains to be confirmed if there were stable mechanisms of exploitation, or what constituted the women-men relationships (Sanahuja *et al.* 1995).

The end of this stage corresponds to the end of the *Argaric* state. Its definitive crisis spelt the end of the *Argaric* political-ideological instances. This occurred when production conditions no longer afforded the contribution of surpluses which were appropriated by the dominant class, nor was it possible to carry out craft production, or to maintain the collectives that assumed the labour. Through revolution or dissolution, the state structures ceased to function in the social reproduction (Castro *et al.* 1999a: 194).

9.5.- 1550/1500 – 1300/1250 CAL BC. Times of autonomy

This stage is problematic right from the start: it was only recognised three decades ago (Molina González 1978; Gil Mascarell 1981), and as such, the documentation is limited, but excavations in sites such as Gatas (Castro *et al.* 1999a) have invited new hypotheses. We now know that there is a reorganisation of production, a renewal of the product models and a restructuring of the social spaces, with the construction of new buildings, predominantly in stone (Castro *et al.* 1999a; Castro 2005). The settlements almost always occupied the same *Argaric* locations, but we know that there were new settlements (Murviedro).

An ongoing debate rages on the *post-Argaric* character of this stage. The disappearance of the *Argaric* state and its political-ideological practices are exemplified in the disappearance of the former funerary rites, which poses the problem of restricting a fundamental basis for sociological studies. However, this is a central argument when referring to a *post-Argaric* situation (Castro 1992; Castro *et al.* 1996; 1999a), which we refer to as the *Villena Horizon*, given the relevance of this locality (Castro 1992; 2005). In contrast, those who affirm the continuity of a "cultural tradition", continue to employ the term *Argaric* (Molina González & Cámara 2004).

The *Villena Horizon* attracts interest in terms of investigating how communities that lived through the disappearance of class dominance and the state acted and also allows us to deal with the rocky path that the collectives in the Southeast followed. This stage can be characterised by the recuperation of the autonomy of the communities, lineages and domestic groups.

This new situation carried consequences in the quality of life of the men and women, as nutrition improved: food became more varied and accessible, with an increased availability of meat in the daily diet, including wild animals from hunt (Castro *et al.* 1999a). Greater capacity of the women to control their bodies and basic production could limit the number of births, resulting in demographic stability.

Autonomy is also expressed in the recuperation of the collective character of the burials. Tombs such as that of Qurénima are typified by inhumation and cremation rites, and by use of individual urns within the common area. Ancient collective burial places have also been reused (megalithic tombs, funerary caves). There are but a few communities of the Vinalopó basin (Alicante) that carried out individual burials within the populated areas. This heterogeneity of the funeral forms distances itself from the regulated norms.

There is specialisation of labour in certain workshops, with some homogeneous models (Castro 1992; 2005). Metallurgy, pottery or thermal processing of materials can be placed equally in a domestic framework as in an extra-domestic one. The autonomous politics of the communities suppose production geared towards self-sufficiency and towards the maintenance of horizontal social networks, in which some goods circulated.

The dissemination of products, in conditions of inter-communitarian symmetry would probably have developed on the basis of reciprocal relations (Castro *et al.* 2003; Castro 2005). However, as in *pre-Argaric* times, we know that allochthonous products arrive to the Iberian Mediterranean (tin, copper, goldsmith pieces, wheel-thrown pottery, amber, iron). Their obtention via interregional networks entailed pluslabour and their access was restricted to some collectives (or some individuals thereof), who amortised them in their tombs. Dissymmetry is probable within some communities or domestic groups, but we cannot ascertain whether we are dealing with owners or a patriarchal form of control.

Among the products pertaining to the *Villena Horizon*, South of the river Ebro, decorative ceramics of the *Cogotas I* style can be found. The explanation for the wide distribution of the *Cogotas I* style throughout the Iberian Peninsula, now does not take into consideration the seasonal migratory movements of shepherds (Jimeno 2001). There are theories that relate this to the practices of the social elites (Contreras & Cámara 2000; Delibes & Abarquero 1997; Harrison 1995). However, its appearance responds more to examples of discontinuity typical of linear social networks, as in the proposals for the *Los Millares Horizons*, than a distribution linked to imbalances of social classes. For this reason, the theory of mobility of products between "relatives" or the dependence of circulation of individuals among domestic groups (exogamy) is maintained (Castro *et al.* 1995).

On the other hand, a series of hypotheses point to the existence of a dominant class. A proposal has introduced the notion of "*post-argaric* principalities", taking the size of certain settlements as a starting point (Arteaga *et al.* 2005), the payment of taxes to the elite is noted (Martínez & Afonso 1998; Molina González & Cámara 2004), or a "class society" is proposed from the management of gold in deposits or funerary grave goods (Jover & López 2004:298). It has even been suggested that the "system of vertical production" survived in specific places (Risch 2002: 281). To evaluate these hypotheses we turn to an area exceptionally well documented, the Villena region, where a relatively large village has been excavated, Cabezo Redondo (Soler 1987), and where deposits of gold objects have been found (Soler 1965; 1987; Almagro 1974).

Cabezo Redondo has some multifunctional workshops, such as the XV Department (milling, metallurgy, textiles), which are highlighted in the context of other units of domestic nature (Soler 1987; Risch 2002). These types of workshop may have been the result of the coordination of labour in an extra-domestic framework, but also part of large domestic units, which do not exclude exploitation relationships.

The accumulation of products of silver, gold and other materials among the Villena "treasures" demands an explanation in this context, concluding the chronology of this moment (Castro 1992; Castro *et al.* 1996). Although they have been treated as treasures of a personal or princely collection, the grouping of heterogeneous pieces and the wear and tear visible in many of them (Perea 2001), point to a more appropriate definition of scrap goods only for recasting. The explanation, therefore, should fall within the framework of specialised forms of handicraft production whose products we find distributed around various regions of the Iberian Peninsula, as in, for example, the Villena-Estremoz-type bracelets or the gold "trumpets" (Armbruster & Perea 1994; Castro 1992). These pieces are among those that appear in some of the Villena tombs, as well as in funerary sites of the Iberian Northeast (Castro 1992). We should only refer to

"princely treasures" after confirming that the conditions of social reproduction allowed the political management of the accumulation of singular products and the appropriation of the surpluses via the exploitation of extensive collectives.

In contrast, demonstrating the existence of social classes and of a centralised territory is somewhat complicated when observing the productive self-sufficiency of the communities (Jover & López 2004: 298). It would indeed be necessary to establish which communities originated the appropriated surplus or the mechanisms to obtain labour from agropastoral groups and how it is managed in such a way as to benefit a dominant class.

Therefore, we uphold the hypothesis that the social inequality discernable from the Villena "treasures" form part of a reality in which privileged subjects in the heart of their communities or domestic groups may have obtained appropriation of handicraft goods (precious metals for example) produced in specialised workshops, or imported via trans-Mediterranean networks (*Mycenaean*). The singular nature of the gold from Villena warrants a closer investigation of this last possibility. The duality of the domestic units displayed by the settlements of the *Villena Horizon* or the co-existence of domestic groups of varying constitution compels us to tackle the mechanisms of coordination of productive labour and access to the goods produced in order to clarify the nature of these units (Castro 2005). The exploitation of relatives or domestic servants, or the patriarchal exploitation of women, does not constitute an adequate condition for approaching the subject of extended exploitation that we could associate with the state (Castro *et al.* 2003: 14).

The attempts to relate the circulation of certain materials (gold, amber, ivory, iron, wheel-thrown pottery) to central-peripheral models also have to be formulated with caution, given that their presence is by no means regular, and is rather quite sporadic. It is important to bear in mind that they may well have circulated within horizontal networks, which were not controlled by a dominant power. If this was the case, the aristocratic administration, if indeed it did exist, must only have been circumscribed in small political territories.

9.6.- 1300/1250 – 900 CAL BC: The Dark Ages and Protohistory

Here, we begin to avail of the evidence of the previous stage, the *Villena Horizon*, bearing in mind that the historical context from 900 cal BC onwards is increasingly better documented, in configuring a social reality influenced by the consolidation of economic-politics administered from coastal epicentres, more precisely, the colonial establishments of the *Phoenician* states. However, the age spanning the XIII-X centuries still eludes us due to the convergence of various factors.

This age corresponds to the beginning of the new settlements where social existence lived on, and the information we have available almost without exception comes from stratigraphic records. Furthermore, the scarce archaeological sites with only one phase of occupation during this age were abandoned without destruction or fire and the centres of activity which were the object of regular strict cleansing hardly offer any materials or remains. On the other hand, the production models, with some exceptions (metallic products), live on beyond 900, which complicates the chronological distinction.

The same is true in the case of the burials. We now know that incineration rites and the burial of the burnt remains predominated, forming quite extensive necropolis, the *Urn-Fields* of the traditional bibliography. But these necropolises will also have a continued existence, which obscures their chronological distinction.

It must be added that, as we pointed out at the beginning, this stage has remained in the hands of research circles with a special interest in the more recent moments (*Protohistory* in academic terms). These circles have a scientific tradition linked more closely to "classical archaeology" and who, more often than not, give special importance to the numerous sources of information of classic writings. Moreover, the wealth of the material production of the stages after 900 cal BC attracts a lot of attention to the consequent detriment of the earlier times.

The analytical procedures and instrumental methodology, which have been incorporated in the research into the earlier periods, have only recently been assumed in these circles of researchers, who favour a more traditional archaeographic approach. To quote an example, we only have to refer to the substantial decrease in the number of radiometric datings available, a consequence of an attitude of scepticism of the independent analysis of the "guide fossils" for establishing chronologies. Thus, in the light of the problems of temporal differentiation of many types of material, a "crushing" effect of the chronologies is produced, and there is the tendency to late-date nearly all of the documented contexts (Castro 1992; Castro *et al.* 1996). The consequence of this research situation is that the XIII to X Centuries cal BC constitute an authentic *Dark Age* for research into eastern peninsular societies.

We also must add that the questions that guide the research no longer centre so much on the dynamics of social change or on crisis situations or the transformation of institutions such as the state. The research circles of *Protohistory* are more concerned with topics of cultural historicism, such as the supposed paths of identity constitution (*ethnogenesis*), when investigating the "peoples" which are cited in written sources.

When this is not the case, and there are concerns around economic and political realities, attention is turned towards circuits of circulation of materials (*colonial* or *indigenous*). Therefore, it has become routine practice to establish sociological explanations whilst availing of pre-established formulas, such as the "economy of prestige goods" (Frankenstein 1997; Frankenstein & Rowlands 1978; Castro 2000), or equally of Braudelian principles (Ruiz-Gálvez 1998) which, when based on formal economic essentials, justify pre-established universals.

The XIII to X centuries currently constitute an "Obscured Age" in research, so much so that the Iberian Mediterranean appear as part of, or antecedent of the ethnically labelled worlds (*Phoenician-Cypriots, Aegeans, Indo-Europeans*), with remnants of a entire Mediterranean, or, at times Atlantic-Mediterranean.

We will conclude our paper here, as tackling sociological questions beyond the problems already highlighted belongs to another cycle of "origins of inequalities", far from the area in which this volume is to be inserted.

9.7.- References

ALMAGRO GORBEA, M. 1974: "Orfebrería del Bronce Final en la Península Ibérica. El tesoro de Abía de la Obispalía, la orfebrería tipo Villena y los cuencos de Axtroki". *Trabajos de Prehistoria* 31: 39-100.

APARICIO, J. 1976: *Estudio económico y social del Bronce Valenciano.* Ayuntamiento de Valencia. Valencia.

ARAUS, J.L.; FEBRERO, A.; BUXO, R.; CAMALICH, M.D.; MARTIN, D.; MOLINA, F.; RODRIGUEZ-ARIZA, M.O. & ROMAGOSA, I. 1997: "Changes in carbon isotope discrimination in grain cereals from different regions of the western Mediterranean Basin during the past seven millennia. Palaeoenvironmental evidence of a differential change in aridity during the late Holocene". *Global Change Biology* 3-2: 107-118.

ARMBUSTER, B. & PEREA, A. 1994: "Tecnología de herramientas rotativas durante el Bronce Final Atlántico: El depósito de Villena". *Trabajos de Prehistoria* 51 (2): 69-87.

ARRIBAS, A. & MOLINA, F. 1978: *El poblado de 'Los Castillejos' en Las Peñas de Los Gitanos (Montefrío, Granada): campaña de excavaciones de 1971. El corte núm. 1.* Cuadernos de Prehistoria de la Universidad de Granada. Serie mongráfica 3. Universidad de Granada. Granada.

ARRIBAS, A.; MOLINA, F.; CARRION, F.; CONTRERAS, F.; MARTÍNEZ, G.; RAMOS, A.; SAEZ, L.; DE LA TORRE, F.; BLANCO, I. & MARTÍNEZ, J. 1987: "Informe preliminar de los resultados obtenidos durante la campaña de excavaciones en el poblado de Los Millares (Santa Fé de Mondújar, Almería). 1985". *Anuario Arqueológico de Andalucía. 1985. II. Actividades Sistemáticas.* Consejería de Cultura. Sevilla: 245-262.

ARTEAGA, O. 2000: "La sociedad clasista inicial y el origen del Estado en el territorio de El Argar". *Revista Atlántica-Mediterránea de Prehistoria y Arqueología Social* 3: 121-219.

ARTEAGA, O.; SCHUBART, H.; PINGEL, V.; ROOS, A.M. & KUNST, M. 2005: "La culminación de las excavaciones arqueológicas en Fuente Alamo (Cuevas de Almanzora, Almería). Campaña de 1999". *Anuario Arqueológico de Anda-*

lucía, 2002, II. Actividades Sistemáticas y Puntuales. Consejería de Cultura. Sevilla: 104-119.

BERNABEU, J. 2002: "The social and symbolic context of Neolithization", *Saguntum-PLAV,* Extra 5: 209-234.

BERNABEU, J.; GUITART, I. & PASCUAL, Ll. 1989: "Reflexiones en torno al patrón de asentamiento en el País Valenciano, entre el Neolítico y la Edad del Bronce". *Saguntum-PLAV* 22: 99-123.

BERNABEU, J.; PASCUAL, J.L.; OROZCO, T.; BADAL, E.; FUAMANAL, M.P. & GARCIA PUCHOL, O. 1994: "Niuet (L´Alquería d´Asnar). Poblado del III milenio a.C.". *Recerques del Museu d´Alcoi* 3: 9-74.

BERNABEU, J.; OROZCO, T.; DÍEZ, A.; GÓMEZ PUCHE, M. & MOLINA HERNÁNDEZ, F.J. 2003: "Mas d´Is (Penàguila, Alicante): Aldeas y recintos monumentales del neolítico inicial en el valle del Serpis". *Trabajos de Prehistoria* 60 (2): 39-59.

BOSCH, J. & ESTRADA, A. 1997: "La minería en Gavá (Bajo Llobregat) en el IV° milenio". *Rubricatum* 1 (1): 265-270.

CÁMARA, J.A. 2001: *El ritual funerario en la Prehistoria Reciente en el Sur de la Península Ibérica*. British Archaeological Reports International Series 913. Oxford.

CARA, L. & RODRIGUEZ, J.M. 1989: "Fronteras culturales y estrategias territoriales durante el III milenio A.C. en el valle medio y bajo del Andarax (Almería)". *Arqueología Espacial* 13: 63-76.

CASTRO MARTÍNEZ, P.V. 1992: *La Península Ibérica entre 1600-900 cal ANE*. Universidad Autónoma de Barcelona. "Tesis Doctorales". Bellaterra.

- 2000: "Book Reviews: Arqueología del colonialismo". *European Journal of Archaeology* 3-2: 281-283.

- 2005: "El Horizonte de Villena. El Sudeste ibérico c. 1550-1250 cal ANE". In press.

CASTRO MARTÍNEZ, P.V.; ESCORIZA MATEU, T. & SANAHUJA YLL, E. 2003: "Trabajo, Reciprocidad y Explotación. Prácticas Sociales, Sujetos Sexuados y Condiciones Materiales". In: *Cultura & Política. IX Congreso de Antropología* (Barcelona 2002). Institut Català d´Antropologia. CD-rom edition. Barcelona.

- 2004: *Soportes simbólicos, prácticas sociales y redes de relación en el Sudeste ibérico*. Unpublished report. Instituto Juan Gil-Albert. Alicante.

CASTRO MARTÍNEZ, P.V.; LULL, V. & MICÓ, R. 1996: *Cronología de la Prehistoria Reciente de la Península Ibérica y Baleares (c. 2800-900 cal ANE)*. British Archaeological Reports International Series 652. Oxford.

CASTRO MARTINEZ, P.V.; MICÓ, R. & SANAHUJA YLL, E. 1995: "Genealogía y cronología de la 'cultura de Cogotas I'. El estilo cerámico y el grupo de Cogotas I en su contexto arqueológico". *Boletín del Seminario de Estudios de Arte y Arqueología* LXI: 51-118.

CASTRO MARTÍNEZ, P.V.; CHAPMAN, R.W.; GILI, S.; LULL, V.; MICÓ, R.; RIHUETE, C.; RISCH, R. & SANA-

HUJA YLL, E 1993-94: "Tiempos sociales de los contextos funerarios argáricos". *Anales de Arqueología y Prehistoria* 9-10: 77-107.

- 1998a: "Teoría de la producción de la vida social: Mecanismos de explotación en el sudeste ibérico". *Boletín de Antropología Americana* 33: 25-77.

- 1998b: *Aguas Project. Palaeoclimatic Reconstruction and the Dynamics of Human Settlement and Land Use in the Area of the Middle Aguas (Almería) in the South-east of the Iberian Peninsula*. European Commission. Luxembourg.

- 1999a: *Proyecto Gatas 2: la dinámica arqueoecológica de la ocupación prehistórica*. Consejería de Cultura. Sevilla.

- 1999b: "Agricultural Production and social change in the Bronze Age of South-east Spain: the Gatas project". *European Journal of Archaeology* 3-2: 147-166.

- 2000: "Archaeology and desertification in the Vera Basin". *European Journal of Archaeology* 3-2: 147-166.

CASTRO MARTÍNEZ, P.V.; ESCORIZA, T.; OLTRA, J.; OTERO, M. & SANAHUJA, E. 2003: "¿Qué es una Ciudad? Aportaciones para su definición desde la Prehistoria". *Geocrítica. Scripta Nova* VII, 146 (10). URL: http://www.ub.es/geocrit/sn/sn-146(010).htm

CASTRO MARTINEZ, P.V.; FREGEIRO, M.I.; OLTRA, J.; SANAHUJA YLL, E. & ESCORIZA, T. 2005: "Trabajo, Producción y 'Neolítico'". In P. Arias, R. Ontañon & C. García-Moncó (eds.): *III Congreso del Neolítico en la Península Ibérica* (Santander 2003). Monografías del Instituto Internacional de Investigaciones Prehistóricas de Cantabria 1. Universidad de Cantabria. Santander: 115-123.

CHAPMAN, R.W. 1978: "The evidence for prehistoric water control in South-east Spain". *Journal of Arid Envionments* 1: 261-274.

- 1982: "Autonomy, ranking and resources in Iberian prehistory". In C. Renfrew & S. Shennan (eds): *Ranking, resources and exchange*. Cambridge University Press. Cambridge: 46-51.

- 1990: *Emerging Complexity: the later prehistory of south-east Spain, Iberia and the west Mediterranean*. Cambridge University Press. Cambridge.

- 2003: *Archaeologies of Complexity*. Routledge. London.

CLOP, X. & FAURA, M. 2002: *El sepulcre megalític de Les Maioles (Rubió, Anoia). Pràctiques funerràries i societat a l´altiplà de Calaf (2000-1600 cal ANE)*. Centre d´Estudis Comarcals. Igualada.

COLOMER, E. 2005: "Cerámica prehistórica y trabajo femenino en el argar: una aproximación desde el estudio de la tecnología cerámica". In M. Sánchez Romero (ed.): *Arqueología y Género*. Monografías. Universidad de Granada 64. Granada: 177-217.

CONTRERAS, F. 2001: "El mundo de la muerte en la edad del bronce. Una aproximación desde la cultura argárica". In M. Hernández (ed.): *... Y acumularon tesoros. Mil años de historia en nuestras tierras*. Caja de Ahorros del Mediterráneo. Alicante: 67-85.

CONTRERAS, F. & CÁMARA, J.A. 2000: "La cerámica". In F. Contreras (ed.): *Proyecto Peñalosa. Análisis histórico de las comunidades de la Edad del Bronce del Piedemonte Meridional de Sierra Morena y depresión Linares-Bailén*. Consejería de Cultura. Junta de Andalucía. Sevilla: 77-128.

- 2002: *La jerarquización social en la Edad del Bronce del Alto Guadalquivir (España). El Poblado de Peñalosa (Baños de la Encina, Jaén)*. British Archaeological Reports International Series 1025. Oxford.

DELIBES, G. & ABARQUERO, F.J. 1997: "La presencia de Cogotas I en el Pais Valenciano: acotaciones al tema desde una perspectiva meseteña". *Saguntum-PLAV* 30: 115-134.

DÍAZ-DEL-RÍO, P. 2001: *La formación del paisaje agrario*. Arqueología, Paleontología y Etnografía 9. Comunidad de Madrid. Madrid.

- 2004a: "Copper Age Ditched Enclosures in Central Iberia". *Oxford Journal of Archaeology* 23 (2): 107-121.

- 2004b: "Factionalism and Collective Labor in Copper Age Iberia". *Trabajos de Prehistoria* 61 (2): 85-98.

ESCORIZA MATEU, T. 2002a: *La Representación del Cuerpo Femenino. Mujeres y Arte Rupestre Levantino del Arco Mediterráneo de la Península Ibérica*. British Archaeological Reports International Series 1082. Oxford.

- 2002b: "Mujeres, Arqueología y Violencia Patriarcal". In M.T. López Beltrán, Mª.J. Jiménez Tomé & E.Mª. Gil Benítez (coords.): *Violencia y Género*. Vol. 1. Diputación Provincial de Málaga. Málaga: 59-74.

FRANKENSTEIN, S. 1997: *Arqueología del colonialismo*. Crítica. Barcelona.

FRANKENSTEIN, S. & ROWLANDS, M.J. 1978: "The internal structure and regional context of Early Irons Age society in south-western Germany". *Bulletin of the Institute of Archaeology* 15: 73-112.

GIBAJA, J.F. 2002: *La función de los instrumentos líticos como medio de aproximación socio-económica. Comunidades neolíticas del V-IV milenios cal BC en el noreste de la Península Ibérica*. Bellaterra. Universidad Autónoma de Barcelona. URL: http://www.tdx.cesca.es/TDX-1128102-182231.

GIL MASCARELL, M. 1981: "El Bronce Tardío y el Bronce Final en el País Valenciano". In *El Bronce Final y el comienzo de la Edad del Hierro en el País Valenciano*. Monografías del Laboratorio de Arqueología de Valencia 1. Universidad de Valencia. Valencia: 9-39.

GILMAN, A. 1976: "Bronze Age dynamics in Southeast spain". *Dialectical Anthropology* 1: 307-319.

- 1987: "El análisis de clase en la Prehistoria del Sureste". *Trabajos de Prehistoria* 44: 27-34.

- 1997: "Como valorar los sistemas de propiedad a partir de datos arqueológicos". *Trabajos de Prehistoria* 54 (2): 81-92.

GILMAN, A. & THORNES, J.B. 1985: *Land use and Prehistory in South-East Spain*. Allen and Unwin. London.

HARRISON, R.J. 1995: "Bronze Age Expansion 1750-1250 B.C.: The Cogotas I Phase in the Middle Ebro Valley". *Veleia* 12: 67-77.

HERNÁNDEZ ALCARAZ, L. & HERNÁNDEZ PÉREZ, M. (eds) 2004: *La Edad del Bronce en tierras valencianas y zonas limítrofes*. Instituto Juan Gil-Albert. Alicante.

JIMÉNEZ BROBEIL, S.A. & GARCÍA SÁNCHEZ, M. 1989-90: "Estudio de los restos humanos de la Edad del Bronce del Cerro de la Encina (Monachil, Granada)". *Cuadernos de Prehistoria de la Universidad de Granada* 14-15: 157-180.

JIMENO, A. 2001: "El modelo de transhumancia aplicado a la cultura de Cogotas I". In M. Ruíz-Gálvez (ed.): *La Edad del Bronce ¿Primera Edad de Oro de España?*. Crítica. Barcelona: 139-178.

JOVER, F.J. 1999: *Un nueva lectura del 'Bronce Valenciano'*. Universidad de Alicante. Alicante.

JOVER, F.J. & LÓPEZ PADILLA, J.A. 2004: "2.100-1.200 BC. Aportaciones al proceso histórico en la Cuenca del río Vinalopó". In L. Hernández Alcaraz & M. Hernández (eds.): *La Edad del Bronce en Tierras Valencianas y Zonas Limítrofes*. Instituto Juan Gil-Albert. Alicante: 285-302.

LEISNER, G., & LEISNER, V. 1943: *Die Megalithgräber der Iberischen Halbinsel. Der Süden*. Walter de Gruyter. Berlin.

LULL, V. 1983: *La 'Cultura' de El Argar. Un modelo para el estudio de las formaciones económico-sociales prehistóricas*. Akal. Madrid.

- 2000: "Argaric society: Death at home". *Antiquity* 74: 581-590.

LULL, V. & ESTÉVEZ, J. 1986: "Propuesta metodológica para el estudio de las necrópolis argáricas". *Homenaje a Luis Siret (1934-1984)*. Consejería de Cultura de la Junta de Andalucía. Sevilla: 441-452.

LULL, V. & RISCH, R. 1995: "El Estado Argárico". *Verdolay* 7: 97-109.

MALGOSA, A.; SUBIRA, E.; BANDERA,R.; SAFONT, S.; EDO, M.; VILLALBA, M. & BLASCO, A. 1996: "Diversidad de estrategias alimentarias en el Neolítico del Baix Llobregat". *Rubricatum* 1 (1): 115-122.

MARTÍ OLIVER, B. 1983: *El naixement de l'agricultura en el Pais Valencià: del Neolític al l'Edat del Bronce*. Universidad de Valencia. Valencia.

MARTÍ OLVIER, B. & HERNÁNDEZ, M. 1988: *El Neolític Valencià. Art rupestre i cultura material*. Servicio de Investigación Prehistórica. Valencia.

MARTÍNEZ, G. & AFONSO, J. 1998: "Las sociedades prehistóricas: de la comunidad al estado", In R. Peinado (ed.): *De Ilurco a Pinos Puente. Poblamiento, economía y sociedad de un pueblo de la Vega de Granada*. Biblioteca de Ensayo 39. Diputación Provincial de Granada. Granada: 21-68.

MATHERS, C. 1984a: "Beyond the grave: the context and wider implications of mortuary practices in south-east Spain". In T.E.C. Blagg, R.E.J. Jones & S.J. Keay (eds.): *Papers in*

Iberian Archaeology. British Archaeological Reports International Series 193. Oxford: 13-46.

- 1984b: "Linear regression, inflation and prestige competition: second millennium transformations in south-east Spain". In W.H. Waldren, R. Chapman, J. Lewthwaite & R-C. Kennard (eds.): *Early settlement in the western Mediterranean Islands and their peripheral areas: The Deya Conference of Prehistory.* British Archaeological Reports International Series. Oxford: 1167-1196.

MICÓ, R. 1993: *Pensamientos y prácticas en las arqueologías contemporáneas. Normatividad y exclusión en los grupos arqueológicos del III y II milenios cal ANE en el sudeste de la península ibérica.* Bellaterra Tesis Doctorales. Universidad Autónoma de Barcelona. Barcelona.

- 1995: "Los Millares and the Copper Age of the Iberian Southeast". In K. Lillios (ed.): *The Origins of Complex Societies in Late Prehistoric Iberia.* Ann Arbor. Michigan: 169-176.

MOLINA BALAGUER, L., GARCÍA-PUCHOL, O. & GARCÍA ROBLES, M.R. 2003: "Apuntes al marco crono-cultural del arte levantino: Neolitico vs neolitización". *Saguntum-PLAV* 35: 51-67.

MOLINA GONZÁLEZ, F. 1978: "Definición y sistematización del Bronce Tardío y Final en el Sudeste de la Península Ibérica". *Cuadernos de Prehistoria de la Universidad de Granada* 3: 159-232.

MOLINA GONZÁLEZ, F. & CÁMARA, J.A. 2004: "Urbanismo y fortificaciones en la Cultura de El Argar. Homogeneidad y patrones de asentamiento". In M.R. García Huerta & J. Morales (eds.): *La Península Ibérica en el IIº milenio A.C.: poblados y fortificaciones.* Universidad de Castilla-La Mancha. Cuenca: 8-56.

MOLINA GONZÁLEZ, F.; CÁMARA, J.A.; CAPEL, J.; NÁJERA, T. & SÁEZ, L. 2004: "Los Millares y la periodización de la Prehistoria Reciente del Sureste". In *Simposio de Prehistoria Cueva de Nerja. II. La problemática del neolítico en Andalucía. III. Las primeras sociedades metalúrgicas en Andalucía.* Fundación Cueva de Nerja. Málaga: 142-158.

MOLIST, M.; RIBE, G. & SAÑA, M. 1995: "La transición del V milenio cal BC en Catalunya". *Rubricatum* 1-2: 781-790.

MONTERO, I.; RIHUETE, C & RUÍZ A. 1999: "Precisiones sobre el enterramiento colectivo neolítico de Cerro Virtud (Cuevas de Almanzora, Almería)". *Trabajos de Prehistoria* 56-1: 119-130.

MUÑOZ, A.M. 1965: *La cultura neolítica catalana de los Sepulcros de Fosa.* Universidad de Barcelona. Barcelona.

NOCETE, F. 2001a: *Tercer milenio antes de nuestra era. Relaciones y contradicciones centro-periferia en el Valle del Guadalquivir.* Bellaterra. Barcelona.

- 2001b: "Entre el colapso de los primeros estados y el final de un desarrollo histórico autónomo. Las formaciones sociales del Sur de la Península Ibérica de inicios del segundo milenio anterior a nuestra era". In M. Hernández (ed.): *...Y acumularon tesoros. Mil años de historia en nuestras tierras.* Caja de Ahorros del Mediterráneo. Alicante: 41-49.

PEREA, A. 2001: "Biografías de escondrijos y tesoros prehistóricos en la Península Ibérica". In M. Hernández (ed.): *...Y acumularon tesoros. Mil años de historia en nuestras tierras.* Caja de Ahorros del Mediterráneo. Alicante: 15-27.

RAMOS, A. 1998: "La minería, la artesanía y el intercambio de sílex durante la Edad del Cobre en el sudeste de la península ibérica". In G. Delibes (coord.): *Minerales y metales en la prehistoria reciente: algunos testimonios de su explotación y laboreo en la Península Ibérica.* Studia Archaeologica 88. Universidad de Valladolid – Fundación Duques de Soria. Valladolid: 13-40.

RISCH, R. 1995: *Recursos naturales y sistemas de producción en el Sudeste de la Península ibérica, entre 3000 y 1000 ANE.* Bellaterra Tesis Doctorales. Universidad Autónoma de Barcelona. Barcelona.

- 2002: *Recursos naturales, medios de producción y explotación social.* Philipp von Zabern. Mainz am Rhein.

ROMÁN, M. P. 1996: *Estudios sobre el Neolítico en el Sureste de la Península Ibérica. Síntesis crítica y valoración.* Universidad de Almería. Almería.

RUIZ-GÁLVEZ, M. 1998: *La Europa Atlántica de la Edad del Bronce.* Crítica. Barcelona.

SANAHUJA YLL, E.; MICÓ, R. & CASTRO MARTÍNEZ, P.V. 1995: "Organización social y estrategias productivas en Catalunya desde el VI milenio hasta el siglo VII cal ANE". *Verdolay* 7: 59-71.

SANCHIDRIÁN, J.L. & VALLADAS, H. 2002: "Dataciones numéricas del Arte Rupestre de la Cueva de La Pileta (Málaga, Andalucía)". *Panel* 1: 104-105.

SCHUHMACHER, T.X. & WENIGER, G.C. 1995: "Continuidad y cambio. Problemas de la neolitización en el Este de la Península Ibérica". *Trabajos de Prehistoria* 52 (2): 83-97.

SIRET, H. & SIRET L. 1890: *Las Primeras Edad del Metal en el Sudeste de España: resultados obtenidos en las excavaciones hechas por los autores desde 1881 a 1887.* Barcelona.

SOLER, J. M. 1965: *El Tesoro de Villena.* Ministerio de Educación Nacional. Dirección General de Bellas Artes. Madrid.

- 1987: *Excavaciones en el Cabezo Redondo (Villena, Alicante).* Instituto Juan Gil-Albert. Alicante.

STOS-GALE, S.; HUNT-ORTIZ, M. & GALE, N. 1999: "Análisis elemental y de isótpos de plomo de objetos metálicos de Gatas". In P.V. Castro *et al.*: *Proyecto Gatas 2: la dinámica arqueoecológica de la ocupación prehistórica.* Consejería de Cultura. Junta de Andalucía. Sevilla: 347-358.

TARRADELL, M. 1969: "La cultura del Bronce Valenciano. Nuevo ensayo de aproximación". *Papeles del Laboratorio de Arqueología de Valencia* 6: 7-30.

VICENT, J.M. 1991: "El neolítico. Transformaciones sociales y económicas". *Boletín de Antropología Americana* 24: 31-62.

CHAPTER 10

The role of the means of production in social development in the Late Prehistory of the Iberian southeast

José Andrés Afonso Marrero
Juan Antonio Cámara Serrano
Universidad de Granada

Abstract

Our work on the development of social hierarchization in Southeast of Iberia has taken into account that throughout history there have been different ways for groups to arrive at unequal accumulation of wealth. Although we emphasise that the control of labour force (female and male) is an initial factor, we also suggest that the control of mobile means of labour (animals) takes on fundamental importance as a condition for ensuring the position of the elites who, from this newly enhanced position, will exercise greater control over the labour force, not only directly, but also through the appropriation by the class-state of the inert means of production (land).

Keywords: Iberia; Late Prehistory; Social Hierarchization; Labour Force; Women; Livestock; Land; Social Classes; State.

Resumen

Nuestra propuesta sobre el desarrollo de la jerarquización social en el Sudeste de la Península Ibérica ha tenido en cuenta que, durante el devenir histórico, diferentes han sido las formas de acceder a la acumulación desigual de riqueza. De esta forma, aunque enfatizamos como factor inicial el control inicial de la fuerza de trabajo (femenina y masculina), mostramos la importancia fundamental que adquiere el control de los medios de trabajo móviles (los animales) como condición para asegurar la posición de las élites que, desde ese nuevo impulso, ejercerán un mayor control no sólo sobre la fuerza de trabajo directamente sino sobre ésta a partir de la apropiación por la clase-estado de los medios de producción inertes (la tierra).

Palabras clave: Península Ibérica; Prehistoria Reciente; Jerarquización social; Fuerza de Trabajo; Mujeres; Ganado; Tierra; Clases Sociales; Estado.

10.1.- Introduction

In the formulation of the various hypotheses regarding the development of social inequality in the Prehistory of Iberian Southeast, it is quite common to characterize the environment as a determinant factor. According to this line of thought, between the Late Neolithic and the Chalcolithic, the adversity of the environment contributed to the adoption of a series of changes that facilitated human settlement. These innovations led, in addition, to a significant increase in social hierarchization, either because managing elites became necessary (Chapman 1982), or because certain people took advantage of the investments to their own benefit (Gilman 1987). This assumption has been shown to be inexact by numerous paleo-environmental studies. The anthracological, carpological and faunal analyses performed have shown that the environment was far from arid and that, although rainfall was not much more abundant than nowadays, the presence of a denser vegetation cover guaranteed the conservation of moisture and the exploitation of certain plant resources, with no need for irrigation (Peters & Driesch 1990; Rodríguez & Vernet 1991; Araus et al. 1997; Buxó 1997). All of this led, in the final two decades of the 20th century, to renewed theoretical reflection on the role that other factors may have played in the extension of inequality beyond that imposed by gender and age.

Within this context, the raising of livestock has been taking into consideration, not just in relation to the use of secondary products (wool, milk, etc.) and traction, but as a means of accumulation and exhibition of wealth. This seems to be the case of the differential consumption patterns, both in terms of the species present and the age of the consumed animals, documented at Los Millares (Navas 2004; Peters & Driesch 1990). Also falling within this context is the analysis of the technical process and the ideological signification of certain craft activities.

The control of metallurgy and the circulation of metal products, both as functional items and as prestige goods, has been a recurring argument in efforts to explain the stratification of prehistoric societies in southeast Iberia. It has been suggested that a series of social and technical conditions existed which facilitated its development. These may have been the search, since Neolithic times, for exotic and attractive raw materials, use of advanced extraction techniques, familiarity with strategies for controlling oven temperatures, and the availability of copper resources, especially in this area. At Los Millares (Santa Fe de Mondújar, Almería) particularly noteworthy are, not only the specialization of certain areas, but the production entity (Molina 1988: 261) and selection of raw materials with a high arsenic content in order to produce certain cutting pieces such as axes (Keesmann *et al.* 1997: 287, 290-291; Montero 1998: 212). However, the role of metallurgy in social development must be understood as an element that, rather than having a triggering effect, may have enhanced it by enabling certain social groups or populations to maintain their privileged positions through the accumulation of means of production, and the exhibition and circulation of certain prestige objects (Molina 1988; Cámara 2001).

During this period, the exploitation of different types of rocks also developed greatly, from quarries for construction materials found by F. Carrión in the surroundings of the settlement of Los Millares, as well as for the manufacture of tools in the surroundings of Cabo de Gata (Carrión *et al.* 1993). These quarries were controlled by Chalcolithic settlements such as El Barronal (Níjar, Almería) (Haro 2004: 56-57), or by others, as the well known flint quarries of La Venta (Orce, Granada) (Ramos *et al.* 1991; Moreno *et al.* 1997), in a process that is also known to happen in Southwest Spain (Nocete *et al.* 1997). More interesting is the exploitation of flint resources in the western Subbetic mountain ranges and the production of large blades for widespread circulation (Martínez 1997; Martínez *et al.* 1998; Nocete *et al.* 2005).

10.2.- Social production

Before setting forth our model of the process of hierarchization (Fig. 10.1), we should briefly reflect on the nature of social evolution, in order to avoid teleological arguments, and the supposed intentionality of social agents in the generation of inequality. One of the first tasks would be to distinguish between the concepts of evolution and change, given the current tendency to use the two terms interchangeably. Thus, while the latter is always provoked, induced, immediate and involves the transformation of some elements of social organization into different ones, the former always occurs gradually over time and is the result of a pseudo combinatorial operation involving the elements comprising all societies. Therefore, it is only possible to determine a line of evolution (phylogeny) when the process has taken place; societies do not have a tendency towards hierarchization, nor is there a simple causality that explains it, so an evolutionary model is never predictive or deductive but rather "postductive".

However, our intention is not to set forth an exhaustive review of the different elements which must be taken into account in drawing up multi-determinate hypotheses on social development, but rather to set forth the general lines that give shape to this type of proposition. Resorting

to causality in the explanation of social phenomena, which the use of the concept social change presupposes, often leads either to determinism (economic, ecological) or to social reductionism that believes that all change is progress. In the evolutionary explanation, explicitly abandoning the line of causal reasoning makes it necessary to turn to a more complex logic, one which accounts for both randomness and peripheral or secondary social phenomena. On this subject, it may be wise to underline the idea that social formations are defined by the coexistence of distinct social relations articulated in a singular, unique structure, although it is true that only one of them is dominant, constituting the referent of the ideological reproduction of the society. The superseding of this particular articulation of social relations is only possible from the subordinate ones, although the "triumph" of one over the others has a "random" nature; that is, it is neither socially, culturally, or economically predetermined. In addition, the creation of a peripheral social action space contributes significantly to the contradictions between social praxis and the ideology that justifies it. The coherence of the system for the ideological justification and reproduction of social action is frequently violated by the everyday action of individuals and groups, and routes are thus opened, although not always followed, towards the superseding of the limits established by the degree of development of the productive forces.

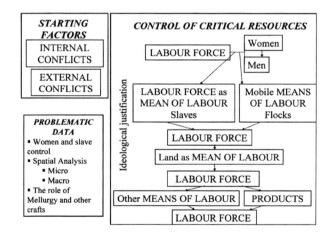

Fig. 10.1. Schematic diagram of our proposed model.

Bearing this in mind, we believe that the development of social inequality in communal systems (beyond the inequality established by gender and age) can only be explained by the success of certain processes that guaranteed differentiated access to the results of production.

These processes are all aimed at the control of the labour force as the only means of amassing goods, although they do function in a three-fold direction: the control of the labour force, the appropriation of herds as products and means of labour and the development of private ownership of land.

The advent of new forms of accumulation of wealth by means of the strengthening of new social relations (through the non-premeditated action of the various social agents), takes place at the limit of the communal system, using that which is only leniently regulated, or which is not considered a threat to the reproduction of the system. Despite this apparent absence of conflict, resistance is produced, mainly at two levels: from the sectors of the population that control the routes giving access to the positions from which the community is led, and from sectors of the population that have become dominated (Ste. Croix 1988). In the case of the superseding the communal system, this is the main area of resistance.

Such resistance is overcome or lessened through the ritual masking of exaction (symbolic, ideological, superstructural). But, if the emerging relations occupy at the beginning of the process a subordinate role in the reproduction of the society, how can it be possible that the ritual systems of the communal society are used in the justification of such relations? This is because, in all social formations, including transitional ones, nothing can be justified outside of the ideological realm that sanctions the socially correct. Therefore, in the justification of exaction and of the social relations that make it possible, previous ideological representation systems are used, often subverting their contents. That is, procedures which highlight the communal nature of production, or even the duty to share, are used (Zvelebil 2002).

10.3.- Control of the labour force

In its initial phase, labour domination is achieved by way of pressure on women and on the non-adult members of the community (Meillassoux 1987; Bender 1989). The communal society finds acceptable this type of division/discrimination because it is at the root of the conditions that enable its reproduction. Soon after, this coercion over female members of the community is channelled towards the control of the kinship system, and especially towards mechanisms for the acquisition of wives, as this permits not only to administer a larger labour force, as in these initial moments its increase is only possible through vegetative growth, but also the accumulation of means of production (labour force, both present and future, and products/means of labour), either produced directly or received in the form of dowry.

In any case, the control of women and their movement, both as labour force and in their capacity as producers of human beings (Castro *et al.* 1999; Estévez *et al.* 1999) is linked to the relationships between the settlements inside social formations originated by integration (synecism – the disappearance of smaller villages), and with the creation of symbols (dowries) to represent the debt of women which are necessary for reproduction (Meillassoux 1987: 94). All of this derives into relationships of inequality, in at least a three-fold way:

1.- Differentiating communities according to their capacity to mobilize labour force if there is no compensation for women-wives, or if the latter are acquired in exchange for elements, basically ideological items, that have acquired an ideal value in themselves (Meillassoux 1987: 103-104). These will eventually become a way of masking the circulation of tribute (Molina 1988) once they have been transformed into prestige items, moving either from the political nucleus, in order to show its capacity to mobilize resources, or towards the political nucleus, as compensation for other services.

2.- Obliging the integrated (conquered) communities to provide women without real compensation (although with imaginary compensation). This links this aspect to the pressure exerted over other groups, and to the tributary movement of other products once power has been consolidated.

3.- Linking animals, as dowry symbols, to women (Martínez & Afonso 1998), and developing a differential price for women according to their origin (Scarduelli 1988). This distinguishes noble families, which had already been able to accumulate products through the development of ownership over herds, and which had acquired a relevant role because of their capacity to provide services to the community, theoretically unsatisfied.

Subsequently, the control of labour force broadens, extending first to other men not belonging to the community (prisoners, e.g. members of integrated [conquered] communities) and, later, to male individuals belonging to the community who have fallen into a situation of dependence because of their incapability to compensate certain services rendered. In this way, two routes of access to servitude are formed, a general one and a limited one.

Understood in a broad sense, the first is earlier and more permanent, and results from the impossibility of accessing to a full possession of the land, due to the inability to give in return for the provided services. This is the first form of what will later be the fiscal and military "burdens" imposed by the state (class instrument). Thus, access to usufruct of the land can only be through ascription to the clan and the community. The limited form of servitude is the result of personal ascriptions and restrictions on mobility, and involves the rendering of personal services to a greater or lesser degree (the former being true servitude, the loss of the condition of community member and the latter being clientele, political association). This last item takes on the nature of an ascription to the lineage (family or individuals who represent it). In this sense, this servitude always implies the rendering of services, payment (Ste. Croix 1988: 163-164), but it also includes the so-called forms of "indirect collective exploitation" (Ste. Croix 1988: 243-246).

10.4.- Appropriation of herds

Herds, especially those comprised of large domestic animals, are in the ideological periphery of what is communal (they are not necessary for the survival and reproduction of the group). This makes their appropriation possible within the framework of an ideological system that emphasizes sharing as an element to guarantee the survival and cohesion of the clan. Also, the very nature of herds endows them with two features that make them easy to appropriate and accumulate. The mobility inherent to this type of product means that larger herds can be handled, and moved through larger and larger territories. Obviously, this generates conflicts with neighbouring communities. But the solution to these conflicts involves the control of more labour force and, through this, of more land as a condition for the monopolization of products based on herd ownership. But livestock have another important particularity; as a movable asset they can easily change from one owner to another. This allows the establishment of relationships between individuals or groups of individuals, and also their violent expropriation. Theft guarantees that maximum benefits are obtained with a minimal investment. There is no need to wait for the animal to grow. It is also a way by which certain people win followers from outside the clan (Cámara *et al.* 1996), therefore generating threats for the social system.

The appropriation of livestock thus constitutes an initial form of accumulation of wealth that is used for the control of the labour force. This allows, first of all, access to a greater number of women, and then to women of "better" quality, which creates the conditions for the foundation of political links between individuals of different sectors of a single social formation and, later, with members of other social formations. In addition, their accumulation enables certain people to hold large events (offerings) involving a large part of the community unable to return received "charity".

On this subject matter, other authors have highlighted that large animals (cattle and horses) are important in the accumulation of wealth, because they can be used as traction (Martínez & Afonso 1998; Criado *et al.* 2001). But livestock, as a means of production, is also important because of the other so-called secondary products (wool, leather, dairy products) and, of course, for meat production. Furthermore, manure could fertilize fields, or animals could have been lent for certain tasks (transport, for example) becoming an investment with substantial return. [1] Nevertheless, it was of course better to obtain means of production/product with no previous investment by theft.

With dependence thus reproduced, and animals being accumulated, a new concentration of means of labour and other products is generated, either by applying the same labour force with a new organization of the technical process of work (through the use of the mobile means of labour), or by increasing the amount of the labour force used in the same work processes. The latter is an important means for controlling a larger fraction of the available labour force. The former constitutes a means for the appropriation of communal land. Thus the appropriation of livestock becomes a way to quickly and permanently accumulate goods and means of production, favoured by the growth of the herds when there are no access restrictions to the communal land, in such a way that, even without real distribution of the land, accumulation differences arise, and also by pillage. At the same time, the administration of a greater volume of production facilitates access to positions of prestige and control of the community, achieved through a process of indebtedness (real or fictitious), that makes it impossible to return the services provided to the community. From such positions of prestige it is possible to intervene more directly in the ritual and the systems of ideological reproduction of the community, which justifies in an indirect way the social relations which permit the acquisition of this new status.

Interest in the appropriation of the labour force led to a more strict control of the movement of women as sources of present and future labour force, and then to other forms of control over female workers, through the union of different groups (clans) in larger settlements. Another influence in this direction was the development of the movable ownership of herds which led to the formation of settlements located in territories offering the necessary resources for extensive livestock exploitation, as well as other economic strategies. These new social formations controlled mountains and plains, exploitation routes and territories for which boundaries would soon be defined, accompanying the rapid development of social classes. Initially, the boundaries would be symbolic, by way of monumental sepulchres or sanctuaries (Cámara 2001). Later on, they would take the form of small dissuasive forts (Nocete 1989; 2001), especially when products were obtained in these territories that could be accumulated, beginning with herds and then, thanks to the impetus of the tributary state, through other forms of wealth.

10.5.- Development of the ownership of land

The usurpation of the ownership of communal land to the benefit of some individuals is a process that, as seen above, cannot be separated from the control of the labour force and the appropriation of livestock. This did not mean the legal expropriation of the community, as the community remained the owner throughout the whole process. Rather, it is this collective nature that allows for the justification of the differential access to usufruct of

---

[1] A similar assessment of the possibilities of livestock accumulation has been presented by R. Peroni (2004:108-109) who makes more central the role of the control of products, of their movement and of craft specialization.

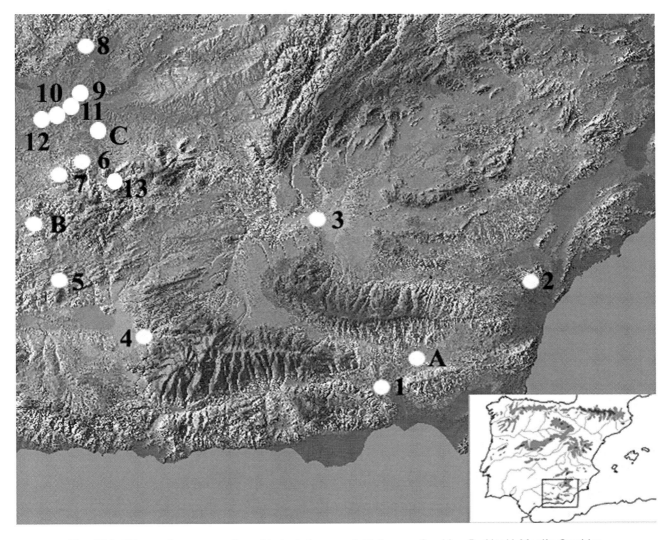

Fig. 10.2. Sites and areas mentioned in text: Areas – A. Tabernas Corridor, B. Alcalá-Moclín Corridor, C. Alto Guadalquivir valley; Sites – 1. Los Millares, 2. Zájara, 3. La Cuesta del Negro, 4. El Cerro de la Encina, 5. Los Castillejos en Las Peñas de los Gitanos, 6. Marroquíes, 7. Polideportivo de Martos, 8. Peñalosa, 9. Sevilleja, 10. Los Pozos, 11. Cerro de la Coronilla (Cazalilla), 12. Cortijo de la Torre, 13. Cerro de la Horca.

the land. First, by acknowledging the possibility that those who have larger families and livestock use more pasture land, and, later, by allowing a larger plot of land to be exploited by those who have acquired control of sufficient labour force and means of labour to do so. In the long run, these changes meant the real expropriation of communal lands and the development of true private ownership, with some individuals assuming the capacity to distribute plots among the members of the community.

Once the sedentarization of the communities had been furthered by the control of the labour force and the appropriation of herds, the conversion of land into a true means of production will only accelerate the process of social hierarchization. This process is favoured since the definition of the community has been based on comparison with exogenous characteristics, paving the way to personal dependence. Also because the control of kinship systems and women exchange has become a means of

other settlement dependency, those settlements that acquire debts because of something that presumably was never given to them.

10.6.- Conclusions

We believe that the threefold process described above, and the interrelation among its components, can be followed throughout the Late Prehistory of the Iberian Southeast (Fig. 10.2). The control of women is undoubtedly the aspect which is most difficult to trace using the archaeological record, especially considering the scarcity not only of anthropological analyses (including paleopathological ones), but also of excavations focusing on the Epipaleolithic and the Neolithic in general, and on the sepulchres in particular (Pellicer 1964; Rubio 1980-81; Pellicer & Acosta 1986; Riquelme 2002). In any case, certain findings do suggest the importance given to fe

137

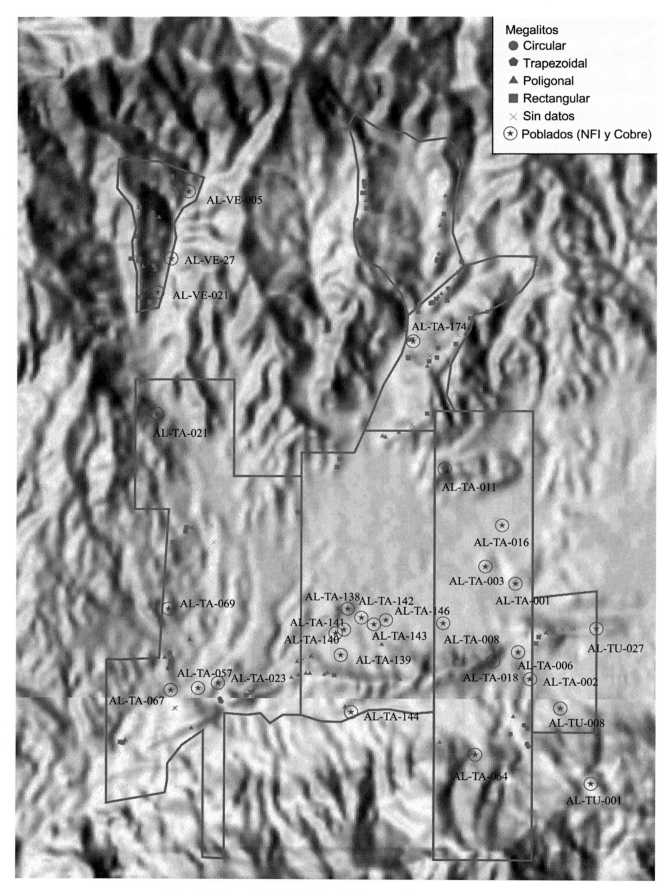

Fig. 10.3. Megalithic distribution in Tabernas Corridor (Almería).

male burials, found in pits within the settlement area, whether in the Late Neolithic as in the case of Martos (Jaén) (Lizcano 1999), or in advanced Chalcolithic times as in Zájara (Cuevas del Almanzora, Almería) (Cámalich *et al.* 1999). This evidence apparently clashes with the hypotheses put forward, although the scarcity of findings makes it impossible, for example, to determine if, as in other areas, differences existed in grave goods in contexts where there are indications of social differences apart from sex and age (Martín *et al.* 1996; Gibaja *et al.* 1997; Blasco *et al.* 1997; Zvelebil 1997) and where there are complex interpretations of the paleo-pathological data, with some authors arguing that there were dietary differences in favour of the men (Zvelebil 2002: 215) and others rejecting this argument (Meiklejohn *et al.* 2002: 231-234).

More interesting in terms of the subordination of women may be to estimate the value attributed to their work, in their two-fold aspect as members of the labour force and means of production as reproducers (Castro *et al.* 1999). On this matter, especially relevant as regards the expression of their undervaluation (Bender 1989; Lerner 1990; Estévez *et al.* 1999), may be the interpretation of the female figurines recovered in Cuccuru S'Arriu (Cabras, Oristano, Sardinia) that, in the published cases, are associated with male burials (Germanà & Santoni 1993; Santoni 1995). If future work confirms this exclusive association, it will be necessary to think that the process of undervaluing women through the appropriation of their productive and reproductive capacities was relatively stronger, or was masked to a lesser degree, in Sardinia, since, again, in Eastern Andalusia there is no evidence of a segregation of women from their reproductive role in terms of its expression in tombs, and in fact in Martos, two women are associated with three young men in tomb 13 (Cámara & Lizcano 1996; Lizcano 1999; Lizcano & Cámara 2004). However, indications of such discrimination can be found in the symbolic ceramics that highlight the reproductive role of men, as seen in the figuration of presumably natural scenes involving animals to which it is easy to give sexual characterization, such as stags (Martínez & Afonso 1998). In the same way, the emphasis placed on the ram's head, used as decoration in one of the dwellings of Martos, has been interpreted as sexual discrimination and the creation of two opposing genders (Cámara & Lizcano 1996).

Similarly, there are no specific studies on the underrepresentation of women in the megalithic tombs of the Southeast, although this has been constantly suggested (Mathers 1984). This is not surprising given the fragmentary nature of data, and the prolonged use of the tombs, making difficult to assess changes through time.

All this means that it is no surprise that, for now, we support our hypothesis concerning the control of the female labour force, regardless of some rituals or indications in other parts of Europe, in the need for demographic control and in ethnographic models (Meillassoux

1987), and stating that its intensification occurs with sedentarization (Lizcano *et al.* 1997), as had already been suggested (Vicent 1993), although emphasizing the need for control as a factor which fomented such sedentarization.

In this sense the process of aggregation was related to the control of the labour force and the control of the territory, but with the latter being understood in an extensive sense, as the medium for pastureland and areas of movement. The system thus represents a way to control men/women and the herds. In the Southeast of Spain, territory is delimited, starting in at least the Late Neolithic, by means of the succession and accumulation of symbols such as megaliths, as studied in Pasillo de Tabernas (Almería) (Fig. 10.3) in relation to routes, folds, and permanent boundaries (Maldonado *et al.* 1997; Cámara 2001), but we can also trace the creation of sacredness through the dispersion of cave paintings (Martínez García 1998) such as those found in Pasillo de Alcalá-Moclín, dating at least to the Middle Neolithic (Martínez & Afonso 1998).

These cave paintings may have constituted a precedent, but also an alternative, to the tumular (megalithic) forms of sacral control, although in a certain way with a greater degree of concealment and reserve which is even more accentuated in the case of burials, of animals and people, in pits or their successors, the artificial caves. This, in turn, like the compartmentalization in chambers and corridors, would link the process of access restrictions with secrets, the classification of persons and hierarchization (Barrett 1990; Thomas 1993; Tilley 1993).

This delimitation cannot be considered in isolation from opposition to the exterior, as a way of drawing together what is interior and of deviating pressure, even using aggression. It is therefore not surprising that early fortifications (ditches and palisades) develop at least at the beginning of the IV Millennium BC (Cámara & Lizcano 1997; Nocete 2001) and that we find the first rituals destined to affirm the community and its continuance. Independent of the extensive delimitation, this is how the particular definition takes place.

In fact, while the most recent excavations in Los Castillejos de las Peñas de los Gitanos (Montefrío, Granada) have shown the transformation of agricultural products in a specialized communal area (Fig. 10.4) in the Initial Neolithic (Ramos *et al.* 1997; Afonso *et al.* 1996), the first ritual forms that can be related to families take place in the Late and Final Neolithic and are related to the delimitation of the dwelling spaces. This is the case both in Montefrío and in Martos (Jaén) and includes, in the latter case, among the various related structures (Lizcano 1999), several which were used at certain times for ritual (Fig. 10.5) that we had principally related to the founding and cohesion of the settlement (Lizcano *et al.* 1997; Cámara & Lizcano 1996; Lizcano & Cámara 2004). On this matter, both stratigraphic and functional data support the domestic nature of most fillings and underground

139

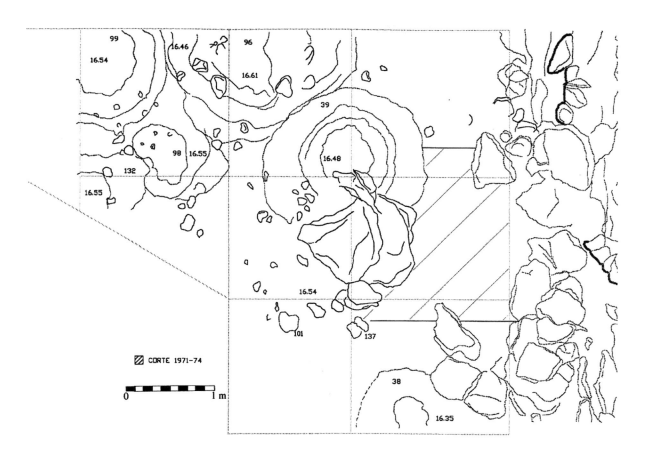

Fig. 10.4. Communal area of ovens at Los Castillejos en Las Peñas de los Gitanos (Montefrío, Granada).

Fig. 10.5. Young cattle burial from the site of Polideportivo de Martos.

structures that contain them, although not all researchers agree (Márquez 2002; Márquez in this volume). This practical nature is even more evident when evaluating the layers recovered from subterranean structures, some of them attributed to the Final Copper Age, found in Marroquíes (Jaén) (Lizcano *et al.* 1995: 65; Burgos *et al.* 2001a: 407; Burgos *et al.* 2001b: 425).

But the different rituals present (Cámara & Lizcano 1996) also show us, firstly, the importance of herds which in addition are consumed in a differential way, involving an association of a pair of bovines to each family unit and a disproportionate ratio of sexes and ages in the case of ovicaprines. This suggests not only the use of secondary products but also seasonal movement of the herds or their separation by sex and age (Lizcano *et al.* 1997) but in a context in which the accent is placed on large animals, especially but not exclusively in the centre of the valley (Nocete 2001) (Fig. 10.6). Secondly, the sacrifice of one of these animals (calf) regardless of its origin could be linked to the beginning of the social ascent of a family, which seems clearer in the case of the tomb (Cámara 2001; Cámara & Lizcano 1996), and which can be ascribed to Phase II of the Polideportivo of Martos.

In Los Millares (Santa Fe de Mondújar, Almería), bovines dominate especially in the outlying areas of the external wall of the settlement, while they are extremely

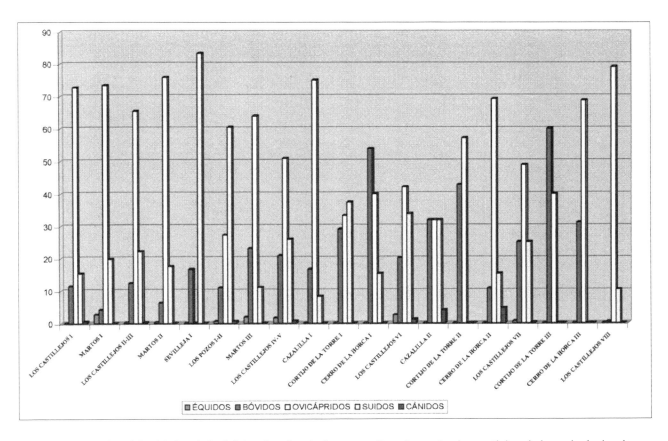

Fig. 10.6. Alto Guadalquivir faunistical data attending to the proportion of remains by spatial and chronological order.

rare in the forts that have been studied (1 and 5), in which there is also almost no presence of wild animal meat. With regard to bovines, areas devoted to carving and disposal have been documented outside the first wall, with the presence especially of parts of the skeleton with little meat, which indicates that carving took place in open areas, outside the living quarters, with the pieces to be consumed being taken elsewhere. This aspect is also supported by the overrepresentation of ovicaprine ribs in fort 5 (Navas 2004). Outside the second wall the presence of bovid phalanx may suggest the tanning of hides. The differences in consumption become even more evident if we look at ages. With regard to bovines the proportion of adults is much greater in the external section of the settlement, between the first and second walls, with the animals being sacrificed between the third and fifth year of life, suggesting their prior use as traction. This contrasts with the high representation of young specimens in the citadel. Pigs occupy the second position among domestic animals and they were generally sacrificed during the first or second year of life, at the end of the autumn or winter; in the citadel we find more adult specimens, mostly male and probably castrated.

It may be useful to remember that in some areas, such as Alentejo, the first megaliths clearly seem to also be associated with individual burials, and that therefore subsequent collectivization is not so much an expression of the

real community as an imposition of masking aimed at control and social classification (Arteaga 1993; Cámara 2001; Guidi 2000), although inequality among lineages, and within them, will soon become evident, as shown not only by Los Millares (Santa Fe de Mondújar, Almería) (Chapman 1981) but also by the presence of certain tombs in the central necropolis of Pasillo de Tabernas (Almería) (Cámara 2001).

Such collectivization could also be related to the proliferation of ditches, mentioned above, aimed at increasing the cohesion of the settlement and also at defence, as shown by their depth and width, their design, their association with walls and palisades and even their continuity, later becoming structures made of non-perishable materials (Arribas & Molina 1984; Cámara & Lizcano 1996; 1997; Pérez & Cámara 1999; Lizcano et al. 2004) and, therefore, a form of exterior opposition that was not only delimiting but also integrating and conquering, as shown by the diffusion of symbols, as an expression of tribute, and the configuration of a landscape comprised of dominating and dominated points in the Bajo Andarax (Molina 1988; Molina et al. 2004) and in the High Guadalquivir (Nocete 1989; Lizcano et al. 1996).

As for the role of such symbols, we have highlighted the case of metal, whose acquisition of exchange value, first as a way of masking tribute, derives, because of its justi-

SITE NAME	KIND OF CONTEXT	DATE B.P.	DATES B.C. (1 σ)	DATES B.C. (2 σ)	LABORATORY REFERENCE	BIBLIOGRAPHICAL REFERENCE
LOS CASTILLEJOS (3)	Hearth. Phase 3. Ancient Neolithic	6120 ± 40	5065-4965	5210-4930	Beta135663	MOLINA et al., 2004
LOS CASTILLEJOS (1)(2)	Hearth. Phase 7. Middle Neolithic	6470 ± 150	5545-5305	5660-5070	Beta135664	MOLINA et al., 2004
LOS CASTILLEJOS (1)(3)	Hearth. Phase 7. Middle Neolithic	6250 ± 80	5310-5070	5365-4985	Beta145302	MOLINA et al., 2004
MARTOS	Phase I. Late Neolithic	5080 ± 40	4036-3706	4239-3542		LIZCANO, 1999
LOS CASTILLEJOS (3)	Collapse. Phase 16b. Final Neolithic	4480 ± 40	3335-3090	3350-3020	Beta135665	MOLINA et al., 2004
LOS CASTILLEJOS (2)	Collapse cañizo-Occupation ground. Phase 20. Middle Calcolithic	3770 ± 70	2295-2050	2445-1975	Beta135666	MOLINA et al., 2004
ALBALATE		4080 ± 100	2860-2491	2895-2348		NOCETE, 1989
ALBALATE		4040 ± 100	2856-2467	2880-2301		NOCETE, 1989
ALBALATE		3890 ± 100	2480-2205	2829-2037		NOCETE, 1989
ALBALATE		3830 ± 100	2459-2147	2568-1980		NOCETE, 1989
CORTIJO DE LA TORRE		3830 ± 90	2457-2150	2562-2028		NOCETE, 1989
LOS CASTILLEJOS (2)	Occupation ground. Phase 22. Late Calcolithic	3910 ± 40	2465-2330	2480-2285	Beta135667	MOLINA et al., 2004
LOS CASTILLEJOS (1)(2)	Collapse cañizo-Occupation ground. Phase 22. Late Calcolithic	3640 ± 120	2190-2165 2150-1880	2340-1695	Beta135668	MOLINA et al., 2004
LOS CASTILLEJOS (1)(3)	Collapse cañizo-Occupation ground Phase 22. Late Calcolithic	3960 ± 50	2555-2535 2490-2445	2580-2310	Beta145303	MOLINA et al., 2004
MARROQUÍES	Fortified Wall UA23. E 2-4.	3910 ± 50	2464-2313	2554-2203	UtC 6458	ZAFRA et al., 1999
MARROQUÍES	Hut UA 23. E-2-4. Phase 3	3942 ±40	2469-2365	2560-2312	UtC 6457	ZAFRA et al., 1999
LOS CASTILLEJOS (2)	Phase 23b. Final Calcolithic	3840 ± 35	2398-2206	2459-2201	GrN 7287	ARRIBAS, 1976
ÚBEDA		3791 ±45	2291-2142	2453-2042	CSIC 1769	NOCETE et al., 2005
MARROQUÍES	House UA23. E-2-4. Phase 4	3706 ±34	2138-1989	2191-1976	CSIC 1346	ZAFRA et al., 1999
MARROQUÍES	Top of the ditch fill. UA23 E-2-4. Phase 4	3705 ± 28	2136-2033	2183-1979	CSIC 1345	ZAFRA et al., 1999
MARROQUÍES	House UA23. E-2-4. Phase 4	3676 ± 30	2127-1978	2135-1953	CSIC 1344	ZAFRA et al., 1999
MARROQUÍES	Rock Bed under Phase 4. UA23 E-2-4	3760 ± 51	2031-1989	2187-1895	CSIC 1240	ZAFRA et al., 1999

Table 10.1. Dates from sites listed in figure 10.6. (1) Dates from the same sample, (2) Samples analysed by Standard radiometric, (3) Samples analysed by AMS

fication of position and not because of intrinsic value, into quite generalized, non mercantile, movement processes, which accentuate the processes of indebtedness and ascription when the only real compensation for the metal is true renewable wealth in the form of work or its results in means of production (herds or land at this point) or other food products and when access to it, in addition to symbolizing "freedom" itself, allowed for its use as a "means for war" with which to theoretically gain access to external benefits.

In this sense the previous accumulation mentioned above, in its generation of different starting points, was the real base of exploitation, based upon this transfer of value that only made sense in a class society, that led to new accumulations thanks to the control of the state and the sanction of inequality, and in which the alternatives were aborted by force or the same force opened the escape valve, although insufficient, of external aggression, continually emphasised, in the absence of true qualitative changes in the productive forces which made it necessary either to extend the territory of domination (colonization or conquest) or to exert greater pressure over dominated groups (Nocete 2001). Given the immediacy of the benefits created by conquest or the increase of tribute, other forms (technical improvements, colonization, etc.) only take place in times of open class conflict, which could explain the concentration of transformations in certain periods like, for example, the transition between the Final Chalcolithic and the Bronze Age, and not separately from new forms of exercising domination, as we shall see.

In this context, social differentiation is increased, as certain archaeological findings show. The differential accumulation of herds can be followed in different Argaric centres like Peñalosa (Baños de la Encina, Jaén), where the differences between the Structural Group X and the rest can be observed, either by the concentration of equine remains, even considering their differential conservation, or by the different proportion of species (Figs. 10.7 and 10.8). Such differential accumulation must be linked not with wealth arising from the exchange related to metal production; rather it should be considered the expression of some peripheral elites associated with the control of metallic items distribution (Contreras & Cámara 2002) and with an intrastate movement of tribute that is especially evident in the territory forming the Vega of Granada in relation to Cerro de la Encina (Monachil, Granada) where horses were abundant (Martínez & Afonso 1998), without forgetting the interstate movement found, almost in its entirety, in the framework of relations among the elites. It is also interesting that the appropriation of agricultural products and their movement as tribute has been suggested (Castro *et al.* 1999), even though the ownership of land is, while ideologically communal, exercised only in benefit of the class-state since the Chalcolithic (Cámara 1998), and for this reason certain authors have used the term "particular ownership" (Arteaga 2001). The separation of communal-state ownership from private ownership (also differential) will only take place very slowly and with the passage from the temporary division and distribution of land to permanent divisions (Peroni 2004)
.

Lastly, in relation to the exploitation of work and progressive indebtedness, the position of the burials within the Argaric settlements, the differences in grave goods, the type of tomb, the relationship they have with the houses where they are located and certain illnesses and malformations documented in the skeletons have enabled us to determine that true serfs existed in the Bronze Age of the South of the Iberian Peninsula (Cámara 2001) in a context in which territory is now defined strictly by means of the fortified hill-top settlements, although in non-Argaric parts of Andalusia the dispersion of external necropolises also means a sacredness of territory through aristocratic routes.

The tombs of these "serfs" are located in the houses of the families to which they were associated, and to whom they owed their work and the resources which would correspond to them in a hypothetical, and now non-existent, community ideal; their ownership clearly becoming a fallacy. This is how we have interpreted the findings of Peñalosa (Baños de la Encina, Jaén) and La

Cuesta del Negro (Purullena, Granada). This phenomenon could be read as a way to "award" their loyalty and to tie them to "service" in the hereafter, while at the same time also linking their descendents in this world, in a two-fold paradox that reveals the duality of the ritual aimed at masking and exhibiting inequality.

Here it would appear that there has been a change from a low rate of exploitation of a broad stratum of the population in the Chalcolithic to a high rate of exploitation of a reduced stratum in the Bronze Age (Cámara 2001; 2004). In no case does this mean a reduction in benefits for the elite, nor the existence of an unexploited middle stratum, since the rest of the population continues to render services in the form of defence of the state, which is also expressed in the possession of metal weapons, as much as these produce relative benefits.

This is the case of the "warrior" stratum: it is not homogenous and constitutes the highest number of Argaric burials. Their children, compared with those of the elite, have limited grave goods, or in any case, different grave goods, although the importance of marriage tends to maintain their position even in the case of the disappearance of the parents, in a context of inheritance and emulation conducive to the acceleration of unequal accumulation and the proliferation of indebtedness with no return, which, at least in advanced times, leads even to perpetuating and justifying inheritance through the appearance of children buried with rich grave goods, as seen in the case of Cerro de la Encina (Monachil) (Molina 1983:104).

This progressive indebtedness, intensified by the amortization costs of elements in the tombs to maintain social position, would provoke a crisis in the Argaric world, as a result of the struggle between classes, to the point that sepulchres completely cease to exist and the only ritual mobilizations of resources are linked to the elite (stelae, deposits...) thus further justifying their position with respect to the growing number of ascribed people (and their resources) which required a new urban system for their control (Cámara 2001).

An explanation of the development of inequality in the Late Prehistory of Andalusia based on the control of the labour force, as has been presented here, is more parsimonious than one based on competition for land because:

1° The latter accepts that such competition occurs only after the complete sedentarization of the populations, but it does not explain the process which leads to this sedentarization. Competition for agricultural land must be emphasized in the consolidation of social classes (Nocete 1989; 2001) but not considered the cause of aggregation. Prior to this phenomenon, pastures and areas for the movement of herds and people bring about certain competition, although, in this case, the accent must be placed on the competition for the elements that circulate and not on the land itself.

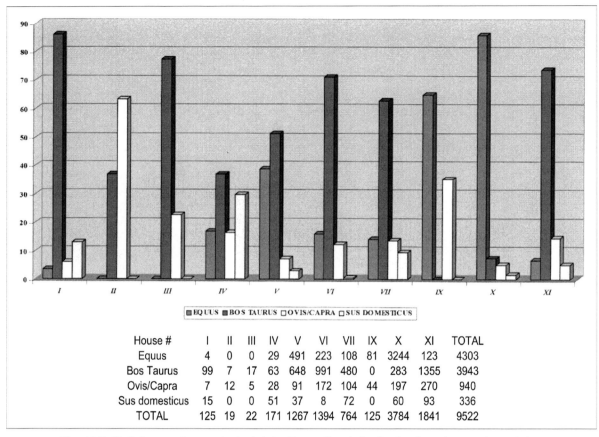

House #	I	II	III	IV	V	VI	VII	IX	X	XI	TOTAL
Equus	4	0	0	29	491	223	108	81	3244	123	4303
Bos Taurus	99	7	17	63	648	991	480	0	283	1355	3943
Ovis/Capra	7	12	5	28	91	172	104	44	197	270	940
Sus domesticus	15	0	0	51	37	8	72	0	60	93	336
TOTAL	125	19	22	171	1267	1394	764	125	3784	1841	9522

Fig. 10.7. Peñalosa archeozoological data. Proportional distribution from houses by weight.

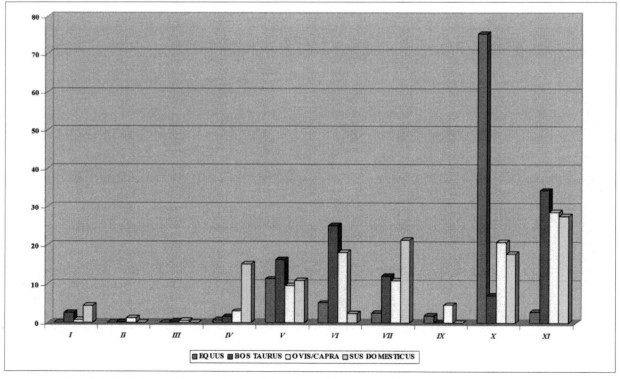

Fig. 10.8. Peñalosa archeozoological data. Proportion in every house on the houses by weight.

144

2º The emphasis on the control of land links the appearance of servitude not to the origin of classes and the beginning of exploitation, but to the appropriation by one of the classes of legal ownership of the land.

3º The emphasis on the labour force explains how the dissolution of the community and the formation of classes come about.

4º This proposal also presents models for how the appropriation of communal land by one class occurs (for example, more land is cultivated by those who have more means of labour, since means of labour allow them to exploit larger plots) and for how distribution is dominated/controlled by those who have come to lead the community through their control of the labour force and of herds.

10.7.- References

AFONSO, J.A.; MOLINA, F.; CÁMARA, J.A.; MORENO, M.; RAMOS, R. & RODRÍGUEZ, Mª.O. 1996: "Espacio y tiempo. La secuencia en Los Castillejos de Las Peñas de Los Gitanos (Montefrío, Granada)". I Congrés del Neolític a la Península Ibérica. Formació e implantació de les comunitats agrícoles (Gavà-Bellaterra 1995). Vol. 1. Rubricatum 1 (1): 297-304.

ARAUS, J.L.; FERRERO, A.; RODRÍGUEZ, Mª.O.; MOLINA, F. & CÁMALICH, Mª.D. 1997: "Identification of ancient irrigation practices based on the carbon isotopes discrimination of plant seeds: a case study form the SE Iberian Peninsula". Journal of Archaeological Science 24: 35-48.

ARRIBAS, A. 1976: "Las bases actuales para el estudio del Eneolítico y la Edad del Bronce en el Sudeste de la Península Ibérica". Cuadernos de Prehistoria de la Universidad de Granada 1: 139-155.

ARRIBAS, A. & MOLINA, F. 1984: "Estado actual de la investigación del megalitismo en la Península Ibérica". In J. Fortea (ed.): Scripta Praehistorica. Homenaje a Francisco Jordá Oblata: 63-112.

ARTEAGA, O. 1993: "Tribalización, jerarquización y Estado en el territorio de El Argar". Spal 1:179-208.

- 2001: "La sociedad clasista inicial y el origen del estado en el territorio de El Argar". Revista Atlántica-Mediterránea de Arqueología Social 3: 121-129.

BARRETT, J.C. 1990: "The monumentality of death: the character of Early Bronze Age mortuary mounds in Southern Britain". Monuments and the Monumental. World Archaeology 22 (2): 179-189.

BENDER, B. 1989: "The roots of inequality." In D. Miller, M. Rowlands & C. Tilley (eds.): Domination and resistance. One World Archaeology 3. Unwin Hyman. London: 83-95.

BLASCO, A.; VILLALBA, Mª.J. & EDO, M. 1997: "Aspectos sociales del Neolítico Medio catalán". In R. de Balbín & P. Bueno (eds.): II Congreso de Arqueología Peninsular (Zamora

1996). T. II. Neolítico. Calcolítico y Bronce. Serie Actas. Fundación Rei Alfonso Henriques. Zamora: 89-97.

BURGOS, A.; PÉREZ, C. & LIZCANO, R. 2001a: "Actuación arqueológica realizada en la piscina comunitaria de los bloques A1, A2, A3, A6, A7 y A8 del Sector UA-23 de Marroquíes Bajos de Jaén". Anuario Arqueológico de Andalucía 1998/III-1. Sevilla: 402-413.

- 2001b: "Actuación arqueológica realizada en el espacio destinado a la instalación del ovoide del vial 4 de la UA-23, Marroquíes Bajos. Jaén". Anuario Arqueológico de Andalucía 1998/III-1. Sevilla: 422-428.

BUXÓ, R. 1997: Arqueología de las plantas. La explotación económica de las semillas y los frutos en el marco mediterráneo de la Península Ibérica. Crítica. Barcelona.

CÁMALICH, Mª.D. & MARTÍN, D. 1999: "Conclusiones". In Mª.D. Cámalich & D. Martín (dirs.): El territorio almeriense desde los inicios de la producción hasta fines de la Antigüedad. Un modelo: La Depresión de Vera y cuenca del río Almanzora. Arqueología Monografías 6. Consejería de Cultura de la Junta de Andalucía. Sevilla: 327-353.

CÁMARA, J.A. 1998: Bases teóricas y metodológicas para el estudio del ritual funerario utilizado durante la Prehistoria Reciente en el sur de la Península Ibérica. Tesis Doctoral Microfilmada. Universidad de Granada. Granada.

- 2001: El ritual funerario en la Prehistoria Reciente en el Sur de la Península Ibérica. British Archaeological Reports International Series 913. Oxford.

- 2004: "Lotta di classe e falso ideologico. L'esempio dei fenomeni funerari della Preistoria Recente del sud della Penisola Iberica". Padusa. Bollettino del Centro Polesano di Studi Storici, archeologici ed etnografici Rovigo XXXIX: 71-90.

CÁMARA, J.A.; CONTRERAS, F.; PÉREZ, C. & LIZCANO, R. 1996: "Enterramientos y diferenciación social II. La problemática del Alto Guadalquivir durante la Edad del Bronce". Trabajos de Prehistoria 53 (1): 91-108.

CÁMARA, J.A. & LIZCANO, R. 1996: "Ritual y sedentarización en el yacimiento del Polideportivo de Martos (Jaén)". I Congrés del Neolític a la Península Ibérica. Formació e implantació de les comunitats agrícoles (Gavá-Bellaterra, 1995). Vol. 1. Rubricatum 1 (1): 313-322.

CARRIÓN, F.; ALONSO, J.M.; RULL, E.; CASTILLA, J.; CEPRIÁN, B.; MARTÍNEZ, J.L.; HARO, M. & MANZANO, A. 1993: "Los recursos abióticos y los sistemas de aprovisionamiento de rocas por las comunidades prehistóricas del S.E. de la península ibérica durante la Prehistoria Reciente". In J.M. Campos & F. Nocete (coords.): Investigaciones arqueológicas en Andalucía. 1985-1992. Proyectos. Consejería de Cultura. Huelva: 295-309.

CASTRO, P.V.; CHAPMAN, R.W.; GILI, S.; LULL, V.; MICÓ, R.; RIHUETE, C.; RISCH, R. & SANAHUJA, Mª.E. 1996: "Teoría de las prácticas sociales". In Mª.A. Querol & T. Chapa (eds.): Homenaje al Profesor Manuel Fernández Miranda I. Complutum Extra 6 (1): 35-48.

CASTRO, P.V.; GILI, S.; LULL, V.; MICÓ, R.; RIHUETE, C.; RISCH, R. & SANAHUJA, Mª.E. 1999: "Teoría de la producción de la vida social. Mecanismos de explotación en el Sudeste ibérico". *Boletín de Antropología Americana* 33: 25-77.

CHAPMAN, R.W. 1981: "Los Millares y la cronología relativa de la Edad del Cobre en el Sudeste de España". *Cuadernos de Prehistoria de la Universidad de Granada* 6: 75-89.

- 1982: "Autonomy, ranking and resources in Iberian prehistory". In C. Renfrew & S. Shennan (eds.): *Ranking, resources and exchange. Aspects of Archeology of Early European Society.* New Directions in Archaeology. Cambridge University Press. Cambridge: 46-51.

CONTRERAS, F. & CÁMARA, J.A. 2002: *La jerarquización social en la Edad del Bronce del Alto Guadalquivir (España). El poblado de Peñalosa (Baños de la Encina, Jaén).* British Archaeological Reports International Series 1025. Oxford.

ESTÉVEZ, J.; VILA, A.; TERRADAS, X.; PIQUÉ, R.; TAULÉ, M.; GIBAJA, J. & RUIZ, G. 1999: "Cazar o no cazar, ¿es ésta la cuestión?". *Boletín de Antropología Americana* 33: 5-24.

GERMANÀ, F. & SANTONI, V. 1993: "La necropoli di Cuccuru S'Arriu (Cabras) e I paleosardi medioneolitici". *Quaderni della Soprintendenza Archeologica per le province di Cagliari e Oristano* 9: 5-30.

GIBAJA, J.F.; CLEMENTE, I. & VILÁ, A. 1997: "Una aproximación a través del análisis funcional a sociedades neolíticas del Noreste Peninsular: las necrópolis de la Bòbila Madurell y el Camí de Can Grau". In R. de Balbín & P. Bueno (eds.): II *Congreso de Arqueología Peninsular* (Zamora 1996). Vol. II. *Neolítico. Calcolítico y Bronce.* Fundación Rei Alfonso Henriques. Zamora: 129-136.

GILMAN, A. 1987: "Regadío y conflicto en sociedades acéfalas". *Boletín del Seminario de Arte y Arqueología* LIII: 59-72.

GUIDI, A. 2000: *Preistoria della complessità sociale.* Quadrante 107. Laterza. Roma.

HARO, M. 2004: "El poblamiento durante la Prehistoria Reciente en el Campo de Níjar". *Arqueología y Territorio* 1: 51-65. http://www.ugr.es/~arqueol/docencia/doctorado/ArqyT/Articulo s%201/Artic4.htm

KEESMANN, I.; MORENO, Mª.A. & KRONZ, A. 1997: "Investigaciones científicas de la metalurgia de El Malagón y Los Millares en el Sureste de España". *Cuadernos de Prehistoria de la Universidad de Granada* 16-17: 247-302.

LERNER, G. 1990: *La creación del patriarcado.* Crítica. Barcelona.

LIZCANO, R. 1999: *El Polideportivo de Martos (Jaén): un yacimiento neolítico del IV Milenio A.C..* Obra Social y Cultural Cajasur. Córdoba.

LIZCANO, R. & CÁMARA, J.A. 2004: "Producción económica y sedentarización. El registro arqueológico del Polideportivo de Martos (Jaén)". *Sociedades recolectoras y primeros productores. Actas de las Jornadas Temáticas Andaluzas de Arqueología* (Ronda 2003). Consejería de Cultura. Junta de Andalucía. Sevilla: 229-248.

LIZCANO, R.; CÁMARA, J. A.; CONTRERAS, F.; PÉREZ, C. & BURGOS, A. 2004: "Continuidad y cambio en comunidades calcolíticas del Alto Guadalquivir". *Simposios de Prehistoria Cueva de Nerja. II. La problemática del Neolítico en Andalucía. III.Las primeras sociedades metalúrgicas en Andalucía.* Fundación Cueva de Nerja. Nerja: 159-175.

LIZCANO, R.; CÁMARA, J.A.; RIQUELME, J.A.; CAÑABATE, Mª.L.; SÁNCHEZ, A. & AFONSO, J.A. 1997: "El Polideportivo de Martos. Estrategias económicas y símbolos de cohesión en un asentamiento del Neolítico Final del Alto Guadalquivir". *Cuadernos de Prehistoria de la Universidad de Granada* 16-17: 5-101.

MALDONADO, Mª.G.; MOLINA, F.; ALCARAZ, F.M.; CÁMARA, J.A.; MÉRIDA, V. & RUIZ, V. 1997: "El papel social del megalitismo en el Sureste de la Península Ibérica. Las comunidades megalíticas del Pasillo de Tabernas". *Cuadernos de Prehistoria de la Universidad de Granada* 16-17: 167-190.

MÁRQUEZ, J.E. 2002: "De los 'Campos de Silos' a los 'Agujeros Negros': Sobre pozos, depósitos y zanjas en la Prehistoria Reciente del Sur de la Península Ibérica". *Homenaje al Profesor Pellicer (I). Spal* 10: 207-220.

MARTÍN, A.; BORDAS, A. & MARTÍ, M. 1996: "Bobila Madurell (St. Quirze del Vallès, Barcelona). Estrategia económica y organización social en el Neolítico Medio". *I Congrés del Neolític a la Península Ibérica. Formació e implantació de les comunitats agrícoles* (Gavá-Bellaterra, 1995). Vol. 1. *Rubricatum* 1 (1): 423-428.

MARTÍNEZ, G. 1997: "Late Prehistory Blade Production in Andalusi (Spain)". In A. Ramos & Mª.A. Bustillo (eds.): *Siliceous rocks and Culture.* Monográfica Arte y Arqueología 42. Universidad de Granada. Granada: 427-436.

MARTÍNEZ, G. & AFONSO, J.A. 1998: "Las sociedades prehistóricas: de la Comunidad al Estado". In R. Peinado (ed.): *De Ilurco a Pinos Puente. Poblamiento, economía y sociedad de un pueblo de la Vega de Granada.* Diputación Provincial de Granada. Granada: 21-68.

MARTÍNEZ, G.; MORGADO, A.; AFONSO, J.A.; SÁNCHEZ, M. & RONCAL, Mª.E. 1998: "Reflexiones sobre la explotación de materias primas para la producción de arfefactos de piedra tallada durante la Prehistoria Reciente de Andalucía Oriental: el caso de Los Castillejos (Montefrío, Granada)". In J. Bosch, X. Terradas & T. Orozco (eds.): *Actes de la 20 Reunió de Treball sobre Aprovisionament de Recursos Lítics a la Prehistòrica* (Barcelona-Gavà, 1997). *Rubricatum* 2: 161-170.

MARTÍNEZ, J. 1998: "Abrigos y accidentes geográficos como categorías de análisis en el paisaje de la pintura rupestre esquemática. El Sudeste como marco". *Arqueología del Paisaje. Arqueología Espacial* 19-20: 543-561.

MATHERS, C. 1984: "Beyond the grave: the context and wider implications of mortuary practices in south-east Spain". In T.F.C. Blagg, R.F.J. Joves & S.J. Keay (eds.): *Papers in Iberian Archaeology* I. British Archaeological Reports International Series 193 (I). Oxford: 13-46.

MEIKLEJOHN, C.; PETERSEN, E.B. & ALEXANDERSEN, V. 2002: "The Anthropology and Archaeology of Mesolithic Gender in the Western Baltic". In M. Donald & L. Hurcombe (eds.): *Gender and Material Culture in Archaeological Perspective.* Studies in Gender and Material Culture 1. Palgrave Macmillan. Basinstoke: 222-237.

MEILLASSOUX, C. 1987: *Mujeres, graneros y capitales. Economía doméstica y capitalismo.* Siglo XXI. México.

MOLINA, F. 1983: "La Prehistoria". In F. Molina & J.M. Roldán: *Historia de Granada I. De las primeras culturas al Islam.* Don Quijote. Granada: 11-131.

- 1988: "El Sudeste" In G. Delibes, M. Fernández-Miranda, A. Martín & F. Molina: El Calcolítico de la Península Ibérica. *Congresso Internazionale L'Età del Rame in Europa* (Viareggio 1987). *Rassegna di Archeologia* 7: 256-262.

MOLINA, F.; CÁMARA, J. A.; CAPEL, J.; NÁJERA, T. & SÁEZ, L. 2004: "Los Millares y la periodización de la Prehistoria Reciente del Sudeste". *Simposios de Prehistoria Cueva de Nerja. II. La problemática del Neolítico en Andalucía. III.Las primeras sociedades metalúrgicas en Andalucía.* Fundación Cueva de Nerja. Nerja: 142-158.

MONTERO, I. 1998: "Interpretación cultural en la investigación arqueometalúrgica: la Edad del Bronce". In J. Fernández & F.J. Sarabia (coords.): *Arqueometalurgia del bronce. Introducción a la metodología de trabajo.* Studia Archaeologica 86. Universidad de Valladolid. Valladolid: 99-108.

MORENO, Mª.A.; CONTRERAS, F. & CÁMARA, J.A. 1997: "Patrones de asentamiento, poblamiento y dinámica cultural. Las tierras altas del sureste peninsular. El pasillo de Cúllar-Chirivel durante la Prehistoria Reciente". *Cuadernos de Prehistoria de la Universidad de Granada* 16-17: 191-245.

NAVAS, E. 2004: "Análisis inicial de los restos faunísticos del yacimiento arqueológico de Los Millares (Santa Fe de Mondújar, Almería) en su contexto espacial". *Arqueología y Territorio* 1: 37-49. http://www.ugr.es/~arqueol/docencia/doctorado/ArqyT/Articulos%201/Artic3.htm

NOCETE, F. 1989: *El espacio de la coerción. La transición al Estado en las Campiñas del Alto Guadalquivir (España). 3000-1500 A.C.* British Archaeological Reports International Series 492. Oxford.

- 2001: *Tercer milenio antes de nuestra era. Relaciones y contradicciones centro/periferia en el Valle del Guadalquivir.* Bellaterra. Barcelona.

NOCETE, F.; ORIHUELA, A.; OTERO, R.; ROMERO, J.C.; ESCALERA, P. & LINARES, J.A. 1997: "Prospección arqueológica en el Andévalo occidental (Presa del Andévalo). Huelva. Informe preliminar". *Anuario Arqueológico de Andalucía* 1993/III: 332-335.

NOCETE, F.; SÁEZ, R.; NIETO, J.M.; CRUZ-AUÑÓN, R.; CABRERO, R.; ALEX, E. & BAYONA, M.R. 2005: "Circulation of silicified oolitic limestone blades in South-Iberia (Spain and Portugal) during the third millennium B.C.: an expression of a core/periphery framework". *Journal of Anthropological Archaeology* 24: 62-81.

PELLICER, M. 1964: *El Neolítico y el Bronce de la Cueva de la Carigüela de Píñar (Granada).* Trabajos de Prehistoria XV. Madrid.

PELLICER, M. & ACOSTA, P. 1986: "Neolítico y calcolítico de la Cueva de Nerja." In J.F. Jordá (ed.): *La Prehistoria de la Cueva de Nerja (Málaga).* Trabajos sobre la Cueva de Nerja 1.

Patronato de la Cueva de Nerja/Universidad de Málaga. Málaga: 377-450.

PÉREZ, C. & CÁMARA, J.A. 1999: "Intervención arqueológica en Marroquíes Bajos (Jaén). Sector Urbanístico RP-4. Parcela G-3". *Anuario Arqueológico de Andalucía* 1995/III: 256-270.

PERONI, R. 2004: *L'Italia alle soglie della storia.* Biblioteca Universale 558. Laterza. Roma.

PETERS, J. & DRIESCH, A. von den. 1990: "Archäozoologische untersuchung der tierreste aus der kupferzeitlichen siedlung von Los Millares (Prov. Almería)". *Studien über frühe Tierknochenfunde von der Iberischen Halbinsel* 12: 49-110.

RAMOS, U.; AFONSO, J.A.; CÁMARA, J.A.; MOLINA, F. & MORENO, M. 1997: "Trabajos de acondicionamiento y estudio científico en el yacimiento de Los Castillejos en Las Peñas de los Gitanos (Montefrío, Granada)". *Anuario Arqueológico de Andalucía* 1993/III: 265-271.

RAMOS, A.; MARTÍNEZ, G.; RIOS, G. & AFONSO, J.A. 1991: *Flint production and exchange in the Iberian Southeast (III Millenium B.C.). (VI International Flint Symposium. Postsymposium field trip).* Universidad de Granada/Instituto Geológico y Minero. Granada.

RIQUELME, J.A. 2002: *Cueva de las Ventanas. Historia y Arqueología.* Ayuntamiento de Píñar. Píñar.

RODRÍGUEZ, Mª.O. & VERNET, J.L. 1991: "Premiers résultats paléocarpologiques de l'établissement Chalcolithique de Los Millares, Almería, d'après l'analyse anthracologique de l'établissement". In W.H. Waldren, J.A. Ensenyat & R.C. Kennard (eds.): *IInd Deya International Conference of Prehistory. Recent developments in Western Mediterranean Prehistory: Archaeological techniques, technology and theory. Vol. I. Archaeological techniques and technology.* British Archaeological Reports International Series 573. Oxford: 1-16.

RUBIO DE MIGUEL, I. 1980-81: "Enterramientos neolíticos de la Península Ibérica". *Cuadernos de Prehistoria y Arqueología de la Universidad Autónoma de Madrid* 7-8: 39-73.

SANTONI, V. 1995: "Il sito preistorico di Cuccuru S'Arriu (Cabras, Oristano)". In A. Moravetti & C. Tozzi (cur.): *Sardegna.* Guide Archeologiche. Preistoria e Protostoria in Italia 2. XIII Congresso Internazionale dell Scienze Preistoriche e Protostoriche. U.I.S.P.P./Ministero per i Beni Culturali e Ambientali/A.B.A.C.O. Edizioni. Forlì: 130-137.

SCARDUELLI, P. 1988: *Dioses, espíritus, ancestros. Elementos para la comprensión de los sistemas rituales.* Siglo XXI. México.

STE. CROIX, G.E.M. de 1988: *La lucha de clases en el Mundo Griego Antiguo. De la Edad Arcaica a las conquistas árabes.* Crítica. Barcelona.

THOMAS, J. 1993: "The Hermeneutics of Megalithic Space". In C. Tilley (ed.): *Interpretative Archaeology.* Explorations in Anthropology Series. Exeter. Berg: 73-97.

TILLEY, C. 1993: "Art, Architecture, Landscape (Neolithic Sweden)". In B. Bender (ed.): *Landscape. Politics and perspectives.* Explorations in Anthropology Series. Exeter. Berg: 49-84.

147

VICENT, J.M. 1993: "El Neolítico. Transformaciones sociales y económicas". *Boletín de Antropología Americana* 24: 31-62.

ZAFRA, N.; HORNOS, F. & CASTRO, M. 1999: "Una macro-aldea en el origen del modo de vida campesino: Marroquíes Bajos (Jaén) c. 2500-2000 cal ANE". *Trabajos de Prehistoria* 56 (1): 77-102.

ZVELEBIL, M. 1997: "Ideology, society and economy of the Mesolithic communities in temperate and northern Europe". *Origini* XX: 39-70.

- 2002: "Fat is a Feminist Issue: On Ideology, Diet and Health in Hunter-Gatherer Societies." In M. Donald & L. Hurcombe (eds.): *Gender and Material Culture in Archaeological Perspective*. Studies in Gender and Material Culture 1, Basinstoke. Palgrave Macmillan: 209-221.

CHAPTER 11

Funerary ideology and social inequality in the Late Prehistory of the Iberian South-West (*c.* 3300-850 cal BC)

Leonardo García Sanjuán
Universidad de Sevilla

Abstract

In this paper I analyse the funerary ideology of the communities which occupied the Southwest of the Iberian Peninsula between c. 3300 and 850 cal BC (Copper and Bronze Age). The definition and critical discussion of the funerary patterns and their evolution over this long period is used as the basis for an analysis of the evolution of social inequality. With this aim in mind, three main groups of evidence are used, corresponding to (i) funerary spaces and architectures, (ii) grave goods deposited as part of the funerary ritual, and (iii) symbology associated with the architecture and portable artefacts. As a result, an interpretation of the dialectic evolution of elements of continuity and rupture within the funerary ideology, and its significance in terms of social relationships, is presented.

Keywords: Neolithic; Copper Age; Bronze Age; Funerary Ideology; Social Inequality; Social Complexity; Megalithism; Artificial Caves.

Resumen

En este trabajo se analiza la ideología funeraria de las comunidades que habitaron el Suroeste de la Península Ibérica entre c. 3300 y 850 cal ANE (Edad del Cobre y Edad del Bronce). La definición y discusión crítica de las pautas funerarias y su evolución en este largo periodo es utilizada como base para examinar la evolución de las formas de desigualdad social. Con este objetivo se utilizan tres grupos principales de indicadores relativos a (i) los espacios y arquitecturas funerarias, (ii) los depósitos de ajuares que forman parte del ritual de la muerte y (iii) la simbología asociada a la arquitectura y objetos portables. Como resultado se propone una interpretación de la evolución dialéctica de elementos de continuidad y ruptura en la ideología funeraria y su significado en términos de relaciones sociales.

Palabras clave: Neolítico; Edad del Cobre; Edad del Bronce; Ideología Funeraria; Desigualdad Social; Complejidad Social; Megalitismo; Cuevas Artificiales.

11.1.- Introduction

The theme of this paper is the analysis of the funerary record left by the societies that occupied the Iberian Southwest during the Copper Age (*c.* 3300-2100 cal BC) and the Bronze Age (*c.* 2100-850 cal BC). This analysis is aimed at interpreting the forms of social inequality that existed among those communities. Therefore, on an epistemological level, an issue which deserves some preliminary consideration is that of the extent to which the funerary archaeological record can be interpreted in terms of social organisation.

In this respect, the modern western society in which we live can be considered as something quite singular within the general framework of human social evolution, given the drastic distance (almost segregation) established between the living and the experience of death.[1] The behav-

iour of prehistoric societies in this aspect could not be more different from our own: death and the dead were actively present in human life in a range of ways. Transformed into ancestors, the dead communicated with the living, legitimising ideological agendas and social and political strategies, leading and maintaining traditions, bringing order to the world and to society. Over the past years, a wealth of empirical data has demonstrated the complexity of the patterns of interaction established between European prehistoric communities and their own ancestors.

Therefore, if the funerary record of prehistoric societies is highly valuable as it establishes the materiality of the funerary ideology, and funerary ideology is important because it shapes the relationships between the sphere of the dead (Past) and the society of the living (Present and Future), why should the funerary ideology be important in the analysis of social organisation - and more specifically of

---

[1] In the capitalist societies of the 21st century, death and the dead have been subtly although effectively separated from the vital human experience, which driven by the irrefrainable impulse of market consumerism, focuses ever more on values of hedonism and eternal youth.

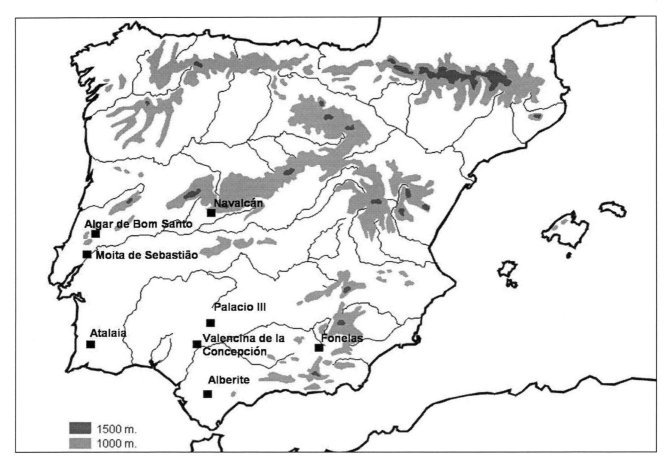

Figure 11.1 Location of main sites discussed in the text.

social inequality? At this point we obviously stumble into one of the central subjects of epistemological and theoretical debate in prehistoric archaeology of the past decades, that is to say, the degree to which the funerary record reflects (or embodies) the structure of social relationships of production to which the members of a community belonged throughout their lives. A large volume of theoretical literature has dealt with this issue in both the English-speaking world – cf. Binford 1972; Chapman & Randsborg 1981; Humphreys & King 1981; Pader 1982; Bartel 1982; Wason 1994; Carr 1995; Tarlow 1999; Parker Pearson 1999; Mchugh 1999; etc. – and within Spanish archaeology – cf. Lull & Picazo 1989; Barceló 1990; Ruiz Zapatero & Chapa 1990; Chapa 1991; Castro et al. 1995; Vicent 1995; Lull 2000.

Given that this is not a theoretical paper, and that therefore it is not my intention to enter here into the details of this wide and complex debate, I will simply establish that by funerary ideology I mean *the systemic framework of symbolic notions which articulate the relationship between the living (present and future) and the ancestors (past), expressed through highly ritualised practices that focus on the treatment of the dead (eschatology) and that display an important material dimension*. The material funerary record of a society is directly connected to the system of symbolic representation of the cosmogonic and religious ideas according to which nature, humankind and society

are interpreted. This ideological and symbolic dimension, materially visible in the funerary record, is often difficult to observe in the settlement record.

The perspective that I have applied in the sociological interpretation of the funerary evidence of the Late Prehistory of the Iberian South-West (García Sanjuán & Hurtado 1997; García Sanjuán 1999a; 1999b; etc.) departs from L. R. Binford's seminal proposal (1972: 235) according to which funerary ideology tends to be *isomorphic* with respect to the structure of the social relations of production of the society, in such a way that its materialisation encapsulates the patterns of symmetry or asymmetry which exist in the society's access to resources. Although perhaps not universally applicable, this premise is of particular interest in the study of hierarchical and class societies in which religious ideology in general (and funerary ideology in particular) is manipulated by the elites in order to maintain and reinforce their power. In general, through empirical observations and the quantitative assessment of the variations of energy or labour investment in the creation of funerary containers and the objects deposited within them as mortuary offerings (grave goods), it is possible to interpret the inequalities at play within an extinct social group (Wason 1994: 84; Bard 1994: 30).

The indicators used in this analysis to assess the patterns of social inequality within the communities belonging to the

Late Prehistory of the Iberian South-West derive from those applied in both settlements and funerary sites in a previous study which focused on the communities of the early phases of the Bronze Age (García Sanjuán 1999a). The application of these indicators in the context of the present paper has been carried out within a broader chronological scope (thus covering greater socio-economic variability). The indicators themselves cover three main axis of variability: (i) the organisation of the funerary containers (space and architecture), (ii) the functional configuration and associations of the ritual deposits (artefacts in particular), and (iii) the symbolic representations associated with the funerary containers.

11.2.- Funerary practices between *c.* 5000 and 3300 cal BC: a short review

Although this paper focuses essentially upon the assessment of the funerary record of the Copper and Bronze Ages, many elements of the funerary ideology of these societies stem from much older traditions that can be traced back in time to the Neolithic, Mesolithic or even Upper Palaeolithic. It is thus necessary to place the discussion within the appropriate diachronic and evolutionary perspective. Moreover, given the current state of Iberian prehistory, it is also highly advisable to place the analysis of forms of social inequality within a broader diachronic framework: indeed, studies of this issue which have focused on limited chronological spans have often led to important misjudgements and erroneous appreciations because of a lack of perspective.

Information regarding the funerary practices of the hunter-gatherer groups of the Iberian Mesolithic is very scarce. A recent review of the available data has shown the predominance of individual inhumations in pits or small cavities of caves, often covered or demarcated by small mounds of stones or earth and almost always accompanied by grave goods of tools, food and ornamental objects (Arias & Álvarez-Fernández 2004: 237). The only data available for the Iberian South-West is provided by the shell-middens spread throughout the Portuguese region of Estremadura, in the estuaries of the Tagus and Sado. Thus, for example, the recent review of the information from the excavations of the large Mesolithic site of Moita do Sebastião (Santarem) carried out by M. Jackes and P. Alvim (in press) estimates in almost one hundred the number of inhumations recorded at the site, forming what in the VI millennium cal BC would have been an open air necropolis, spatially structured by a horseshoe of burials with its opening facing the highest point of the hill where the settlement was located. However, the degree to which the *advanced* funerary practices observed at this site are pristine (and representative of the cultural patterns of the local late hunter-gatherer groups) or influenced by the acculturating contact with the communities which in the same chronological framework had already developed an economy of production in other

regions of southern Iberia, is not clear (Arias & Álvarez-Fernández 2004: 240).

Indeed, from the mid-VI millennium cal BC (perhaps late VII millennium), Neolithic communities appear in the South of Spain, occupying caves such as Cueva de La Dehesilla (Cádiz), Cueva Chica de Santiago (Seville), Cueva del Toro (Málaga) or Cueva de los Murciélagos (Córdoba), as well as small open air settlements such as El Retamar (Cádiz) or Los Castillejos de Las Peñas de los Gitanos (Granada), to name but those which have received most detailed study and for which radiocarbon dates are available. The most common funerary pattern among these communities appears to have been burial in caves (in the same caves that were used as dwellings and in other caves with a more specialised ritual and funerary function). The funerary use of natural caves during the early Neolithic is well documented in many locations of Central and Eastern Andalusia, especially in Málaga and Granada, although unfortunately their chronology has not been established through absolute dating methods (*cf.* discussion in Rubio 1981: 55-58; González-Tablas 1990). In such cases, the spatial and architectural organisation of the burials follows three main trends:

(i)   the use of natural hollows or crevices in the rock to place the bodies.
(ii) the excavation of small burial pits.
(iii) the emplacement of bodies lying or sitting leaning against the cave walls.

In some cases, the burials are further marked by large stones or mounds of small stones, thus implying the continuity of Mesolithic practices such as the incipient demarcation or monumentalisation of the burial space (although in this case with very limited visibility and no impact upon the landscape). The composition of the grave good assemblage is almost always found to resemble that of the Mesolithic burials.

In the regions of Southern and Western Portugal, where the Neolithic process takes place at a comparatively later date than in the Spanish Mediterranean regions, the use of natural caves as funerary spaces by the first agrarian communities has been established spanning the whole of the IV millennium cal BC. An important series of radiocarbon dates confirms the use of cave sites in the Portuguese regions of Alentejo (Gruta do Escoural), Estremadura (Lapa do Fumo, Lapa do Bugio, Algar do Barrão and Algar de Bom Santo) and Ribatejo (Gruta dos Ossos) (Tables 11.1 and 11.3). At the site of Algar de Bom Santo, which benefits from excellent conditions of preservation, a minimum of 121 individuals have been recorded that represent but a small fraction of the population buried in this cave over a period of five centuries (Duarte 1998).

A strong Neolithic tradition can thus be observed regarding the use of natural cavities as funerary spaces. During the Copper and Bronze Ages, this tradition (with roots that can be traced back to the Upper Palaeolithic) gradu-

SITE	REGION	BP	BC (1 σ)	REF. LAB.	REFERENCE
Anta da Cabeçuda	Alentejo (PO)	7660 ± 60	6590-6430	ICEN-978	Oliveira, 1998
Anta das Castelhanas	Alentejo (PO)	6360 ± 110	5480-5210	ICEN-1264	Oliveira, 1998
Anta da Figueira Branca	Alentejo (PO)	6210 ± 60	5260-5060	ICEN-823	Oliveira, 1998
Menhir da Meada	Alentejo (PO)	6022 ± 40	4950-4800	UtC-4452	Oliveira, 1996
Anta de Joaninha	Alentejo (PO)	5400 ± 210	4460-3980	Sac-1380	Oliveira, 1998
Alberite	Cádiz (SP)	5320 ± 70	4255-4000	Beta-80602	Ramos Muñoz & Giles Pacheco, 1996
Alberite	Cádiz (SP)	5110 ± 140	4035-3760	Beta-80600	Ramos Muñoz & Giles Pacheco, 1996
Lapa do Fumo	Estremadura (PO)	5040 ± 160	3980-3650	KN-361	Monge Soares & Peixoto Cabral, 1984
Alberite	Cádiz (SP)	5020 ± 70	3940-3715	Beta-80598	Ramos Muñoz & Giles Pacheco, 1996
El Palomar	Sevilla (SP)	4930 ± 70	3780-3640	Beta-75067	Cabrero García et al, 1997
Vale de Rodrigo	Alentejo (PO)	4905 ± 60	3760-3640	Ua-10830	Larsson, 1997
Algar de Bom Santo	Estremadura (PO)	4860 ± 100	3770-3520	OxA-5513	Duarte, 1998
Lapa do Bugio	Estremadura (PO)	4850 ± 45	3700-3530	GrN-5628	Monge Soares y Peixoto Cabral, 1984
Algar de Bom Santo	Estremadura (PO)	4780 ± 50	3650-3520	Beta-120048	Duarte, 1998
Algar de Bom Santo	Estremadura (PO)	4705 ± 65	3630-3370	OxA-5511	Duarte, 1998
Gruta do Escoural	Alentejo (PO)	4689 ± 80	3630-3360	ICEN-861	Soares, 1994
Algar do Barrão	Estremadura (PO)	4660 ± 70	3620-3360	ICEN-740	Carvalho et al, 2003
Gruta dos Ossos	Ribatejo (PO)	4630 ± 70	3630-3130	ICEN-465	Carvalho et al, 2003
Algar de Bom Santo	Estremadura (PO)	4630 ± 60	3520-3340	OxA-5512	Duarte, 1998
Monte do Castelo	Estremadura (PO)	4630 ± 45	3510-3350	ICEN-738	Soares, 2003
Gruta do Escoural	Alentejo (PO)	4610 ± 60	3520-3130	Lv-1923	Soares, 1994
Viera	Málaga (SP)	4550 ± 140	3510-3020	GrN-16067	Ferrer Palma & Marqués Merelo, 1993
Gruta do Escoural	Alentejo (PO)	4500 ± 60	3350-3090	Lv-1922	Soares, 1994
Gruta do Escoural	Alentejo (PO)	4460 ± 70	3340-3020	Lv-1924	Soares, 1994
Gruta dos Ossos	Ribatejo (PO)	4460 ± 110	3340-2930	I-17368	Carvalho et al, 2003
Gruta do Escoural	Alentejo (PO)	4420 ± 60	3310-2920	Lv-1925	Soares, 1994

Table 11.1. Radiocarbon dates for Neolithic funerary contexts of SW Iberia. Bibliographic and laboratory references

ally looses its cultural and ideological significance, although it does never disappear completely. Alongside the tradition of the funerary use of caves, the first megalithic monuments emerge and see their initial stages of development. This process has been dated between c. 4500 and 4000 cal BC, although dates recently provided from the Portuguese region of Alentejo suggest dates within the first half of the V millennium and even late VI millennium cal BC (Table 11.1). Similarly, a recent assessment based on relative chronologies has placed several menhirs from the Portuguese region of Algarve between the late VI and early V millennium cal BC (Calado 2000). Regardless of the precise date of the earliest emergence of monumental stone architecture, it seems clear that the new forms of religious ideology are associated with (and derived from) the transition to an agricultural and livestock based mode of production. With increasing economic security (storage of surplus, lesser vulnerability faced with bad years and poor harvests) and a fairly low demographic density (which spared them the territorial conflicts that would appear in later periods), the agrarian societies of the Iberian Southwest disposed between c.

4500 and 3300 cal BC of sufficient energetic resources and time to tackle the erection of magnificent stone monuments for the glory of the gods and the ancestors. As has been discussed on many occasions, megalithic architecture functioned for the early European farming societies as a mechanism of ideological reproduction, establishing and ensuring the principles that vertebrate the social and natural orders (Sherratt 1990: 334; 1995: 355). It is thus extremely interesting that, throughout this period, megalithic funerary architecture and the funerary use of natural caves coexisted so intensely. The information currently available is insufficient for the formulation of interpretations of whether the use of the two is accounted for by ethnic (different communities with different cultural traditions), or socio-ideological factors (not all groups had the capacity or legitimacy to build megalithic monuments). In any case, it seems clear that in the early stages of development of the farming way of life, funerary ideology induced the coexistence of a highly innovative form of funerary ritual based around megalithic constructions alongside elements of great antiquity (even millennia) such as cave burials.

SITE	REGION	BP	BC (1 σ)	REF. LAB.	REFERENCE
Monte Canela	Algarve (PO)	4460 ± 110	3340-2930	ICEN-1159	Soares, 2003
Algar de Bom Santo	Estremadura (PO)	4430 ± 50	3310-2920	Beta-120047	Duarte, 1998
Monte Canela	Algarve (PO)	4420± 60	3310-2920	OxA-5515	Soares, 2003
Lapa do Fumo	Estremadura (PO)	4420 ± 45	3260-2930	ICEN-240	Monge Soares & Peixoto Cabral, 1984
Los Millares (Sep.19)*	Almería (SP)	4380 ± 120	3330-2880	KN-72	Almagro Gorbea, 1970
Covão do Poço	Ribatejo (PO)	4360 ± 60	3090-2900	Beta-134407	Carvalho et al, 2003
Bola da Cera	Alentejo (PO)	4360 ± 50	3090-2900	ICEN-66	Oliveira, 1998
El Barranquete (Sep.7)*	Almería (SP)	4300 ± 130	3100-2650	CSIC-82	Alonso et al, 1978
El Barranquete (Sep.7)*	Almería (SP)	4280 ± 130	3090-2660	CSIC-81	Alonso et al, 1978
Praia das Maças	Estremadura (PO)	4260 ± 60	2930-2690	H-2049/148	Sousa, 1998
La Paloma	Huelva (SP)	4220 ± 40	2890-2700	Beta-150153	Nocete Calvo et al, 2005
La Venta	Huelva (SP)	4200 ± 70	2870-2660	Beta-150157	Nocete Calvo et al, 2005
La Pijotilla (Tumba 3)	Badajoz (SP)	4130 ± 40	2865-2595	Beta-121143	Hurtado Pérez et al, 2002
Amarguillo II	Sevilla (SP)	4070 ± 60	2860-2490	Beta-75066	Cabrero García et al., 1997
La Paloma	Huelva (SP)	4070 ± 70	2860-2490	Beta-150154	Nocete Calvo et al, 2005
Quinta do Anjo (H-3)	Estremadura (PO)	4050 ± 60	2840-2470	OxA-5508	Soares, 2003
Quinta do Anjo	Estremadura (PO)	4040 ± 70	2830-2460	GrN-10744	Soares, 2003
Alcaide	Málaga (SP)	4030 ± 110	2900-2350	GrN-16062	Marqués Merelo et al, 2004
Gruta dos Ossos	Ribatejo (PO)	3970 ± 140	2850-2200	I-17248	Carvalho et al, 2003
Los Gabrieles (Tumba 4)	Huelva (SP)	3920 ± 50	2470-2300	Beta-185649	Linares Catela, 2006
Vale de Rodrigo	Alentejo (PO)	3905 ± 75	2470-2300	Ua-10831	Larsson, 1997
Herdade dos Cebolinhos	Alentejo (PO)	3900 ± 40	2470-2310	Beta-176899	Gonçalves, 2003
La Pijotilla (Tumba 1)	Badajoz (SP)	3860 ± 70	2460-2280	BM-1603	Hurtado Pérez, 1981
Los Gabrieles (Tumba 4)	Huelva (SP)	3850 ± 40	2410-2200	Beta-185648	Linares Catela, 2006
Herdade dos Cebolinhos	Alentejo (PO)	3840 ± 40	2400-2200	Beta-177471	Gonçalves, 2003
Anta de Joaninha	Alentejo (PO)	3840 ± 170	2600-2000	Sac-1381	Oliveira, 1996
Alcaide	Málaga (SP)	3830 ± 180	2600-1950	GrN-19198	Marqués Merelo et al, 2004
Alcaide	Málaga (SP)	3755 ± 210	2500-1850	GrN-19197	Marqués Merelo et al, 2004
Anta da Cabeçuda	Alentejo (PO)	3720 ± 45	2200-2030	ICEN-979	Oliveira, 1998
Huerta Montero	Badajoz (SP)	3720 ± 100	2300-1970	GrN-16954	Blasco & Ortiz, 1991
Praia das Maças	Extremadura (PO)	3650 ± 60	2140-1930	H-2048/1458	Sousa, 1998
Anta da Cabeçuda	Alentejo (PO)	3650 ± 110	2200-1830	ICEN-977	Oliveira, 1997
Cortijo de El Tardón	Málaga (SP)	3530 ± 60	1940-1740	UGRA-260	Fernández Ruiz et al, 1997
Setefilla	Sevilla (SP)	3520 ± 95	2010-1690	I-11070	Aubet Semmler et al, 1983
La Traviesa	Sevilla (SP)	3520 ± 60	1940-1760	RCD-2110	García Sanjuán, 1997
Herdade do Pomar	Alentejo (PO)	3510 ± 140	2030-1630	ICEN-87	Barceló Álvarez, 1991
Cerro de la Corona	Málaga (SP)	3490 ± 120	2010-1630	Beta-93020	Recio Ruiz et al, 1998
Setefilla	Sevilla (SP)	3470 ± 95	1920-1640	I-11069	Aubet Semmler et al, 1983
Las Minitas	Badajoz (SP)	3430 ± 50	1880-1640	Beta-68668	Pavón Soldevilla, 2003
La Traviesa	Sevilla (SP)	3420 ± 60	1880-1670	RCD-2111	García Sanjuán, 1997
Herdade do Pomar	Alentejo (PO)	3330 ± 45	1690-1520	ICEN-85	Barceló Álvarez, 1991
Anta dos Tasos	Alentejo (PO)	3320 ± 200	1900-1300	SA-199	Leisner & Veiga Ferreira, 1963
Pessegueiro	Alentejo (PO)	3270 ± 45	1620-1460	ICEN-867	Soares & Tavares, 1995
Herdade de Belmeque	Alentejo (PO)	3230 ± 60	1600-1420	ICEN-142	Monge Soares, 1994
Anta das Castellanas	Alentejo (PO)	3220 ± 65	1660-1410	OXA-5432	Oliveira, 1997
Loma del Puerco	Cádiz (SP)	2940 ± 90	1290-1000	UBAR-346	Giles Pacheco et al, 1994
La Encantada 1	Almería (SP)	2830 ± 60	1110-890	CSIC-249	Alonso et al, 1978
Atalaia	Algarve (PO)	2770 ± 50	990-850	KN-1201	Schubart, 1975
Palacio III	Sevilla (SP)	2660 ± 90	980-660	Beta-165552	García Sanjuán, 2005a
El Barranquete (Sep. 11)*	Almería (SP)	2570 ± 100	830-520	CSIC-201b	Almagro Gorbea, 1973

Table 11.2. Radiocarbon dates for Copper and Bronze Age funerary contexts of SW Iberia.
Bibliographic and laboratory references (*) Spanish South-East

PERIOD	SITE	CONTEXT	BC (1 σ)
Early Neolithic (c. 6000-4500 cal BC). Natural caves, very early megalithic architecture (?).	Anta da Cabeçuda	Megalith	6590-6430
	Anta das Castelhanas	Megalith	5480-5210
	Anta da Figueira Branca	Megalith	5260-5060
	Menhir da Meada	Menhir	4950-4800
Late Neolithic (c. 4500-3300 cal BC). First megalithic tradition; expansion of stone monuments; very frequent use of natural caves and early use of artificial caves.	Anta de Joaninha	Megalith	4460-3980
	Alberite	Megalith	4255-4000
	Alberite	Megalith	4035-3760
	Lapa do Fumo	Natural cave	3980-3650
	Alberite	Megalith	3940-3715
	El Palomar	Megalith	3780-3640
	Vale de Rodrigo	Megalith	3760-3640
	Algar de Bom Santo	Natural cave	3770-3520
	Lapa do Bugio	Natural cave	3700-3530
	Algar de Bom Santo	Natural cave	3650-3520
	Algar de Bom Santo	Natural cave	3630-3370
	Gruta do Escoural	Natural cave	3630-3360
	Gruta dos Ossos	Natural cave	3630-3130
	Algar do Barrão	Natural cave	3620-3360
	Algar de Bom Santo	Natural cave	3520-3340
	Monte do Castelo	Artificial cave	3510-3350
	Gruta do Escoural	Natural cave	3520-3130
	Viera	Megalith	3510-3020
	Gruta do Escoural	Natural cave	3350-3090
	Gruta do Escoural	Natural cave	3340-3020
	Gruta dos Ossos	Natural cave	3340-2930
	Gruta do Escoural	Natural cave	3310-2920

Table 11.3. Radiocarbon dates for Neolithic funerary contexts of SW Iberia. Context types

Between *c.* 3300 and 3100 cal BC, important changes began to take place within the societies of the Iberian South-West. The accumulated demographic growth and the processes of colonisation of new lands (in many cases areas of secondary or marginal agricultural productivity) through mechanisms of tribal fission, led to the emergence of completely new inter-group strategic relationships - and conflict dominated ones. The fortification of settlements in the Centre (Leceia, Zambujal) and South of Portugal (Santa Justa, Monte da Tumba), at the same time as that which takes place in the Southeast of Spain (Los Millares), constitutes quite a solid indicator of the kind of new balance that is being defined between communities and territories. The increasing economic and socio-cultural importance of warfare in this period (Monks 1997; Kunst 2001) is evidenced by several indicators. Among these, cases of massacres or collective killings are not the least expressive (*cf.* for example the hypogeum of Longar in Navarra, and San Juán Ante Portam Latinam, in the Basque Country). On the other hand, it is possible that the development of copper metallurgy was itself an important element of techno-economic and social transformation, stimulating greater interregional integration for the supply and exchange of mineral resources and finished objects, although it yet remains necessary to determine to what extent this technological development feeds back into the dynamics of social organisation.

The changes in the economic and territorial spheres which take place from the late IV millennium cal BC onwards imply patterns of social organisation relying heavily on hierarchical structures in which inequality becomes more visible and prominent in the sphere of funerary ideology. In the following sections I will attempt to analyse these changes, and their evolution in terms of social inequality between the III and II millennium cal BC. In the process, I shall make use of the epistemological premises and the three groups of empirical indicators described above.

11.3.- The late megalithic tradition (*c.* 3300-2100 cal BC)

11.3.a.- Spaces and architectures

From the point of view of the funerary practices, several significant transformations take place from the late IV millennium cal BC onwards. Among the most visible changes in relation with the conceptualisation of funerary spaces and architectures, it is possible to outline (i) an important decrease in the frequency of use of natural caves, (ii) an increase of hypogeum type burials (the so-called *artificial caves*), and (iii) the emergence of *tholos* type tombs.

The tables of radiocarbon dates included in this study show how natural caves, which were a very important element of funerary practices in the Neolithic, experience a sharp decline. Indeed, while 64% (14 out of a total of 22) of the radiocarbon-dated funerary contexts of the Late Neolithic (*c.* 4500-3300 cal BC) are located within natural caves, this frequency drops to 3% (1 out of 30) when dealing with the funerary sites of the Copper Age (*c.* 3300-2100 cal ANE) (Table 11.3). None of the radiocarbon dates provided by Bronze Age funerary sites (Table 11.4) correspond to natural caves.

Despite its permanence within the funerary behaviour of the prehistoric communities of the III and II millennia cal BC in the South-West (as is indicated by a series of data that has not been dated scientifically), it is quite clear that the long (millenary) tradition of the funerary use of natural caves declines from the beginning of the Copper Age. It is significant that this decline appears to coincide with the development and expansion of a new type of funerary container: the artificial cave (*hypogeum* in the Portuguese literature).

The third most significant change taking place in the sphere of funerary ideology at the beginning of the Copper Age is the emergence of *tholos* type monuments, with a circular chamber and corbelled vaulted roof. The earliest cases of this type of construction according to the radiocarbon chronology currently available are tombs number 19 of Los Millares and number 7 of El Barranquete (both located in Almería), within the first centuries of the III millennium BC. Other dates such as those provided by the tomb 3 of La Pijotilla and Huerta Montero (Badajoz) are later and correspond to the mid-III millennium.

The *tholos* represents an innovative conception of the funerary space, associated with a funerary tradition also different in part from that which surrounded the previous development of megalithism. Three aspects of the *tholoi* are of particular interest and deserve further discussion in the context of the analysis presented in this article:
1) First of all, the architecture of these constructions displays a lesser emphasis on the transportation and emplacement of huge monolithic blocks, given that the corbelled vault is generally built out of dry-stone of small sized stones (dry-stone technique is also documented in the construction of some access passages). The use of large uprights and cover slabs is maintained in many *tholoi*, thus coexisting with dry-stone architecture. The difference, however, stems from the degree of protagonism given to this constructive element. Even in the largest *tholoi* such as those of La Pastora or Matarrubilla in the province of Seville and El Romeral in the province of Málaga, whose passages are covered by large slabs, the visibility and protagonism of the huge monolithic blocks is lesser than in the monuments of the early megalithic tradition.

2) A second significant aspect derives from the coexistence on a micro-spatial level of *tholoi* and earlier megalithic chambers. Cases in which *tholoi* appear built alongside pre-existing megalithic monuments, at times even sharing the same mound, are numerous in the Iberian Southwest. In the study of the chamber 2 of Herdade de Cebolinho, V. dos Santos Gonçalves (2003) lists some of the cases identified in the area of Reguengos de Monsaraz (Évora). Recently, another similar case has been identified in Almadén de la Plata (Seville) (García Sanjuán & Wheatley 2006). The dynamic and complex relationship between tradition and innovation in the funerary ideology is observed once again: on one hand, some degree of rupture is established, illustrated by the fact that the dead are put to rest in a new space (a chamber physically independent and formally different from that of the ancestors), while on the other hand, the location of the burial place, which implies a genealogical bond, represents a strong element of continuity. This particular interaction of factors of continuity and discontinuity is in fact a constant in the evolution of the funerary ideology of the communities of the peninsular Southwest – and, I believe, of all of the Iberian prehistory: see for example Ontañón Peredo in this volume. As we shall see below, new and traditional eschatological concepts are overlapped, thus forming a complex puzzle of cultural practices which we archaeologists have tended to oversimplify.

3) A third characteristic aspect of the design of the *tholoi* is their accessibility. In this aspect too, these constructions display an essential dialectic between continuity and discontinuity with respect to the previous megalithic tradition. On one hand, since they share the same general traits as all megalithic architecture, *tholoi* are funerary constructions designed to enable the movement of people within them, thus illustrating the dynamic symbolic and ritual relationship between the living and the material remains of the ancestors (that is also reflected by the use of relics made out of human bone). This point is an important element of differentiation between the funerary architectures of the Copper Age and those of the Bronze Age: the latter do not allow internal movement. On the other hand however, the accessibility of many *tholos* type tombs is nuanced by the architectural design itself. In many cases there is a marked contrast between the height of the passage (which prevents the visitor from walking upright and in some case force him/her into crawling) and the height of the chamber in which a person of average height is able to stand upright (most of the well recorded monuments appear to present a one to one proportion between chamber diameter and roof height). Numerous *tholos* type tombs appear to have been designed in such a way that the chamber enables the agents to stand, whilst the passage deliberately forces them to crouch or even crawl along the floor. This deliberate duality in the design reinforces the symbolism of the passage as a space of transition between two worlds, outside (open) and inside (subterranean), connected by a 'journey' or 'transition' in which the human visitor looses temporarily his/her *human* condition (García Sanjuán & Hurtado 2001: 45).

PERIOD	SITE	CONTEXT	BC (1 σ)
Copper Age (c. 3300-2200/2100 cal BC). Second megalithic tradition. Continued use and construction of orthostatic monuments. Earliest *tholoi* (T) towards 3100-2900 cal BC. Intense development of artificial caves that seem to replace natural caves (which, despite what this table suggests, are still being used for funerary purposes).	Monte Canela	Artificial cave	3340-2930
	Monte Canela	Artificial cave	3310-2920
	Lapa do Fumo	Natural cave	3260-2930
	Los Millares (Sep.19)*	Megalith (*Tholos*)	3330-2880
	Bola da Cera	Megalith	3090-2900
	Covão do Poço	Natural cave	3090-2900
	El Barranquete (Sep.7)*	Megalith (*Tholos*)	3100-2650
	El Barranquete (Sep.7)*	Megalith (*Tholos*)	3090-2660
	Praia das Maças	Artificial cave	2930-2690
	La Pijotilla (Tumba 3)	Megalith (*Tholos*)	2865-2595
	Alcaide	Artificial cave	2900-2350
	La Paloma	Megalith	2890-2700
	La Venta	Megalith	2870-2660
	Amarguillo II	Pit	2860-2490
	La Paloma	Megalith	2860-2490
	Quinta do Anjo (H-3)	Artificial cave	2840-2470
	Quinta do Anjo	Artificial cave	2830-2460
	Alcaide	Artificial cave	2600-1950
	Anta de Joaninha	Megalith	2600-2000
	Vale de Rodrigo	Megalith	2470-2300
	Herdade dos Cebolinhos	Megalith	2470-2310
	Los Gabrieles (Tumba 4)	Megalith	2470-2300
	Alcaide	Artificial cave	2500-1850
	Los Gabrieles (Tumba 4)	Megalith	2410-2200
	Herdade dos Cebolinhos	Megalith	2400-2200
	La Pijotilla (Tumba 1)	Megalith (*Tholos*)	2460-2280
	Huerta Montero	Megalith (*Tholos*)	2300-1970
	Anta da Cabeçuda	Megalith	2200-2030
	Anta da Cabeçuda	Megalith	2200-1830
	Praia das Maças	Artificial cave	2140-1930
Early/Middle Bronze Age (c. 2200/2100-1300 cal BC). Megalithic traditions continue in various ways. Individual burials become widespread. The *de-monumentalization* process of funerary architecture becomes consolidated. Use of artificial caves becomes less prominent. Use of natural caves seems to become marginalised.	Herdade do Pomar	Cist	2030-1630
	Setefilla	Pit, triple	2010-1690
	Cerro de la Corona	Megalith	2010-1630
	Cortijo de El Tardón	Megalith	1940-1740
	La Traviesa	Cist	1940-1760
	Setefilla	Pit, triple	1920-1640
	Anta dos Tasos	Megalith	1900-1300
	Las Minitas	Cist	1880-1640
	La Traviesa	Cist	1880-1670
	Herdade do Pomar	Cist	1690-1520
	Pessegueiro	Cist	1620-1460
	Herdade de Belmeque	Cist	1600-1420
	Anta das Castelhanas	Megalith	1660-1410
	Loma del Puerco	Artificial cave	1290-1000
Late Bronze Age (c. 1300-850 cal BC). The *de-monumentalization* process of funerary architecture peaks. Funerary containers are hardly visible.	La Encantada 1*	Megalith (*Tholos*)	1110-890
	Atalaia	Cist	990-850
	Palacio III	Megalith (*Tholos*) (cremation)	980-660
	El Barranquete (Sep. 11)*	Megalith (*Tholos*) (cremation)	830-520

Table 11.4. Selection of radiocarbon dates for Copper and Bronze Age funerary contexts of SW Iberia. Context types Some dates with excessively large standard deviations have been suppressed. (*) Spanish South-East

In general terms, it could be argued that the emergence of a concept based upon the idea of a passage + circular chamber + corbelled vault, with a lesser emphasis on the movement of large stones, did not have any major significance beyond the use of innovative architectural techniques. However, in the context of ceremonial and funerary functions, spatial design and shape (or size) rarely exclusively depend upon some random whim to apply a technical innovation or experiment *per se*. Normally, it is religious ideology (with the limitations of the available technology), as a conceptual expression of the world and society, which dictates the criteria according to which the formal designs are elaborated - on the basis of the functions to be fulfilled. In this sense, the introduction of *tholos* type monuments must be understood as part of an authentic *second megalithic tradition*. The precise ideological meaning of the emergence of *tholoi* could only be reached through either (1) an exhaustive contextual analysis, in relation with the possible changes in other important variables of funerary ideology (for instance patterns in the selection and deposition of grave goods), or (2) through a diachronic assessment. The first suggestion would require a systematic analysis which has not yet been carried out and that would exceed by far the limits of the present article. However, regarding the second option, it is possible to present some general observations.

The funerary ideology of which *tholoi* and artificial caves are part places less emphasis on collective cooperation and the effort of technical and logistic (inter-clan or inter-group rivalry) problem solving than that implied in the transportation and emplacement of very large stone monoliths that have deeply symbolical connotations in themselves (as various kinds of evidence show). For a construction design of similar scale, the labour force required to build a dry-stone wall out of small stones is not the same as that required to move large blocks weighing several dozens of tons. I will refer here to the incipient tendency towards the reduction of labour investment (and degree of inter-group cooperation) in the construction of funerary containers as the process of *demonumentalisation* of funerary architecture. This process experiences a first impulse with the emergence and expansion of the *tholoi*, is later consolidated by the appearance of individual burials towards the end of the III millennium or early II millennium cal BC, and reaches its acutest expression in the Late Bronze Age, when funerary architecture (and spaces) became almost invisible.

Hypothetically, this observation could lead to the interpretation of the emergence and expansion of *tholos* type megalithic constructions as a reflection of a weakening of one of the main mechanisms of symbolic competition among Neolithic parental and tribal groups: namely the erection of monuments using huge monolithic blocks. It is significant, in this respect, that according to the absolute chronology currently available, the expansion of *tholoi* coincides (or closely follows) the emergence of fortified settlements and inter-territorial tensions. At least

in some regions of southern Iberia, competition no longer operates in the domain of the symbolic, instead turning seriously war-like.

Another expression of the gradual decline of social and ideological communalism is the subtle tendency towards the differentiation of specific areas within the collective funerary container. Thus, for instance, in some megalithic collective tombs (such as the *tholos* 7 of the necropolis of Alcalar, in the Portuguese region of the Algarve), or in some artificial caves, niches or small chambers have been documented which correspond to the deposit of relatively individualised persons. Similarly, in the southeast of Spain, at Fonelas and Majadillas (Granada), megalithic constructions have been identified in which individual bodies are placed in individualised spaces (defined by slabs of stone) and marked with decorated stele (Ferrer 1997; Castellano *et al.* 2001). This type of occasional special treatment of the funerary space suggests the emergence of incipient forms of leadership which require formal and material expression in the funerary ideology.

11.3.b.- Objects and deposits

Artificial caves, *tholoi* and the chambers of the first megalithic tradition all share the basic characteristic of clustering together a number of deceased which can vary greatly between a small number and several dozens, in some exceptional cases up to one or two hundred. In all of the Iberian South-West, the composition of the grave goods of the collective burials shares common characteristics among which the diversity of the artefacts stands out. A problem in dealing with the issue of the meaning of these funerary assemblages in terms of social inequality is that there have been no trustworthy quantitative studies. On the basis of the data collected in a previous synthesis (García Sanjuán 1999a: 190), and including data from two *tholos* tombs excavated over the past decade (García Sanjuán & Hurtado 2002), it is possible to verify (at least in the Southwest of Spain) the existence of some quite consistent patterns in the distribution of the artefacts of the grave good assemblages, according to some basic functional categories (Table 11.5).

On the one hand, objects which could be generically classified as means of production and consumption (pottery and knapped or polished stone tools) dominate by far the funerary assemblages, representing around 90% of all of the objects in the assemblages included in Table 11.5. Objects of personal adornment (necklace beads) and of magic/religious nature (idols and precious or rare stones used as amulets) are characterised by percentages below 10% in all of the monuments under consideration - except La Pijotilla in which the assemblage of idols reaches 21,6% of the total.[2]

---

[2] It is noteworthy that the Copper Age site of La Pijotilla (with an outstanding extension of c. 80 hectares) has yielded one of the largest and most varied collections of idols of the Iberian Peninsula. This frequency can thus not be considered as representative of the normal frequency of this artefact type in Copper Age collective burials of the Iberian South-West.

ASSEMBLAGE	SITE	POTTERY	STONE TOOLS	IDOLS AND AMULETS	PERSONAL ORNAMENTS	METAL OBJECTS
Copper Age collective burials	El Pozuelo y La Zarcita (Huelva)	19,5%	68,8%	02,8%	10,0%	00,2%
	Las Plazuelas I (Huelva)	30,0%	60,0%	00,0%	10,0%	00,0%
	Palacio III (Sevilla)	29,1%	66,1%	02,6%	01,0%	00,5%
	La Pijotilla (T3) (Badajoz)	31,2%	22,3%	21,6%	22,6%	00,3%
Bronze Age individual burials	339 individual tombs	79,5%	08,0%	00,0%	04,5%	08,0%

Table 11.5. Grave goods in Copper Age and Bronze Age burials of SW Spain Source: García Sanjuán, 1999

A particularly interesting aspect of this composition is the very small volume of metal objects in all the monuments included in Table 11.5, which never exceeds 1%. This suggests that the possession and ostentation of metal objects has not yet become integrated into the paraphernalia manipulated by the elite. In this respect, the functional distribution of this small group of copper artefacts must also be considered. According to the data presented in Table 11.6, the metal objects from the Copper Age collective burials of Southwest Spain (artificial caves and megaliths have been included) are dominated (49%) by means of production and tools (awls, saws), followed by the group composed of axes and arrow heads (29%) which can be considered as both tools and prestige warrior items, and finally by daggers (22%). Attributes of personal adornment (bracelets, arm rings, diadems, etc) are completely absent. In the particular case of the large settlement of Valencina de la Concepción, the distribution of the metal objects identified within the funerary containers appears to deviate slightly from this tendency. Indeed, ornaments and daggers together (39%) exceed the volume of tools (22%) and the group formed by axes and arrow heads (39%). This pattern could suggest that the dynamic of association between status and prestige objects was more developed among the elite of the settlement which appears to play the role of a *matrix village* in the context of the lower Gualdalquivir (a similar case to that of the idols of the funerary context of La Pijotilla).

Comparatively, the much larger sample taken from several sites of the Spanish South-East displays an even greater predominance of means of production (60%), alongside fewer prestige objects (weapons and objects of personal adornment). This contrasts sharply with the role played by metal objects, within the funerary ideology of Bronze Age communities, as markers of social rank and prestige.

On the other hand, the recent study of the funerary deposits of the Palacio III *tholos* tomb (García Sanjuán & Wheatley 2006) found the number of ceramic vessels and arrowheads to be identical (55 of each), while the number of knapped blades and various stone tools is of around

60-65 (depending on the particular functional classification of some of the objects). Given that this funerary context was found in an excellent state of preservation, that on several occasions small slate slabs were identified below the pottery vessels (acting as a kind of offering *tray*), and that various blades and arrowheads were found *inside* the vessels, it seems possible to define the existence of a fairly standardised grave good assemblage that accompanied all of the individuals interred within this tomb.[3] In terms of social organisation, the standardisation of the funerary assemblage observed in the Palacio III *tholos* suggests a sharp sense of equality in the symbolic treatment of the dead.

Previously, I mentioned the existence of some architectural traits which appear to reflect, more or less subtly, the presence of individuals with singular attributes of power during the Copper Age. Are these functions of leadership and social hierarchy reflected in the funerary assemblages of grave goods? A particularly interesting artefact type is the so-called *staff*, identified essentially in tombs of the South of Portugal (although, among the monuments described in Table 11.5, one is present in the assemblage of tomb 3 of El Pozuelo). The *staff* is an elongated stone object, with one curved and wider extremity, occasionally decorated. Although a recent review has suggested that they may represent stone copies of throwable wooden weapons which have both archaeological and ethnographic parallels (Bradherm 1995), this type of artefact has often been interpreted as a personal attribute of prestige and power (*staff of power* or sceptre) inspired by the shepherd's staff (Bueno *et al.* 1998: 120). Indeed, this object is depicted on one of the lateral sides of the magnificent stele-menhir of the Dolmen of Navalcán (Toledo), a phallus-shaped stone also engraved with a snake representation (Bueno & Balbín 1994: 340), thus suggesting an object of overwhelming symbolic meaning

---

[3] The number of funerary assemblages can thus be determined as between 55 and 60 although unfortunately it is impossible to test this number against the osteological record in order to establish whether this number indeed corresponds to the number of burials within the tomb, given that the human bones had been completely destroyed by the high acidity of the soil.

	CONTEXT (*)	TOOLS (AWLS, CHISELS, SAWS)	AXES, ARROW HEADS	DAGGERS, SWORDS AND HALBERDS	PERSONAL ORNAMENTS
IBERIAN SOUTH-WEST	Collective burials, general (27)	49%	29%	22%	0%
	Collective burials, Valencina de la Concepción, Sevilla (23)	22%	39%	13%	26%
	Individual burials (26)	0%	5%	55%	39%
	CONTEXT	TOOLS (AWLS, CHISELS, SAWS)	AXES, DAGGERS, ARROW HEADS	SWORDS AND HALBERDS	PERSONAL ORNAMENTS
SPANISH SOUTH-EAST	Chalcolithic (587)	60.5 %	26.4 %	0 %	0.6 %
	Argaric (2888)	15.7 %	27.4 %	1.7 %	53.3 %

Table 11.6 Distribution of metal artefacts according to functional groups in funerary contexts of the Copper and Bronze Age in Southern Spain. Sources: South-East: Montero Ruiz, 1994; South-West: García Sanjuán, 1999a (*) Raw number of objects included in the assessment

that indicated the high hierarchical position of the particular individual (and/or parental unit) with whom it was associated – cf. discussion below.

11.3.c.- Symbolism

The symbolism of the Copper Age societies in the Iberian South-West is quite rich and is reflected upon a range of different materials and functional spaces, including portable artefacts, rock art and funerary chambers. The fact that particular motives sometimes appear in all three of these spheres of expression, in quite distant regions, is evidence of the existence of shared ideological principles among geographically separated groups.

Perhaps the most studied form of symbolic expression has traditionally been the group of representations named *idols*, that include small figurines made from a range of materials (animal bone, stone, fired clay) and display a wide variety of expressions (plaques, cylinders, anthropomorphic forms, etc.). In general, by means of a series of formal concomitances and similarities, this group of representations has been connected to the mother earth goddess cult which constituted a central element in the religious ideology of the European Neolithic (Gimbutas 1974; 1989). This cult is itself bound to the development among the Iberian communities IV-III millennium cal BC of what has been called the *second Neolithic revolution* (or *secondary products revolution*), basically the definitive technological consolidation of the agro-pastoral economy and open-air settlement (Harrison & Moreno 1985).

In many cases, the idols appear as part of the funerary assemblages, thus suggesting the existence of a connection between the divinity (or divinities) which they represent and the act of deposition of the dead in the underground funerary chamber, what may have been conceived of as a return to the mother's womb. In this respect, the

Copper Age communities remain more closely culturally and ideologically to the Neolithic than to the Bronze Age communities, which as we shall see below, hold in the Iberian South-West a markedly *aniconic* religious ideology (Hurtado 1990: 170).

On the other hand, painted and carved graphical representations in funerary and ritual contexts are currently no longer considered as more or less sporadic expressions reduced to particular regions of the Iberian Peninsula. Instead, they have become considered as recurrent cultural expressions, widely spread among the megalith building societies and highly associated with schematic parietal art through its main techniques and symbols – cf. Bueno Ramírez and Balbín Behrmann in the present volume for a good summary of this process.

Megalithic art, through its contextual development and symbolic nature, is inextricably linked to the funerary ideology of the Neolithic and Copper Age communities of the Iberian Peninsula. Moreover, megalithic art must be considered within a broader diachronic perspective, in terms of the evolution of the graphical representations of the prehistoric communities of the Iberian Peninsula, not only in terms of its connection to parietal art (in rock shelters and caves), but also in terms of its relationship to the representations of the Bronze and Iron Ages (essentially stelae). In a similar way as the designs and concepts relative to monumental architecture, the codes of graphic symbolism established by the first agrarian societies gain a huge strength as *tradition* among the later social formations.

In both the first (Neolithic) and second (Chalcolithic) megalithic traditions, the carved or painted representations appear to be dominated by a well defined series of geometric and naturalist themes. While the former are of complex interpretation, among the latter anthropomorphic motives (and their personal attributes, occasionally weapons), quadrupeds (sometimes figured in hunting scenes involving anthropomorphic figures) and snake-like motives, are the most frequent (Bueno & Balbín 1997: 701-702; Vázquez Varela 1997: 16-18). Taken as a whole, the organisation and association of the naturalist motives suggest two main thematic axes: (i) divinities and mythological beings associated with the earth and fertility or with the celestial bodies and (ii) foundational characters or ancestors. Both themes appear to be closely related as complementary aspects of the foundational cosmogony of the megalith building societies.

Perhaps the best example of the first of these two themes can be found not in the peninsular Southwest but in Central Spain, in the already mentioned statue-menhir which dominates the entrance of the chamber of the dolmen Navalcán (Toledo) (Bueno et al. 1998). This sculpture displays an impressive carving of a snake which runs up one of its lateral sides while an object resembling the staffs discussed above is depicted on the other side. Given its location within the monuments architecture and the complexity of its symbolism (phallus, male symbol; snake, earth and ctonic symbol associated with female fertility and death; staff, symbol of ancestral clan authority), this figure becomes the guardian and protector of the ancestral bones and remains deposited within the monument. The second thematic axis appears to place greater emphasis on the anthropomorphic figure. Good examples are provided by the stelae of the dolmens of Alberite and Toconal (Cádiz) in which anthropomorphic elements (eyes, arms, hands) are associated with personal attributes belonging to warriors, particularly stone halberds, again fulfilling an apotropaic role (Bueno & Balbín 1996: 296).

Taken as a whole, the funerary symbolism of Copper Age megalithic architecture (in connection with the Neolithic tradition of which it is part) places great emphasis on the basic elements of the cosmogony of the first European agrarian societies: fertility, earth and foundational ancestors. The small figurines (idols) underline the articulation within funerary ideology between the powerful ancestral cult of the mother goddess of the Neolithic, present in all agrarian societies of Anatolia, the Aegean and Balkans, from at least the VI millennium BC. The stelae bearing anthropomorphic figures integrated in the organisation of the funerary space (either inserted within the body of the architecture or placed outside) constitute authentic *totems* which represent powerful mythical characters or foundational ancestors who protect by their presence the peaceful rest of the ancestors (Barceló 1991; Vázquez Varela 1994: 51-53).

From the perspective of its sociological significance, this symbolism draws on codes and messages that are shared by the community as a whole and fulfil the function of protecting the general well-being of the ancestral community – and, by extension, of the living community.

11.4.- Individualisation and de-*monumentalisation* (*c.* 2100-850 cal BC)

11.4.a.- Spaces and architecture

From around 2200-2100 cal BC, a series of substantial changes begin to emerge in the sphere of the funerary ideologies. The spatial and architectural organisation of the funerary places erected by the communities of the Iberian South-West display new conceptions, the most notable being, (i) a considerable decline in the construction of collective containers (especially of megalithic monuments, although also of artificial caves) and their gradual replacement by individual containers, and (ii) a marked process of *demonumentalisation* of the architecture of the dead. In parallel, as mentioned previously, the long tradition of funerary use of natural caves becomes marginalised.

1) The first of these trends implies (at least apparently) a rather drastic change: the previously predominant ideological rule which led to the clustering of the deceased according to their family or community unit within a collective chamber (whose constructive complexity was obviously the same for all of those buried within it), dissolves in favour of a shift towards individualisation.[4] From the point of view of funerary ideology, the consolidation of the notion of an individual mortuary container can be firstly interpreted as a devaluation of the communalist ideology, and a possible decline of the traditional principle of solidarity in the access to the means of production and the collective product. Secondly, as a greater emphasis on personal success and prestige as mechanisms of identification of the social individual (in opposition to the parental mechanisms typical of the clan), that is both cause and effect of the former.

2) The second most distinguishable change in the funerary practices of the Bronze Age is the drastic reduction of the size of the containers, a process that I have previously described as *demonumentalisation* of the funerary architecture. The funerary ideology of the Bronze Age societies places much less emphasis on the creation of large spaces (chambers) defined by large monolithic blocks, reducing the scale of funerary architecture to the point that, in its later phases (late II millennium, early I millennium cal BC), the identification of funerary architecture as such is very problematic (if not impossible).

A trait of the large megalithic monuments was the collective and cooperative nature of their enterprise. In contrast, from around *c.* 2100 cal BC onwards, the much smaller Bronze Age containers (small and simple cists, or pits,

---

[4] In actual fact, as was discussed above, the shift towards the personalisation of the architecture of the funerary container of particular individuals (of significant religious importance and/or high social status) was already expressed in previous centuries in a range of ways, although always within the context of the collective container.

only rarely accompanied by a funerary mound) require but a humble investment of time and labour. In a small number of communities, the individual containers are monumentalised by a circle of stones: examples of this have been identified mainly in the South of Portugal at sites such as Atalaia, Provença Alfarrobeira or Corte Cabreira, while in the South-West of Spain the single studied case is that of La Traviesa (Sevilla). In these cemeteries, the spatial location and the formal characteristics of some burials suggest the presence of stronger forms of leadership. At Atalaia this can be observed materially in the burials accompanied by a complete individual ring/mound structure which reflects comparatively greater labour investment.

The generalised reduction of the size of the funerary containers has quite unmistakable implications in terms of physical access, given that it implies the end of the concept of a continually used funerary space. While the previous megalithic funerary spaces (both the first and second traditions) were based upon their fluid and permanent use, which implied people moving in and out of the funerary container and their direct and constant contact with the ancestors, the individual containers of the Bronze Age appear to place much greater emphasis on the single use of the tomb. The great majority of the individual containers are prepared, used once (or a limited number of times) and sealed definitively.

This shift towards a greater degree of social hierarchy and towards the decline (but not disappearance as we shall now see) of the cult of the ancestors also appears to have been expressed in a short (although significant) casuistic in which individual funerary containers were made *within* settlement areas, in association with particular dwellings. In the South-West, this practice is recorded in (at least) 7 sites in Western Andalusia (El Trastejón, Llanete de los Moros, El Picacho, El Berrueco, Setefilla and Cerro del Castillo de Alange) (García Sanjuán 1999a: 74). However, given the reduced number of excavated settlement sites belonging to the early phases of the Bronze Age, it is difficult to define the extent and significance of this practice. One must remember that one of the most clearly marked changes that can be observed in the funerary ideology of the people of the Spanish Southeast from around c. 2100 cal BC onwards is the practice of burials below the floor of the dwellings. This widespread practice among Argaric communities lies in sharp contrast with the predominant pattern of collective burials megalithic monuments located outside of the settlements (as at Los Millares) and has been interpreted as evidence of an evolution towards an ideological framework in which the broad family (clan) has lost strength with respect to the nuclear family.

Thus in terms of social inequality, three processes appear to function in parallel in the architectural and spatial expressions of the funerary ideology during the Bronze Age: (i) the loss of importance of the idea of inter-group cooperation in the construction of large orthostatic monuments, (ii) greater architectural visibility of the leaders through the

occasional construction of more expensive and monumental special funerary containers and (iii) the collapse of the concept of the funerary container as the temple of the ancestors.

As mentioned above, perhaps the most incontrovertible aspect of the funerary ideology of the societies of the Late Prehistory of the peninsular South-West is the constant interaction between elements of tradition and change. Several important elements of continuity exist alongside the innovative characteristics already described, the most distinguishable of which are: (i) the reuse (or continued use) of collective burials belonging to the previous Neolithic and Chalcolithic communities, and (ii) the recreation in individual burials built *ex novo* of some characteristic elements of megalithic architecture.

Until very recently, cases of reuse of earlier megalithic monuments had been treated as *anomalies* of limited cultural significance, despite evidence of their frequency[5]. Two recent reviews, one for the South-East (Lorrio & Montero 2004) and one for the South-West (García Sanjuán 2005b) have pointed out that the casuistic is much more widespread and regular than had been hitherto assumed, and that it involves different patterns of interaction with the ancestors and the Past. The conscious act of carrying out a burial upon or inside an earlier megalithic monument can represent an explicit wish to establish genealogical ties with the Past: perhaps particular Bronze Age groups or individuals considered themselves to be linked by consanguinity to the particular lineages or clans buried (supposedly or actually) in particular megalithic chambers (García Sanjuán 2005b).

The Bronze Age communities thus find themselves immersed in a process of change which also possesses an anchor in tradition. Having lost the communalist ideology that motivated the construction of temple-houses for the ancestors, replaced in most cases by small burials of little or nil monumentality which emphasise the power of some warrior leaders, the old ideology of ancestor worship is maintained through the reuse or imitation (on a smaller scale) of the millenary architecture of the large stones.

From around 1300 cal BC onwards, the definition of the funerary ideology of the communities of the Iberian South-West (and by extension the whole of the Atlantic façade) becomes more complicated. As is illustrated in Table 11.4, the number of radiocarbon dates of funerary contexts belonging to the period between c. 1300 and 850 cal BC is limited to two. There seems to be a sense of agreement in the fact that this period is characterised by the generalisa-

---

[5] There are several examples of this. Cases of morphologically *late* materials (belonging basically to the first part of the Bronze Age) identified in the megalithic monuments of the Alentejo were described as "frequent" by H. Schubart (1973a: 188), while in a study of the megalithism of the bassin of the river Sever (Alentejo), "secondary" Bronze Age deposits were described as "innumerable" (Oliveira, 1998: 487).

tion of funerary practices which barely leave any material trace (Barceló 1991; Belén Deamos *et al.* 1991; Parreira 1995). It is possible that forms of cremation which do not leave archaeologically visible remains are responsible for the drop in the *number* of burials recorded for this period. On the other hand evidence persists of the continuity of the patterns consolidated during the Bronze Age, as for example the use of individual containers or the reuse of megalithic monuments.[6]

Something which in any case appears indubitable is that the trend toward *de-monumentalisation* of the funerary architecture, which began in the early III millennium cal BC with the emergence of *tholoi* and continued later (from around c. 2100 on), with the spread of individual containers, reached its full expression during the Late Bronze Age. Indeed, the very concept of funerary architecture appears to suffer a drastic decline in all of the Iberian South-West during this period.

11.4.b.- Objects and deposits

Once again, in comparison with other important regions of the Iberian Peninsula (especially the South-East), the funerary artefactual record of the south-western Bronze Age presents a fairly high degree of internal homogeneity. In terms of the pattern described above with regards to collective burials, the predominant funerary ideology from around 2100 cal BC onwards displays a series of elements of continuity, although it also establishes some significant changes. Among the elements of continuity, the composition of the grave good assemblages according to functional categories is significant (Table 11.5). Pottery vessels and stone tools (knifes, blades, microliths, etc.) prevail, although the latter generally correspond to a much lower percentage than in the collective burial record.

The most sharply marked elements of change are (i) the *complete* disappearance of ideotechnic artefacts, in particular idols and amulets (exotic stones, etc.), (ii) the global growth of metal objects and (iii) the substantial alteration of the functional nature of the metal artefacts, given that tools (means of production) diminish or disappear while personal attributes, weapons and ornamental objects, increase significantly. This evolution itself speaks clearly of the change produced in the funerary ideology: the emphasis on the representation of divinities and ancestors represented by idols (collective, communal ideas) which were previously abundant in collective burials, now shifts towards objects of personal adornment and warrior prestige made of bronze and silver.

However, this increase of the presence of prestige metal goods must be nuanced, given that it does not come even near to what can be observed in the South-East where both

metallurgy (as an economic activity) and the dynamic of status exhibition through the use of prestige objects in tombs are much more developed. As an example of the limited impact of the use of prestige metal objects among the Bronze Age communities of the South-West, it is worth mentioning the data compiled for the Western Sierra Morena (Table 11.5). In this set of 339 individual burials, a total of nine artefacts, five weapons (one halberd and four daggers) and four personal ornaments (three spiral bracelets and one diadem) have been identified; other metal objects such as axes, awls or arrowheads which are common in Argaric necropolis are absent from this sample (García Sanjuán 1999: 199). The differences between the frequencies of the different categories of prestige metal objects in the Argaric area and in the South-West of Spain are huge. To mention but one example, over 250 copper and arsenic alloy or bronze daggers have been recorded in funerary contexts of the Argaric area (Lull 1983: 157) while in the Western Sierra Morena, only three such items have been discovered; in the case of halberds, 32 are recorded in Argaric burials (Lull 1983: 190) compared to just one from western Sierra Morena and barely a dozen from the rest of the Iberian South-West.

The generalisation of individual burials in the Bronze Age, on the other hand, enables the analysis of statistical co-variations in order to establish the existence of possible *funerary classes* (associations of artefacts) on the basis of which to define *social classes* (Brown 1981: 28). In societies which practice forms of collective burial the analysis of co-variations between the categories of artefacts is complicated by the issue of establishing the relationship between each individual and its particular grave goods within funerary deposits which seem to be jumbled up.

In this respect, the analysis of the individual Bronze Age burials of the Iberian South-West enables us to establish that, in terms of social organisation, from around 2100 cal BC, an increase in the degree of internal hierarchisation of the social groups of the Iberian South-West takes place, leading to the definition of a category of leaders who were buried alongside prestige goods of bronze and silver (García Sanjuán 1999: 214-226). However, this process of growing social inequality is bound by some fairly well defined limitations. On one hand, it is limited by the relative frequency and poverty of the funerary deposits that include prestige objects, thus suggesting that the dynamic of status ostentation by the elites is limited by the rules of funerary ideology. In comparison with other social formations peripheral to the State-Empires of the Near East (such as Central European or Danish societies), the dynamics of accumulation of bronze weapons in the tombs of the Iberian South-West can be considered minute. On the other hand, there is no systematic stratification of the distribution of the prestige grave good assemblages within the necropolis according to funerary classes, nor is there evidence of a system of adscription of status by birth as would be demonstrated by child burials accompanied by prestige goods. This, again, lies in contrast to what can be observed in Argaric social groups in

---

[6] This is precisely the situation observed in the area of Viseu in the North of Portugal. In the necropolis of Paranho, six cist burials were identified containing incinerations which have been dated by radiocarbon between c. 1300 and 1000 cal BC (Cruz, 1997: 97).

which the stratified distribution of grave goods suggests a possible example of a pristine class society (Lull & Estévez 1986).

These observations support the trends previously observed in the analysis of funerary space and architecture, thus confirming the partial decomposition of the notions of solidarity and communalism present among the Copper Age societies.

From around 1300 cal BC onwards, the *invisibilisation* of the funerary architecture in all of the Iberian South-West (and indeed in all of Atlantic Iberia), seems to find a counter-balance in the shift towards the deposition of metal objects in particular points of the landscape with special significance. The distribution of artefact categories within these deposits experiences such a radical change as that experienced by the mutation of the funerary spaces and architectures themselves. Lithic tools and pottery vessels disappear completely while metal weapons and personal ornaments reach almost 90% of the total volume of votive artefacts. It is particularly significant that metal tools (saws, awls, etc.) which were frequent in Copper Age funerary assemblages are completely absent from the Late Bronze Age deposits. In many cases, the deposits evolve into authentic *hoards* of objects of great ideological value which according to the functional nature of the objects can be divided into two groups:

- Those composed of objects of adornment such as torques, bracelets, spiral arm rings, ankle bracelets and rings, of which the best known of the South-West are the *hoards* of Mérida, Bodonal de la Sierra, Orellana, Alange, Azuaga, Sagrajas, São Martinho, Montes Claros and Olivar de Melcón. Regarding their ideological and social function, these deposits have been interpreted as true female funerary assemblages (Ruiz Gálvez 1995: 23).

- Those composed of weapons, in particular axes of different description, spears and swords. In the peninsular South-West, deposits of this type come from the Portuguese Alentejo, Montijo, Guareña and Orellana in Badajoz and from the mouths of the Guadalquivir and Guadalete rivers in Spain. Taking into account the analogy of many weapons recovered from deposits of the second group and those represented on the so-called warrior-stelae (see below), the weapon deposits could be remains of equivalent male rituals.

Assuming their funerary nature, such deposits of weapons and valuable objects clearly reflect the ideological glorification of the possession and exhibition of expensive metal artefacts by the social elites as a means of ostentation and a reinforcing mechanism of their status. This in turn suggests that the control and manipulation of the metallurgic processes and networks of exchange of finished objects has become a source of social power. For the first time in the later prehistory of the South-West, metallurgy seems to fulfil a decisive role in support of social inequality.

11.4.c.- Symbolism

From around 2100 cal BC onwards, the graphical representations in funerary contexts in the Iberian South-West undergo a very marked transformation. Not only do the ideas represented change completely, but the articulation of the representation and its architectural context is also substantially altered. Conceptually, the notions of mother earth, fertility, earth forces, regeneration and mythical protective ancestors, disappear. In their place, a single idea appears to take over: warrior prestige. Indeed, from the beginning of the II millennium cal BC, all that is left of the rich repertoire of concepts present in the previous megalithic traditions are the weapons. This spectacular thematic impoverishment is reflected on the one hand by the complete disappearance of figurines of the divinities of the tombs and on the other hand by the appearance of slabs and stelae decorated with carvings of weapons placed on top of or alongside the funerary containers of particular individuals.

The stelae carved with weapons have been one of the main focuses of Bronze Age studies of the peninsular South-West over the past 40 years, various in-depth monographs having been published on this issue (Almagro Basch 1966; Barceló 1991; Galán 1993; Celestino 2001). Paradoxically, however, although these monographs have presented increasingly elaborate hypotheses regarding their functional contexts and evolution over time, the study of the stelae is still faced with some important gaps that make their interpretation in terms of social inequality rather difficult. There are two main collections of stele of this type, referred to in the literature using somewhat confusing terminologies. On the one hand, those known as *type I stelae or Alentejo slabs* (since they are found across the South of Portugal) according to the terminology used by M. Almagro Basch (1966). On the other hand, the so-called *basic warrior stelae* following the terminology of S. Celestino Pérez (2001), which are found across the North of the Spanish region of Extremadura. Those constitute a subgroup (of early development) of the *type II stelae* (or *warrior stelae*, sometimes also called *Tartesian stelae*, typical of the Late Bronze Age and Iron Age). Summarising, individual burials of the first part of the II millennium cal BC are associated with:

- Alentejan slabs or group I stelae (engraved with panoply of weapons and placed as cover stones of individual cists).
- Basic warrior stelae, with panoplies of weapons, associated spatially as markers of funerary places.

Independently of the specific problems of context raised by these materials (and the fundamental problem of their chronological scope), it appears to be the case that at some point (currently undetermined) during the first half of the II millennium cal BC, in some areas of the Iberian South-West, particular individuals began to make use in their funerary containers of decorated slabs and stele showing swords, shields, daggers, halberds or axes (as well as anchor-shaped object). These representations no longer function merely as apotropaic symbols (that is to say, symbols serving the well-being of the ancestors and with the benefit that this may have for the living), but are associated with individuals of particularly important social status, underlining their personal prestige and power. The emphasis of the predominant symbolism within the funerary ideology is no longer focused upon the communal (cosmogony, ancestors), but on the individual panoply of military objects, indicators of the leader function of certain individuals.

Once again however, as was the case of the architectural designs and of the composition of the grave good assemblages, several indicators present in the sphere of symbolic expression suggest the limitations of the power of the individuals displaying such warrior prestige. On one hand, it seems that the symbolic association with particular bronze weapons is more symbolic that real: the objects represented in the tombs do not always appear among the objects deposited in the tomb (Belén *et al.* 1991: 232). This suggests that the ability of the community leaders to associate their functions with particular prestige items is socially and ideologically restricted and that their political power is insufficient in order to monopolise these items as part of their grave good assemblages (Barceló 1991: 242). In this sense, it is possible that the objects were too valuable for the ideological reproduction of the social system for them to be deposited definitively within a tomb and thus be put out of circulation, hence the symbolic rather than real nature of the offering.

This contrast between the frequency of graphical and symbolical presence of weapons and their actual physical presence in funerary deposits is important in terms of the analysis of forms of social inequality. In the Northwest of Spain (Galicia) there is a similar case to that of the Alentejan dressed slabs: since the Bronze Age, one central theme of rock art (whether painted or engraved), centred on the celebration of warrior prestige items (daggers and halberds) which, despite their profuse representation, are in fact an exceptional find in the funerary deposits (Bradley 1998: 247). Paradoxically, in the Argaric area (South-East Spain), where the funerary assemblages containing prestige metal items are, as mentioned above, much more common than in the South-West (and by far more numerous than in the North-West), graphical representations of weapons are extremely rare or do not exist at all, neither as rock art nor as stelae. This pattern seems to suggest that within Argaric society, metal weapons expressed a very *real* coercive power (displayed by a social class which controls a tributary system), whereas in the societies of the South-West and North-West weapons were essentially valued as fetish-like elements of a personal power (part real and part figurative) that was rarely sufficient to justify their deposition within the funerary assemblage of particular individuals.

The changes in the funerary pattern which take place from around 1300 cal BC do not appear to affect much the essence of the symbolism associated with death. The so-called warrior stelae (*Group II* according to the terminology of Almagro Basch), display the same panoplies of weapons listed above, with the only difference that these objects now appear to centre on a male anthropomorphic representation characterised as a hero-like war faring leader. Although our current knowledge of these remains is limited by problems derived from their difficult contextualisation, on the basis of what is known it is possible that they may have been used as funerary stelae and/or territorial markers. In either case, in terms of the evolution of forms of social inequality since the Copper Age, these stelae reflect a clearly marked rupture in the process of increasing social hierarchisation reflected in the funerary record: the glorification of chiefs or leaders who appear to display their power through the complete range of elements provided by a sophisticated military technology (including war chariots). Thus, the Late Bronze Age stelae are far from the megalithic statue-menhirs doted with representations of mythological beings and symbols of patriarchal power which were understood by the Neolithic and Copper Age societies as the protectors of the houses of the dead. The symbols no longer serve common ancestors but are manipulated to the glory of particular warrior leaders.

11.5.- In way of conclusion

The evidence handled throughout this article has shown that between c. 3300 and 850 cal BC, the funerary ideologies of the social groups of the Iberian South-West are subjected to an intense dialectic of change and continuity. This dialectic expresses the transformations taking place in the structures of social relations of production of these societies. In general terms, this evolution implies the gradual decomposition of the primigenial social system, based upon inter-group solidarity and communalism as well as inter-group symbolic competition. This social system is slowly replaced by a new system in which an elite, which draws partly its power from the exercise of warfare, controls for its own benefit essential elements of economic production, for example metallurgy. Table 11.7 attempts to summarise the particular evidence, based on the analysis of funerary ideology, which supports this hypothesis.

The funerary ideology of the social groups of the Copper Age is characterised by: (i) the conceptual (and often spatial) continuity of the collective funerary practices of the first megalithic tradition, despite some significant transformations in particular in the decreasing focus on the prowesses of the transportation and emplacement of constructive elements that require cooperation; (ii) the tendency towards indifferentiation and standardisation of the artefactual and symbolic representation of the social status of the individual, with greater emphasis on the personal attributes related with work and production and lesser emphasis on personal attributes of prestige (especially metal weapons); (iii) a low visibility of leadership,

Indicators	Continuity vs. change	Copper Age c. 3300-2100 cal BC	Early Bronze Age c. 2100-1300 cal BC	Late Bronze Age c. 1300-850 cal BC
Architecture and spaces	Tradition	- Occasional use of natural caves. - Monumentality. - Use of monuments of early megalithic tradition - Re-use of *locii* of early megalithic tradition for location of *tholoi* - Accessibility, movement inside/outside the funerary architecture	- Re-utilisation of chambers of both early and late megalithic traditions - Megalith-like architecture - Re-use of *locii* of megalithic traditions for location of individual tombs	- Re-utilisation of megaliths and megalithic sites - Re-utilisation or continuity of individual burials
	Change	- Late megalithic tradition (*tholoi*) - Artificial caves	- Decline of natural and artificial caves - Individual burials. - Demonumentalization - Inaccesibility: no movement inside/outside funerary architecture - Hierarchization of containers in some cemeteries	- Further demonumentalization (often no funerary architecture at all)
Objects and deposits	Tradition	- Predominance of means of production - Standardization of grave sets - Invisibility or low-visibility of leadership - High presence of idols representing collective beliefs - Symbols of clanship (staffs)	- Presence of means of production	-Break with tradition
	Change	- Low number of metallic items – Metallic items frequently or predominantly characterised as tools.	- No idols. - No symbols of clanship - Higher number of metallic items - Metallic items predominantly weapons and ornaments - Hierarchization of grave sets	- No idols - No means of production - Higher number of metallic items - Metallic items only weapons and ornaments - ¿ Hierarchization of grave sets?
Symbols	Tradition	- Cosmogony and mythology: images of deities and ancestors - Protection for the houses of the ancestors	- Sharp break with tradition	- Personal military prestige - Further glorification of warriors
	Change	- ¿No change?	- Weapons - Personal military prestige	

Table 11.7 Continuity and change in the funerary ideologies of SW Iberian populations (c. 3300-850 cal BC)

occasionally insinuated by architectural or artefactual traits - an example of the latter being the *staffs* which allude to the symbolic power handed down from the ancestors, whether real or mythical; (iv) the strong presence of representations of the primigenial mother earth goddess; (v) a funerary symbolism inspired in representations alluding to cosmogony and the ancestors, that fulfils an essentially apotropaic function.

The funerary containers and spaces of the Copper Age, as places of ancestral cult, bear more similarities to those of the Neolithic than to those of the Bronze Age. The living (possibly through specialists in dealing with the Beyond) move in and out of the chamber-ossuary, manipulating and organising the physical remains of the ancestors according to ritualised schemes. The long periods of use of the chambers, as well as the evidence of constant redeposition (including selection and discard) of the human

bones and grave goods, indicate the presence and importance of the ancestors among the living. It is probably not a coincidence that, within Iberian Prehistory, cases of relics made of human bones and the manipulation of human bones for magic or cult purposes[7] reach their maximum frequency in contexts spanning the Late Neolithic and Copper Age, thus representing the peak of ancestor worship within the funerary ideology.

From around 2100 cal BC onwards, this funerary ideology undergoes important changes, that can be summarised according to the following points: (i) rupture with the collective funerary practices of the first megalithic tradition, by means of the *demonumentalisation* and individualisation of the containers, thus implying the devaluation of the concept

---

[7] This is the case of skull vessels, idols made of human long bone, or trepanated or incised skulls (Campillo Valero, 1980; García Sánchez & Carrasco Rus, 1981; Delibes de Castro & De Paz Fernández, 2000; etc.).

165

valuation of the concept of the funerary container as the temple-house of the ancestors; (ii) continuity, despite (i), of a significant pattern of reuse of earlier megalithic spaces; (iii) an increasing shift towards the visible display of leadership through the hierarchical organisation of the design of individual funerary spaces and containers; (iv) a shift towards a homologous display of leadership in the form of prestige grave goods composed of metal weapons and ornaments (arsenic alloyed copper, bronze, silver); (v) a simultaneous and sudden disappearance of the images of the divinities associated with the primigenial mother earth, as well as that of the staffs that symbolised the ancestors; (vi) the radical replacement of the beneficent apotropaic images by panoplies of weapons that symbolise the individual prestige of the leaders.

The funerary ideology of the Bronze Age breaks with the notion of the funerary container as the temple-house of the ancestors. Although the funerary ideology is no longer dominated by the worship of the ancestors, the ancestors maintain an important religious and social position as is illustrated for instance by the numerous cases of reuse of megalithic monuments. The funerary iconography and grave good assemblages of the Bronze Age suggest the abode of the ideological emphasis previously placed on the ancestors: the cult of warfare.

Finally, the funerary ideology of the social groups of the Late Bronze Age is characterised by: (i) the peak of the *demonumentalisation* of funerary architecture, which becomes almost invisible, thus implying the loss of the idea of the funerary container as the temple-house of the ancestors; (ii) a reduction in the frequency of reuse of earlier megalithic spaces for funerary purposes; (iii) the disappearance of means of production from the grave good assemblages and the total predominance of prestige metal objects (weapons and personal ornaments), thus indicating an important manipulation of the funerary ideology by the elites who possess and exhibit these valuable goods; (iv) the consolidation of the shift towards the glorification of individual warrior prestige in the symbolism associated with funerary practices. The funerary ideology of the late and early phases of the Bronze Age display substantial continuity in the gradual devaluation of ancestor worship and its progressive replacement by a personality cult to military leaders.

11.6.- References

ALMAGRO BASCH, M. 1966: *Las Estelas Decoradas del Suroeste Peninsular*. Bibliotheca Praehistorica Hispana 8. Instituto Español de Prehistoria. C.S.I.C. Madrid.

ALMAGRO GORBEA, M. 1970: "Las fechas del C14 para la prehistoria y la arqueología peninsular". *Trabajos de Prehistoria* 27: 9-42.

ALMAGRO GORBEA, M. J. 1973: *El Poblado y la Necrópolis de El Barranquete*. Acta Arqueológica Hispánica IV. Madrid.

ALONSO, F.; CABRERA VALDÉS, V.; CHAPA BRUNET, T. & FERNÁNDEZ MIRANDA, M. 1978: "Índice de fechas arqueológicas de C-14 en España y Portugal". In M. Almagro & M. Fernández Miranda (eds.): *C14 y Prehistoria de la Península Ibérica*. Serie Universitaria, 77. Fundación Juan March. Madrid: 155-183.

ARIAS CABAL, P. & ÁLVAREZ FERNÁNDEZ, E. 2004: "Iberian foragers and funerary ritual: a review of Paleolithic and Mesolithic evidence on the Iberian Peninsula". In M. González Morales & G.A. Clark (eds.): *The Mesolithic of the Atlantic Façade. Proceedings of the Santander Symposium*. Arizona State University Anthropological Research Paper 55. Arizona State University. Tempe: 225-248.

AUBET SEMMLER, M. E.; SERNA, M. R.; ESCACENA CARRASCO, J. L. & RUIZ DELGADO, M. M. 1983: *La Mesa de Setefilla (Lora del Rio, Sevilla). Campaña de 1979*. Excavaciones Arqueológicas en España 122. Madrid.

BARCELÓ ÁLVAREZ, J. A. 1990: "La Arqueología y el estudio de los ritos funerarios: métodos matemáticos de análisis". *Actas del I Coloquio Internacional sobre Religiones Prehistóricas de la Península Ibérica (Salamanca, 1987). Zephyrus* 43: 181-187.

- 1991: *Arqueología, Lógica y Estadística. Un Análisis de las Estelas de la Edad del Bronce en la Península Ibérica*. Universidad Autónoma de Barcelona. Barcelona.

BARD, K.A. 1994: *From Farmers to Pharaos. Mortuary Evidence for the Rise of Complex Society in Egypt*. Academic Press. Sheffield.

BARTEL, B. 1982: "A historical review of ethnological and archaeological analysis of mortuary practice". *Journal of Anthropological Archaeology* 1: 32-58.

BELEN DEAMOS, M.; ESCACENA CARRASCO, J. L. & BOZZINO, M. I. 1991: "El mundo funerario del Bronce Final en la fachada atlántica de la Península Ibérica. I. Análisis de la documentación". *Trabajos de Prehistoria* 48: 225-256.

BINFORD, L.R. 1972: "Mortuary practices: their study and their potential". In L.R. Binford: *An Archaeological Perspective*. Academic Press. New York.: 210-243.

BLASCO, F. & ORTIZ, M. 1991: "Trabajos arqueológicos en Huerta Montero (Almendralejo, Badajoz)". *Actas de las I Jornadas de Prehistoria y Arqueología en Extremadura (1986-1990). Extremadura Arqueológica* II: 129-138.

BRADLEY, R. 1998: "Invisible warriors. Galician weapon carvings in their Iberian context". In R. Fábregas Valcarce (ed.): *A Idade do Bronze en Galicia. Novas Perspectivas*. Cadernas do Seminario de Sargadelos 77. Edicios do Castro. A Coruña: 243-258.

BRANDHERM, D. 1995: "Os chamados báculos. Para uma interpretacao simbólico-funcional". *Actas do I Congresso de Arqueologia Peninsular. Trabalhos de Antropologia e Etnologia* 35 (1): 89-94.

BROWN, J. A. 1981: "The search for rank in prehistoric burials". In R. Chapman, I. Kinnes & K. Randsborg (eds.): *The Archaeology of Death*. Cambridge University Press. Cambridge: 25-37.

BUENO RAMÍREZ, P. & BALBÍN BEHRMANN, R. 1994: "Estatuas-menhir y estelas antropomorfas en megalitos ibéricos. Una hipótesis de interpretación del espacio funerario". In J.A. las Heras (ed.): *Homenaje al Dr. Joaquín González Echegaray*. Ministerio de Cultura. Madrid: 337-347.

-. 1996: "La decoración del Dólmen de Alberite". In J. Ramos Muñoz & F. Giles Pacheco (eds.): *El Dolmen de Alberite (Villamartín). Aportaciones a las Formas Económicas y Sociales de las Comunidades Neolíticas en el Noroeste de Cádiz*. Universidad de Cádiz. Cádiz.

- 1997: "Ambiente funerario en la sociedad megalítica ibérica: arte megalítico peninsular". In C. Rodríguez Casal (ed.): *O Neolítico Atlántico e as orixes do Megalitismo*. Consello da Cultura Galega. Santiago de Compostela: 693-718.

BUENO RAMÍREZ, P.; BALBÍN BEHRMANN, R.; BARROSO, R.; ALCOLEA, J.J.; VILLA, R. & MORALEDA, A. 1998: *El Dolmen de Navalcán. El Poblamiento Megalítico en el Guadyerbas*. Instituto Provincial de Investigaciones y Estudios Toledanos. Toledo.

CABRERO GARCÍA, R.; RUIZ MORENO, M. T.; BLAS CUADRADO, L. & SABATÉ DIAZ, I. 1997: "El poblado metalúrgico de Amarguillo II en Los Molares (Sevilla) y su entorno inmediato en La Campiña. Últimas analíticas realizadas". *Anuario Arqueológico de Andalucía/1993*. Tomo II. Junta de Andalucía. Sevilla: 131-141.

CALADO MENDES, D. 2000: "Poblados con menhires del extremo SW peninsular. Notas para su cronología y economía. Una aproximación cuantitativa". *Revista Atlántica-Mediterránea de Prehistoria y Arqueología Social* 3: 47-99.

CAMPILLO VALERO, D. 1980: "Incisiones rituales en un cráneo de Montblanc". *Ampurias* 41-42: 367-370.
CARR, C. 1995: "Mortuary practices: their social, philosophical-religious, circumstancial and physical determinants". *Journal of Archaeological Method and Theory* 2: 105-200.

CARVALHO, A. F.; ANTUNES-FERREIRA, N. & VALENTE, M. J. 2003: "A gruta-necrópole neolítica do Algar do Barrão (Monsanto, Alcanena)". *Revista Portuguesa de Arqueología* 6 (1): 101-119.

CASTELLANO GÁMEZ, M.; FRESNEDA PADILLA, E.; LÓPEZ LÓPEZ, M.; PEÑA RODRIGUEZ, M. & BUENDÍA ROMERO, A. F. 2001: "El paisaje megalítico de Gorafe (Granada, España)". *Territorios megalíticos del Mediterráneo. Gorafe (Granada, España). Sa Corona Arrúbia (Cagliari, Cerdeña, Italia)*. Lider Comarca de Guadix. Granada: 4-68.

CASTRO MARTÍNEZ, P.; LULL, V.; MICO, R. & RIHUETE, C. 1995: "La Prehistoria Reciente en el sudeste de la Península Ibérica. Dimensión socio-económica de las prácticas funerarias". In R. Fábregas, F. Pérez & c. Fernández (eds.): *Arqueologia da Morte Na Peninsula Iberica desde as Orixes ata o Medievo*. Ayuntamiento de Xinzo de Limia. Xinzo de Limia: 129-167.

CELESTINO PÉREZ, S. 2001: *Estelas de Guerrero y Estelas Diademadas: La Precolonización y Formación del Mundo Tartésico*. Bellaterra. Barcelona.

CHAPA BRUNET, T. 1991: "La Arqueología de la muerte: planteamientos, problemas y resultados". In D. Vaquerizo Gil (ed.): *Arqueología de la Muerte: Metodología y Perspectivas Actuales*. Diputación Provincial. Córdoba: 13-38.

CHAPMAN, R. & RANDSBORG, K. 1981: "Approaches to the archaeology of death". In R. Chapman, I. Kinnes & K. Randsborg (eds.): *The Archaeology of Death*. Cambridge University Press. Cambridge: 1-10.

CRUZ, D.J. 1997: "A necrópole do Bronze Final do Paranho (Molelos, Tondela, Viseu)". *Estudos Pré-Históricos* 5: 85-109.

DELIBES DE CASTRO, G. & DE PAZ FERNÁNDEZ, F. J. 2000: "Ídolo-espátula sobre radio humano en el ajuar de un sepulcro megalítico de la Meseta". *Spal* 9: 341-349.

DUARTE, C. 1998: "Necrópole neolítica de Algar de Bom Santo: contexto cronológico e espaço funerario". *Revista Portuguesa de Arqueología* 1 (2): 107-118.

FERNÁNDEZ RUIZ, J.; MARQUÉS MERELO, I.; FERRER PALMA, J. E. & BALDOMERO NAVARRO, A. 1997: "Los enterramientos colectivos de El Tardón (Antequera, Málaga)". In R. de Balbín & P. Bueno (eds.): *II Congreso de Arqueología Peninsular. Tomo II. Neolítico, Calcolítico y Bronce (Zamora, 24-27 de Septiembre de 1996)*. Fundación Rei Afonso Henriques. Zamora: 371-380.

FERRER PALMA, J. E. 1997: "Aproximación al estado actual de la investigación sobre el megalitismo en Andalucía". In *Actas del 1° Congresso de Arqueología Peninsular* (Porto, 1993), *Trabalhos de Antropología y Etnología*, XXXV, Fasc. 1. Porto: 71-80.

FERRER PALMA, J. E. & MARQUÉS MERELO, I. 1993: "Informe de las actuaciones realizadas en la necrópolis megalítica de Antequera (Málaga) durante 1991". *Anuario Arqueológico de Andalucía/1991*, III: 358-360.

GALÁN DOMINGO, E. 1993: *Estelas, Paisaje y Territorio en el Bronce Final del Suroeste de la Península Ibérica*. Complutum Extra 3. Universidad Complutense de Madrid. Madrid.

GARCÍA SÁNCHEZ, M. & CARRASCO RUS, J. 1981: "Cráneo-copa eneolítico de la cueva de la Carigüela de Piñar (Granada)". *Zephyrus* 32-33: 121-131.

GARCÍA SANJUÁN, L. 1997: "Segunda intervención de urgencia en el yacimiento de la Edad del Bronce de La Traviesa (Almadén de la Plata, Sevilla)". *Anuario Arqueológico de Andalucía/1993*. Tomo III. Junta de Andalucía. Sevilla: 619-634.

- 1999a: *Los Orígenes de la Estratificación Social. Patrones de Desigualdad en la Edad del Bronce del Suroeste de la Península Ibérica (Sierra Morena Occidental c. 1700-1100 a.n.e./2100-1300 A.N.E.)*. British Archaeological Reports International Series S823. Oxford.

- 1999b: "Expressions of inequality. Settlement patterns, economy and social organisation in southwest Iberia Bronze Age (c. 1700-1100 BC)". *Antiquity* 72 (279): 337-351.

- 2005a: "Grandes piedras viejas, memoria y pasado. Reutilizaciones del Dolmen de Palacio III (Almadén de la Plata, Sevilla) durante la Edad del Hierro". In *Actas del III Simposio Internacional de Arqueología de Mérida. Congreso de Proto-*

167

historia del Mediterráneo Occidental. El Periodo Orientalizante (Mérida 2003). CSIC. Mérida.

- 2005b: "Las piedras de la memoria: la permanencia del megalitismo en el Suroeste de la Península Ibérica durante el II y I milenios ANE". *Trabajos de Prehistoria* 62 (1): 85-109.

GARCÍA SANJUÁN, L. & HURTADO PÉREZ, V. 1997: "Los inicios de la jerarquización social en el suroeste de la Península Ibérica (*c.* 2500-1700 a.n.e.). Aspectos conceptuales y empíricos". *Saguntum* 30. *Homenatge a la Pra. Dra. Milagros Gil-Mascarell Boscá*. Volum II. *La Península Ibérica entre el Calcolítico y la Edad del Bronce*. Universitat de Valencia & Generalitat Valenciana. Valencia: 135-152.

- 2002: "La arquitectura de las construcciones funerarias de tipo *tholos* en el Suroeste de España". In D. Serrelli & D. Vacca (eds.): *Aspetti del Megalitismo Prehistórico. Incontro di Studio Sardegna-Spagna (Museo del Territorio, Lunamatrona, Cagliari, Italia, 21-23 de Septiembre de 2001)*. Grafica del Parteolla. Cagliari: 36-47.

GARCÍA SANJUÁN, L. & WHEATLEY, D. W. 2006 - in press: "Recent investigations of the megalithic landscapes of Sevilla province, Spain, Andalucía: Dolmen de Palacio III". *Proceedings of the Colloquium Origin and Development of the Megalithic Phenomenon in Western Europe (Bougon, France, October 26th-30th 2002)*.

GILES, F.; MATA ALMONTE, E.; BENÍTEZ MOTA, R.; GONZÁLEZ TORAYA, B. & MOLINA, I. 1994: "Fechas de radiocarbono 14 para la Prehistoria y Protohistoria de la Provincia de Cádiz". *Boletín del Museo de Cádiz* 6: 43-52.

GIMBUTAS, M. 1974: *The Gods and Goddesses of Old Europe, 7000-3500 BC. Myths, Legends and Cult Images*. Thames and Hudson. London.

- 1989: *The Language of the Goddess. Unearthing the Hidden Symbols of Western Civilization*. Thames and Hudson. London.

GONZÁLEZ-TABLAS SASTRE, F. J. 1990: "La cueva de Nerja como santuario funerario". *Zephyrus* 43. *Actas del I Coloquio Internacional de Religiones Prehistóricas de la Península Ibérica* (Salamanca 1987). Universidad de Salamanca. Salamanca: 61-64.

HARRISON, R. J. & MORENO, G. (1985): "El policultivo ganadero o la revolución de los productos secundarios". *Trabajos de Prehistoria* 42: 51-82.

HUMPHREYS, S.C. & KING, H. (eds.) 1981: *Mortality and Inmortality. The Anthropology and Archaeology of Death*. Academic Press. London-New York.

HURTADO PÉREZ, V. 1981: "Las figuras humanas del yacimiento de La Pijotilla (Badajoz)". *Madrider Mitteilungen* 22: 78-88.

- 1990: "Manifestaciones rituales y religiosas en la Edad del Bronce". *Zephyrus* 43: 165-174.

HURTADO PÉREZ, V.; MONDEJAR FERNÁNDEZ DE QUINCOCES, P. & PECERO ESPÍN, J. C. 2002: "Excavaciones en la Tumba 3 de La Pijotilla". In J.J. Jiménez Ávila & J.J. Enríquez Navascués (eds.): *El Megalitismo en Extremadura.*

Homenaje a Elías Diéguez Luengo. Extremadura Arqueológica VIII: 249-266.

JACKES, M. & ALVIM, P. in press: "Reconstructing Moita do Sebastião, the first step". Actas IV Congreso de Arqueología Peninsular, Faro (2004)

KUNST, M. 2001: "A guerra no Calcolítico na Península Ibérica". *Era Arqueologia* 2: 128-142.

LARSSON, L. 1997: "Die untersuchung des megalithgrabes Vale de Rodrigo 2, Concelho Evora, Portugal. Vorbericht über die ausgrabungen 1991-1995". *Madrider Mitteilungen* 38: 36-48.

LEISNER, V. & VEIGA FERREIRA, O. da 1963: "Primeiras datas de radiocarbono 14 para a cultura megalitica portuguesa". *Revista de Guimaraes* 73: 358-366.

LEVY, J. 1982: *Social and Religious Organization in Bronze Age Denmark: an Analysis of Ritual Hoard Finds*. British Archaeological Reports International Series 142. Oxford.

LINARES CATELA, J. A. 2006: "Documentación, consolidación y puesta en valor del conjunto dolménico de Los Gabrieles (Valverde del Camino, Huelva). 2ª Fase." *Anuario Arqueológico de Andalucía/2003*. Sevilla. Junta de Andalucía: 250-264.

LORRIO ALVARADO, A. J. & MONTERO RUIZ, I. 2004: "Reutilización de sepulcros colectivos en el Sureste de la Península Ibérica: la colección Siret". *Trabajos de Prehistoria* 61 (1): 99-116.

LULL, V. 1983: *La "Cultura" de El Argar. Un Modelo para el Estudio de las Formaciones Económico-Sociales Prehistóricas*. Akal. Madrid.

- 2000: "Death and society: a Marxist approach". *Antiquity* 74: 576-80.

LULL, V. & STEVEZ, J. 1986: "Propuesta metodológica para el estudio de las necrópolis argáricas". In *Homenaje a Luis Siret (1934-1984)*. Consejería de Cultura de la Junta de Andalucía. Dirección General de Bellas Artes. Sevilla: 441-452.
LULL, V. & PICAZO, M. 1989: "Arqueología de la muerte y estructura social". *Archivo Español de Arqueología* 62: 5-20.

MARQUÉS MERELO, I.; AGUADO MANCHA, T.; BALDOMERO NAVARRO, A. & FERRER PALMA, J. E. 2004: "Proyectos sobre la Edad del Cobre en Antequera (Málaga)." In *III Simposio de Prehistoria Cueva de Nerja: Las Primeras Sociedades Metalúrgicas en Andalucía. Homenaje al Profesor Antonio Arribas Palau*. Fundación Cueva de Nérja. Nérja: 238-260.

McHUGH, F. 1999: *Theoretical and Quantitative Approaches to the Study of Mortuary Practice*. British Archaeological Reports International Series 785. Oxford.

MONGE SOARES, A. 1994: "O Bronze do Sudoeste na margem esquerda do Guadiana. As necropoles do Concelho de Serpa". *Actas das V Jornadas Arqueológicas (Lisboa, 1993)*. Asociaçao dos Arqueólogos Portugueses. Lisboa: 179-184.

MONKS, S. 1997: "Conflict and competition in Spanish Prehistory: the role of warfare in societal development from the Late Fourth to Third Millenium BC". *Journal of Mediterranean Archaeology* 10 (1): 3-32.

NOCETE CALVO, F.; LIZCANO PRESTEL, R.; NIETO LIÑÁN, J. M.; ÁLEX TUR, E.; INACIO FRANCO, N. M.; BAYONA, M.; DELGADO HUERTAS, A.; ORIHUELA PARRALES, A. & LINARES CATELA, J. A 2005: "El desarrollo del proceso interno: el territorio megalítico del Andévalo Oriental." In F. Nocete Calvo (Ed.): *Odiel. Proyecto de Investigación Arquelógica para el Análisis del Origen de la Desigualdad Social en el Suroeste de la Península Ibérica*. Sevilla. Junta de Andalucía: 129-232

OLIVEIRA, J. M. 1996: "O megalitismo de xisto na bacia do Sever (Montalvao-Cedillo)". In V. dos Santos Gonçalves (ed.): *Muitas Antas, Pouca Gente? Actas do I Colóquio Internacional sobre Megalitismo (Reguengos de Monsaraz, Outubro de 1996)*. Trabalhos de Arqueologia 16. Lisboa: 135-158.

- 1997: "Datas absolutas de monumentos megalíticos da bacia hidrográfica do río Sever". *Actas del II Congreso de Arqueología Peninsular. Tomo II. Neolítico, Calcolítico y Bronce*. Zamora: 229-240.

- 1998: *Monumentos Megalíticos da Bacia Hidrográfica do Río Sever*. Colibrí. Lisboa.

PADER, E. J. 1982: *Symbolism, Social Relations and the Interpretation of Mortuary Remains*. British Archaeological Reports International Series 130. Oxford.

PARKER PEARSON, M. 1999: *The Archaeology of Death and Burial*. Sutton. London.

PARREIRA, R. 1995: "Aspectos da Idade do Bronze no Alentejo Interior". In AAVV: *A Idade do Bronze em Portugal. Discursos de Poder*. Secretaria de Estado da Cultura. Lisboa: 131-134.

PAVÓN SOLDEVILLA, I. 2003: "Muerte en Los Barros. Aproximación a la dinámica demográfica, ritual y social de una necrópolis de cistas de la Baja Extremadura." *Estudos Pré-Históricos* 10-11: 119-144.

RAMOS MUÑOZ, J. & GILES PACHECO, F. (eds.) 1996: *El Dolmen de Alberite (Villamartín). Aportaciones a las Formas Económicas y Sociales de las Comunidades Neolíticas en el Noroeste de Cádiz*. Universidad de Cádiz. Cádiz.

RECIO RUIZ, A.; MARTÍN CÓRDOBA, E.; RAMOS MUÑOZ, J.; DOMÍNGUEZ-BELLA, S.; MORATA CÉSPEDES, D. & MACÍAS LÓPEZ, M. 1998: *El Dolmen del Cerro de la Corona de Totalán. Contribución al Estudio de la Formación Económico-Social Tribal en la Axarquía de Málaga*. Diputación Provincial de Málaga. Málaga.

RUBIO DE MIGUEL, I. 1981: "Enterramientos neolíticos de la Península Ibérica". *Cuadernos de Prehistoria y Arqueología de la Universidad Autónoma de Madrid* 7-8: 39-73.

RUIZ GALVEZ, M. 1995: "Depósitos del Bronce Final ¿Sagrado o profano? ¿Sagrado y, a la vez profano?". In M. Ruiz Galvez (ed.): *Ritos de Paso y Puntos de Paso. La Ría de Huelva en el Mundo del Bronce Final Europeo*. Complutum Extra 5: 21-32.

RUIZ ZAPATERO, G. & CHAPA BRUNET, T. 1990: "La Arqueología de la Muerte. Perspectivas teórico-metodológicas". *Actas del III Simposio sobre los Celtíberos* (Daroca 1991). Zaragoza: 357-373.

SANTOS GONÇALVES, V. 2003: "A Anta 2 da Herdade dos Cebolinhos (Reguengos de Monsaraz, Évora): sinopse das intervençoes de 1996-97 e duas dataçoes de radiocarbono para a última utilizaçâo da câmara ortostática". *Revista Portuguesa de Arqueologia* 6 (2): 143-166

SHERRATT, A. 1990: "The genesis of megaliths: monumentality, ethnicity and social complexity in Neolithic North-West Europe". *World Archaeology* 22 (2): 147-167.

- 1995: "Instruments of conversion: the role of megaliths in the Mesolithic-Neolithic transition in North-West Europe". *Oxford Journal of Archaeology* 14 (3): 245-260.

SCHUBART, H. 1973: "Tumbas megalíticas con enterramientos secundarios de la Edad del Bronce de Colada de Monte Nuevo de Olivenza". *Actas del XII Congreso Nacional de Arqueología* (Jaén, 1971). Zaragoza: 175-191.

- 1975: *Die Kultur der Bronzezeit in Sudwesten der Iberischen Halbinsel*. Berlin.

SOARES, A. M. 1994: "Dataçao absoluta da necrópole 'neolítica' da Gruta do Escoural." In A.C. Araujo & M. Lejeune (eds.): *Gruta da Escoural. A Necrópole Neolítica e a Arte Rupestre Paleolítica*. Trabalhos de Arqueologia 8: 111-119.

SOARES, J. 2003: *Os Hipogeus Pré-históricos da Quinta do Anjo (Palmela) e as Economías do Simbólico*. Museo de Arqueología e Etnografia do Distrito de Setúbal. Setúbal.

SOARES, J. & TAVARES, C. 1995: "O Alentejo Litoral no contexto da Idade do Bronze do Sudoeste Peninsular". In VVAA: *A Idade do Bronze em Portugal. Discursos de Poder*. Secretaria de Estado da Cultura. Lisboa: 136-139.

TARLOW, S. 1999: *Bereavement and Commemoration. An Archaeology of Mortality*. Blackwell. Oxford.

VICENT GARCÍA, J. M. 1995: "Introducción. Problemas fundamentales de la Arqueología de la Muerte". In R. Fábregas, F. Pérez & C. Fernández (eds.): *Arqueologia da Morte Na Peninsula Iberica desde as Orixes ata o Medievo*. Ayuntamiento de Xinzo de Limia. Xinzo de Limia: 15-31.

VÁZQUEZ VARELA, J. M. 1994: "Función y significado de la escultura megalítica en Galicia". *Brigantium* 8: 49-56.

- 1997: "Ideología en el arte megalítico de la Península Ibérica". *Brigantium* 10: 15-22.

WASON, P. K. 1994: *The Archaeology of Rank*. Cambridge University Press. Cambridge.

CHAPTER 12

Neolithic and Copper Age ditched enclosures and social inequality in the south of the Iberian peninsula (IV-III millennia cal BC)

José E. Márquez Romero
Universidad de Málaga

Abstract

In this paper I argue that, in the South of the Iberian Peninsula, ditched enclosures are but another feature of the Monumental Landscape between the IVth and IIIrd millennia BC. First, I make a general description of the archaeological record available for these sites: general morphological characterisation, deposits, chronological span of the sites and interpretative approaches. Second, I discuss the central role of ditched enclosures in the origin and develeopment of social inequality in southern Iberia's Late Prehistory.

Keywords: Southern Iberia; Neolithic; Copper Age; Ditched Enclosures; Structured Deposits; Potlatch; Social Inequality; Monumental Landscape.

Resumen

Este artículo muestra como, en el sur de la Península Ibérica, los recintos de fosos son una característica más del Paisaje Monumental del IV al III milenio cal. a.C. En primer lugar, se presenta la problemática de estos yacimientos meridionales: características morfológicas generales, naturaleza del registro arqueológico, vigencia cronológica de los yacimientos y propuestas interpretativas más interesantes. En segundo lugar, se discute el papel central atribuido a estos yacimientos en el origen y desarrollo de la desigualdad social en la Prehistoria Reciente del sur peninsular.

Palabras Clave: Sur de Iberia; Neolítico; Edad del Cobre; Recintos de Foso; Depósitos Estructurados; Potlatch; Desigualdad Social; Paisaje Monumental.

> *... the moment he saw the inn he pictured it to himself as a castle with its four turrets and pinnacles of shining silver, not forgetting the drawbridge and moat...*
> Don Quixote
> Miguel de Cervantes

12.1.- Introduction: gaps in the maps

In the various thematic and synthetic studies carried out on the theme of Neolithic enclosures (Burgess *et al.* 1988; Andersen 1997; Darvill & Thomas 2001; Varndell & Topping 2002), references to the Iberian Peninsula are almost absent and even seem anecdotic. Moreover, the only Iberian sites recognised as *enclosures* in European catalogs (Fig. 12.1) are the Los Millares and Vila Nova de Sao Pedro fortified settlements located in southeast Spain and the estuary of the Tagus respectively (Whittle 1988: 2; Andersen 1997: 143; Darvill & Thomas 2001: 2), when in reality both meet few of the classical characteristics of this type of site (causewayed ditch system, structured deposits, palisades, etc). Paradoxically, a series of sites have been identified in the south of the Iberian Peninsula displaying V-shaped ditches and an area exceeding at times 90 hectares. These sites have been interpreted since the outset as fortified settlements, leading them to be marginalised in the discussion of the nature and func-tion of Neolithic ditched enclosures that has taken place in much of central and Western Europe over the past 40 years. What is more, these sites have been used as the central argument to defend: a) the early emergence of fully sedentary settlements from the IV millennium cal BC, and b) the hierarchical structure of the territory and the emergence of the first centres of power during the III millennium cal BC This unfortunate conjuncture has exacerbated the lack of north-south communication be-tween European researchers of different latitudes and continues to provide a fragmentary and incomplete per-ception of an archaeological issue that defies the spatial limits initially estimated.

As an alternative, this article deals with the question of Neolithic-Copper Age ditched enclosures in the south of the Iberian Peninsula from a non-local perspective. In this study, we consider the current state of the question in Western Europe and discuss the ways in which the inter-pretation of the archaeological record has been used to

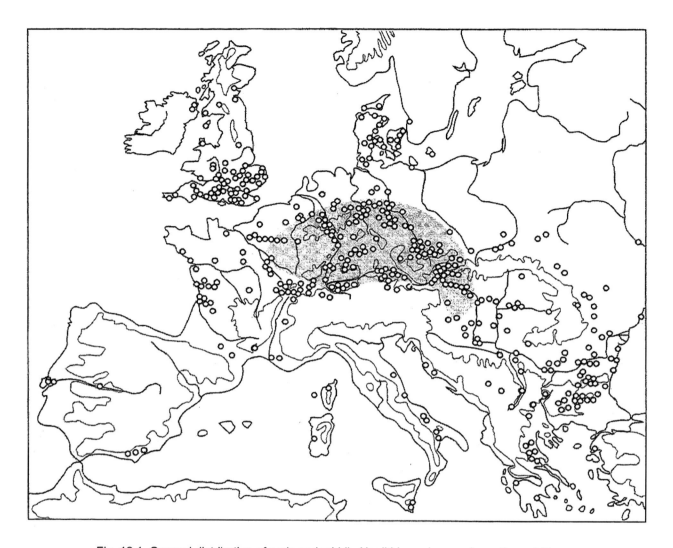

Fig. 12.1. General distribution of early and middle Neolithic enclosures in north-west Europe after Andersen 1999 with addition of Darvill and Thomas 2001.

support the hypothesis of the early emergence of social inequality in Iberian prehistory.

12.2.- Describing sites

Over the past 25 years, numerous sites have been identified that display ditch systems: Valencina de la Concepción (Sevilla) (Ruiz Mata 1983; Fernández & Oliva 1985); Papa Uvas (Huelva) (Martín de la Cruz 1985; 1986); Peñón Gordo (Benaocaz, Cádiz) (Perdigones & Guerrero 1987: 29); Los Pozos (Higuera de Arjona, Jaén) (Hornos *et al.* 1987); Ciavieja (El Ejido, Almería) (Suarez *et al.* 1987); La Minilla, (La Rambla, Córdoba) (Ruiz Lara 1990); La Pijotilla (Badajoz) (Hurtado 1991); Les Jovades (Concentaina, Alicante) and Arenal de la Costa (Onteniente, Valencia) (Bernabeu 1993); Polideportivo (Martos, Jaén) (Lizcano *et al.* 1991-92; Lizcano 1997); Povado dos Perdigoes (Reguengos de Monsaraz) (Lago 1998); Marroquíes Bajos (Jaén) (Zafra *et al.* 1999); Cabeço do Torrao (Elvas) (Lago and Albergaria 2001);

Carmona –Sevilla- (Gómez 2003); and Porto Torrao (Ferreira do Alentejo) (Valera & Filipe 2004). In other cases, the evidence is limited to a series of scoops, pits and unenclosed shafts (e.g. see the *Anuarios Arqueológicos de Andalucía* Series 1986-2001), some of which were identified towards the end of the 19th century (e.g. Bonsor 1899) (Fig. 12.2).

In Southern Iberia (for other regions see Díaz-del-Río 2003) the information regarding Neolithic and Copper Age ditched enclosures remains fairly patchy and their identification has often not been corroborated by aerial photography or geophysical surveys. As far as is currently known, their location tends to have a low strategic value in the surrounding landscape and their morphology is similar to those of other European regions: large circular or sub-circular spaces defined by a single circuit or sometimes double lines of V-shaped ditches. The only accurately calculated surface areas available are those of La Pijotilla with 70-90 hectares (Hurtado 2004: 247) and Povoado do Perdigoes which does not exceed 16 hectares

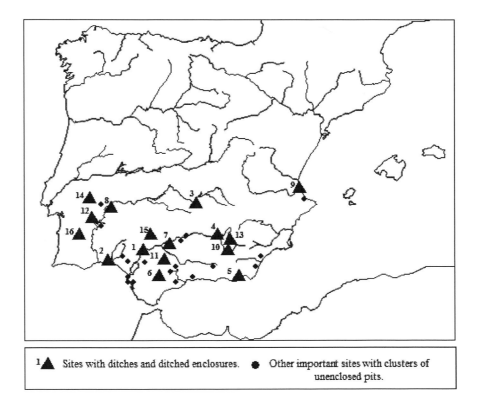

Fig.12.2. General distribution of Neolithic and Early/Middle Copper Age ditched Enclosures in Southern Iberian Peninsula:
1 Valencina; 2 Papauvas; 3 Vega de los Morales; 4 Los Pozos; 5 Ciavieja; 6 Peñón Gordo; 7 La Minilla; 8 La Pijotilla; 9 Arenal de la Costa; 10 Polideportivo Martos; 11 El Negrón; 12 Povoado dos Perdigoes; 13 Marroquíes; 14 Cabeço do Torrao; 15 Carmona y, 16 Porto Torrao .

Fig.12.3. Povoado do Perdigoes, aerial view. Lago *et al.* 1998 (Manuel Ribeiro. Photograph August 1997).

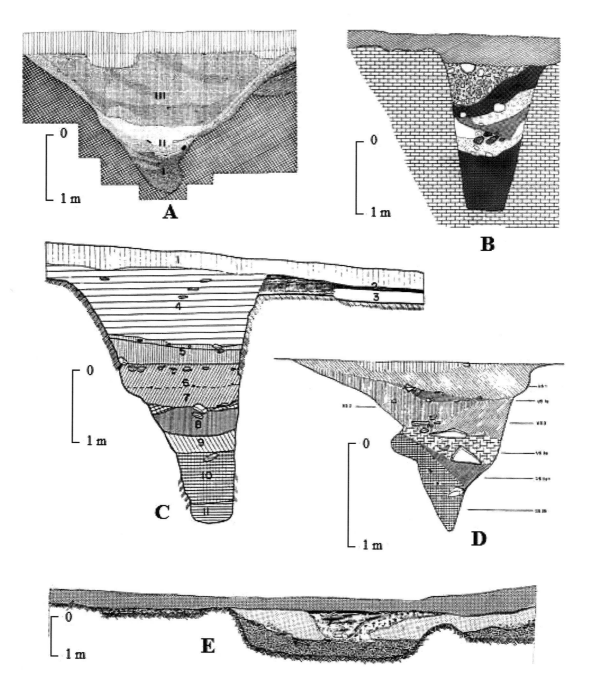

Fig.12.4. V/U-shaped ditches from Iberian sites: A. Papa Uvas (Martín de la Cruz 1985) ; B. La Minilla (Ruiz Lara 1990); C. Los Pozos (Hornos *et al.* 1987); D. Polideportivo Martos (Lizcano 1999) y E. La Pijotilla (Hurtado 1991).

(Valera 2003: 136) (Fig. 12.3). The remaining sites offer only rough size-estimates, some of which point towards areas between 100 and 300 hectares (Ruiz 1983; 184; Vargas 2003: 141; Valera & Filipe 2004: 30). The ditches display very variable width and depth (Fig. 12.4); for example, the ditch of Valencina de la Concepción reaches a depth of 7 metres (Ruiz 1983: fig. 5) while that of Peñon Gordo barely exceeds 0.8 metre (Perdigones & Guerrero 1987: 32). The width of the ditches ranges between 2 and 4 metres. In some cases, the ditches display a discontinued layout (Ruiz Lara 1990: fig. 6; Berbabeu 1993 fig. 3.15; Lago *et al.* 1998: 71) although it is difficult for the moment to talk about true causewayed enclosures. Evidence of associated palisade enclosures has not yet been observed. Within the area defined by the ditch systems, there are no standing or walled structures that can be directly associated with the ditches, but hundreds of scoops, pits, "refuse pits", "dwellings-pits", "silos" containing many cubic metres of fill (Fig. 12.5). The ditches and these features are in many cases filled intentionally, either in one event or as sequence of deposits. Finds typically include potsherds, prismatic blades and

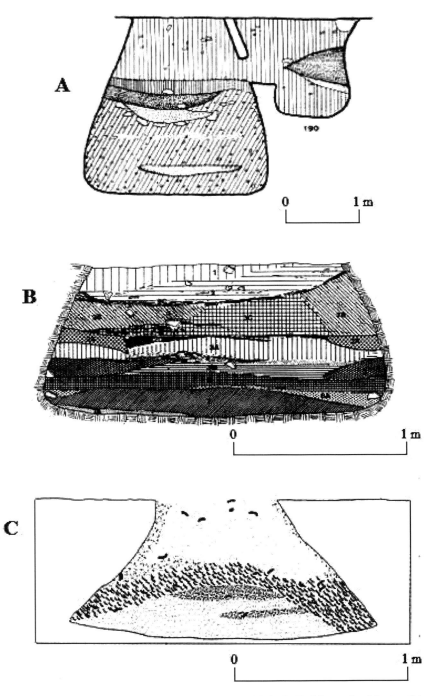

Fig.12.5. Pits from Iberian sites: A. Les Jovades (Bernabeu 1993); B. Polideportivo Martos (Lizcano 1999); C. Papa Uvas (Martín de la Cruz y Lucena 1985)

other flint tools, flint knapping waste and broken quern stones. Large open vessel forms (dishes, plates) (Fig. 12.6) are abundant while decorated sherds are very scarce. Alongside the artefacts, remains of large mammals such as sheep, goat, pig and dog are particularly numerous. Shell remains are important at some sites such as Papa Uvas (Martín de la Cruz 1985). Finally, it is worth noting the presence of human remains, both complete and incomplete, that appear articulated or disarticulated in the base of many structures (e.g. Fernández & Oliva 1985: 20; Zafra *et al.* 2003: 83).

The chronology of the ditched enclosures of the south of the Iberian peninsula appears to span from the IV millennium up until the last third of the III millennium, thus encompassing the Late Neolithic and Early/Middle Copper Age (Table 12.1), although some cases are known in the Spanish Southeast that date to the Cardial period (Bernabeu *et al.* 2003). In any case, the emergence of the Bell-beaker phenomenon, in the second half of the III millennium, appears to bring an end to these ditched systems (e.g. Ruiz Mata 1983:192, fig. 5; Valera & Filipe 2004: 37 and fig 3).

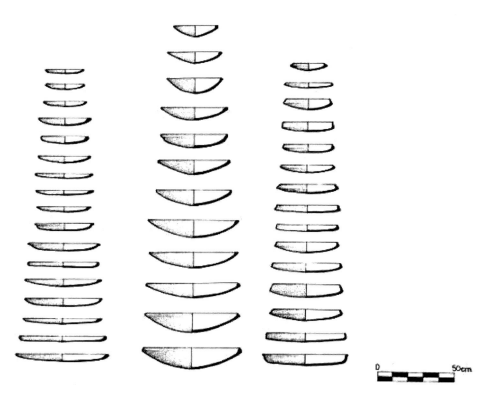

Fig.12.6. Characteristic types of pottery from the ditched enclosures in Southern Iberian Peninsula.
Valencina de la Concepción. (Fernández y Oliva 1985).

Site	Context	BP	Cal BC 1 σ	Cal BC 2 σ	Lab. Nº	References
ARENAL DE LA COSTA	"Dwelling-pit" A II	3890 ± 80	2473 - 2212	2573 – 2140	BETA-43237	Bernabeu 1993
CIAVIEJA	Pit nº 4	4170 ± 100	2886 - 2628	3008 – 2473	I-15011	Carrilero y Suárez 1989-90
EL NEGRÓN	Ditch	4330 ± 35	3010 - 2898	3078 – 2890	~	Cruz-Auñón et al. 1992
EL NEGRÓN	~	4300 ± 35	2996 - 2885	3012 – 2880	~	Nocete 2001
EL NEGRÓN	Ditch	4250 ± 35	2910 - 2781	2919 – 2702	~	Cruz-Auñón et al. 1992
LES JOVADES	Pit nº 129	4810 ± 60	3654 - 3523	3705 – 3379	BETA-43236	Bernabeu 1993
LES JOVADES	Pit nº 129	4660 ± 90	3629 - 3353	3640 – 3105	BETA-43235	Bernabeu 1993
LES JOVADES	Pit nº 165	4370 ± 60	3087 - 2908	3326 – 2888	BETA-57293	Bernabeu 1993
LOS VILLARES	Pit nº 2	4510 ± 50	3344 - 3106	3363 – 3029	GrN-27023	Márquez y Fernández 2002
MARROQUIES	Ditch VI	3775 ± 45	2286 - 2138	2344 – 2036	Ua 21455	Zafra et al. 2003
MARROQUIES	Ditch V	3707 ± 28	2136 - 2033	2183 - 1979	CSIC-1345	Zafra et al. 2003
MARROQUÍES	Ditch VI	3885 ± 40	2459 - 2309	2472 - 2210	Ua 20267	Zafra et al. 2003
PAPA UVAS	~	4840 ± 120	3765 - 3384	3942 - 3365	CSIC-485	Martín de la Cruz 1985
PAPA UVAS	~	4480 ± 70	3338 - 3034	3362 - 2930	CSIC-812	Martín et al. 2000
PAPA UVAS	~	4470 ± 70	3335 - 3028	3353 - 2929	CSIC-811	Martín et al. 2000
PAPA UVAS	"Dwelling-pit" nº 10	4110 ± 50	*	*	CSIC-654	Martín de la Cruz 1986
PAPA UVAS	~	4330 ± 50	*	*	CSIC-814	Martín et al. 2000
POLIDEPORTIVO MARTOS	"Dwelling-pit" XIIa	5080 ± 140	4036 - 3706	4239 - 3542	I-17083	Lizcano et al 1997
VALENCINA Cerro de la Cabeza	Pit nº 31	4050 ± 105	2858 - 2470	2886 - 2301	I-10187	Fernández y Oliva 1986
VALENCINA Cerro de la Cabeza	Pit nº 1	3910 ± 110	2566 - 2208	2849 - 2038	GIF-4028	Fernández y Oliva 1986
VIÑAS - CANTARRANAS	Pit nº 16	4950 ± 60	*	*	UGRA-370	Giles et al. 1993-1994
VIÑAS - CANTARRANAS	Pit nº 50	4800 90	*	*	UGRA-369	Giles et al. 1993-1994

Table 12.1. Calibrated radiocarbon dates from sites with ditches, "dwelling-pits" and pits of Southern Iberia.
(All calibration with CALIB REV 5.0.1.) * Shells / not calibrated

12.3.- The genealogy of the southern Iberian ditched enclosures

Numerous unenclosed pit-sites (so-called "silos") have been identified since the end of the 19th century (e.g. Bonsor 1899). During the 1970's, these sites were attributed to the *"Cultura de los Silos del Guadalquivir"* (Collantes de Terán 1969: 6; Bübner 1981: 141). In general terms, this cultural group was characterised as an agricultural community, not one of megalithic builders, living in settlements formed of huts and using bell-shaped storage pits in which they also carried out burials (Carrilero *et al.* 1982). This cultural hypothesis was still favoured until well into the 1980's when the existence of ditches surrounding these pit-sites was identified, thus opening path for a new hypothesis: that of large scale fortified settlements. From then on, the idea grew that the ditches were part of the constructive elements of large settlements, serving a defensive and/or drainage purpose, which having lost their initial function were backfilled with domestic refuse (e.g. Ruiz Lara 1990: 157; Alcazar *et al.* 1992: 22; Gómez 2003: 1253). The distribution of numerous features (scoops, pits, large pits and shafts) interpreted as semi-troglodyte dwellings within the area defined by the ditches has thus led to the reconsideration of the cultural definition of these communities on the basis of the artefacts and ecofacts produced by domestic activities and accumulated in these structures, forming a sequence of cultural levels (e.g. Lizcano 1999). In contrast to the hypothesis of the *"Cultura de los Silos"*, these large sites have become widely accepted as the settlements of megalithic cultures (Arribas & Molina 1984: 90-91).

At the beginning of the 1990's, these sites were recognised as an important indication of the early concentration of populations in the IV millennium cal BC (Lizcano *et.al.* 1991-92: 48-49; Zafra *et.al.* 1999: 88; Nocete 2001: 67), the result of which would be the emergence of fully sedentary communities. The defensive ditch systems were understood as precursors of the stone walls of Los Millares-VNSP type settlements of the third millennium (Lizcano 1999: 10; Calado 2000: 38; Nocete 2001: 50), while the coexistence of these large sites alongside numerous small hamlets was interpreted as evidence of a hierarchical structure, at least from the late IV millennium onwards (Lizcano 1999: 238-239; Calado 2000: 39), and during the III millennium BC (Hurtado 2000: 389-390; Nocete 2001: 95; Varela 2003: 136). The proliferation of pits within these sites characterises them as true *"silo fields"* where agricultural surpluses were accumulated and distributed on a macro-territorial scale, from a centre of power -Valencina de la Concepción- to the whole of lower Andalusia (Cruz-Auñón & Arteaga 1999: 604-605).

This short summary is sufficient to expose the suggested relationship between the emergence of some Iberian ditch systems and the existence of an early complex settlement pattern and singular political processes shaped by social inequality since the IV millennium cal BC Notwithstanding, this argument is supported by a well-known archaeological record in the rest of Western Europe. Without any doubt, the critique that could be made of these arguments would reflect the stereotypes of European historiography of the last decades and would be superfluous in the general discussion. In any case, we feel that it would be pertinent to develop these themes at this point of the discussion in order to meet the final objectives of the publication of which this study is part. We will therefore develop under the two following subheadings the main critiques that have been shed upon these historical arguments (e.g. Márquez 2001; 2002a; 2002b; 2003; Márquez & Fernández 2002).

12.4.- Non-farm enclosures

The hypothesis of the "large settlements" in the south of the Iberian Peninsula mentioned above in turn required the reconciliation of an idealised image of the Neolithic farmer with an inadequate archaeological record. This was achieved through a series of biases, namely:

a) The sites are fortified settlements with defensive ditch systems.

b) The absence of domestic structures with their corresponding walls and post-holes is due to the subterranean or semi-subterranean nature of the huts,

c) The proliferation of silos reflects consolidated farming communities capable of producing a large agricultural surplus.

d) Many of the excavated structures were reused as refuse pits once their initial function had been lost.

e) The subterranean nature of the features of the archaeological record of these sites is the result of post-depositional processes leading to the destruction of other domestic remains on the surface of the site.

As is well-known, as early as the 1960's, I. Smith (1996: 471) questioned the interpretation of prehistoric enclosures as settlements and suggested the social dimensions of their use. From then on, the critique of the large fortified settlements with defensive ditch systems has taken place all over Europe. For instance, the study of the site of Etton by F. Pryor, pointed out "the evident and calculated inefficiency of these ditches" as defensive systems and their deliberately open nature (1988: 124). Along the same line, a number of authors have argued against the supposedly dissuasive function that has traditionally been attributed to ditches (e.g. Drewett 1976: 223; Andersen 1998: 303; Edmonds 1999: 113). In accord with this idea, the irregularity of the layout and the nature of the fills of the ditch systems of southern Iberia do not support the interpretations formulated regarding their supposedly defensive function.

The hypothesis of the "dwelling-pits" is just as questionable. In this case too, it has been forgotten that since the hypothesis formulated by Cecil Curwen in 1930 who talked about the "subterranean homes of pit-dwellers" up until the present, a long-running debate in European prehistory on the use of pits as semi-subterranean houses has taken place. The insurmountable difficulties of evacuating rain water from inside these dwelling-pits, or the rapid insect invasion that these structures are subjected to just weeks after their construction (Chapman 2000: 87), have not been taken into account. Moreover, it has been a serious mistake to confuse the accumulation of archaeological deposits within these subterranean structures with true "cultural layers" resulting from the gradual deposition of domestic materials by the dwellers. Apart from the limited dimensions of the "hut floors", which rarely reach 3 metres in width, and their slight bell shape that without a doubt hindered the majority of the domestic activities which are supposed to have taken place inside, the fact that, within normal circumstances, an occupation of several decades would have been necessary to produce a deposit ranging between 0.5 and 1 metre or more has not been considered. The gradual sedimentation of these semi-subterranean houses, up to the ground-level as is displayed for example at the site of Polideportivo de Martos (Lizcano 1999: 83-90), would also reduce considerably the usable living space, making them impracticable. However, this scenario does not explain why the structures were not periodically recut and the levels of domestic refuse evacuated from within. Finally, it is noteworthy that the nature of each one of the "cultural layers" appearing in ditches, pits and "hut floors" is very heterogeneous, thus indicating a series of stratigraphically successive deposits of artefactual and ecofactual evidence, dissimilar to the continuous discard of artefacts and animal bones which typify truly domestic cultural levels (Fig. 12.7).

The interpretation of the pits as "silos" is not unheard of in other European regions (e.g. Field *et al.* 1964). In the sphere of the present study, it has been generally assumed that since the beginning of the Neolithic (end of the VI/beginning of the V millennium cal BC), the early farmers already *enjoyed* most of aspects of agrarian life (so-called Neolithic *package*) and that such economic and technological resources, through the intensification and optimisation of agriculture and livestock, were developed during the following cultural phases (Late Neolithic and Early Copper Age – IV and part of the III millennium cal BC). In this case, it appears coherent to recognise the Neolithic enclosures as the first large scale settlements with storage-pit systems. However, the sparse carpological and archaeological record does not confirm this hypothesis. And, as Bradley pointed out for other European regions (1998: 3), agricultural activities are poorly reflected in the archaeological record of the Neolithic and first moments of the metal ages of the south of the Iberian Peninsula (see Márquez 2002)

Collaterally to the previous argument, it has been suggested that after loosing their initial function many "silos" were reused as refuse pits, confronting us with the classical problem raised by prehistoric rubbish deposits. Archaeologists tend to assume that broken and disarticulated artefacts or bones simply represent rubbish. We thus project our Cartesian principles: the complete is superior to the incomplete, the symmetrical is superior to the asymmetrical, the oriented to the disoriented, etc, in the classification of "disorganised" contexts such as refuse deposits. As has been pointed out in various occasions (e.g. Moore 1982: 75; Brück 1999: 153; Chapman 2000: 63; Whittle *et al.* 1999: 361), the term "rubbish" is heavily conditioned by an ethnocentric bias in such a way that it is not necessarily applicable to the study of prehistoric societies. The issue appears to be subject to a modern-day

Fig.12.7. Los Villares de Algane, Pit n° 2. A clear series of stratigraphically succesive collections of artetactual and ecofactual evidence characteristic of structured depositions.

perception that past societies must have produced a large volume of rubbish which they must have disposed of in some orderly fashion, or else would have accumulated within the human dwelling areas, regardless of the fact that only Taphonomic studies can establish the truth of the matter *i.e.* how and how much rubbish created at a prehistoric site ever entered the archaeological record.

Finally, and as a consequence of the latter, there is a tendency to consider that apparently empty sites must be the result of heavy erosion since prehistoric times rather than the absence of domestic activities during their occupation. However, the nature and magnitude of these erosive processes, which paradoxically appear to affect all and everyone of the known pit sites, are rarely discussed in publications In any case, if this hypothesis were to be true, and independently of whether a specific site was finally erased through erosive processes, we believe that the subterranean structures composing such sites would have been filled according to a similar pattern of deposition and sedimentation as that displayed in the archaeological record of all of the remaining types of domestic structures considered to be coetaneous. Nonetheless, when this type of contingency has been rigorously sought, for instance at the sites of Papa Uvas (Martín de la Cruz & Lucena 2003: 159) or Ferreira do Alentejo. (Valera & Filipe 2004: 33), the fills of the ditches and pits did not ever reveal a stratigraphic sequence enabling to compare one type of structure with another.

For all of the reasons presented above, the notion of farming settlements occupied over many generations is difficult to sustain in the case of these Neolithic and Copper Age enclosures, where there is little or no evidence for dense palimpsests of walls or related features. It is thus logical that these sites should lack true vertical stratigraphy, and that in any case they never grew into "tells".

12.5. Non-inequalitarian societies

During the 1980's and well into the 1990's, an evolutionist tripartite scheme was explicitly and implicitly shared by many researchers who consequently interpreted the increasing social inequality in the south of the peninsula according to three different "sceneries": early farmer ditch settlements (IV-III millennia) – Los Millares-VNSP type walled settlements (III millennium) – hillforts of the Argaric culture (II millennium). In this rigid scheme, the final phase would have led to an advanced form of social hierarchies, if not the emergence of full-blown State structures, while the initial phase on the other hand would have reflected early farming practices and storage. This function was thus attributed, as presented above, to the Neolithic and Copper Age enclosures. Notwithstanding, over the past decade, more elaborate arguments have been formulated which give greater importance to the early enclosures in the origin and initial development of the south of the Iberian Peninsular. Here,

we shall critically present some of the more interesting cases.

The site of Marroquíes Bajos for instance (Zafra *et al.* 1999) (displaying archaeological remains from the Neolithic up until historical times) is an example of a prehistoric settlement whose development reflects a process of agricultural intensification which led to the construction of a Late Copper Age "macro-village". The phases ZAMB 1 y ZAMB2 (defined by a generalised pattern of scoops, dwelling-pits, storage pits, refuse deposits and shafts) correspond to the first occupation of the site and are the consequence of a severe process of demographic concentration. ZAMB 3 is related with six enclosure ditches, interpreted as a circular water capture and distribution system, a fortified wall and huts with post-holes and foundation trenches. Finally, houses with stone foundations and clay walls are found within ZAMB4 (Zafra *et. al.* 1999: 77-88). In contrast, and independently from the chronological adscription of the ditches and wall (see discussion by Lizcano *et al.* 2004: 164-166), it could be argued that one or several Neolithic-Early Copper Age enclosures may have initially overlapped (ZAMB1; ZAMB2 and possibly ZAMB3), and upon them, and only since the mid-III millennium, a settlement was built with domestic structures with associated walls and postholes. This was not a simple change in the architectural nature of the site over time as the result of the historical processes leading up to the emergence of farmers, but a clear-cut differentiation between two completely different types of site. This example enables us to point out that although some ditched enclosures continued to be the focus of attention in the Late Copper Age and Early Bronze Age, there is no evidence indicating that new enclosures were built after 2500-2200 cal. B.C in southern Iberia. As is the case in other European regions, non-contemporary associations (e.g.. Bell-beaker / Late Copper Age, Bronze Age) are fairly common at ditch enclosure sites but we deem their assimilation with models of local pre-urban evolution to be inadequate.

In some cases, the early emergence of social complexity is demonstrated by the existence of differentiated functional areas within the ditched enclosures, as is the case at Valencina de la Concepción, La Pijotilla or Perdigoes where dwelling areas (dwelling pits), areas of storage and production (storage pits) and burial areas are clearly defined (Arteaga & Cruz-Auñón 1999: 590-598; Hurtado 2004: 247-248; Lago *et al.* 1998: 145). The emergence of *specialised areas* can be traced back to the end of the IV millennium cal BC or beginning of the IIIrd millennium BC, with the appearance of settlements with clearly proto-urban characteristics, although the historical processes leading to these circumstances, that are not shared across all of Western Europe at this date, are not easily identified. The archaeological record does not however support this hypothesis given that the magnitude of the social and political activities implied by these *proto-urban settlements* is not accompanied by other indicators such as monumental entrances, ceremonial buildings, architectural differentiation, stables, irrigation, water storage or public spaces. Moreover, clear evidence of the *secondary products revolution* defined by A. Sherrat (1981), such as signs of ploughing, animal traction and others, is barely present.

A third debatable parameter regards the emergence of a hierarchical territory around the enclosures. In these terms, the large sites of Valencina de la Concepción, Ferreira do Alentejo, La Pijotilla and Perdigoes have usually been interpreted in terms of their political and economic centrality during the IV-III millennia, and in relationship with smaller dependent neighbouring sites (Lizcano 1999: 238-239; Nocete 2001: 95, 137; Varela 2003: 136). As was pertinently observed by Díaz-del-Río it has been assumed that "the variability in size between settlements necessarily reflects relations of political dependence", despite that "the contemporaneity and permanence of all of these Copper Age settlements, large and small, remains to be demonstrated" (2004: 95-96). My reticence goes further still, as I share this criticism and take one step more: the large ditched enclosures are not farming settlements.

Finally, a further argument in the identification of social inequality at these sites deserves mention: the frequent presence of human remains within pits and ditches. As was set out above, the cultural perspectives of the 1980's regarded this phenomenon as a funerary practice distinct from the megalithic tradition (Carrilero *et al.* 1982). More recently, it has been suggested that the variety of types of ritual inhumations is the reflection of important social asymmetries between the members of the same community, leading to the exclusion of some members from megalithic rituals and their deposition in refuse pits and unused subterranean structures without any grave-goods (Alcázar *et al.* 1992: 26; Arteaga & Cruz-Auñón 1999: 613; García & Fernández 1999: 118; Nocete 2001: 99). Notwithstanding, it is worth noting that the presence of articulated and disarticulated human remains is a constant, if not one of the main characteristics, in the majority of Late prehistoric European *enclosures* (e.g. Drewett 1977: 225; Whittle *et al.* 1999: 361-362; Andersen 2002: 5). The anthropocentrism of our perspectives and the tendency to recognise evidence of funerary ritual in any archaeologically recovered human remains, have caused other possible social and symbolic practices dealing with the treatment of the human body to be undervalued (Barret 1994: 91).

In summary, the argument of the local emergence of social inequalities and large-scale political changes in the south of the Iberian Peninsula, based on an archaeological phenomenon such as the Neolithic-Copper Age ditched enclosures (otherwise widespread in all of Western Europe during the IV and III millennia BC) is unsustainable.

12.6. The genesis of the sites: depositional episodes

Among the first prehistoric settlements and the Iberian ditched enclosures we believe that there existed, above all, a marked difference in the formation of the archaeological record. While a settlement is the result of similar forms of domestic activities which implies a period of constant use drawn out over years or centuries from their foundation up until their final abandonment, the ditched enclosures are the result of a rather different genesis. I thus think that in the formation of the Neolithic-Copper Age enclosures in the south of Iberia the influences of two architectural traditions, widely spread in continental Late Prehistory, are at play:

a) Firstly, the construction in the landscape of large circular enclosures, either drawn in the ground or defined on the surface (e.g. *henges*, palisade enclosures, *causewayed enclosures, erdenlegens, rondells, cromlech, enceintes interrompues*, etc).

b) Secondly, the structured deposition in the ground of artefacts and human and animal remains. In any case, we are confronted with a specific formation of the archaeological record quite different from that of a strict settlement site.

Similarly, by the IV millennium BC, the Neolithic groups living in southern Iberia began to shape a circular microcosmos, opening large ditches whose meaning clearly represented the *ownership* between those who had access to or dwelled within them, and the *exclusion* of those whose access, presence and transit through the site was denied. The active permanence of these groups within the site was made manifest by the structured deposit of *goods* or *gifts* within the ditches and many other subterranean structures that did not function as constructive features but as a means of recording in the ground the events or special activities that were punctually carried out.

Morphologically, we can distinguish between bell-shaped pits (the so-called "silos"), displaying greater depth than width and hallows, and the so-called "hut floors", displaying greater width than depth (Fig. 12.8), although the two types of features do not display differences in their fills. In either case, the structures were filled up to the ground level, finally leading them to disappear. In most cases, the filling took place over a very short period of time, through the accumulation of a series of stratigraphically successive collections of artefactual and ecofactual assemblages, levels of ash and in rare cases, levels of natural sedimentation. As is the case in many other European sites, potsherds, broken quern stones, prismatic blades and other flint tools are the most common materials, alongside a large volume of pebbles deposited *ex profeso*. Another type of commonly deposited object are cones of unfired clay.

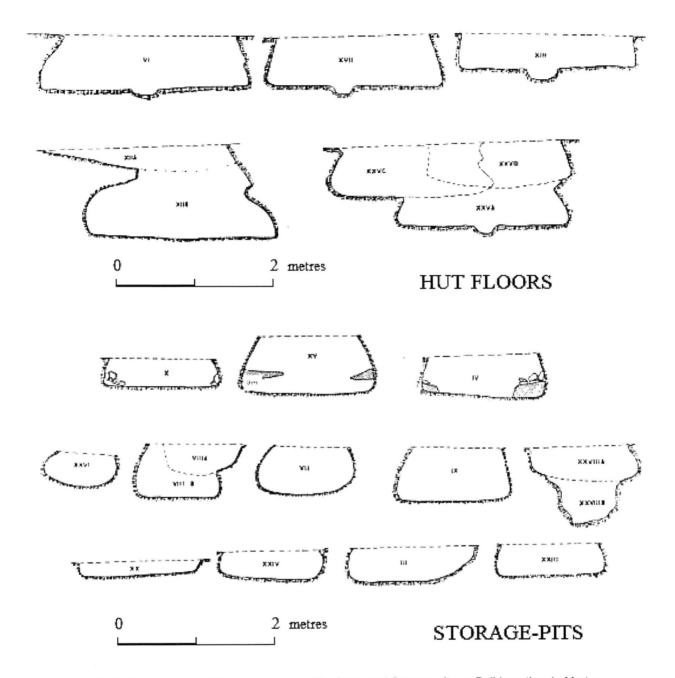

Fig.12.8. Morphological differences between Hut floors and Storage-pits on Polideportivo de Martos after R. Lizcano (1999).

The analysis of the faunal remains deposited within these structures (Márquez in press b) has enabled the identification of numerous examples of Bos Taurus; capra hircus and ovis aries; canis familiaris; sus domesticus and cervus elaphus (deer), although the latter are only represented by their antlers. In most cases, all of these species are incomplete and disarticulated, although some cases of complete and articulated bovid and dogs have documented (Fig. 12.9) (Hurtado 1991: 54; Lizcano 1999: 112, 117; Conlin 2004: 373). In such cases, the remains of these animals are very frequently covered by a layer of stones and/or broken quern stones. In the fill of a single structure, alternate "levels" of articulated and disarticu-lated animals can sometimes be observed. Within the same level, individual specimens can even be treated in different ways (e.g. see structure XV of Polideportivo de Martos, Lizcano 1999: 115). Finally, skeletal elements of a single individual have been observed in spatially distinct features, as is the case of an adult male sheep whose skull was found in structure XXV of Polideportivo de Martos while the cervical vertebrae were located in the base of feature XIIb (Lizcano 1999: 112).

The deposition of human remains at these sites also presents some common features (Márquez in press a). Firstly, there is no indication of the differential or preferential of fleshed bodies, and previously unfleshed skeletons and/or disarticulated remains. At times, the bones appear below a single large stone, or as is the case of bovid and dog burial, covered by a layer of pebbles and/or pieces of quern stone. Lastly, it is worth noting that the remains of people and animals are nothing more than another undifferentiated part of larger depositional episodes involving important volumes of artefacts and ecofacts.

Finally, it is interesting to point out the absence of spatial planning in the distribution of these deposits within the Neolithic-Copper Age enclosures whilst the cultural uniformity of the contents of each feature is displayed by the absence of any stratiphied remains of any other period within the deposits. Features frequently overlap, cutting one another and thus forming a complex palimpsest within the site, suggesting that the deposits appear to have been placed in the area during a small number of successive punctual episodes, most probably during the period in which the ditches were open and the symbolic area defined by the ditched in use (Márquez 2003: 276). Some ditched enclosures were even modified and in some cases extended through multiple phases of complete ditch circuits, enlarging or modifying the circumference of the enclosures (e.g. Papa Uvas or Ferreira do Alentejo).

Based on the patterns outlined above, we believe that there is a sufficient basis supporting the existence of structured deposition in the Neolithic-Copper Age ditched enclosures of the south of the Iberian Peninsula. However, structured deposits are not necessarily ritual deposits. Domestic activities also display a great degree of structure (Richards & Thomas 1984: 215). It would thus be a mistake to fall into the trap of replacing the profane interpretation of these sites as a metaphor of the Neolithic farmer by an alternative sacred perception of the sites as archaic sanctuaries or temples (Márquez 2003: 277). It would therefore be useful to talk of the "ritualisation of the Domestic Sphere" (Bradley 2003), thus avoiding the false dichotomies between sacred and profane, ceremonial and every-day, or public and private.

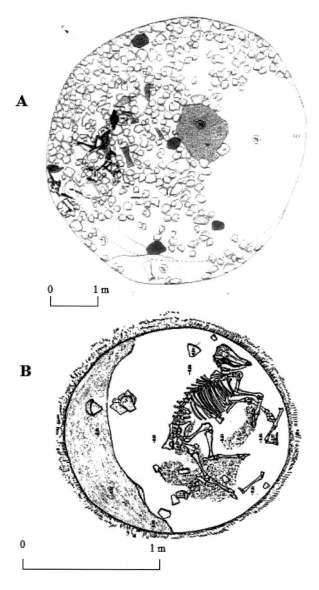

Fig.12.9. Dog and cattle skulls deposited in the interior of neolithic pits. A. Carmona (Colin 2004) ; B. Polideportivo Martos (Lizcano 1999)

treatment of human remains compared with other types of deposition. They are never accompanied by grave-goods, and along with bovid and dogs, they are the only species that appear complete and articulated. In ditches they are uncommon, as examples are only known at the sites of Valencina de la Concepción and Marroquíes Bajos (Fernández & Oliva 1986: 20; Zafra et al. 2003: 83). On the other hand, many bell-shaped pits contain one or two individuals, while as many as five individuals may appear in some hallows. When the bodies are complete, they generally adopt a foetal or crouched position. In the hallows, some kind of centrifugal process seems to be applied to the remains which are shifted towards the periphery of the huts. In many other cases, human bones appear disarticulated and intentionally piled up within these features. This in turn leads us to believe that we are observing symbolic practices which integrate the deposition

12.7.- Monumental landscape as resistance landscape

The ditched enclosures are but one element of the monumental landscape of the IV-III millennia BC in the south of the Iberian Peninsula. In the surroundings of the enclosures, small scattered mobile Neolithic groups raised various types of megalithic constructions and monumentalised natural places through the use of rock carvings and schematic paintings. They were in fact groups based around a relatively mobile economy, composed of non-intensive agriculture, the exploitation of forest resources, for example acorns, the breeding of livestock including pig, cattle, sheep and goat, and the use of primary raw materials, flint in particular. The monumentality mentioned previously contrasts sharply with the ephemeral and non-permanent nature of the settlements. As was pointed out by J.C. Barrett (1994: 136-146) for other European regions, in the south of the Iberian peninsula, the group identity of these societies also appears to be shaped by their movement through a landscape loaded with meaning rather than through their ties with a specific place (*i.e.* the settlement).

However, if as we have been arguing, the Neolithic-Copper Age enclosures and the monumental landscape of which they are part do not reflect sedentary communities, the consolidation of a mixed land and livestock based economy, nor the emergence of social inequality in the Late Prehistory of the southern peninsula, this could be because they precisely, and paradoxically, reflect the opposite situation: the resistance of farming and social fracture. In accord with J. Vicent (1998: 828), we believe that very few Neolithic societies, through endogenous processes, replaced parentship relations by class relationships as the main dynamic of production, and that in the south of the peninsula there is no archaeological evidence able to argue otherwise. Moreover, we consider primitive societies as ones which resist the emergence of a separate organ of political power, as would be the State (Clastres 1996: 111-116), a factor that has not been given sufficient importance in the interpretation of the archaeological record. The social mechanisms of resistance which could have led to internal tensions between families or lineages of some segmentary Neolithic societies have not been sought. This hypothesis, in contrast with Renfrew's functionalism, could help redefine megalithism as a *landscape of resistance* faced with the consolidation of the farming way of life and would allow us to explore its particular mechanisms of economic and social organisation which not only distances it from the traditional image of the Neolithic, but also delays the introduction of the first farming communities in Western Europe (Márquez 2003: 279). Let us present an interpretation of the role that the ditched enclosures may have played within this new scenario.

We consider that Neolithic-Copper Age enclosures like Valencina de la Concepción and many others throughout the continent may not make much sense as settlements, although they were a focus for a considerable number of people, reflected first and foremost by the simple fact that their scale implies the labour of many. Therefore, it is evident that these sites involved important aggregations. They thus appear as the setting of large-scale meetings of people, during which a series of activities and events took place: gatherings, sacrifices, feasts and complex rites of passage, that is in brief the creation of a specific space for various social transactions (e.g. Richards & Thomas 1984: 190-191; Evans 1988: 88; Edmonds 1999: 98; Whittle *et al.* 1999: 384-385). Such meetings must have been guided by cycles of social visits. However, once the objectives of the gathering had been fulfilled, the groups involved returned to their particular distribution in the surrounding landscape. We are thus observing a dynamic of social "to and fro", repeated over generations and

which implies an intense level of social interaction between small scattered mobile Neolithic-Copper Age groups. This would explain the magnitude and monumentality of these sites as the result of communal work projects organised without the use of coercive force (Edmonds 1999: 101). Even distant populations could be regular participants in events at "non-local" ceremonial complexes.

The construction of monuments, such as henges and enclosures, by distant groups is not only frequent in the European prehistory since similar social dynamics have been attributed to the construction of the conical burial mounds of the Woodland Period in the east of the United State, the geometric Hopewell earthworks in southern Ohio, the Chacoan houses and the great kivas of the American Southwest (Bernardini 2004: 331). The repetition of the visits to these sites during generations and the generalised deposition events that were carried out supports the phenomenon defined by C. Evans as a "discourse of redefinition of an original social space" (1988: 85). Some of these ditched enclosures were also recut on several occasions, thus emphasising and reinforcing the sense of place experienced by those who gathered and helping to create and reinforce a feeling of group identity (Bradley 1998: 72; Edmonds 1999: 110). This argument explains the magnitude of many of these sites, which in any case, are accumulative. The *extension* of some southern sites, such as Valencina de la Concepción, Papa Uvas or La Pijotilla can therefore be satisfactorily explained by these same dynamics of accumulation without the need of hypothetical suggestions of social complexity and/or larger scale urban settings.

Viewed in this way, the megalithic landscape becomes polyhedral and dynamic, never static, and can only be perceived as a whole with all of its nuances, from the perspective of the marked mobility of the Neolithic groups who moved through it alongside their herds. In any case, the social, economic and symbolic mechanisms which justify these particular historical processes have not been studied in too much detail. Here, we limit our work to the presentation of a historical rather than evolutionist explanation, which defends the universal resistance of undivided societies to a power structure which sets itself apart from the society itself (Clastres 1996: 112). Any landscape implies above all "the imposition of human order" (Ingold 1993: 154), and we believe that megalithism is no exception: part of it reflects resistance to social fracture. Thus within a subsistence economy which must have been successful (abundant domesticated, woodland and raw material resources), the megalithic people were "forced" to move throughout the territory, guided by strictly planned social rhythms. The gatherings are not coincidental: they are severely programmed. The sendentarisation of a population would perhaps have started a process of accumulation of unequal wealth, and thus was avoided through almost obsessive mechanisms of social fission. However, this centrifugal tendency could easily have divided the society if it were not for the counteraction of punctual and ceremonial social relations which united the scattered groups. This took place through reversible aggregations, for which the Neolithic enclosures were the ideal setting.

In these societies, a *system of total lending* as defined by M. Mauss (1991: 160) must have been general practice: a system of reciprocal gifts. It can therefore be assumed that such meetings were based around the gift, without rivalries or strategies. We could almost be talking about a form of secular exchange between groups through which goods and/or women were put into circulation. In these terms, we can explain the non-local nature of many of the materials deposited in Neolithic enclosures (e.g. Edmonds 1999: 128). As was pointed out by Mauss (1991: 160-161), this generalised scheme of gifts also enabled the tensions and rivalries between groups to be channelled, not through the appropriation of material items but through the sumptuary and *agonistic* donation and destruction of material items: the so-called Potlatch. Obviously, and as is widely recognised, the prestige reached during these events is directly proportional to the volume of goods consumed and wasted, thus leading to the "impoverishment" of the group holding the ceremony, effectively preventing the accumulation of wealth and surpluses and postponing social fracture. However, this must not mask the fact that in such practices forms of appropriation of labour may have existed, but we think that they would have taken place according to the *parental mode of surplus extraction* defined by Vicent (1998: 832-839).

In the peninsular context, Criado already pointed out some years ago that the construction of megaliths could be considered as mechanisms of anti-power resistance (1989: 89-92). In such terms, the builders of monumental landscapes can be identified as societies in which since "power threatened to become separated from the society, anti-power strategies were developed, among which figured ritual and sumptuary consumption (potlatches)". Moreover, the monumental constructions implied a "means of consuming the surplus during symbolically loaded events, which reinforced the ties between groups and avoided the accumulation or personal use of the surplus" (Criado in press). Along a similar line, Díaz-del-Río pointed out that "monumental architecture is the main and earliest form of conspicuous consumption" (2004: 86). We can also add that in other regions it has been observed that the enclosures seem to have witnessed intense levels of conspicuous consumption and been the possible source of local scale tensions, competition and negotiation (e.g. Harding 1997: 286; Thomas 1999: 42; Edmonds 1999: 117; Whittle & Pollard 1999: 388). This possibility has also been considered in the study of the structured deposits of the southern Iberian peninsula (Marquez & Fernández 2002: 319). In any case, and following the argument of M. Mauss, we cannot forget that potlatches are but an evolved although fairly rare practice within a much broader system of generalised non-competitive lending (1991: 160), in such a way that

they cannot be considered the unique explicative "key" to all of these sites.

In summary, the Monumental Landscape of the IV-III millennia BC appears as a landscape of resistance to the consolidation of the farming way of life, capable not only of delayed full-blown sedentarisation and the emergence of social divisions, but of coherently resolving the first social tensions which arise in the segmentary societies of the Neolithic and Copper Age of southern Iberia. Their crisis (c. mid-III – early II millennia BC), as in other European regions, was marked by new landscapes in which the centre of the group identity is shifted to the farmer settlements which would be occupied, now permanently, and in which a previously unseen agricultural intensification would take place. New forms of monumentality would thus become necessary and would become centred for the first time within the settlement itself or in its immediately surrounding landscape.

Acknowledgements

The author would like to thank Juan Fernández Ruiz, Francisco Rodríguez Vinceiro and Víctor Jiménez Jáimez for discussing the present paper; Felipe Criado and Antonio C. Varela for providing access to graphical documentation and unpublished texts.

12.8.- References

ALCAZAR, J.; MARTÍN, A. & RUIZ, M.T. 1992: "Enterramientos Calcolíticos en zonas de hábitat". *Revista de Arqueología* 137: 18-27.

ANDERSEN, N.H. 1997: *Sarup volumen 1. The Sarup enclosures*. Jutland Archaeological Society. Moesgaard.

ARTEAGA, O. & CRUZ-AUÑON 1999: "El sector funerario de Los Cabezuelos (Valencina de la Concepción, Sevilla). Resultados preliminares de una excavación de urgencia". *Anuario Arqueológico de Andalucía* 1995, III: 589-599.

ARRIBAS, A. & MOLINA, F. 1978: "Nuevas aportaciones al inicio de la metalurgia en la península ibérica. El Poblado de los Castillejos de Montefrío (Granada)". En M. Ryan (ed.): *The origins of metallurgy in Atlantic Europe, Proceedings of the fifth atlantic colloquium*. Dublin: 7-32.

BARRETT, J. C. 1994: *Fragments from Antiquity. An archaeology of social life in Britan, 2900-1200. B.C.* Blackwell. Oxford.

BERNABEU, J. (dir) 1993: *El III milenio a.C. en el País Valenciano. Los poblados de Jovades (Concentaina) y Arenal de la Costa (Ontinyent)*. Saguntum 26. Universidad de Valencia. Valencia.

BERNABEU, J.; OROZCO, T.; DÍEZ, A. GÓMEZ, M. & MOLINA, F.J. 2003: "Mas D'Is (Penàguila, Alicante): Aldeas y recintos monumentales del Neolítico Inicial en el Valle del Serpis". *Trabajos de Prehistoria* 60 (2): 239-259.

BERNARDINI, W. 2004: "Hopewell geometric earthworks: a case study in the referential and experimental meaning of monuments". *Journal of Antrhopological Archaeology* 23: 331-356.

BONSOR, G. 1899: *Les colonies agricoles pré-romaines de la Vallée du Betis. Revue Archéologique* XXXV. Paris.

BRADLEY, R. 1993: *Altering the Earth: The origins of monuments in Britain and Continental Europe.* Society of antiquaries of Scotland 8. Edinburgh.

- 1998: *The Significance of Monuments. On the shaping of human experience in Neolithic and Bronze Age Europe.* Routledge. London.

- 2003: "A life less ordinary: the ritualization of the domestic sphere in Later Prehistoric Europe". *Cambridge Archaeological Journal* 13 (1): 5-23.

BRÜCK, J. 1999: "Houses, lifecycles and deposition on Middle Bronze Age settlements in Southern England". *Proceeding of the Prehistoric Society* 65: 145-166.

BUBNER, T. 1981: "Endneolithikum und Frühbronzezeit im uteren Guadalquivirbecken". *Zephyrus* XXXII-III: 133-155.

BURGESS; C.; TOPPING, P.; MORDANT C. & MADDISON, M. (eds) 1988: *Enclosures and defences in the Neolithic of Western Europe.* BAR International Series 403.

CALADO, D. 2000: "Neolitizaçao e Megalitismo no Alentejo Central: Uma leitura espacial". *Actas do 3º Congresso de Arqueología Peninsular* III: 35-45.

CARRILERO, M.; MARTÍNEZ, G. & MARTÍNEZ, J. 1982: "El yacimiento de los Morales (Castro del Río, Córdoba). La Cultura de los Silos en Andalucía Occidental". *Cuadernos de Prehistoria de la Universidad de Granada* 7: 171-208.

CARRILERO, M. & SUAREZ, A. 1989-90: "Ciavieja (El Ejido, Almeria): Resultados obtenidos en las campañas de 1985 y 1986. El poblado de la Edad del Cobre". *Cuadernos de Prehistoria Universidad de Granada* 14-15: 109-136.

CLASTRES, P. 1996: *Investigaciones en antropología política.* Gedisa. Barcelona.

COLIN, E. 2004: "El poblado calcolítico de Carmona (Sevilla)". *Simposios de Prehistoria Cueva de Nerja. II. La problemática del Neolítico en Andalucía. III. Las primeras sociedades metalúrgicas en Andalucía.* Fundación Cueva de Nerja. Nerja: 370-378.

COLLANTES DE TERÁN, M. 1969: "El Dolmen de Matarrubilla". *Tartesos o sus problemas: Vº Simposium Internacional de Prehistoria Peninsular* (Jerez de la Frontera 1968). Universidad de Barcelona. Barcelona: 47-62.

CRIADO, F. 1989: "Megalitos, espacio, pensamiento". *Trabajos de Prehistoria* 46: 75-98

- In press: "Memorias de espacio: La construcción del Paisaje en la Prehistoria". *Revista TAPA.* Santiago de Compostela.

CRUZ-AÑON, R.; MORENO, E.; CACERES, P. & VALVERDE, Mª. 1995: "Informe provisional de la excavación sistemática en el yacimiento de El Negrón (Gilena, Sevilla). Campaña de 1991". *Anuario Arqueológico de Andalucía* 1992, II : 347-351.

CRUZ-AUÑON, R. & ARTEAGA, O. 1999: "Acerca de un campo de silos y un foso de cierre prehistóricos ubicados en la Estacada Larga (Valencina de la Concepción, Sevilla), Excavación de urgencia de 1995". *Anuario Arqueológico de Andalucía* 1995, III: 600-607.

CHAPMAN, J. 2000: "Pit-digging and structured deposition in the Neolithic and Copper Age". *Procedings of the Prehistoric Society* 66: 61-87.

DARVILL, T. & THOMAS, J. (eds.) 2001: *Neolithic enclosures in Atlantic Nortwest Europe.* Oxbow Books. Oxford.

DIAZ-DEL-RIO, P. 2003: "Recintos de fosos del III milenio a.C. en la Meseta Peninsular". *Trabajos de Prehistoria* 60 (2): 61-78.

- 2004: "Factionalism and collective labor in Copper Age Iberia". *Trabajos de Prehistoria* 61 (2): 85-98.

DREWETT, P. 1977: "The excavation of a Neolithic Causewayed Enclosure on Offham Hill, East Sussex, 1976". *Proceedings of the Prehistoric Society* 43: 201-241.

EDMONS, M. 1999: *Ancestral Geographies of the Neolithic. Landscape, monuments and memory.* Routledge. London.

EVANS, C. 1988: "Acts of enclosure: A consideration of concentrically-Organised causewayed enclosures". In J.C. Barret & I.A. Kinnes (eds.): *The archaeology of context in the Neolithic and Bronze Age. Recent trends.* University of Sheffield. Sheffield: 85-96.

FERNÁNDEZ, J. OLIVA, D. 1985: "Excavaciones en el yacimiento Calcolítico de Valencina de la Concepción (Sevilla). El corte C La Perrera". *Noticiario Arqueológico Hispánico* 25: 7-131.

FIELD, N.H., MATTHEWS, C.L. & SMITH, I.F. 1964: "New Neolithic sites in Dorset and Bedfordshire, with a note on the distribution of Neolithic Storage-Pits in Britain". *Proceding Prehistoric Society* 15: 352-381.

GARCÍA, C. & FERNÁNDEZ, J 1999: "La época calcolítica de San Bartolomé de Almonte". *Huelva Arqueológica* 15: 6-153.

GÓMEZ, Mª. T. 2003: "Excavaciones arqueológicas realizadas en el solar de la Plazuela de Santiago nº 6-7 de Carmona (Sevilla)". *Anuario Arqueológico de Andalucía 2000* III (2): 1245-1256.

HARDING, J. 1997 : "Interpreting the Neolithic : The Monuments of North Yorkshire". *Oxford Journal of Archaeology* 16 (3): 279-295.

HORNOS, F.; NOCETE, F. & PEREZ, C. 1987: "Actuación arqueológica de urgencia en el yacimiento de los pozos en Higuera de Arjona (Jaén)". *Anuario Arqueológico de Andalucía 1986* III :198-202.

HURTADO, V. 1991: "Informe de las excavaciones de urgencia en la Pijotilla. Campaña de 1990". *Extremadura Arqueológica* II : 45-67.

- 2000: "El proceso de transición a la Edad del Bronce en la Cuenca Media del Guadiana. Ruptura o continuidad". *Actas del 3º Congresso de Arqueología Peninsular* (4): 381-397.

- 2004: "Fosos y fortificaciones entre el Guadiana y el Guadalquivir en III milenio A.C: evidencias del registro arqueológico". S. En Oliveira Jorge (ed.): *Recintos murados da pré-historia recente*. Facultad de Arte. Porto: 239-268.

INGOLD, T. 1993: "The temporality of the lanscape". *World Archaeology* 25 (2): 152- 174.

LAGO, M.; DUARTE, C.; VALERA, A.; ALBERGARIA, J. ALMEIDA, F. & CARVALHO, A. 1998: "Povoado dos Perdigoes (Reguengos de Mosaraz): dados preliminares dos trabalhos arqueológicos realizados em 1997". *Revista portuguesa de Arqueología* 1 (1): 45-152.

LAGO, M. & ALBERGARIA, J. 2001: "O cabeço do Torrao (Elvas): contextos e interpretaçoes previas de um lugar do Neolítico alentejano". *ERA-Arqueologia* 4: 39-63.

LIZCANO, R.; CAMARA, J.A.; RIQUELME, J.A.; CAÑABATE, Mª. L.; SANCHEZ, A. & AFONSO, J.A. 1991-92: "El polideportivo de Martos. Producción económica y símbolo de cohesión en un asentamiento del Neolítico final en las campiñas del Alto Guadalquivir". *Cuadernos de Prehistoria de Granada* 16-17: 5-101.

LIZCANO, R. 1999: *El Polideportivo de Martos (Jaén): un yacimiento neolítico del IV milenio a.C. Nuevos datos para la reconstrucción del proceso histórico del Alto Guadalquivir.* Obra Social y Cultural Cajasur. Córdoba.

LIZCANO, R.; CÁMARA, J.A.; CONTRERAS, F.; PÉREZ, C. & BURGOS, A. 2003: "Continuidad y cambio en comunidades calcolíticas del Alto Guadalquivir". *Simposios II y III de Prehistoria Cueva de Nerja*: 159-175.

MÁRQUEZ, J.E. 2001: "De los campos de silos a los agujeros negros: Sobre pozos, depósitos y zanjas en la Prehistoria Reciente del Sur de la Península Ibérica". *Spal Revista de Prehistoria y Arqueología* 10: 207-220.

- 2002: "Megalitismo, agricultura y complejidad social: algunas consideraciones". *Baetica* 24: 193-222.

- 2003: "Recintos Prehistóricos Atrincherados (RPA) en Andalucía (España): Una propuesta interpretativa". En S. Oliveira Jorge (ed.): *Recintos murados da Pré-história recente*. Facultad de Arte. Porto: 269-284.

- In press a: "Muerte ubícua: sobre deposiciones de esqueletos humanos en zanjas y pozos en la prehistoria reciente de Andalucía". *Mainake* XXVI.

- In press b: "Sobre los depósitos estructurados de animales en yacimientos de fosos del sur de la Península Ibérica". In E. Weiss-Krejci (coord): *Hombre y animal en la Prehistoria e Historia peninsular*, IV Congreso de Arqueología Peninsular.

MÁRQUEZ, J.E. & FERNÁNDEZ, J. 2002: "Viejos depósitos, nuevas interpretaciones: La estructura nº 2 del yacimiento prehistórico de los Villares de Algane (Coín, Málaga)". *Mainake* XXI-XXII: 301-333.

MARTÍN DE LA CRUZ, J.C. 1985: *Papa Uvas I. Aljaraque, Huelva Campañas de 1976 a 1979.* Excavaciones Arqueológicas en España 136. Madrid.

- 1986: *Papa Uvas II. Aljaraque, Huelva Campañas de 1981 a 1983.* Excavaciones Arqueológicas en España 149. Madrid.

MARTÍN DE LA CRUZ, J.C .; SANZ, Mª. P. & BERMÚDEZ, J. 2000: *La Edad del Cobre en El Llanete de los Moros (Montoro). El origen de los pueblos en la Campiña cordobesa.* Revista de Prehistoria 1. Córdoba.

MARTÍN DE LA CRUZ, J.C. & LUCENA, A. 2003: "Problemas metodológicos e interpretativos que plantean los depósitos sedimentarios del yacimiento arqueológico de Papa Uvas (Aljaraque, Huelva)". *Trablhos de Antropología e Etnologia* 43 (1-2): 151-170.

MAUSS, M. 1991: *Sociología y Antropología. Ensayo sobre los dones, motivo y forma del cambio en las sociedades primitivas.* Tecnos. Madrid.

MOORE, H.L. 1982: "The interpretation of spatial patterning in settlement residues". In I. Hodder (ed.): *Symbolic and structural archaeology.* Cambridge University Press. Cambridge: 74-79.

NOCETE, F. 2001: *Tercer milenio antes de nuestra era. Relaciones y contradicciones centro/periferia en el Valle del Guadalquivir.* Bellaterra. Barcelona.

PERDIGONES, L. & GUERRERO, L.J. 1987: "Excavaciones de urgencia en el Peñón Gordo (Benaocaz, Cádiz), 1985". *Anuario Arqueológico de Andalucía* 1985, III: 29-33.

RICHARDS, C. & THOMAS, J. 1984: "Ritual activity and structured deposition in Later Neolithic Wessex". In R. Bradley & J. Gardiner (eds): *Neolithic Studies: a review of some recent reserch.* British Archaeological Report 133: 189-214.

RUIZ LARA, D. 1990: "Excavación arqueológica de urgencia en la Minilla, La Rambla, Córdoba. Campaña de 1989". *Anuario Arqueológico de Andalucía* 1989, III: 157-163.

RUIZ MATA, D. 1983: "El yacimiento de la Edad del Bronce de Valencina de la Concepción (Sevilla) en el marco cultural del Bajo Guadalquivir". *Actas del I Congreso de Historia de Andalucía.* Monte de Piedad y Caja de Ahorros. Córdoba: 183-208.

SHERRAT, A. 1981: "Plough and pastoralism: aspects of the secondary products revolution". In I. Hodder, G. Isaac & N. Hammond (eds): *Pattern of the Past. Studies in honour of David Clarke.* Cambridge Universty Press. Cambridge: 261-306.

SMITH, I. F. 1966: "Windmill Hill and its implications". *Palaeohistoria* XII: 469-481.

SUAREZ, A; CARRILERO, M.; MELLADO, C. & SAN MARTÍN, C. 1987: "Memoria de la excavación de urgencia realizada en Ciavieja, El Ejido (Almería)". *Anuario Arqueológico de Andalucía* 1986 III: 20-24.

THOMAS, J. 1999: *Understanding the Neolithic.* Routledge. London.

VALERA, A.C. 2003: "Mobilidade estratégica e prolongamento simbólico: problemátics do abandono no povoamento calcolítico do occidente peninsular". *ERA-Arqueologia* 5: 126-149.

VALERA, A.C. & FILIPE, I. 2004: "O povoado do Porto Tor-rao (Ferreira do Alentejo)". *ERA-Arqueologia* 6: 28-61.

VALLESPÍ, E; CIUDAD, A; HURTADO, V.; GARCÍA, R. & CABALLERO, A. 1985: "Materiales del Neolítico Final-Calcolítico de la Vega de los Morales (Aldea del Rey, Ciudad Real)". *Estudios y Monografías* 15. Ciudad Real.

VARGAS, J.M. 2003: "Elementos para la definición territorial del yacimiento prehistórico de Valencina de la Concepción (Sevilla)". *Spal* 12: 125-144.

VARNDELL, G. & TOPPING, P. (eds) 2002: *Enclosures in Neolithic Europe. Enssays on Causewayed and Non-Causewayed sites*. Oxbow Books. Oxford.

VICENT, J.M. 1998: "La prehistoria del modo tributario de producción". *Hispania* LVIII/3 200: 823-839.

WHITTLE, A. 1977: "Earlier neolithic enclosures in North-West Europe". *Proceeding of the Prehistoric Society* 43: 329-348.

- 1988: "Contexts, Activities, Events – Aspect of Neolithic and Copper Age Enclosures in Central and Western Europe". In C. Burgess (eds): *Enclosures and defences in the Neolithic of Western Europe*. British Archaeological Reports International Series 403 (ii): 1-19.

WHITTLE, A; POLLARD, J. & GRIGSON, C. 1999: *The armony of symbols. The Windmill Hill causewayed enclosure*. Oxbow Books. Oxford.

ZAFRA, N.; HORNOS, F. & CASTRO. M. 1999: "Una macro-aldea en el origen del modo de vida campesino: Marroquíes Bajos (Jaén) c. 2500-2000 cal. ANE". *Trabajos de Prehistoria* 56 (1): 77-102.

ZAFRA, N.; CASTRO, M. & HORNOS, F. 2003: "Sucesión y simultaneidad en un gran asentamieno: La cronología de la macro-aldea de Marroquíes Bajos, Jaén. C. 2500-2000 Cal. Ane". *Trabajos de Prehistoria* 60 (2): 79-90.

Name Index